Twilight of the American Century

TWILIGHT
OF THE
AMERICAN
CENTURY

ANDREW J. BACEVICH

University of Notre Dame Press

Notre Dame, Indiana

University of Notre Dame Press
Notre Dame, Indiana 46556
undpress.nd.edu
All Rights Reserved

Published in the United States of America

Library of Congress Cataloging-in-Publication Data

Names: Bacevich, Andrew J., author.
Title: Twilight of the American century / Andrew J. Bacevich.
Description: Notre Dame, Indiana : University of Notre Dame Press, [2018] |
Includes index. |
Identifiers: LCCN 2018021921 (print) | LCCN 2018040612 (ebook) |
ISBN 9780268104870 (pdf) | ISBN 9780268104887 (epub) |
ISBN 9780268104856 | ISBN 9780268104856 (hardback : alk. paper) |
ISBN 0268104859 (hardback : alk. paper) | ISBN 9780268104863
(paperback : alk. paper) | ISBN 0268104867 (paperback : alk. paper)
Subjects: LCSH: United States—Politics and government—21st century.
Classification: LCC E902 (ebook) | LCC E902.B33   2018 (print) |
DDC 320.973/0905—dc23
LC record available at https://lccn.loc.gov/2018021921

∞ *This paper meets the requirements of
ANSI/NISO Z39.48-1992 (Permanence of Paper).*

To Steve Brown, Tom Engelhardt, and John Wright

—

Irrepressible New Yorkers,

Irreplaceable Friends

Jerusalem has sinned grievously; therefore, she has become an
    object of scorn.
All who honored her now despise her, for they have seen her
    nakedness.

—Lamentations, chapter 1, verse 8

Contents

Part 2. History and Myth

Part 3. War and Empire

Part 4. Politics and Culture

Introduction
Straying from the Well-Trod Path

Everyone makes mistakes. Among mine was choosing at age seventeen to attend the United States Military Academy, an ill-advised decision made with little appreciation for any longer-term implications that might ensue. My excuse? I was young and foolish.

Yet however ill-advised, the decision was all but foreordained. At least so it appears to me in retrospect. Family background, upbringing, early schooling: all of these, along with the time and place of my birth, predisposed me to choose West Point in preference to the civilian schools to which I had applied. Joining the Corps of Cadets in the summer of 1965 was a logical culmination of my life's trajectory to that point.

West Point exists for one reason only: to produce soldiers. Not all graduates become career military officers, of course. Many opt out after a few years of service and retool themselves as lawyers, bankers, business executives, stockbrokers, doctors, dentists, diplomats, and the like. But the nation doesn't need federally funded service academies to fill the ranks of these occupations. For such purposes, America's multitude of colleges and universities, public and private, more than suffice.

My alma mater is — or at least was — a different sort of place. At the West Point I attended, education per se took a backseat to socialization.

As cadets we studied the arts and sciences, thereby absorbing knowledge much like our peers at Ohio State or Yale. Yet mere learning was not the object of the exercise. West Point's true purpose was to inculcate a set of values and a worldview, nominally expressed in the academy's motto Duty, Honor, Country.

Virtually all institutional mottos—Google's now-defunct "Don't be evil" offers a good example—contain layers of meaning. Apparent simplicity conceals underlying ambiguity, which only the fully initiated possess the capacity to decipher.

Embedded in West Point's motto are two mutually reinforcing propositions that we aspiring professional soldiers were expected to absorb. According to the first, the well-being of the United States as a whole is inextricably bound up with the well-being of the United States Army. Much as Jesuits believe that the Society of Jesus not only defends but also embodies the Faith, so too does West Point inculcate into its graduates the conviction that the army not only defends but also embodies the nation. To promote the army's interests is therefore to promote the national interest and, by extension, all that America itself signifies.

According to the second proposition, individual standing within the military profession is a function not of what you are doing but of who you give evidence of becoming. Upward trajectory testifies to your potential for advancing the army's interests. In this regard, "promotability"—prospects for ascending the hierarchy of rank and position—becomes the ultimate measure of professional status. Thus does the code of professional values incorporate and indeed foster personal ambition and careerism.

I was, to put it mildly, slow to grasp the tension between the values that West Point professed and those that it actually imparted. Appreciating the contradictions would have required critical faculties that in my passage from adolescence to adulthood I did not possess. After all, I was not given to questioning institutional authority. Indeed, my instinct was to defer to institutions and to take at face value the word handed down from podium, pulpit, or teacher's desk, whatever that word might be. Spending four years at West Point powerfully reinforced that tendency.

Born during the summer of 1947 in Normal, Illinois, of all places, I was, as it were, marked from the outset with the sign of orthodoxy. From an early age, as if by instinct, I deferred to convention, as I was brought up to do.

My roots are in Chicagoland, the great swathe of the Midwest defined by the circulation area of Colonel Robert McCormick's *Chicago Tribune*, which in those days proclaimed itself the "World's Greatest Newspaper." My father, the son of Lithuanian immigrants, had grown up in East Chicago, Indiana, a small, charmless city known chiefly as the home of the now-defunct Inland Steel. My mother came from an undistinguished farm town situated alongside the Illinois River, a hundred miles from the Windy City. Both of my parents were born in the early 1920s, both were cradle Catholics, and both were veterans of World War II. Within a year of returning from overseas once the war ended, they had met, fallen in love, and married. Theirs was a perfect match. Eleven months later, with my father now enrolled in college courtesy of the G.I. Bill, I arrived on the scene.

Ours was an upwardly mobile family at a moment when opportunities for upward mobility were plentiful, especially for white Americans willing to work hard. And ours was a traditional family — my Dad as breadwinner, my Mom as "housewife" — at a time when such arrangements seemed proper, natural, and destined to continue in perpetuity.

After my father graduated from college and then from medical school — years during which my parents struggled financially — we returned to East Chicago and began our ascent into a comfortable middle-class existence: a small home, then a bigger one; first one car, then two; black-and-white TV, then color; lakeside summer vacations in Wisconsin; a single sibling, and eventually a houseful. Big families were the order of the day, especially among Catholics. That within the confined spacing defining our existence, things occurred as they were meant to occur was a proposition that I accepted without question. This was, after all, the 1950s.

I attended the local parochial school, staffed by the Poor Handmaids of Jesus Christ, and committed to memory the Baltimore Catechism, as required. Upon finishing eighth grade, I was off to an all-boys

Benedictine high school situated among the cornfields of Illinois, the very school that my father had attended back in the 1930s. I was a boarding student and here commenced a long journey away from home, even though in some indefinable sense I was to remain a son of the Middle Border.

In the American church, the years following World War II had produced a windfall in vocations and this particular monastic community had reaped its share of that harvest. In my four years as a high school student, I had a single lay teacher—all the rest were priests. Fifty years later my old school survives, but the abbey community has dwindled to a shadow of its former self. With virtually the entire school faculty now consisting of laypeople, the character of the place has radically changed. Truth to tell, I no longer think of it as "my school."

The monks who taught and mentored us were an extraordinary lot, varying widely in age, ability, and temperament. Whenever possible, we students gave them grief, as adolescent boys inevitably do in the face of authority. Yet they were, in our eyes, objects of fascination, from whom we learned much. For me at least, real religious formation began here as a direct consequence of daily exposure to imperfect men striving to live a godly life.

Although not nearly as bright as I imagined myself to be, I was a good student. I tested well, this at a time when performance on standardized exams counted for much. I also read a lot, mostly escapist fiction, albeit with attention to writers—Hemingway, Fitzgerald, John O'Hara, and J. D. Salinger—who in some scarcely fathomable way touched on what it meant to be a man. I dabbled in poetry, briefly fancying myself heir to Carl Sandburg. All in all, I was a brooding self-centered twit, beset by hormone-fueled insecurities.

Yet for whatever reason, that one lay teacher took a particular interest in me. Mr. Burke was not Mr. Chips. He was a Chicagoan through and through: whip smart, sophisticated (at least in my eyes), funny, impatient, and sarcastic to the point of outright cruelty. He taught history, a subject I thought I liked without actually understanding. Mr. Burke cared about books and ideas and thought I should too. Through him I glimpsed, ever so briefly, the life of the mind, which implied a future altogether different from the one toward which I imagined myself heading. I dimly recall Mr. Burke advising against me choosing a service academy. I ought to have listened to him. As it was, for me at least, the life of the mind was about to go on long-term hiatus.

Apart perhaps from those who had attended West Point back when the Civil War erupted, few cadets, if any, passed through the United States Military Academy at a more disconcerting time than my own class experienced. We joined the Corps of Cadets in July 1965, just as the first increments of US combat troops were deploying to South Vietnam. We received our diplomas and accepted our commissions in June 1969, with fighting still very much underway. Increasingly viewed as misguided and unwinnable, the war had waited for us.

In the interim, the country and certainly the generation to which we belonged had all but split in two. To prepare for entry into the military profession during that interval was to be simultaneously exposed to and insulated from the profound upheaval that was affecting all aspects of American society. Protest, unrest, riots, and the backlash they induced: to all of this, from our fortress-like campus just upriver from New York City, we were perplexed witnesses rather than participants.

Graduation meant release, but also donning harness. After pausing to marry my very young Chicago-born bride, I departed for a yearlong tour of duty in Vietnam. The war was now winding down and the army was falling apart, beset by widespread drug use, acute racial tension, and indiscipline. The implicit mission was to contain these pathologies while preventing the soldiers in your charge from getting killed to no purpose. For a young officer, it did not pay to reflect too deeply about the predicament into which the army and the nation as a whole had gotten itself. The demands of duty were enough; thinking could wait.

I returned home in one piece, even if somewhat unsettled by my experiences. After a stint of stateside soldiering, with my service obligation about to expire, we contemplated "getting out" and trying our hand at civilian life. But with the economy doing poorly, a family to care for, and the army offering graduate school followed by a tour teaching at West Point, we opted to "stay in." Short-term expediency had prevailed.

So it was off to Princeton to study history under the tutelage of an illustrious and learned faculty. I arrived completely unprepared and spent two years trying to conceal my ignorance. I read hundreds of pages a day, testing my wife's patience while giving too little attention to our young daughters. Fearing failure, I somehow concluded that my task was to absorb as much information as possible; my fellow graduate students knew better. Mastering the arguments mattered as much as or more than mastering the facts. Historiography rather than history per se was the name of the game.

I was not particularly interested in or attuned to the ideas then in fashion on university campuses. But this was the mid-1970s, still the heyday of the New Left, and ideas were interested in me. Those that I encountered in seminar challenged and subverted my worldview, particularly regarding the course of American statecraft. I both resisted these ideas and absorbed them. They became lodged in my subconscious.

Much as I had survived Vietnam, I survived Princeton. I worked hard, showed up on time for class, met deadlines, and followed the rules. Perhaps suspecting that a dour, but compliant, army captain was unlikely to cause permanent harm to the historical profession, my mentors allowed me to graduate.

Returning to West Point where our family continued to grow, I tried my hand at teaching. It did not go well. For some bizarre reason, I set out to provide the young cadets assigned to my section room with an experience comparable to a Princeton graduate seminar when all they wanted was sufficient knowledge to pass the course—precisely what I had wanted a dozen years earlier.

Once again, we contemplated "getting out." I applied for the Foreign Service and satisfied all the necessary requirements for joining the State Department. From career soldier to career diplomat sounded like an attractive move. But when the offer of an appointment actually materialized, it involved taking a cut in pay. We now had three very young children. Again, expediency won out.

After West Point came a decade of troop duty, including two tours in what was then West Germany. Assignments as a commander or operations officer alternated with fellowships and attendance at army schools.

The Cold War was winding down, but in the field we found it convenient not to notice. After Vietnam, the Cold War had provided the army with its principal raison d'être. Preparing to defend against an all-out attack by the Warsaw Pact, which we pretended to think could come at any minute, infused everything we did with urgency and a sense of purpose. We worked as if freedom's very survival hung in the balance.

That said, I did not much care for the day-to-day routine of soldiering. I disliked being away from home for long stretches, sitting up half the night on gunnery ranges, and being cold, wet, tired, and miserable on field training exercises. Most of all, I hated the exorbitant waste of time: mindless meetings that went on for hours; the pre-briefings that preceded the briefings that were anything but brief; the pre-rehearsals that preceded the rehearsals that preceded the actual event; the drafting and endless revision of dull, jargon-filled documents that nobody ever read.

I had begun to write, at first by contributing occasional articles to service journals. Then over the course of a three-year period, I wrote an interpretive history of the army during the interval between Korea and Vietnam, co-authored a monograph about US military involvement in El Salvador during the 1980s, and converted my Princeton dissertation into a publishable book. In each of these projects, I found considerable satisfaction.

This is not to say that anyone noticed. Yet I was discovering that here was something I liked to do very much. I enjoyed the challenge of formulating an argument. I enjoyed the hard work of composition. Most of all, I enjoyed drawing connections between past and present, employing history as an instrument of illumination.

In 1989, with the fall of the Berlin Wall, the Cold War ended. My own military career likewise ended soon thereafter, abruptly and ingloriously.

Command, I had learned, is something of a juggling act. It requires closely attending to all that is happening today even while putting the finishing touches on what is to happen tomorrow and next week while simultaneously preparing for what should occur next month or next year. When the synchronization works, the results are gratifying, almost magical. Maintain that synchronization and you've got a disciplined, high-performing outfit in which all involved can take pride.

But as with juggling, just one miscalculation can produce catastrophe. In the summer of 1991, I dropped a ball. And in the immortal words of Bruce Springsteen, "man, that was all she wrote."

Soon after the Cold War had ended, I assumed command of one of the army's more storied units. Not long thereafter, Saddam Hussein foolishly invaded Kuwait. In the subsequent campaign to liberate that country, we remained at our home stations, mortified at being left behind in Germany while friends went off to fight. Shortly after Operation Desert Storm ended, however, and with Kuwaitis still eyeing Saddam nervously, we received orders to deploy to the Gulf. Although a second Iraqi assault on Kuwait was even less likely than a Soviet invasion of Western Europe had been, the Emir of Kuwait needed reassurance and my regiment was tagged to provide it.

The mission went well until it didn't. I did not take seriously any threat posed by Saddam. I took very seriously the possibility of a terrorist attack of the sort that had befallen the US Marines in Beirut, Lebanon, less than a decade earlier. I failed completely to anticipate the real threat: a vehicular fire touching off massive explosions that destroyed millions of dollars of equipment and caused dozens of casualties among my own soldiers.

With my unit committed to what was still nominally a war zone, I had directed that our ammunition be stored so that we could engage the enemy on a moment's notice. This, of course, is what we were meant to convey to the Kuwaiti government. The very purpose of our mission required that we maintain a ready-to-fight posture. In retrospect, I took that requirement way too literally.

In any event, at a time when it appeared that the United States Army could do no wrong, I had presided over a spectacular failure. Of greater significance to me personally, I had brought dishonor to the regiment entrusted to my care.

Over the course of some two decades on active duty, I had on several occasions observed commanders dodging responsibility for misfortunes that had occurred on their watch, usually by fingering some subordinate to take the fall. I had vowed never to do that.

Only one recourse appeared available: accept responsibility for what had occurred, finish out my command tour, and quietly leave the service, confident that the army would do just fine without me. This is the course I proceeded to follow.

How well I could do without the army was a different question altogether. We now had four children, two of them of college age. There were bills to pay. Although hiring on with a defense contractor might have been a possibility, the mere prospect of doing so was highly disagreeable. Now in my mid-forties, I needed to find a new calling.

In truth, even during my last years in the army, I had begun to feel increasingly restless and out of place. I had mastered the art of striking a soldierly pose, which largely involved attitude, posture, vocabulary, and dubious personal habits. (I drew the line at chewing tobacco.) However belatedly, I sensed that I had drifted into the wrong vocation. To some of us, self-knowledge comes slowly.

That said, I had no clear sense of what my new calling might be. I had spent countless hours planning training exercises and tactical operations. I had no plan for my own life and my family's future, however.

I knew I liked to write. And I felt vaguely drawn to that life of the mind that I had long ago glimpsed under Mr. Burke's tutelage. Might these inclinations enable me to make a living? Buoyed by the generosity of friends and the kindness of strangers willing to take a chance on me, I now tested that proposition.

As a direct result, I gained entry into academic life, albeit through the side door. A stint at Johns Hopkins served as an apprenticeship of sorts during which I learned how to teach (finally) and started writing for wider audiences. In 1998, Boston University offered me a senior faculty appointment, an unearned and undeserved opportunity with transformative implications. I accepted with alacrity. Our wandering days now finally ended. We became New Englanders.

As a serving officer, I had remained studiously apolitical. Now, however, I was no longer a servant of the state. Prior inhibitions about expressing my own views regarding the state of American politics, statecraft, and culture fell away. Soon enough, events drew me to four broad issues that with the passing of the Cold War deserved far more critical attention than they were receiving, at least in my view.

The first of those issues related to changes in the prevailing understanding of what freedom should permit, require, or disallow. The second dealt with the tensions between America's conception of itself as freedom's principal champion and its proper role as a global power. The focus of the third issue was the use of US military might, not infrequently justified by citing the nation's ostensible duty to advance the cause of freedom. Finally, there was the system devised to raise and sustain the nation's armed forces, thereby fostering a specific (and to my mind problematic) relationship between soldiers and society.

By the time I took up my position at Boston University, these were already becoming central to my writing agenda. Yet in ways that I had not anticipated, moving to Boston sharpened my thinking. To escape from the orbit of Washington was to see its narrowly partisan preoccupations and imperial pretensions for what they were. With distance came clarity and focus.

Given the terms of my appointment, I had no need to worry about tenure or promotion. So I could write what I wanted and publish where I wanted without having to consider whether I was chalking up the requisite number of scholarly points. Here was freedom, indeed.

Much to my surprise, invitations to write books materialized. Beginning soon after 9/11 and continuing over the course of the next decade-and-a-half, I published a series of volumes, along with dozens of articles and reviews, that critically assessed American imperialism, militarism, civil-military relations, and the changing meaning of freedom. I developed an abiding interest in understanding why the United States does what it does in the world and concluded that the answers were to be found by looking within rather than abroad. No doubt US policy draws on multiple sources. Yet ultimately it expresses the conviction that we are God's new Chosen People.

Roughly midway through that period my only son was killed in action in Iraq. Just about everyone sooner or later suffers the loss of loved ones. Certainly, I had. While I was still attending West Point, my father had died in an accident. My wife's brother, my closest friend in high school, had died much too soon, having been badly wounded in Vietnam and never thereafter really getting his life on track. But my son's death was excruciatingly painful, not only for me, but also for my wife and our daughters. Nor did I find it a faith-enhancing experience. But we endured.

I had by this time become accustomed to describing myself as a conservative. That said, I had little use for what passed for conservatism in the Republican Party or among pundits of an ostensibly conservative persuasion. I had over the years come to my own understanding of the term by reading a mix of thinkers not easily pigeon-holed as belonging exclusively to the Right or the Left. These included Henry Adams, Randolph Bourne, Charles Beard, Dorothy Day, Dietrich Bonhoeffer, Evelyn Waugh, Reinhold Niebuhr, C. Wright Mills, James Baldwin, William Appleman Williams, Walker Percy, and Christopher Lasch.

The position I eventually staked out for myself was as a non-partisan conservative who saw much to admire among progressives. That from time to time I was able to publish in periodicals associated with the Left pleased me to no end.

In a 2008 article, urging principled conservatives to vote for Barack Obama rather than John McCain in the upcoming presidential election, I offered my own list of conservative tenets. They included the following:

- a commitment to individual liberty, tempered by the conviction that genuine freedom entails more than simply an absence of restraint;
- a belief in limited government, fiscal responsibility, and the rule of law;
- veneration for our cultural inheritance combined with a sense of stewardship for creation;
- a reluctance to discard or tamper with traditional social arrangements;
- respect for the market as the generator of wealth combined with a wariness of the market's corrosive impact on humane values;
- a deep suspicion of utopian promises, rooted in an appreciation of the sinfulness of man and the recalcitrance of history.

I should have added recognition of a collective responsibility to promote the common good. But apart from that omission, I stand by what I wrote (and, given the alternatives on offer, have no regret for having twice voted for Obama).

In 2014, I retired from teaching. Whether my students knew it or not, I was going stale and they deserved better than I was able to give. Besides, I wanted to spend time with my wife, while turning to new writing projects. On matters of particular interest to me, there is much that I still want to say and that needs to be said, even if the likelihood of making a dent in prevailing opinion appears negligible.

I could hardly have anticipated the political earthquake triggered by the election held to choose Obama's successor. Yet in retrospect, a series of tremors—some large, others small—had offered ample warning. The essays reprinted below recall and reflect on some of those tremors dating back to 9/11. Yet they by no means constitute the last word. There remains much more that needs saying.

Walpole, Massachusetts
January 2018

PART 1

Poseurs and Prophets

1

A Letter to Paul Wolfowitz

Occasioned by the Tenth Anniversary of the Iraq War

(2013)

Dear Paul,

I have been meaning to write to you for some time, and the tenth anniversary of the beginning of the Iraq war provides as good an occasion as any to do so. Distracted by other, more recent eruptions of violence, the country has all but forgotten the war. But I won't and I expect you can't, although our reasons for remembering may differ.

Twenty years ago, you became dean of the Johns Hopkins School of Advanced International Studies and hired me as a minor staff functionary. I never thanked you properly. I needed that job. Included in the benefits package was the chance to hobnob with luminaries who gathered at SAIS every few weeks to join Zbigniew Brzezinski for an off-the-record discussion of foreign policy. From five years of listening to these insiders pontificate, I drew one conclusion: people said to be smart—the ones with fancy résumés who get their op-eds published in the *New York Times* and appear on TV—really aren't. They excel mostly in recycling bromides. When it came to sustenance, the sandwiches were superior to the chitchat.

You were an exception, however. You had a knack for framing things creatively. No matter how daunting the problem, you contrived a solution. More important, you grasped the big picture. Here, it was apparent, lay your métier. As Saul Bellow wrote of Philip Gorman, your fictionalized double, in *Ravelstein*, you possessed an aptitude for "Great Politics." Where others saw complications, you discerned connections. Where others saw constraints, you found possibilities for action.

Truthfully, I wouldn't give you especially high marks as dean. You were, of course, dutiful and never less than kind to students. Yet you seemed to find presiding over SAIS more bothersome than it was fulfilling. Given all that running the place entails—raising money, catering to various constituencies, managing a cantankerous and self-important faculty—I'm not sure I blame you. SAIS prepares people to exercise power. That's why the school exists. Yet you wielded less clout than at any time during your previous two decades of government service.

So at Zbig's luncheons, when you riffed on some policy issue—the crisis in the Balkans, the threat posed by North Korean nukes, the latest provocations of Saddam Hussein—it was a treat to watch you become so animated. What turned you on was playing the game. Being at SAIS was riding the bench.

Even during the 1990s, those who disliked your views tagged you as a neoconservative. But the label never quite fit. You were at most a fellow traveler. You never really signed on with the PR firm of Podhoretz, Kristol, and Kagan. Your approach to policy analysis owed more to Wohlstetter Inc.—a firm less interested in ideology than in power and its employment.

I didn't understand this at the time, but I've come to appreciate the extent to which your thinking mirrors that of the nuclear strategist Albert Wohlstetter. Your friend Richard Perle put the matter succinctly: "Paul thinks the way Albert thinks." Wohlstetter, the quintessential "defense intellectual," had been your graduate-school mentor. You became, in effect, his agent, devoted to converting his principles into actual policy. This, in a sense, was your life's work.

Most Americans today have never heard of Wohlstetter and wouldn't know what to make of the guy even if they had. Everything about him exuded sophistication. He was the smartest guy in the room before anyone had coined the phrase. Therein lay his appeal. To be admitted to discipleship was to become one of the elect.

Wohlstetter's perspective (which became yours) emphasized five distinct propositions. Call them the Wohlstetter Precepts.

First, liberal internationalism, with its optimistic expectation that the world will embrace a set of common norms to achieve peace, is an illusion. Of course virtually every president since Franklin Roosevelt has paid lip service to that illusion, and doing so during the Cold War may even have served a certain purpose. But to indulge it further constitutes sheer folly.

Second, the system that replaces liberal internationalism must address the ever-present (and growing) danger posed by catastrophic surprise. Remember Pearl Harbor. Now imagine something orders of magnitude worse—for instance, a nuclear attack from out of the blue.

Third, the key to averting or at least minimizing surprise is to act preventively. If shrewdly conceived and skillfully executed, action holds some possibility of safety, whereas inaction reduces that possibility to near zero. Eliminate the threat before it materializes. In statecraft, that defines the standard of excellence.

Fourth, the ultimate in preventive action is dominion. The best insurance against unpleasant surprises is to achieve unquestioned supremacy.

Lastly, by transforming the very nature of war, information technology—an arena in which the United States has historically enjoyed a clear edge—brings outright supremacy within reach. Of all the products of Albert Wohlstetter's fertile brain, this one impressed you most. The potential implications were dazzling. According to Mao, political power grows out of the barrel of a gun. Wohlstetter went further. Given the right sort of gun—preferably one that fires very fast and very accurately—so, too, does world order.

With the passing of the Cold War, global hegemony seemed America's for the taking. What others saw as an option you, Paul, saw as something much more: an obligation that the nation needed to seize, for its own good as well as for the world's. Not long before we both showed up at SAIS, your first effort to codify supremacy and preventive action as a basis for strategy had ended in embarrassing failure. I refer here to the famous (or infamous) Defense Planning Guidance of

1992, drafted in the aftermath of Operation Desert Storm by the Pentagon policy shop you then directed. Before this classified document was fully vetted by the White House, it was leaked to the *New York Times*, which made it front-page news. The draft DPG announced that it had become the "first objective" of US policy "to prevent the re-emergence of a new rival." With an eye toward "deterring potential competitors from even aspiring to a larger regional or global role," the United States would maintain unquestioned military superiority and, if necessary, employ force unilaterally. As window dressing, allies might be nice, but the United States no longer considered them necessary.

Unfortunately, you and the team assigned to draft the DPG had miscalculated the administration's support for your thinking. This was not the moment to be unfurling grandiose ambitions expressed in indelicate language. In the ensuing hue and cry, President George H. W. Bush disavowed the document. Your reputation took a hit. But you were undeterred.

The election of George W. Bush as president permitted you to escape from academe. You'd done yeoman work tutoring candidate Bush in how the world works, and he repaid the debt by appointing you to serve as Donald Rumsfeld's deputy atop the Pentagon hierarchy. You took office as Osama bin Laden was conspiring to attack. Alas, neither Rumsfeld nor you nor anyone else in a position of real authority anticipated what was to occur. America's vaunted defense establishment had left the country defenseless. Yet instead of seeing this as evidence of gross incompetence requiring the officials responsible to resign, you took it as an affirmation. For proof that averting surprise through preventive military action was now priority number one, Americans needed to look no further than the damage inflicted by nineteen thugs armed with box cutters.

You immediately saw the events of 9/11 as a second and more promising opening to assert US supremacy. When riding high a decade earlier, many Americans had thought it either unseemly or unnecessary to lord it over others. Now, with the populace angry and frightened, the idea was likely to prove an easier sell. Although none of the hijackers were Iraqi, within days of 9/11 you were promoting military action against Iraq. Critics have chalked this up to your supposed obsession with Saddam. The criticism is misplaced. The scale of your ambitions was vastly greater.

In an instant, you grasped that the attacks provided a fresh opportunity to implement Wohlstetter's Precepts, and Iraq offered a made-to-order venue. "We cannot wait to act until the threat is imminent," you said in 2002. Toppling Saddam Hussein would validate the alternative to waiting. In Iraq, the United States would demonstrate the efficacy of preventive war.

So even conceding a hat tip to Albert Wohlstetter, the Bush Doctrine was largely your handiwork. The urgency of invading Iraq stemmed from the need to validate that doctrine before the window of opportunity closed. What made it necessary to act immediately was not Saddam's purported WMD program. It was not his nearly nonexistent links to al-Qaeda. It was certainly not the way he abused his own people. No, what drove events was the imperative of claiming for the United States prerogatives allowed no other nation.

I do not doubt the sincerity of your conviction (shared by President Bush) that our country could be counted on to exercise those prerogatives in ways beneficial to all humankind—promoting peace, democracy, and human rights. But the proximate aim was to unshackle American power. Saddam Hussein's demise would serve as an object lesson for all: Here's what we *can* do. Here's what we *will* do.

Although you weren't going to advertise the point, this unshackling would also contribute to the security of Israel. To Wohlstetter's five precepts you had added a silent codicil. According to the unwritten sixth precept, Israeli interests and US interests must align. You understood that making Israelis feel safer makes Israel less obstreperous, and that removing the sources of Israeli insecurity makes the harmonizing of US and Israeli policies easier. Israel's most effective friends are those who work quietly to keep the divergent tendencies in US-Israeli relations from getting out of hand. You have always been such a friend. Preventive war to overthrow an evil dictator was going to elevate the United States to the status of Big Kahuna while also making Israelis feel just a little bit safer. This audacious trifecta describes your conception. And you almost pulled it off.

Imagine—you must have done so many times—if that notorious "Mission Accomplished" banner had accurately portrayed the situation on the ground in Iraq in May 2003. Imagine if US forces had achieved a clean, decisive victory. Imagine that the famous (if staged) photo of Saddam's statue in Baghdad's Al Firdos Square being pulled down had actually presaged a rapid transition to a pro-American liberal democracy, just as your friend Ahmed Chalabi had promised. Imagine if none of the ensuing horrors and disappointments had occurred: the insurgency; Fallujah and Abu Ghraib; thousands of American lives lost and damaged; at least 125,000 Iraqis killed, and some 3 million others exiled or displaced; more than a trillion dollars squandered.

You expected something different, of course. Shortly before the war, you told Congress,

> It's hard to conceive that it would take more forces to provide stability in post-Saddam Iraq than it would take to conduct the war itself and to secure the surrender of Saddam's security forces and his army. Hard to imagine.

Your imagination led you to foresee a brief conflict, with Iraqis rather than US taxpayers footing the bill for any mess left behind.

After all, preventive war was supposed to solve problems. Eliminating threats before they could materialize was going to enhance our standing, positioning us to call the shots. Instead, the result was a train wreck of epic proportions. Granted, as you yourself have said, "the world is better off" with Saddam Hussein having met his maker. But taken as a whole, the cost-benefit ratio is cause for weeping. As for global hegemony, we can kiss it goodbye.

What conclusions should we draw from the events that actually occurred, rather than from those you hoped for? In a 2003 *Boston Globe* interview, Richard Perle called Iraq "the first war that's been fought in a way that would recognize Albert's vision for future wars." So perhaps the problem lies with Albert's vision.

One of Wohlstetter's distinguishing qualities, you once told an interviewer, was that he "was so insistent on ascertaining the facts. He had a very fact-based approach to policy." Albert's approach was ruthlessly pragmatic. "It derived from saying, 'Here's the problem, look at it factually, see what the questions are that emerged from the thing itself,' so to speak." Then confront those questions.

One of the questions emerging from the Iraq debacle must be this one: Why did liberation at gunpoint yield results that differed so radically from what the war's advocates had expected? Or, to sharpen the point, *How did preventive war undertaken by ostensibly the strongest military in history produce a cataclysm?*

Not one of your colleagues from the Bush Administration possesses the necessary combination of honesty, courage, and wit to answer these questions. If you don't believe me, please sample the tediously self-exculpatory memoirs penned by (or on behalf of) Bush himself, Cheney, Rumsfeld, Rice, Tenet, Bremer, Feith, and a small squad of eminently forgettable generals.

What would Albert Wohlstetter have done? After Iraq, would he have been keen to give the Bush Doctrine another go, perhaps in Iran? Or would he have concluded that preventive war is both reckless and inherently immoral? That, of course, had been the traditional American view prior to 9/11.

Would Albert endorse Barack Obama's variant of preventive war, the employing of unmanned aircraft as instruments of targeted assassination? Sending a Hellfire missile through some unsuspecting jihadist's windshield certainly fits the definition of being proactive, but where does it lead? As a numbers guy, Albert might wonder how many "terrorists" we're going to have to kill before the "Mission Accomplished" banner gets resurrected.

And what would Albert make of the war in Afghanistan, now limping into its second decade? Wohlstetter took from Vietnam the lesson that we needed new ways "to use our power discriminately and for worthy ends." In light of Afghanistan, perhaps he would reconsider that position and reach the conclusion others took from Vietnam: Some wars can't be won and aren't worth fighting.

Finally, would Albert fail to note that US and Israeli security interests are now rapidly slipping out of sync? The outcome of the Arab Spring remains unknown. But what the United States hopes will emerge from that upheaval in the long run differs considerably from what will serve Israel's immediate needs.

Given the state of things and our own standing ten years after the start of the Iraq war, what would Albert do? I never met the man (he died in 1997), but my guess is that he wouldn't flinch from taking on these questions, even if the answers threatened to contradict his own long-held beliefs. Neither should you, Paul. To be sure, whatever you might choose to say, you'll be vilified, as Robert McNamara was vilified when he broke his long silence and admitted that he'd been "wrong, terribly wrong" about Vietnam. But help us learn the lessons of Iraq so that we might extract from it something of value in return for all the sacrifices made there. Forgive me for saying so, but you owe it to your country.

Give it a shot.

Andy

2

David Brooks

Angst in the Church of America the Redeemer

(2017)

Apart from being a police officer, firefighter, or soldier engaged in one of this nation's endless wars, writing a column for a major American newspaper has got to be one of the toughest and most unforgiving jobs there is. The pay may be decent (at least if your gig is with one of the major papers in New York or Washington), but the pressures to perform on cue are undoubtedly relentless.

Anyone who has ever tried cramming a coherent and ostensibly insightful argument into a mere 750 words knows what I'm talking about. Writing op-eds does not perhaps qualify as high art. Yet, like tying flies or knitting sweaters, it requires no small amount of skill. Performing the trick week in and week out without too obviously recycling the same ideas over and over again—or at least while disguising repetitions and concealing inconsistencies—requires notable gifts.

David Brooks of the *New York Times* is a gifted columnist. Among contemporary journalists, he is our Walter Lippmann, the closest thing we have to an establishment-approved public intellectual. As was the case with Lippmann, Brooks works hard to suppress the temptation to rant. He shuns raw partisanship. In his frequent radio and television appearances, he speaks in measured tones. Dry humor and ironic references abound. And like Lippmann, when circumstances change, he makes at least a show of adjusting his views accordingly.

For all that, Brooks remains an ideologue. In his columns, and even more so in his weekly appearances on NPR and PBS, he plays the role of the thoughtful, non-screaming conservative, his very presence affirming the ideological balance that, until November 8 of last year, was a prized hallmark of "respectable" journalism. Just as that balance always involved considerable posturing, so, too, with the ostensible conservatism of David Brooks: it's an act.

Praying at the Altar of American Greatness

In terms of confessional fealty, his true allegiance is not to conservatism as such, but to the Church of America the Redeemer. This is a virtual congregation, albeit one possessing many of the attributes of a more traditional religion. The Church has its own Holy Scripture, authenticated on July 4, 1776, at a gathering of fifty-six prophets. And it has its own saints, prominent among them the Good Thomas Jefferson, chief author of the sacred text (not the Bad Thomas Jefferson who owned and impregnated slaves); Abraham Lincoln, who freed said slaves and thereby suffered martyrdom (on Good Friday no less); and, of course, the duly canonized figures most credited with saving the world itself from evil: Winston Churchill and Franklin Roosevelt, their status akin to that of saints Peter and Paul in Christianity. The Church of America the Redeemer even has its own Jerusalem, located on the banks of the Potomac, and its own hierarchy, its members situated nearby in High Temples of varying architectural distinction.

This ecumenical enterprise does not prize theological rigor. When it comes to *shalts* and *shalt nots*, it tends to be flexible, if not altogether squishy. It demands of the faithful just one thing: a fervent belief in America's mission to remake the world in its own image. Although in times of crisis Brooks has occasionally gone a bit wobbly, he remains at heart a true believer.

In a March 1997 piece for the *Weekly Standard*, his then-employer, he summarized his credo. Entitled "A Return to National Greatness," the essay opened with a glowing tribute to the Library of Congress and, in particular, to the building completed precisely a century earlier to house its many books and artifacts. According to Brooks, the structure itself embodied the aspirations defining America's enduring purpose. He called particular attention to the dome above the main reading room decorated with a dozen "monumental figures" representing the advance of civilization and culminating in a figure representing America itself. Contemplating the imagery, Brooks rhapsodized,

> The theory of history depicted in this mural gave America impressive historical roots, a spiritual connection to the centuries. And it assigned a specific historic role to America as the latest successor to Jerusalem, Athens, and Rome. In the procession of civilization, certain nations rise up to make extraordinary contributions. . . . At the dawn of the 20th century, America was to take its turn at global supremacy. It was America's task to take the grandeur of past civilizations, modernize it, and democratize it. This common destiny would unify diverse Americans and give them a great national purpose.

This February, twenty years later, in a column with an identical title, but this time appearing in the pages of his present employer, the *New York Times*, Brooks revisited this theme. Again, he began with a paean to the Library of Congress and its spectacular dome with its series of "monumental figures" that placed America "at the vanguard of the great human march of progress." For Brooks, those twelve allegorical figures convey a profound truth.

> America is the grateful inheritor of other people's gifts. It has a spiritual connection to all people in all places, but also an exceptional role. America culminates history. It advances a way of life and a democratic model that will provide people everywhere with dignity. The things Americans do are not for themselves only, but for all mankind.

In 1997, in the midst of the Clinton presidency, Brooks had written that "America's mission was to advance civilization itself." In 2017, as Donald Trump gained entry into the Oval Office, he embellished and expanded that mission, describing a nation "assigned by providence to spread democracy and prosperity; to welcome the stranger; to be brother and sister to the whole human race."

Back in 1997, "a moment of world supremacy unlike any other," Brooks had worried that his countrymen might not seize the opportunity that was presenting itself. On the cusp of the twenty-first century, he worried that Americans had "discarded their pursuit of national greatness in just about every particular." The times called for a leader like Theodore Roosevelt, who wielded that classic "big stick" and undertook monster projects like the Panama Canal. Yet Americans were stuck instead with Bill Clinton, a small-bore triangulator. "We no longer look at history as a succession of golden ages," Brooks lamented. "And, save in the speeches of politicians who usually have no clue what they are talking about," America was no longer fulfilling its "special role as the vanguard of civilization."

By early 2017, with Donald Trump in the White House and Steve Bannon whispering in his ear, matters had become worse still. Americans had seemingly abandoned their calling outright. "The Trump and Bannon anschluss has exposed the hollowness of our patriotism," wrote Brooks, inserting the now-obligatory reference to Nazi Germany. The November 2016 presidential election had "exposed how attenuated our vision of national greatness has become and how easy it was for Trump and Bannon to replace a youthful vision of American greatness with a reactionary, alien one." That vision now threatens to leave America as "just another nation, hunkered down in a fearful world."

What exactly happened between 1997 and 2017, you might ask? What occurred during that "moment of world supremacy" to reduce the United States from a nation summoned to redeem humankind to one hunkered down in fear?

Trust Brooks to have at hand a brow-furrowing explanation. The fault, he explains, lies with an "educational system that doesn't teach civilizational history or real American history but instead a shapeless multiculturalism," as well as with "an intellectual culture that can't imagine providence." Brooks blames "people on the left who are uncomfortable with patriotism and people on the right who are uncomfortable with the federal government that is necessary to lead our project."

An America that no longer believes in itself—that's the problem. In effect, Brooks revises Norma Desmond's famous complaint about the movies, now repurposed to diagnose an ailing nation: it's the politics that got small.

Nowhere does he consider the possibility that his formula for "national greatness" just might be so much hooey. Between 1997 and 2017, after all, egged on by people like David Brooks, Americans took a stab at "greatness," with the execrable Donald Trump now numbering among the eventual results.

Invading Greatness

Say what you will about the shortcomings of the American educational system and the country's intellectual culture, they had far less to do with creating Trump than did popular revulsion prompted by specific policies that Brooks, among others, enthusiastically promoted. Not that he is inclined to tally up the consequences. Only as a sort of postscript to his litany of contemporary American ailments does he refer even in passing to what he calls the "humiliations of Iraq."

A great phrase, that. Yet much like, say, the "tragedy of Vietnam" or the "crisis of Watergate," it conceals more than it reveals. Here, in short, is a succinct historical reference that cries out for further explanation. It bursts at the seams with implications demanding to be unpacked, weighed, and scrutinized. Brooks shrugs off Iraq as a minor embarrassment, the equivalent of having shown up at a dinner party wearing the wrong clothes.

Under the circumstances, it's easy to forget that, back in 2003, he and other members of the Church of America the Redeemer devoutly supported the invasion of Iraq. They welcomed war. They urged it. They did so not because Saddam Hussein was uniquely evil—although he was evil enough—but because they saw in such a war the means for the United States to accomplish its salvific mission. Toppling Saddam and transforming Iraq would provide the mechanism for affirming and renewing America's "national greatness."

Anyone daring to disagree with that proposition they denounced as craven or cowardly. Writing at the time, Brooks disparaged those opposing the war as mere "marchers." They were effete, pretentious, ineffective, and absurd. "These people are always in the streets with their banners and puppets. They march against the IMF and World Bank one day, and against whatever war happens to be going on the next. . . . They just march against."

Perhaps space constraints did not permit Brooks in his recent column to spell out the "humiliations" that resulted and that even today continue to accumulate. Here, in any event, is a brief inventory of what that euphemism conceals: thousands of Americans needlessly killed; tens of thousands grievously wounded in body or spirit; trillions of dollars wasted; millions of Iraqis dead, injured, or displaced; this nation's moral standing compromised by its resort to torture, kidnapping, assassination, and other perversions; a region thrown into chaos and threatened by radical terrorist entities like the Islamic State that US military actions helped foster. And now, if only as an oblique second-order bonus, we have Donald Trump's elevation to the presidency to boot.

In refusing to reckon with the results of the war he once so ardently endorsed, Brooks is hardly alone. Members of the Church of America the Redeemer, Democrats and Republicans alike, are demonstrably incapable of rendering an honest accounting of what their missionary efforts have yielded.

Brooks belongs, or once did, to the Church's neoconservative branch. But liberals such as Bill Clinton, along with his secretary of state Madeleine Albright, were congregants in good standing, as were Barack Obama and his secretary of state Hillary Clinton. So, too, are putative conservatives like Senators John McCain, Ted Cruz, and Marco Rubio, all of them subscribing to the belief in the singularity and indispensability of the United States as the chief engine of history, now and forever.

Back in April 2003, confident that the fall of Baghdad had ended the Iraq War, Brooks predicted that "no day will come when the enemies of this endeavor turn around and say, 'We were wrong. Bush was right.'" Rather than admitting error, he continued, the war's opponents "will just extend their forebodings into a more distant future."

Yet it is the war's proponents who, in the intervening years, have choked on admitting that they were wrong. Or when making such an admission, as did both John Kerry and Hillary Clinton while running for president, they write it off as an aberration, a momentary lapse in judgment of no particular significance, like having guessed wrong on a TV quiz show.

Rather than requiring acts of contrition, the Church of America the Redeemer has long promulgated a doctrine of self-forgiveness, freely available to all adherents all the time. "You think our country's so innocent?" the nation's forty-fifth president recently barked at a TV host who had the temerity to ask how he could have kind words for the likes of Russian President Vladimir Putin. Observers professed shock that a sitting president would openly question American innocence.

In fact, Trump's response and the kerfuffle that ensued both missed the point. No serious person believes that the United States is "innocent." Worshippers in the Church of America the Redeemer do firmly believe, however, that America's transgressions, unlike those of other countries, don't count against it. Once committed, such sins are simply to be set aside and then expunged, a process that allows American politicians and pundits to condemn a "killer" like Putin with a perfectly clear conscience while demanding that Donald Trump do the same.

What the Russian president has done in Crimea, Ukraine, and Syria qualifies as criminal. What American presidents have done in Iraq, Afghanistan, and Libya qualifies as incidental and, above all, beside the point.

Rather than confronting the havoc and bloodshed to which the United States has contributed, those who worship in the Church of America the Redeemer keep their eyes fixed on the far horizon and the work still to be done in aligning the world with American expectations. At least they would, were it not for the arrival at center stage of a manifestly false prophet who, in promising to "make America great again," inverts all that "national greatness" is meant to signify.

For Brooks and his fellow believers, the call to "greatness" emanates from faraway precincts—in the Middle East, East Asia, and Eastern Europe. For Trump, the key to "greatness" lies in keeping faraway places and the people who live there as faraway as possible. Brooks et al. see a world that needs saving and believe that it's America's calling to do just that. In Trump's view, saving others is not a peculiarly American responsibility. Events beyond our borders matter only to the extent that they affect America's well-being. Trump worships in the Church of America First, or at least pretends to do so in order to impress his followers.

That Donald Trump inhabits a universe of his own devising, constructed of carefully arranged alt-facts, is no doubt the case. Yet, in truth, much the same can be said of David Brooks and others sharing his view of a country providentially charged to serve as the "successor to Jerusalem, Athens, and Rome." In fact, this conception of America's purpose expresses not the intent of providence, which is inherently ambiguous, but their own arrogance and conceit. Out of that conceit comes much mischief. And in the wake of mischief come charlatans like Donald Trump.

3

Arthur M. Schlesinger Jr. and the Decline of American Liberalism

(2017)

Arthur M. Schlesinger Jr., the subject of a briskly readable and instructive new biography, would probably have taken issue with its title.[1] He did not see himself as a chronicler of empire or as an agent of imperial ambition. The cause to which he devoted his professional life was the promotion of US liberalism, in his view "the vital center" of US politics.

As a prodigiously gifted historian, Schlesinger celebrated the achievements of those he deemed liberalism's greatest champions, notably Andrew Jackson, Franklin D. Roosevelt, and the martyred Kennedy brothers. As a skillful polemicist, he inveighed against those

---

1. Richard Aldous, *Schlesinger: The Imperial Historian* (New York: W. W. Norton, 2017).

he saw as enemies of liberalism, whether on the communist left or the Republican right. As a Democratic operative, he worked behind the scenes, counseling office seekers of a liberal persuasion and drafting speeches for candidates he deemed likely to advance the cause (and perhaps his own fortunes).

Arthur Schlesinger lived a rich and consequential life, and had fun along the way. He died just a decade ago at the ripe old age of eighty-nine. Yet as this account makes abundantly clear, Schlesinger comes to us from an altogether different time, far removed from our own in terms of attitudes, aspirations, and fears. Indeed, Donald Trump's elevation to the office once occupied by Schlesinger's heroes signifies the repudiation of all that Schlesinger, as scholar and public intellectual, held dear.

The Schlesinger depicted by Richard Aldous, a professor of history and literature at Bard College, resembles Trump in just one respect: each, born into privilege, demonstrated a knack for translating privilege into opportunities for personal advancement. But the privileges granted to Arthur Bancroft Schlesinger, born on October 15, 1917, had less to do with money than with his father's prominence as a renowned historian.

A distinguished member of the Harvard faculty, Arthur M. Schlesinger Sr. took it for granted that his son would follow in his footsteps and spared no effort toward that end. It was therefore all but inevitable that "Young Arthur," as he was known among family friends in Cambridge, should attend the university where his father taught, should concentrate in US history, and should be mentored by his father's accommodating colleagues. In 1938 he graduated from Harvard with unusual scholarly promise and, to quote Aldous, a "highhanded sense of entitlement," both very much in evidence. Young Arthur had by then jettisoned Bancroft, his mother's family name, in favor of Meier, thereby becoming Schlesinger Jr.

While Schlesinger was spending a postgraduate year at Cambridge University, his undergraduate thesis, a biography of the idiosyncratic scholar-activist Orestes Brownson, appeared in print with none other than the august Henry Steele Commager providing an effusive review in the *New York Times*. Meanwhile, back home, his father was pulling the necessary strings to secure his son's three-year appointment with Harvard's Society of Fellows. By 1940 Arthur seemed a made man.

Soon enough, however, complications slowed his upward trajectory. They came in two forms: family and war. In August 1940 Schlesinger married Marian Cannon, daughter of another Harvard professor. The union was an ill-fated one. For Arthur, the responsibilities of being a husband and, soon enough, a father became a source of annoyance and consternation. Then in December 1941, the United States entered World War II, with Harvard Yard instantly transformed from the center of Schlesinger's universe into a backwater. Unless tied to the war effort, scholarly pursuits now seemed superfluous and even self-indulgent.

Intent on being part of the action but medically disqualified from military service, Schlesinger was soon off to Washington. There he contributed to the war effort, first by producing government propaganda for the United States Office of War Information and then by editing a classified weekly journal for the Office of Strategic Services (OSS). Neither assignment proved rewarding. In the summer of 1944, he wangled an overseas posting with the OSS. But rather than espionage and skullduggery, his labors in London and subsequently in liberated Paris involved pushing paper. Snobbish and impatient with bosses he considered his intellectual inferiors, he found the experience suffocating.

The end of the war brought release and a sudden restoration of Schlesinger's fortunes. In October 1945 his second book, written during his abbreviated term as a Harvard fellow, appeared. *The Age of Jackson* proved to be a monumental success, spending twenty-five weeks on the *New York Times* best-seller list and, with his father's help behind the scenes, winning the 1946 Pulitzer Prize for history. Soon enough Schlesinger was contributing essays to *Fortune*, *Life*, and the *New York Times Magazine*, hobnobbing with members of Washington DC's "Georgetown set," and collaborating with Eleanor Roosevelt, Reinhold Niebuhr, and other luminaries to found the Americans for Democratic Action (ADA), which became in short order the leading voice of Cold War liberalism. With his father running interference, he also accepted a tenured appointment to Harvard's Department of History, despite not having a PhD.

His time now divided between teaching, scholarship, journalism, and politics—with sporadic attention to family—Schlesinger's life became dizzyingly busy. He embarked on an ambitious multi-volume history of the "Age of Roosevelt," envisioned as his life's work, but destined never to be finished. At regular intervals he penned attention-grabbing polemics such as *The Vital Center* (1949), which depicted New Deal-style liberalism as the only legitimate alternative to right-wing or left-wing totalitarianism, and *The General and the President* (1951), written with Richard Rovere, which castigated Douglas Mac-Arthur as a threat to the Constitution.

Schlesinger also "developed a near addiction to the narcotic of political battle," writes Aldous. In 1952 and again in 1956, he hitched his wagon to Adlai Stevenson's ambivalent star, writing speeches during each of Stevenson's two presidential campaigns and offering advice to a candidate who remained unsure as to whether he really wanted the top job. Then in 1960, he fell for the seductive charms of a candidate who entertained none of Stevenson's ambivalence.

John F. Kennedy's liberal bona fides were dubious at best. To be fair, by this time Schlesinger's own conception of liberalism was not especially easy to define. Rather than an ideology or set of fixed principles, his liberalism was more akin to an attitude or temperament. For Schlesinger flexibility, pragmatism, and the vigorous exercise of state power, especially by the chief executive, were among liberalism's defining attributes. To be a liberal was to revere the New Deal and to hold Big Business and communism in equal contempt. Notwithstanding Schlesinger's friendship with and enduring admiration for Niebuhr, he was uninterested in religion and oblivious to transcendence. Yet his liberalism was also a matter of style. It implied intellect, wit, and savoir faire, qualities not found in loathsome politicians like Joseph McCarthy or Richard Nixon or among the dour figures presiding over the Soviet Politburo.

Of course Kennedy had style to spare. That, combined with the fact that Nixon was the GOP presidential nominee in 1960, enabled Schlesinger to climb aboard the Kennedy bandwagon without any qualms of conscience. When the president-elect subsequently invited Schlesinger to join the "action intellectuals" being recruited to work in the White House, he jumped at the chance and took leave from Harvard, as it turned out, for good.

Schlesinger was to serve as Special Assistant to the President. No one had more than a murky understanding of what that title was meant to entail. Aldous describes Schlesinger's status as that of a "gadfly." Perhaps *kibitzer* works as well. Schlesinger had no staff and no fixed responsibilities. Although his office was in the déclassé East Wing, he did enjoy occasional access to the Oval Office. He served as a sort of liaison to Ambassador Stevenson at the United Nations and pitched in on some of the First Lady's projects. With or without invitation, he dashed off memos advising Kennedy on sundry matters. Yet on critical issues such as Cuba, Vietnam, and relations with the Soviet Union, Schlesinger was "at best distant, at worst completely out of the loop." He was by no means a central player.

His actual function—and the reason Kennedy wanted him around in the first place—was to serve as a sort of court historian in waiting. Between the president and his special assistant, writes Aldous, there was an "implicit understanding" that Schlesinger's real work would begin once JFK left the White House. His long-term assignment was to "establish the Age of Kennedy as a worthy successor to the Age of Roosevelt."

When Kennedy's assassination brought his presidency to a premature end, Schlesinger went immediately to work to secure his legacy. Throughout his long career, Schlesinger suffered from the inverse of writer's block. Put him in front of a typewriter and words, sentences, and whole paragraphs gushed forth: graceful, abundant, and laced with exquisitely apposite quotations from a wide array of sources.

In just over a year, he crafted a massive memoir-history of the Kennedy administration that appeared in 1965 under the title of *A Thousand Days*. It was a bravura performance, delivering precisely what Kennedy himself and the Kennedy family had counted on Schlesinger to produce.

Upon publication the thousand-plus page tome rocketed to the top of the *New York Times* best-seller list. It won both the National Book Award and the Pulitzer Prize. Above all, it imparted to the now-emerging legend of Camelot a historian's imprimatur. A grateful

Jacqueline Kennedy sent Schlesinger a congratulatory note comparing him to Plutarch and Thucydides.

Kennedy, Schlesinger wrote, had "reestablished the republic as the first generation of our leaders saw it—young, brave, civilized, rational, gay, tough, questing, [and] exultant." He had "transformed the American spirit," thereby "wiping away the world's impression of an old nation of old men, weary, played out, fearful of ideas, change, and the future." All this over the course of a presidency that had lasted less than three years.

In reality Schlesinger's labors had yielded something other than a history. *A Thousand Days* was more akin to an epic poem in prose form. Schlesinger depicted JFK as more than a mere mortal and his assassination as something more than a politically motivated murder—in his telling, it was an incomparable historical tragedy affecting all of humankind. That so many Americans still accept Schlesinger's rendering as true testifies to his extraordinary artistry, which concealed blemishes, erased shadows, and cast its subject in a soft golden glow.

Intent on returning to his Roosevelt project, Schlesinger accepted a position with the City University of New York—the teaching duties were light, the amenities generous—and moved to Manhattan. Newly divorced and something of a celebrity in his own right, Schlesinger soon emerged as a man about town. All was not frivolity, however. With the Vietnam War now in full swing, he dashed off a blistering critique of Lyndon Johnson's policy, titled *The Bitter Heritage* (1967), insisting that had Kennedy lived he would have avoided war. At the same time, as a leading figure of the liberal Democratic establishment, Schlesinger himself came in for sharp criticism from the New Left. In some quarters, "liberal" had become an epithet. After all, the "best and brightest" who had presided over America's plunge into Vietnam in the first place had possessed impeccably liberal credentials.

Unsurprisingly, as both Kennedy family loyalist and sharp critic of Johnson, Schlesinger threw himself into Robert Kennedy's abbreviated 1968 presidential campaign. Although Kennedy's assassination ended Schlesinger's own behind-the-scenes political career, it created a further opportunity to be of service to the Kennedy family. Just a month after her husband's murder, Ethel Kennedy approached

Schlesinger about writing his biography. After only the briefest hesitation, he accepted the invitation.

In this instance, however, the project took far longer to complete than expected. Distractions intervened. One was Schlesinger's marriage to the much younger, much taller, and (in comparison with the nerdy-looking Arthur) more glamorous Alexandra Emmet. Starting a new family while in his fifties, he became a devoted father. A second distraction came in the form of Schlesinger's old nemesis Richard Nixon, now occupying the White House. Nixon inspired Schlesinger to rethink his enthusiasm for an activist chief executive in the mold of FDR. His anti-Nixon brief found expression in his 1973 book *The Imperial Presidency*.

When *Robert Kennedy and His Times* finally appeared in 1978, it pleased Kennedy acolytes but struck others as overly long and uncritical. In truth, Schlesinger now found himself increasingly out of step with the prevailing political and cultural climate. Although he kept writing, he increasingly came across as something of a crank. *The Disuniting of America*, his 1991 attack on multiculturalism and what he called "the cult of ethnicity," offers a good illustration.

In his later years he retained his ability to provoke. Yet his views now seemed retrograde, a throwback to another time. After a long period of physical decline during which he demonstrated a continuing zest for life, Schlesinger died abruptly of a heart attack in February 2007.

Elegant in expression, his pen ever at the ready to serve causes in which he believed, Schlesinger was undoubtedly "one of the finest narrative historians America has ever produced," as Aldous concludes. Yet with very rare exceptions, historians themselves are a disposable commodity, their work destined to be superseded or simply forgotten. On the very first page of *Orestes Brownson* (1939), the first of his many books, Schlesinger himself had written, "The measure of what is historically important is set by the generation that writes the history, not by the one that makes it." Yet each generation in turn claims the prerogative to decide what qualifies as historically important, almost inevitably rendering obsolete the judgments of prior generations. By the time of Schlesinger's death, the writing of history had long since passed to a generation other than his own.

Yet to read this account is to appreciate that Schlesinger's America, shaped by the Great Depression, World War II, and the Cold War, has also vanished. And with it so too has Schlesinger's brand of liberalism. In the era of Donald Trump, a seemingly unbridgeable divide exists where the "vital center" once stood. You don't have to be a liberal to mourn all that has been lost as a consequence.

4

George Kennan
Kennan Kvetches

(2014)

Pity the man's poor wife. To peruse this generous selection from a diary totaling, according to the volume's editor, some "twenty thousand pages of elegant, insightful prose" is to come away with a heightened appreciation for Annelise Sørensen Kennan. To share a breakfast table, much less a life, with George Kennan must have been a trial.

We know from John Gaddis's biography of Kennan, which won the Pulitzer Prize in 2012, that his penchant for philandering tested Annelise's patience. Judging from this account, spanning almost nine decades—the first entry is by an eleven-year-old, the last by a near-centenarian—a wandering eye may have ranked as least among Kennan's personal shortcomings. The widely regarded diplomat turned scholar was a bigoted crank given to feeling sorry for himself.

The George Kennan cherished in public memory is a figure representing a rare combination of prescience and sagacity. As a Foreign Service officer, he alerted the American people to the threat posed by Soviet expansionism after World War II. Yet he also stood foursquare against the excesses to which the ensuing anticommunist crusade gave rise, opposing the militarization of US policy, speaking out against the folly of Vietnam, and warning of the risk of nuclear holocaust.

As edited by Frank Costigliola, a noted diplomatic historian who teaches at the University of Connecticut, *The Kennan Diaries* do contain stray bits of sagacity.[1] There are also occasionally elegant passages recalling Kennan's trenchant and melancholic *Memoirs*, the best of his many books. But the overall tone of this new collection is one of bellyaching. Kennan pissed and moaned incessantly and at length. Although the list of complaints raising his ire is long, heading that list was an abiding resentment at being (by his own estimation) insufficiently appreciated.

Kennan, of course, was the recipient of a warehouse full of honors, but he yearned for more than prizes and honorary degrees. Sure, his books sold well. All the top journals opened their pages to his opinions. Invitations to testify or lecture or occupy some cushy sinecure arrived by the bushel. What Kennan sought above all, however, was power, along with the deference and respect commanded by those exercising it.

According to one of his colleagues, Kennan possessed "a strong messianic streak." In a modern world hell-bent on destroying itself, he fancied himself assigned the role of savior. Apart from an exhilarating but fleeting moment in the immediate wake of World War II, however, when he played a central part in formulating the Cold War strategy of "containment," real power eluded Kennan. As ostensibly the wisest and certainly the most durable of the postwar Wise Men, he enjoyed respect without wielding much in the way of immediate influence, leaving him in the twilight of his long life to mourn that in his self-designated role as prophet he had failed. "It was for this that I was born," he insisted in 1982, at age seventy-seven. Yet he found himself "standing as a witness at the final, apocalyptic self-destruction of this marvelous Western civilization." His resulting sense of deprivation was all but unendurable.

---

1. George F. Kennan, *The Kennan Diaries*, ed. Frank Costigliola. (New York: W.W. Norton, 2014).

More often than not, the marvels of Western civilization impressed Kennan less than did its deficiencies. Writing in 1937, he described man as "a skin-disease of the earth." The passage of time reinforced this view. Technology, principally represented by automobiles, which he loathed, and by nuclear weapons, which he came to fear, served only to make matters worse. "Modern urban-industrial man," he reflected some forty years later, "is given to the raping of anything and everything natural on which he can fasten his talons. He rapes the sea; he rapes the soil. . . . He rapes the atmosphere. He rapes the future of his own civilization. . . . [H]e goes on destroying his own environment like a vast horde of locusts."

When Kennan turned his gaze to his country, his views were equally bleak and unsparing. As a young man fresh out of Princeton, he characterized Americanism as a "disease" and likened it explicitly to Bolshevism. American society as a whole was cheap, vulgar, and materialistic. Middle age found him railing against "the chrome, the asphalt, the advertising, the television sets, the filling stations, [and] the hot dog stands" that embodied the "trancelike, unreal" American way of life. As an old man, he denounced "the shameless pornography, the pathological preoccupation with sex and violence, [and] the weird efforts to claim for homosexuality the status of a proud, noble, and promising way of life" that "in significant degree" had made America a "sick society." But when it came to eliciting paroxysms of indignation, nothing topped California. "I find myself really wishing," he wrote en route from San Francisco to Monterey in 1966, "that some catastrophe might occur that would depopulate this region & permit it to heal its scars & return to its natural state." In his dotage, he wrote of America, "I am in utter despair about this country." He "long[ed] for the day of the catastrophe" that would allow the "atrocities of man's handiwork to decay into the ruins they deserve to become."

In the 1950s, Kennan contemplated the possibility of simply fleeing, "even to the Soviet Union"—any alternative seemed preferable to allowing his children to "grow up in this cradle of luxury that corrupted and demoralized them before they even reached maturity." Cold War expectations that the United States could deflect the forces of darkness while leading the free world toward some promised land were, to Kennan, the height of absurdity.

I read this book while visiting Fort Lauderdale, a place peculiarly suited to Kennan's denunciations of chrome and asphalt, overcrowding and overdevelopment. To contemplate the strip malls lining traffic-clogged US 1, the high-rises crowding the beach, and the fleets of gaudy megayachts cluttering the Intercoastal Waterway is to entertain Kennanesque views. Is this what the signers of the Declaration of Independence had in mind when they staked their claim to "certain unalienable Rights"? You don't have to be a believer or a cultural conservative—Kennan was both—to endorse his view that there's something fundamentally amiss with American-style freedom as actually exercised.

But when it comes to proposing remedies for the ills of modernity, the Kennan of the diaries comes across not as a thoughtful conservative but as a slightly unhinged reactionary. To reduce overpopulation, he insisted in 1984, "Men having spawned more than 2 children will be compulsively sterilized." (With Annelise, Kennan had spawned four.) To purge the culture of corrupting influences, he wanted television to "be sacrificed," with broadcasts limited to "perhaps one or two public channels operating only in the evening hours." (Watching tennis was a favorite Kennan diversion, so presumably one of those channels would be reserved for suitably high-toned sporting events.) Intent on reducing oil consumption and slowing the pace of life, he proposed that air travel be "throttled down & eventually restricted to hardship & urgent cases." (Of course, Kennan was constantly jetting around the world for reasons unlikely to satisfy either criterion.)

Even when it comes to statecraft, the arena in which Kennan's reputation as a sage ultimately rests, the diary does as much to diminish as to enhance his standing. Basic policy, Kennan believed, should "be created and pursued only by specialists and professionals"—members of the guild to which he belonged. He lamented the American practice of "placing foreign affairs in the hands of amateurs." And no fan of the *demos*, he. The masses, he wrote in 1932 as a young member of the Foreign Service, "should be properly clothed and fed and sheltered, but not crowned with a moral halo, and above all not allowed to have anything to do with government." He never budged from that dim assessment.

Yet the analyses and prescriptions offered by Kennan as the ur-professional are mixed at best. Sometimes, pros commit errors of judgment that would make even amateurs blush. Were Joseph Stalin's lieutenants quietly easing him out of power immediately after World War II? Kennan, relying apparently on gut instinct, thought so. In a diary entry dated November 26, 1945, he described himself as "one of the few foreigners in Moscow, if not the only one, who feels that it is questionable whether Stalin is still the dictator that people think he is."

As early as the 1950s, Kennan had disconcerted officials in Washington by publicly calling for negotiations to pull all NATO and Soviet forces out of Germany. Mutual withdrawal would allow that divided country to reunite, thereby removing the primary cause of Cold War rivalry. American officials denounced the scheme as both reckless and implausible. Not without reason, Kennan believed that the offhand rejection of his proposal had less to do with its viability than with a desire, tacitly shared by Washington and Moscow, to prolong the status quo. A divided Germany suited both sides just fine, he suspected.

But when the fall of the Berlin Wall in 1989 offered up peaceful reunification on a platter, Kennan had a sudden change of heart. A big, powerful Germany was sure to have a destabilizing effect, he now contended. Although Kennan dashed off an op-ed in favor of perpetuating the division he had so forcefully argued against, German reunification proceeded anyway. Thin-skinned as usual, he took the setback personally. On a matter of high policy, authorities in Washington had once again ignored his views. "Very well," Kennan pouted. "Agreed. They win; I lose. I am defeated." In fact, to a considerable extent, subsequent developments vindicated the argument he had made decades earlier: German unification has made a European war less likely.

Then there is Kennan the Chicken Little of nuclear armageddon. Did his 1951 prediction that war with the Soviets would "break out within two years" hold any water? No more than did his insistence the following year that war had become "inevitable, or very nearly so." More such pronouncements followed. Close to despair in 1988, Kennan confessed to having "no hope that a nuclear disaster can be avoided." Within months, the Cold War ended.

On all matters related to race and ethnicity, Kennan harbored views that could charitably be described as unseemly, if not morally obtuse. He considered apartheid unobjectionable in theory, if a tad harsh in practice, advocating a gentler approach that would allow each side to preserve "the integrity of its own social life . . . rather than being subjected to a process of forced homogenization."

And for all the abuse he heaped on Western civilization, Kennan held the non-West in even lower regard. If nothing good could come of modern civilization, he wrote in 1932, the "situation is essentially a biological one. No amount of education and discipline can effectively improve conditions as long as we allow the unfit to breed copiously and to preserve their young." Visits to virtually every part of the world had persuaded him that the unfit—by which he meant "the Mediterraneans, the Moslems, the Latinos, the various non-WASPS of the third and not-quite-third worlds"—were "destroying civilization with their proliferation." As for immigrants entering the United States, he adamantly opposed "the reckless importation into our society . . . of masses of people of wholly different cultural habits, traditions, and outlooks, incompatible with our own." Assimilating such groups would dilute the pedigreed Northern European stock that had formed the basis of a bygone America worthy of respect—the America of the nineteenth century, a time of "meaning, thought, beauty"—which was now lost forever.

Whether Kennan's off-the-wall inclinations aided or undermined his performance in office is difficult to say. Kennan was to statecraft what James Dean was to acting or Sylvia Plath was to poetry. Once "discovered," he burned brightly, but burned out quickly. Kennan had gained access to the inner circle of political power in February 1946, when his "long telegram," written from Moscow, sounded the alarm about an emerging Soviet threat and took Washington by storm. Summoned home, he became a key adviser to Secretary of State George C. Marshall, helping to frame early Cold War strategy. He also won wide acclaim as the mysterious "Mr. X," author of "The Sources of Soviet Conduct," the most famous article ever to appear in the journal *Foreign Affairs*.

But by January 1949 Kennan's star was already in decline. Dean Acheson, who had replaced Marshall, found Kennan's attitude toward power "rather mystical" and therefore less than helpful. After an interval when he had seemingly called the tune, Kennan suddenly found himself out of step.

During this interlude, *The Kennan Diaries* are all but silent. In 1946, Costigliola tells us, Kennan kept no diary. The following year there was a single entry—a poem. (It urged the seeker after Fortune who "Has heard the rustling of the Time-God's raiment / And has contrived to touch the gleaming hem" to rest content, expecting no more—advice that Kennan himself declined to follow.) Only in 1949, with Kennan now increasingly marginalized, did the regularly scheduled rumination resume. So when Kennan mattered most as a historical figure, his diaries have the least to offer. It's as if Samuel Pepys had skipped over the Great Plague or Henry Adams had omitted from his *Education* any mention of his visit to the Paris Exposition of 1900.

In 1953, Kennan retired from government service, embarking on a storied career as a scholar and public intellectual. A brief, ill-starred term in 1952 as US ambassador to the Soviet Union had left him *persona non grata* in Moscow. Back in Washington, his standing was roughly comparable. John Foster Dulles, the hard-liner who was now secretary of state, shared Acheson's aversion to mystical thinking and had no interest in providing meaningful employment to someone tainted by his association with the Democrats. Kennan concluded in retrospect that the years when he and the foreign-policy apparatus had "found ourselves momentarily on the same wave length" had been "accidental, fortuitous."

Still, even though unceremoniously shown the door, Kennan never ceased hoping that he might one day be summoned back to Washington. From the 1950s through the 1980s, as presidents rotated in and out of the White House, he waited expectantly for the phone to ring, for Washington to call on him to save his unworthy countrymen and the teeming millions of wretches with whom Americans collaborated in besmirching the planet. Unless an abbreviated tour as John F. Kennedy's ambassador to Yugoslavia qualifies, the summons never came.

Instead, Kennan whiled away his time in leafy Princeton, New Jersey. There for several decades he occupied a comfortable position at the Institute for Advanced Study, surveying the past and commenting on the present. To stay in the limelight, he wrote and lectured compulsively. "I fire my arrows into the air," he commented with a hint of weariness.

> Sometimes they strike nothing; sometimes they strike the wrong things; sometimes one or another of them strikes a bell and rings it, loud and clear. And then, if no other purpose is served, people are at least stimulated and helped to think.

The people Kennan wanted to stimulate, of course, were those who could get him back into the thick of things.

As he aged—he lived to be 101—a return to active diplomatic service became ever less likely. At the same time, accolades piled up at an accelerating rate. By the 1980s, Kennan wagered that he had become "the most extensively honored private person in the country." Yet as with many of those on whom the world showers recognition, what Kennan now symbolized had eclipsed who Kennan actually was. He himself recognized the problem. "I am being honored, in large part, not for what I really am but for what people think I am," he wrote in 1990. "[L]ike an actor acting the part of someone other than himself, I must try to live up to the costume and to the part. My role is to sustain other people's illusions." Chief among these was the illusion, nurtured in elite political and academic circles, that effective and morally defensible statecraft remains possible. Kennan represented the lingering hope, despite abundant evidence to the contrary, that policies formulated by wise men (and women) can tame or at least redirect historical currents.

That Kennan accomplished this after World War II is the central illusion propping up the Kennan myth. In fact, Costigliola sees the illusion for what it is, writing in his introduction that the "emotionally charged, exaggerated depictions of the Soviet Union as an existential threat" that Kennan penned in 1946 and 1947 simply "spurred administration officials along the route they were already taking."

Under Kennan's watch, that route led directly to the Truman Doctrine, the Marshall Plan, and the founding of NATO, policy initiatives that defined the parameters of the early Cold War. Yet in subsequent years it also led to the very nuclear-arms race Kennan later decried, to a rash of CIA-instigated coups and assassinations, and to a pattern of armed intervention that found US troops fighting in places like Korea and Vietnam, not to mention, in our own day, Iraq and Afghanistan.

Kennan's successors appropriated concepts he had articulated and applied them in ways that went far beyond anything their author had imagined. Larger forces—personal ambition, collective paranoia, domestic politics, bureaucratic inertia, and corporate interests— combined, in different proportions at different times, to determine the actual character of US policy. The memos and speeches of those ostensibly charged with "making" policy served largely as window dressing.

To explain actual outcomes, whether for good or ill, in terms of what some individual achieved or might have achieved if given the authority to act is clearly to misunderstand the workings of history. As an explanation for why the United States does what it does in the world, the original sin of American exceptionalism or the machinations of the national security state offer a closer approximation to truth than do the scribblings of wise men, whether "architects" inside the policy apparatus or self-proclaimed prophets on the outside looking in.

The Kennan Diaries reveal in excruciating detail what made one such architect, or prophet, tick. But Kennan himself makes plain just how limited, flawed, and unwise he was. In that revelation may be found whatever redeeming value this book possesses.

5

———————————

Tom Clancy
Military Man

(2014)

Word of Tom Clancy's passing in October reached me at a local gym. Peddling away on an elliptical trainer, I welcomed the distraction of this "breaking news" story as it swept across a bank of video monitors suspended above the cardio machines. On cable networks and local stations, anchors were soon competing with one another to help viewers grasp the story's significance. Winning the competition (and perhaps an audition with Fox News) was the young newsreader who solemnly announced that "one of America's greatest writers" had just died at the relatively early age of sixty-six.

Of course, Tom Clancy qualifies as a great writer in the same sense that Texas senator Ted Cruz qualifies as a great orator. Both satisfy a quantitative definition of eminence. Although political historians are unlikely to rank Cruz alongside Clay, Calhoun, and Webster, his recent twenty-one-hour-long denunciation of Obamacare, delivered before a near-empty Senate chamber, demonstrated a capacity for narcissistic logorrhea rare even by Washington standards.

So too with Clancy. Up in the literary Great Beyond, Faulkner and Hemingway won't be inviting him for drinks. Yet, as with Ted Cruz, once Clancy got going there was no shutting him up. Following a slow start, the works of fiction and nonfiction that he wrote, cowrote, or attached his moniker to numbered in the dozens. Some seventeen Clancy novels made it to the top of the *New York Times* best-seller list, starting with his breakthrough thriller *The Hunt for Red October*. A slew of titles written by others appeared with his imprimatur. Thus, for example, *Tom Clancy's Ghost Recon: Choke Point* or *Tom Clancy's Splinter Cell: Blacklist Aftermath*.

Similarly, on those occasions when Clancy partnered with some retired US four-star to craft the officer's memoirs, the result was a tome "by" Tom Clancy "with" General So-and-So, the difference in font size signaling who was the bigger cheese. And then there is Tom Clancy's Military Reference series, another product line in the realm of fictive nonfiction. Each title—*Fighter Wing*, for example, or *Armored Cav*—promises a Clancy-led "guided tour" of what really goes on in the elite corners of the United States military.

Clancy did for military pop-lit what Starbucks did for the preparation of caffeinated beverages: he launched a sprawling, massively profitable industrial enterprise that simultaneously serves and cultivates an insatiable customer base. Whether the item consumed provides much in terms of nourishment is utterly beside the point. That it tastes yummy going down more than suffices to keep customers coming back.

If Clancy was a hack, as he surely was, he was a hack who possessed a remarkable talent for delivering what his fans craved. Nor did the Tom Clancy brand confine itself to the written word. His oeuvre has provided ideal fodder for Hollywood too. Movie adaptations chronicling the exploits of Jack Ryan, Clancy's principal protagonist, and starring the likes of Harrison Ford, Alec Baldwin, and Ben Affleck became blockbuster hits. Then there are the testosterone-laced video games, carrying titles like *Tom Clancy's Ghost Recon: Future Soldier* and *Tom Clancy's Rainbow Six: Vegas 2*.

Clancy-approved video games captured the Pentagon's fancy. In 2007, Red Storm Entertainment, the gaming arm of Clancy's empire, released *America's Army: True Soldiers*, advertised as an "Official U.S.

Army Game." ("Created by Soldiers. Developed by Gamers. Tested by Heroes.") The accompanying copy assures prospective purchasers/ recruits that "combat action doesn't get any more authentic than this."

> Become one of America's bravest in this game developed in con-
> junction with the U.S. Army. See what it's like to live life as an
> infantryman. Take on the role of a Rifleman, Grenadier, Auto-
> matic Rifleman, or Sniper. Develop skills including Valor,
> Marksmanship, Stealth, and more.

Here profit and propaganda blend into a seamless package.

Did I mention Clancy-themed board games, music CDs, toys, and apparel? There is even a Clancy line of pseudo-military collectibles. Among the items available for purchase is the *Ghost Recon* "Future Soldier" — your choice: statuette or stuffed toy.

Don't expect Clancy's departure to stem this tsunami of stuff. Although the founder himself may have left the scene, Clancy Inc. gives every indication of carrying on. A new Clancy novel called *Command Authority* arrived in December. And a new Jack Ryan movie, this one not based on previously published material, is in the works.

Yet to argue that Clancy's books and ancillary byproducts offer little in terms of lasting value is not to say that they have lacked influence. Indeed, just the reverse is true. As a shaper of the zeitgeist, Tom Clancy may well rate as one of the most influential creative entrepreneurs of the last several decades.

In whatever medium, Clancy's abiding theme is the never-ending struggle between good guys and bad guys. His bad guys tend to be irredeemably bad. His good guys are invariably very, very good — Americans devoted to the cause of keeping their countrymen safe and the world free. As good guys, they subscribe to old-fashioned virtues while making skillful use of the latest technology. Whether garbed in battledress or trenchcoats, they are cool, professional, dedicated, resourceful, and exceedingly competent. These are, of course, the very qualities that Americans today ascribe to those who actually serve in uniform or who inhabit the "black world," whether as CIA agents or members of highly specialized units such as Delta Force or SEAL Team Six.

What's worth recalling is that the prevailing view of America's warriors was not always so favorable. In the wake of Vietnam, shortly before Clancy burst onto the scene, the books that sold and the scripts attracting Hollywood's attention told a different story. Those inhabiting positions of responsibility in the United States military were either venal careerists or bunglers out of their depth. Those on the front lines were victims or saps. When it came to military-themed accessories, the preferred logo was FTA.

Clancy was among the first to intuit that the antimilitary mood spawned by Vietnam represented an opportunity. The legions who did not find *Catch-22* particularly amusing, who were more annoyed than entertained by *M*A*S*H*, and who classified Jane Fonda as a traitor were hungry to find someone to validate their views—someone who still believed in the red, white, and blue and who still admired those fighting to defend it. Clancy offered himself as that someone.

To be more accurate, Ronald Reagan had already offered himself as that someone. What Clancy did was seize the role of Reagan's literary doppelgänger—what the Gipper might have become had he chosen writing instead of politics after ending his acting career.

Clancy's own career took off when President Reagan plugged *Red October* as "my kind of yarn." As well he might: Clancy shared Reagan's worldview. His stories translated that worldview into something that seemed "real" and might actually become real if you believed hard enough. Reagan was famous for transforming the imagined into the actual; despite never having left Hollywood during World War II, he *knew*, for example, that he had personally witnessed the liberation of Nazi death camps. Similarly, Clancy, who never served in the military, imagined a world of selfless patriots performing feats of derring-do to overcome evil—a world that large numbers of Americans were certain had once existed. More to the point, it was a world they desperately wanted to restore. Clancy, like Reagan, made that restoration seem eminently possible.

Soon after Clancy's death, the *Washington Post* published an appreciation entitled "How Tom Clancy Made the Military Cool Again," written by a couple of self-described Gen-Xer policy wonks. "Clancy's legacy lives on in the generations he introduced to the military," they gushed, crediting Clancy with having "created a literary bridge across the civil-military divide." His "stories helped the rest of society understand and imagine" the world of spooks and soldiers. Perhaps not surprisingly, those who served or aspired to serve found those stories to be especially gratifying. Clancy depicted American soldiers and would-be soldiers precisely as they wished to see themselves.

But any understanding gained by either soldiers or society, whether engaged in *Patriot Games* or fending off *The Sum of All Fears*, was illusory, rooted in fantasies that sanitized war and conveyed a false sense of what military service really entails. Instead of bridging the civil-military divide, Clancy papered it over, thereby perpetuating it. By extension, he contributed in no small way to the conditions breeding the misguided and costly military adventurism that has become the signature of US policy.

Clancy did prove to be a figure of consequence. Alas, almost all of those consequences have proven to be pernicious. And there's no Jack Ryan anywhere in sight to come to our rescue.

6

Robert Kagan
The Duplicity of the Ideologues

(2014)

"Almost seventy years ago, a new world order was born from the rubble of World War II, built by and around the power of the United States." Yet today, Robert Kagan laments, "that world order shows signs of cracking, and perhaps even collapsing." Wherever he looks, Kagan sees evidence that "something is changing, and perhaps more quickly than we may imagine," as he writes in the *New Republic* ("Superpowers Don't Get to Retire"). Indeed, "the signs of the global order breaking down are all around us."

These changes "signal a transition into a different world order," one bearing troubling similarities to the 1930s. The origins of this prospective calamity are plain to see. Don't bother to look for material explanations. "If a breakdown in the world order that America made is occurring," Kagan writes, "it is not because America's power is declining." The United States has power to spare, asserts the author of *The World America Made*. No, what we have here is "an intellectual problem, a question of identity and purpose." Feckless, silly Americans, with weak-willed Barack Obama their enabler, are abdicating their obligation to lead the planet. The abyss beckons.

Writing in the *New York Times*, columnist David Brooks hails Kagan's *New Republic* essay as "brilliant." A more accurate appraisal would be slickly mendacious. Still, Kagan's essay also qualifies as instructive: Here, in some 12,700 carefully polished words, the impoverished state of foreign-policy discourse is laid bare. If the problem hobbling US policy is an intellectual one, then Kagan himself, purveyor of a fictive past, exhibits that problem in spades.

That Robert Kagan, a bona fide Washington insider currently housed at the Brookings Institution, possesses very considerable talents is doubtless the case. A well-regarded historian, he is also a skilled polemicist and an ideologue. Here he combines all three callings to fashion a historical narrative that advances two claims. The first enshrines the entire period since 1945 — until Obama sounded retreat, anyway — as a kind of golden age when freedom, democracy, and liberal values flourished as never before. The second attributes this golden age almost entirely to enlightened American leadership. Policymakers in Washington, he writes, manifested a "sense of global responsibility that equated American interests with the interests of many others around the world."

Neither one of these claims stands up to even casual scrutiny. Rather than describing the prevailing realities of the post-1945 era, phrases like "world order" and "global responsibility" obfuscate. Purporting to clarify, they merely gloss over. Kagan employs these as devices to beguile, while constructing a version of "truth" that ignores inconvenient facts. There's a name for this technique: It's called propaganda.

The "world order" of the decades following World War II exists only in Kagan's imagination. You'd hardly know it from reading his essay, but the postwar world was divided into three distinct camps: the American-led West, the Soviet-led Communist bloc, and the so-called Third World, which had its own problems, unrelated to the East-West rivalry, to worry about.

Furthermore, even to refer to these as camps involves considerable oversimplification. Within each, sharp divisions existed. Nominally allies, France and the United States frequently found themselves at odds, for example. Although Communists ruled Yugoslavia, Josip Broz Tito refused to take orders from the Kremlin. Some countries—Yugoslavia offers one example, Castro's Cuba another—consciously sought to keep a foot in more than one camp. Then there was Israel, which occupied a camp all its own. After President Richard Nixon's famous visit, so too did China, openly antagonistic toward the USSR, but by no means part of the West.

To the extent that we can credit this disorderly conglomeration with producing anything worthy of note, its chief accomplishment was to avoid a cataclysmic third world war. Here, the United States, sole practitioner of nuclear warfare and possessor of the world's largest nuclear arsenal, did play a role. Yet apart from sheer dumb luck, what kept Armageddon at bay was not farsighted global leadership on Washington's part but prudent self-restraint.

In October 1962, when Nikita Khrushchev's rashness handed John F. Kennedy the chance to liberate Cuba from communism, the president judged it the better part of valor to cut a deal instead. Rather than confrontation, he opted for negotiation, offering the Soviets an unearned concession—in exchange for their missiles out of Cuba, ours would come out of Turkey. Cubans remained unliberated.

Similarly, when brave Europeans under the boot of Soviet dominion periodically rose up—East Germans in 1953, Poles and Hungarians in 1956, Czechs in 1968—Washington's commitment to freedom and democracy took a backseat to its preference for avoiding a potentially climactic East-West showdown. In each case, the United States stood by as the Kremlin brutally restored discipline in its empire.

Of course, much like the Soviets in Eastern Europe, Washington asserted the prerogative of policing its own sphere of influence. When it did so—overthrowing regimes not to its liking in Guatemala, Iran, and South Vietnam, for example—the "promotion of a liberal world order" did not rank high on the list of American motives. So too with the roster of despots, dictators, and kleptocrats that the United States assiduously supported. From Batista and Somoza in the 1950s to Musharraf and Mubarak in the past decade, a regime's adherence to liberal values seldom determined whether it was deemed a worthy American ally.

Such matters do not qualify for inclusion in Kagan's celebration of American global leadership, however. Guatemala he simply ignores—

not worth the bother. Iran gets mentioned only as a "rogue state" with an inexplicable hankering to acquire nuclear weapons. As for Vietnam, Kagan contents himself with an ambiguous reference to its "uncertain and unsatisfying" outcome, as if the war were a risky stock purchase that still might show a modest profit.

Other disruptions to a "world order" ostensibly founded on the principle of American "global responsibility" included the 1947 partition of India (estimated 500,000 to 1 million dead); the 1948 displacement of Palestinians (700,000 refugees); the exodus of Vietnamese from north to south in 1954 (between 600,000 and 1 million fled); the flight of the pied noir from Algeria (800,000 exiled); the deaths resulting directly from Mao Zedong's quest for utopia (between 2 million and 5 million); the mass murder of Indonesians during the anti-Communist purges of the mid-1960s (500,000 slaughtered); the partition of Pakistan in 1971 (up to 3 million killed; millions more displaced); genocide in Cambodia (1.7 million dead); and war between Iran and Iraq (at least 400,000 killed). Did I mention civil wars in Nigeria, Uganda, Burundi, Ethiopia, Mozambique, Sudan, Congo, Liberia, and Sierra Leone that killed millions? The list goes on.

Kagan mentions none of those episodes. Yet all occurred during the Cold War, when the United States was, in his words, "vigilant and ready to act, with force, anywhere in the world."

By what standard does a system in which such things occur qualify as a "world order"? With the United States reacting passively to human misery on an epic scale (where not actively abetting the perpetrators), what is the operative definition of "global responsibility" that squares with US behavior? If, as Kagan argues, "the American project has aimed at shaping a world different from what had always been, taking advantage of America's unique situation to do what no nation had ever been able to do," then how can it be that such awful events persist?

The answers to these questions are clear. First, to the extent that a postwar liberal order existed, it was fragile, tentative, and incomplete. It was a club. Membership criteria were strictly enforced. Residents of the Anglosphere were in, of course. So too were certain favored Europeans. After a time, Japan and South Korea gained entry. As far as Washington was concerned, however, most others could fend for themselves.

Second, in defending this less-than-global order, American leaders by-and-large understood what Kagan refuses to acknowledge: The United States wielded limited power and influence. For the most part, these leaders sought to husband that power. Rather than "ready to act, with force, anywhere in the world," they confined their actions to places and situations thought to matter.

At least they did most of the time, with Vietnam an especially telling exception. The Vietnam War was not uncertain and unsatisfying. It was stupid and catastrophic. An accounting of what the United States got wrong in Vietnam would require an essay longer than Kagan's. The things that the United States got right in Vietnam can be reduced to a single sentence: Cynically proclaiming that "peace with honor" had been achieved, it left.

Now back in the late 1960s and early '70s, the intellectual forebears of Robert Kagan decried this decision to cut American losses. Leaving implied the acceptance of failure. Such a failure, they insisted, would hand the Communists a great victory. United States credibility would suffer permanent damage. The Soviets would seize the initiative. Dominoes would topple. The United States would find itself isolated and alone.

None of those gloomy predictions—similar in tone to Kagan's own forecast of "increasing conflict, increasing wars over territory, greater ethnic and sectarian violence, and a shrinking world of democracies" as the inevitable price for any lapse in American globalism—turned out to be accurate, of course.

Instead, the nation that Kagan describes as committed to doing "what no nation had ever been able to do" actually did what every great power does when it loses a war. It licked its wounds and left it to others to lick their own. That the United States made next to no effort to aid the Vietnamese and others adversely affected by the war speaks volumes about the definition of "global responsibility" that actually prevailed in Washington. But however cynical, leaving—more accurately abandoning—South Vietnam turned out to be a smart move. Doing so facilitated this nation's military, economic, and political recovery.

With the end of the Cold War, according to Kagan, Washington's commitment to promoting a liberal world order reached new heights.

The signature of US foreign policy during the 1990s was renewed activism. A series of armed interventions ensued. "All aimed at defending and extending the liberal world order," Kagan writes, "by toppling dictators, reversing coups, and attempting to restore democracies."

As Hemingway's Jake Barnes might put it, "Isn't it pretty to think so?" In fact, during the post–Cold War decade, with the Persian Gulf now the epicenter of US military activity, "extending the liberal world order" lagged well behind other, more pressing considerations. Priority number one was to ensure the safety and well-being of the distinctly illiberal Saudi monarchy. Priority number two was to contain Shiite-majority Iran. Fear of delivering Sunni-controlled Iraq into the hands of its own Shiite majority muted US enthusiasm for democratizing that country. If the choice was between stability and democracy, Washington preferred the former.

Still, if as Kagan regretfully notes (and recent polls affirm), Americans today show signs of being "world weary," it's not the events of the 1990s that have induced this weariness. No, if Americans appear disinclined to have a go at overthrowing Syria's Assad or at restoring the Crimea to Ukrainian control, it's due to their common-sense assessment of what US policy in very recent years has produced.

On this subject, astonishingly, Kagan has almost nothing to say. "A generation that does not remember the Cold War," he observes, "but grew up knowing only Iraq and Afghanistan, is going to view America's role in the world differently." But what *should* this generation (not to mention generations that *do* remember the Cold War) make of the wars in Iraq and Afghanistan? What lessons does Kagan himself take from those wars? On this he is mute.

The reticence is uncharacteristic. Back in 1996, in a famous *Foreign Affairs* article co-authored with William Kristol, Kagan identified "benign global hegemony" as the proper basis for US policy. It was incumbent upon the United States to exploit its Cold War victory. Armed with a combination of "military supremacy and moral confidence," Washington needed to put existing and potential adversaries in their place. The idea was "to make clear that it is futile to compete with American power." Permanent dominion was the goal. To settle for anything less, Kagan and Kristol wrote, was to embrace "a policy of cowardice and dishonor."

Even before September 11, 2001, Kagan was among those fixing their sights on Saddam Hussein's Iraq as the place to validate this approach. The events of 9/11 reinforced his determination along with his sense of self-assurance. Writing with Kristol in April 2002, he declared flatly that "the road that leads to real security and peace" is "the road that runs through Baghdad."

George W. Bush took that road. Yet much to his considerable chagrin, Bush discovered that it led to rather considerable unpleasantness. As it dragged on, the Iraq War exposed as hollow any American aspirations to global hegemony. Left behind when US troops finally withdrew was their reputation for military supremacy. Meanwhile, as reports of prisoner abuse, torture, and the killing of noncombatants mounted, American moral confidence lost its luster. As for the Iraqis themselves, although few Americans are inclined to take notice, today they enjoy neither security nor peace.

On all of these matters, Kagan chooses to stay mum. That is his privilege, of course. Yet in exercising that privilege he forfeits any claim to be taken seriously. As with members of the Catholic hierarchy who hoped that the clergy sex-abuse scandal would just blow over or investment bankers who shrug off the economic collapse of 2008 as just one of those things, without accountability there can be no credibility.

William Buckley once remarked that the country would be better off governed by the first two thousand names in the Boston phone book than by the faculty of Harvard University. Here's a corollary: When it comes to foreign policy, the president of the United States would be better served to consult a few reasonably informed citizens from Muncie, Indiana, than to take seriously advice offered by seers such as Robert Kagan.

If experience has brought President Obama to share in this view—as his recent ruminations on foreign policy appear to suggest—then more power to him.

7

Boykinism

Joe McCarthy Would Understand

(2012)

First came the hullaballoo over the "Mosque at Ground Zero." Then there was Pastor Terry Jones of Gainesville, Florida, grabbing headlines as he promoted "International Burn-a-Koran Day." Most recently, we have an American posting a slanderous anti-Muslim video on the Internet with all the ensuing turmoil.

Throughout, the official US position has remained fixed: the United States government condemns Islamophobia. Americans respect Islam as a religion of peace. Incidents suggesting otherwise are the work of a tiny minority—whackos, hatemongers, and publicity-seekers. Among Muslims from Benghazi to Islamabad, the argument has proven to be a tough sell.

And not without reason: although it might be comforting to dismiss anti-Islamic outbursts in the United States as the work of a few fanatics, the picture is actually far more complicated. Those complications in turn help explain why religion, once considered a foreign policy asset, has in recent years become a net liability.

Let's begin with a brief history lesson. From the late 1940s to the late 1980s, when Communism provided the overarching ideological rationale for American globalism, religion figured prominently as a theme of US foreign policy. Communist antipathy toward religion helped invest the Cold War foreign policy consensus with its remarkable durability. That Communists were godless sufficed to place them beyond the pale. For many Americans, the Cold War derived its moral clarity from the conviction that here was a contest pitting the God-fearing against the God-denying. Since we were on God's side, it appeared axiomatic that God should repay the compliment.

From time to time during the decades when anti-Communism provided so much of the animating spirit of US policy, Judeo-Christian strategists in Washington (not necessarily believers themselves), drawing on the theologically correct proposition that Christians, Jews, and Muslims all worship the same God, sought to enlist Muslims, sometimes of fundamentalist persuasions, in the cause of opposing the godless. One especially notable example was the Soviet-Afghan War of 1979–89. To inflict pain on the Soviet occupiers, the United States threw its weight behind the Afghan resistance, styled in Washington as "freedom fighters," and funneled aid (via the Saudis and the Pakistanis) to the most religiously extreme among them. When this effort resulted in a massive Soviet defeat, the United States celebrated its support for the Afghan Mujahedeen as evidence of strategic genius. It was almost as if God had rendered a verdict.

Yet not so many years after the Soviets withdrew in defeat, the freedom fighters morphed into the fiercely anti-Western Taliban, providing sanctuary to al-Qaeda as it plotted—successfully—to attack the United States. Clearly, this was a monkey wrench thrown into God's plan.

With the launching of the Global War on Terror, Islamism succeeded Communism as the body of beliefs that, if left unchecked, threatened to sweep across the globe with dire consequences for freedom. Those whom Washington had armed as "freedom fighters" now became America's most dangerous enemies. So at least members of the national security establishment believed or purported to believe, thereby curtailing any further discussion of whether militarized globalism actually represented the best approach to promoting liberal values globally or even served US interests.

Yet as a rallying cry, a war against Islamism presented difficulties right from the outset. As much as policymakers struggled to prevent Islamism from merging in the popular mind with Islam itself, significant numbers of Americans—whether genuinely fearful or mischief-minded—saw this as a distinction without a difference. Efforts by the Bush administration to work around this problem by framing the post-9/11 threat under the rubric of "terrorism" ultimately failed because that generic term offered no explanation for motive. However the administration twisted and turned, motive in this instance seemed bound up with matters of religion.

Where exactly to situate God in post-9/11 US policy posed a genuine challenge for policymakers, not least of all for George W. Bush, who believed, no doubt sincerely, that God had chosen him to defend America in its time of maximum danger. Unlike the communists, far from denying God's existence, Islamists embrace God with startling ferocity. Indeed, in their vitriolic denunciations of the United States and in perpetrating acts of anti-American violence, they audaciously present themselves as nothing less than God's avenging agents. In confronting the Great Satan, they claim to be doing God's will.

Waging War in Jesus's Name

This debate over who actually represents God's will is one that the successive administrations of George W. Bush and Barack Obama have studiously sought to avoid. The United States is not at war with Islam per se, US officials insist. Still, among Muslims abroad, Washington's repeated denials notwithstanding, suspicion persists and not without reason.

Consider the case of Lieutenant General William G. ("Jerry") Boykin. While still on active duty in 2002, this highly decorated Army officer spoke in uniform at a series of some thirty church gatherings during which he offered his own response to President Bush's famous question: "Why do they hate us?" The general's perspective differed markedly from his commander-in-chief's: "The answer to that is because we're a Christian nation. We are hated because we are a nation of believers."

On another such occasion, the general recalled his encounter with a Somali warlord who claimed to enjoy Allah's protection. The warlord was deluding himself, Boykin declared, and was sure to get his comeuppance: "I knew that my God was bigger than his. I knew that my God was a real God and his was an idol." As a Christian nation, Boykin insisted, the United States would succeed in overcoming its adversaries only if "we come against them in the name of Jesus."

When Boykin's remarks caught the attention of the mainstream press, denunciations rained down from on high, as the White House, the State Department, and the Pentagon hastened to disassociate the government from the general's views. Yet subsequent indicators suggest that, however crudely, Boykin was indeed expressing perspectives shared by more than a few of his fellow citizens.

One such indicator came immediately: despite the furor, the general kept his important Pentagon job as deputy undersecretary of defense for intelligence, suggesting that the Bush administration considered his transgression minor. Perhaps Boykin had spoken out of turn, but his was not a fireable offense. (One can only speculate regarding the fate likely to befall a US high-ranking officer daring to say of Israeli Prime Minister Benjamin Netanyahu, "My God is a real God and his is an idol.")

A second indicator came in the wake of Boykin's retirement from active duty. In 2012, the influential Family Research Council (FRC) in Washington hired the general to serve as the organization's executive vice-president. Devoted to "advancing faith, family, and freedom," the council presents itself as emphatically Christian in its outlook. FRC events routinely attract Republican Party heavyweights. The organization forms part of the conservative mainstream, much as, say, the American Civil Liberties Union forms part of the left-liberal mainstream.

So for the FRC to hire as its executive vice-president someone espousing Boykin's pronounced views regarding Islam qualifies as noteworthy. At a minimum, those who recruited the former general apparently found nothing especially objectionable in his worldview. They saw nothing politically risky about associating with Jerry Boykin. He's their kind of guy. More likely, by hiring Boykin, the FRC intended to send a signal: on matters where their new executive VP claimed expertise — above all, war — thumb-in-your eye political incorrectness was becoming a virtue. Imagine the NAACP electing Nation of Islam leader Louis Farrakhan as its national president, thereby endorsing his views on race, and you get the idea.

What the FRC's embrace of General Boykin makes clear is this: to dismiss manifestations of Islamophobia simply as the work of an insignificant American fringe is mistaken. As with the supporters of Senator Joseph McCarthy, who during the early days of the Cold War saw communists under every State Department desk, those engaging in these actions are daring to express openly attitudes that others in far greater numbers also quietly nurture. To put it another way, what Americans in the 1950s knew as McCarthyism has reappeared in the form of Boykinism.

Historians differ passionately over whether McCarthyism represented a perversion of anti-Communism or its truest expression. So, too, present-day observers will disagree as to whether Boykinism represents a merely fervent or utterly demented response to the Islamist threat. Yet this much is inarguable: just as the junior senator from Wisconsin in his heyday embodied a non-trivial strain of American politics, so, too, does the former special-ops-warrior-turned-"ordained minister with a passion for spreading the Gospel of Jesus Christ."

Notably, as Boykinism's leading exponent, the former general's views bear a striking resemblance to those favored by the late senator. Like McCarthy, Boykin believes that, while enemies beyond America's gates pose great dangers, the enemy within poses a still greater threat. "I've studied Marxist insurgency," he declared in a 2010 video. "It was part of my training. And the things I know that have been done in every Marxist insurgency are being done in America today." Explicitly comparing the United States as governed by Barack Obama to Stalin's Soviet Union, Mao Zedong's China, and Fidel Castro's Cuba, Boykin charges that, under the guise of health reform, the Obama administration is secretly organizing a "constabulary force that will control the population in America." This new force is, he claims, designed to be larger than the United States military, and will function just as Hitler's Brownshirts once did in Germany. All of this is unfolding before our innocent and unsuspecting eyes.

Boykinism: The New McCarthyism

How many Americans endorsed McCarthy's conspiratorial view of national and world politics? It's difficult to know for sure, but enough in Wisconsin to win him reelection in 1952 by a comfortable 54 percent to 46 percent majority—enough to strike fear into the hearts of politicians who quaked at the thought of McCarthy fingering them for being "soft on Communism."

How many Americans endorse Boykin's comparably incendiary views? Again, it's difficult to tell. Enough to persuade FRC's funders and supporters to hire him, confident that doing so would burnish, not tarnish, the organization's brand. Certainly, Boykin has in no way damaged its ability to attract powerhouses of the domestic right. FRC's recent "Values Voter Summit" featured luminaries such as Republican vice-presidential nominee Paul Ryan, former Republican Senator and presidential candidate Rick Santorum, House Majority Leader Eric Cantor, and Representative Michele Bachmann—along with Jerry Boykin himself, who lectured attendees on "Israel, Iran, and the Future of Western Civilization." (In early August, Mitt Romney met privately with a group of "prominent social conservatives," including Boykin.)

Does their appearance at the FRC podium signify that Ryan, Santorum, Cantor, and Bachmann all subscribe to Boykinism's essential tenets? Not any more than those who exploited the McCarthyite moment to their own political advantage—Richard Nixon, for example—necessarily agreed with all of McCarthy's reckless accusations. Yet the presence of leading Republicans on an FRC program featuring Boykin certainly suggests that they find nothing especially objectionable or politically damaging to them in his worldview.

Still, comparisons between McCarthyism and Boykinism only go so far. Senator McCarthy wreaked havoc mostly on the home front, instigating witch-hunts, destroying careers, and trampling on civil rights, while imparting to American politics even more of a circus atmosphere than usual. In terms of foreign policy, the effect of McCarthyism, if anything, was to reinforce an already existing anti-communist consensus. McCarthy's antics didn't create enemies abroad. McCarthyism merely reaffirmed that communists were indeed the enemy, while making the political price of thinking otherwise too high to contemplate.

Boykinism, in contrast, makes its impact felt abroad. Unlike McCarthyism, it doesn't strike fear into the hearts of incumbents on the campaign trail here. Attracting General Boykin's endorsement or provoking his ire probably won't determine the outcome of any election. Yet in its various manifestations Boykinism provides the kindling that helps sustain anti-American sentiment in the Islamic world. It reinforces the belief among Muslims that the Global War on Terror really *is* a war against them.

Boykinism confirms what many Muslims are already primed to believe: that American values and Islamic values are irreconcilable. American presidents and secretaries of state stick to their talking points, praising Islam as a great religious tradition and touting past US military actions (ostensibly) undertaken on behalf of Muslims. Yet with their credibility among Iraqis, Afghans, Pakistanis, and others in the Greater Middle East about nil, they are pissing in the wind.

As long as substantial numbers of vocal Americans do not buy the ideological argument constructed to justify US intervention in the Islamic world—that *their* conception of freedom (including religious freedom) is ultimately compatible with *ours*—then neither will Muslims. In that sense, the supporters of Boykinism who reject that proposition encourage Muslims to follow suit. This ensures, by extension, that further reliance on armed force as the preferred instrument of US policy in the Islamic world will compound the errors that produced and have defined the post-9/11 era.

8

Henry Luce
The Elusive American Century

(2012)

As contemplated by average Americans, sitting in their living rooms and leafing through their favorite magazine, the outside world in mid-February 1941 seemed nothing if not troubled. Occupying the center of attention was Great Britain, its people stoic in the face of a widely expected invasion. Although the intensity of German air raids had diminished in recent weeks (a pause that some called the "Lullablitz"), Londoners were still spending their nights in underground shelters. British newspapers buzzed with stories "of gas clouds to be blown across the Channel, of paralyzing gas, of inaudible sound waves that make people sick, of 40,000 troop gliders, of air-troop landings in 500 places at once." Although small numbers of demonstrators, "alleged to be Communists," were complaining that food-rationing arrangements favored the well-to-do, the British upper lip remained admirably stiff.

These reports appeared—along with much else—in the February 17, 1941, issue of *Life* magazine. *Life* was the latest franchise of Time Inc., the journalistic juggernaut that had propelled the young

Henry R. Luce to a position of wealth and power. Raised in China by missionary parents, Luce retained throughout his life a missionary inclination, determined to have a hand in great deeds. This found expression in various enthusiasms, yet, by early 1941, one cause took precedence: supporting Great Britain in its lonely struggle against Nazi Germany. With President Roosevelt proceeding by half steps, Luce sought to force the issue. The result, a lengthy editorial in that same issue of *Life*, carried the evocative title "The American Century."

Luce began his essay by assuming the role of national shrink. "We Americans are unhappy," he wrote. "We are nervous—or gloomy—or apathetic." For Luce, the contrast between Americans and Britons was striking. Fighting for their very existence, the people of Great Britain "are profoundly calm. There seems to be a complete absence of nervousness." With the onset of war, "all the neuroses of modern life had vanished from England." Why were Americans feeling so out of sorts? The role that the United States had come to play in the ongoing European war—involved yet less than fully committed—offered a clue. The times called for action, but Americans persisted in dithering. The "cure" was self-evident. In an immediate sense, duty required the United States to ally itself with Great Britain as a full-fledged belligerent in the European war. Yet this amounted to hardly more than a first step. Duty implied a mission of transforming the entire global order, with the United States assuming unequivocally and permanently the mantle of global leadership. In the course of performing that duty, Luce fully expected the United States to transform—and perfect— itself.

"The American Century" was sandwiched between a feature on women's fashion ("Shoe Fair Features Casual Styles Inspired by US Navy and Cowboys") and a profile of Betty Carstairs, oil heiress, adventuress, and speedboat racer. The vision of American global leadership that Luce advanced in his essay and the vision of personal gratification that his magazine extolled had this much in common: each represented an aspiration, not to be confused with an actually existing reality. The tension between these two visions of an American Century first became evident with the Korean War. A decade later, the Vietnam War brought that tension fully into the open, revealing the limits of both Washington's capacity to police the American Century and the American people's willingness to underwrite that effort. More or less simultaneously, the foundations of US economic primacy began to erode. The terms of trade tipped from black to red and stayed there. The oil needed to sustain the mobile lifestyle that Americans prized came increasingly from abroad. So, too, did the manufactures—including automobiles—that Americans coveted, acquired, used, and discarded with abandon.

The decline and eventual collapse of the Soviet empire—interpreted in Washington as the vindication and renewal of the American Century—disguised the significance of these developments. As the Cold War wound down, politicians and pundits vied with one another to replicate Luce's feat, attempting to capture in a single phrase what "victory" over Communism signified. In a nod to Luce, the most ardent proponents of deploying US power "for such purposes as we see fit and by such means as we see fit" called their enterprise simply the Project for the New American Century. While PNAC agitated for the more aggressive use of US military muscle, the advocates of globalization unleashed rhetorical flourishes that would have made Luce himself blush. Few observers paid much attention to the fact that when the United States now employed armed force, it rarely achieved decisive results, or that globalization, while making some people very rich indeed, left many ordinary Americans hurting.

After 9/11, President George W. Bush launched an all-out effort to realize the American Century throughout the Islamic world, without mobilizing his country or even adjusting its domestic priorities. Rather than collective sacrifice, the wartime role assigned to the American public was uninhibited consumption, encouraged by reduced taxes. The costs, fiscal as well as human, absorbed by the American people turned out to be vastly greater than anticipated. Instead of transforming the Middle East, simply extricating the United States from Iraq soon became the priority. Then, in the midst of war, the economy went into a tailspin, producing a crisis not seen since the Great Depression. PNAC quietly closed up shop, but politicians and ideologues continued to identify themselves with Luce's dream.

As a presidential candidate, Senator Barack Obama called upon his supporters "to unite in common purpose, to make this century the next American century." This was akin to promising that world peace or a cure for cancer lies just around the corner: a pleasant thought with little basis in reality. Were there any doubts in that regard, the disappointments associated with Obama's presidency soon quashed them. By the seventieth anniversary of Luce's famous essay, the gap between what he had summoned Americans to do back in 1941 and what they were actually willing or able to do had become unbridgeable. Contemplating the implications of President Obama's decision to begin withdrawing US troops from Afghanistan during the summer of 2011, *Washington Post* columnist Richard Cohen observed that "the American Century just ended." Although, like most observers in Washington, Cohen lagged considerably behind events, his verdict is likely to stand. To the extent that an American Century ever did exist—a point on which historians are not in unanimous agreement— that era has now definitively passed.

Was the "American Century" ever more than a figment of a publisher's fevered imagination? Incorporating the events of the era into Luce's narrative poses a challenge. Exertions undertaken to benefit ourselves and all humanity have so often produced unforeseen, unintended, and even perverse consequences. Defenders of the American Century insist that repeated failures to export democracy (with sundry other errors and disappointments along the way) reveal nothing essential about the United States or its ability to direct the course of events. To rebut the claim that trying to remake the world in America's image is a fool's errand, they cite the results of World War II and the outcome of the Cold War. Framed as chapters in a longer narrative of liberation, these two events invest the ambitions inherent in the vision of an American Century with a modicum of plausibility. Yet sustaining that narrative requires the careful selection and arrangement of facts, with inconvenient or uncomfortable truths excluded, suppressed, or simply ignored.

With regard to World War II, the many facts that don't fit include the following: in the destruction of Nazi Germany, US forces played at best a supporting role, with Stalin's Red Army—the vanguard of a totalitarian police state—doing most of the fighting, killing, and dying; as a result, the price of liberating Western Europe included delivering Eastern Europe to Stalin and his henchmen. Meanwhile, in its aerial bombing campaign against German and Japanese cities, the United

States engaged in the conscious, intentional, wholesale slaughter of noncombatants. In the aftermath of the European war, the Allies collaborated in enforcing a massive involuntary transfer of populations—that is, a policy of ethnic cleansing. When they found it expedient to do so, US officials allowed Nazi war criminals—rocket scientists and intelligence officials, for example—to escape prosecution and to enter the service of the United States. Then there is this: at no time prior to or during the war did the United States make any substantive effort to prevent, or even disrupt, the Nazi persecution of Jews that culminated in the "Final Solution." In Washington the fate of European Jewry never figured as more than an afterthought. As much as or more than the promotion of American ideals—that "sharing with all peoples of our Bill of Rights, our Declaration of Independence, [and] our Constitution" that Luce dearly hoped to see—these decisions, along with the priorities they reflect, laid the basis for the interval of American primacy that followed.

The "Disneyfication" of World War II, to use Paul Fussell's term, finds its counterpart in the Disneyfication of the Cold War, reduced in popular imagination and the halls of Congress to Ronald Reagan's demanding "Mr. Gorbachev, tear down this wall!" The Soviet leader meekly complied, and freedom erupted across Europe. Facts that complicate this story—assassination plots, dirty tricks gone awry, cozy relations with corrupt dictators—provide endless fodder for scholarly articles and books but ultimately get filed under the heading of Things That Don't Really Matter. The Ike Americans like even today is the one who kept the Soviets at bay while presiding over eight years of peace and prosperity. The other Ike—the one who unleashed the CIA on Iran and Guatemala, refused to let the Vietnamese exercise their right to self-determination in 1956, and ignored the plight of Hungarians, who, taking seriously Washington's rhetoric of liberation, rose up to throw off the yoke of Soviet power—remains far less well known. Similarly, Americans today continue to cherish John F. Kennedy's charisma, wit, and eloquence. When it comes to the Bay of Pigs, Operation Mongoose, and the murder of Ngo Dinh Diem, they generously give the martyred president a pass.

The way that Americans choose to remember World War II and the Cold War—evil overthrown thanks chiefly to the United States—

invests the American Century with reassuring moral clarity. Fixing December 7, 1941, as the start date of the struggle for Pacific domination, for example, saddles the Japanese aggressors with responsibility for all that followed. The high-handedness of Commodore Matthew Calbraith Perry in coercing Japan to open itself to the outside world nearly a century earlier; systematic American discrimination against Japanese immigrants, codified in insulting state and local laws; Washington's refusal to acknowledge a Japanese sphere of influence in East Asia, while asserting American primacy throughout the Western Hemisphere; and, more immediately, the impact of US-imposed sanctions intended to strangle Japan economically: for most Americans, Pearl Harbor renders all these irrelevant.

Self-serving mendacities—that the attacks of September 11, 2001, reprising those of December 7, 1941, "came out of nowhere" to strike an innocent nation—don't enhance the safety and well-being of the American people. To further indulge old illusions of the United States presiding over and directing the course of history will not only impede the ability of Americans to understand the world and themselves but may also pose a positive danger to both. No one opens an old issue of *Life* today in the expectation of unearthing truths with contemporary relevance. They do so to satisfy their taste for nostalgia, resurrecting memories, real or imagined, of an America that was good and getting better, a land and people overflowing with promise. Something of the same can be said of Luce's other great creation: his vision of an American Century likewise survives as an artifact, encapsulating an era about which some (although by no means all) Americans might wax nostalgic—a time, real or imagined, of common purpose, common values, and shared sacrifice. Only by jettisoning the American Century and the illusions to which it gives rise will the self-knowledge and self-understanding that Americans urgently require become a possibility. Whether Americans will grasp the opportunity that beckons is another matter.

9

Donald Rumsfeld
Known and Unknown

(2011)

Sometimes you *can* judge a book by its cover. Adorning the dust jacket of *Known and Unknown* is a carefully staged photograph of its author, decked out in jeans, work shirt and sleeveless fleece jacket.[1] He leans against a gate, mountains in the background. The image is quintessentially American.

Well into his seventies, the only man to serve two terms as US secretary of defense exudes vigor. Donald Rumsfeld's smile, familiar from his days of jousting with reporters covering the Pentagon, still conveys combativeness rather than warmth. The cover photo captures the essence of the man and of the memoir he has composed: assured, confident, not given to second thoughts or apologies.

The book's title refers to one especially memorable encounter with the press, in which Rumsfeld seized on a reporter's question to riff on

---

1. Donald Rumsfeld, *Known and Unknown: A Memoir* (New York: Sentinel, 2011).

the distinctions between known knowns, known unknowns and un-known unknowns. According to Rumsfeld, insufficient attention to this last category—the things "we don't know we don't know"—gets people in trouble.

In fact, this very thick account of his public life points to an alto-gether different conclusion. The known knowns turn out to be the real problem. When the "things we know we know" prove to be false or misleading, statesmen drive their country off a cliff. Yet being alert to truths that are not true requires a capacity for introspection, a quality manifestly absent from Rumsfeld's make-up. He remains stubbornly, even defiantly, someone who knows what he knows.

What he knows above all else is this: "Weakness is provocative." Here is the essence of Rumsfeld's worldview and the *leitmotif* that runs through his book. To be safe, the US must be strong, with strength measured by readily available military might. Yet merely possessing military power does not suffice. Since perceptions shape reality, the US must leave others in no doubt as to its willingness to use power. Passivity invites aggression. Activism, if successful, enhances credi-bility. Rather than the negation of peace, war becomes its essential antecedent.

Rumsfeld takes pains to portray himself as a regular guy: the son of a Second World War vet who made his living selling real estate near Chicago; an Eagle Scout and high-school wrestler who went east for college, where he joined the Naval Reserve Officer Training Corps to pay the bills. After graduation, Rumsfeld married his high school sweetheart, Joyce, and served a tour as a naval aviator. He then headed home to Chicago and went into politics, joining Congress in 1962 as a twenty-nine-year-old novice.

A Republican, he supported limited government, low taxes, and strong defense, but also racial equality. In 1964, as Rumsfeld notes proudly, he voted for the Civil Rights Act. That same year, he also voted in favor of the Gulf of Tonkin Resolution, which paved the way for full-scale military intervention in Southeast Asia without any fur-ther action by Congress.

If Rumsfeld had a problem with Vietnam, it was with the way Lyndon Johnson conducted the war. "We were fighting dedicated ideo-logical revolutionaries," he writes, but fighting with US troops had proven a mistake. By sending even more Americans to the war zone, "we were increasing the number of targets" and "creating a dependency on the part of the South Vietnamese." The draft also imposed constraints. Had the country relied on volunteers rather than conscripts, "the level of violence and protest" on the home front "would have been considerably less," allowing policymakers a freer hand.

But the biggest problem was that the US wasn't winning. As the war dragged on, Rumsfeld's talents attracted the attention of Johnson's successor, Richard Nixon. This "thoughtful, brilliant man" employed Rumsfeld in several capacities, culminating in his appointment as US ambassador to NATO. As an insider, Rumsfeld was still a regular guy who took his kids to Redskins games, befriended Sammy Davis Jr., and was a fan of Elvis Presley. (Backstage in Las Vegas late one night, Presley pulled Rumsfeld aside. "He wanted to share his thoughts about the armed forces," an encounter serving as "a welcome reminder that patriots can be found anywhere.")

Steadfast in his commitment to Vietnam, Rumsfeld supported Nixon's policy of drawing down the US troop presence there while returning responsibility for the war to the South Vietnamese. The implosion of Nixon's presidency, culminating in his resignation, robbed this "Vietnamization" policy of whatever slight congressional support it had enjoyed.

Nixon's resignation brought a job change for Rumsfeld, who was recruited to become Gerald Ford's White House chief of staff in 1974. In this post, he witnessed the Saigon regime's final collapse, which he blames on a spineless Congress. Even now, Rumsfeld does not question Vietnam's necessity, referring to the war not as a mistake or a failure but, instead, describing the outcome as a "withdrawal" and "retreat."

With the passing of time, Vietnam looks more and more like an inexplicable march to folly or at best a vast, sorrowful tragedy. To Rumsfeld, it became "a symbol of American weakness" and "an invitation to further aggression." In Asia, Africa and Latin America, the Soviet Union wasted no time in exploiting that weakness, with academic and opinion leaders turning a blind eye. Rumsfeld was not surprised. "Sympathy for the Soviets," he writes, had been "a longstanding sentiment among the American elite."

In late 1975, Rumsfeld moved again, this time to the Pentagon as defense secretary. His aim was to slow the Soviet onslaught and to restore US military credibility, an effort that found him at cross-purposes with just about everyone: hidebound generals, congressmen in hock to defense contractors and devotees of détente such as secretary of state Henry Kissinger.

Ford's defeat by Jimmy Carter sent Rumsfeld back to Chicago and private life. For the next two decades, he made money as a successful chief executive of Searle pharmaceuticals, served as an occasional envoy (including a notorious mission in 1983 "to cultivate warmer relations with Saddam Hussein's Iraq"), and agitated from the sidelines against any hint of pusillanimity. Rumsfeld's brisk account of his years out of power form an awkwardly inserted parenthesis. His eagerness to get back in the game is palpable, as suggested by his own abortive bid for the presidency in 1988.

In 2001, that chance finally came when George W. Bush returned him to the Pentagon as defense secretary. All the old problems remained: the previous administration had gutted defense, responded ineffectually to provocations, and allowed itself to be cowed by generals who remained stuck in the past. Rumsfeld's initial charge was to fix all that, investing US forces with greater "agility, speed, deployability, precision, and lethality." Preoccupied with this task—the enemy he worried about most was a change-averse bureaucracy—Rumsfeld failed to anticipate and did nothing to thwart the events of September 11, 2001.

Still, the 9/11 attacks reaffirmed his thesis: once again, weakness had proven provocative. The overarching purpose of "the war on terror"—Rumsfeld now regrets the name, preferring war against "violent Islamists"—was to demolish once and for all the perception that the US was some sort of patsy. Projecting toughness, rather than promoting democracy, defined the object of the exercise. Rumsfeld simply wanted to show the locals who was boss—the Bush Doctrine of "anticipatory self-defense" conferring the necessary grant of authority—and then move on. Transforming the US military to assert unquestioned global supremacy ranked well ahead of transforming the Muslim world by exporting liberal values.

Although Rumsfeld is fond of using the term *strategy*, what becomes apparent is that the Bush administration never developed anything resembling an actual strategy after 9/11. To get its message across, Rumsfeld simply wanted the US to crack heads whenever and wherever the need arose. If that implied a military effort lasting decades, that was all right with him.

The initial success achieved by the 2001 invasion of Afghanistan seemingly demonstrated the feasibility of this approach. Even so, Rumsfeld struggles to explain the haste with which Bush shifted his attention to Iraq. Two weeks after 9/11, he reports, the president was privately urging his Pentagon chief to put Saddam at the top of the list of those needing to have their heads cracked. That Saddam was actively stockpiling weapons of mass destruction (WMD) fell into the category of "known knowns," with the question of when to pass a nuclear device to terrorists his to decide. In any event, no such weapons existed. Rejecting charges that the administration lied about the Iraqi WMD program, Rumsfeld writes, "The far less dramatic truth is that we were wrong." Acquitting the administration of dishonesty, he enters a plea of incompetence. The emphasis on WMD turned out to be a "public relations error."

Much the same applies to his cursory treatment of matters such as torture and detention. He says critics misunderstood or willfully distorted the truth, or misleadingly implied that unfortunate incidents such as Abu Ghraib were more than mere aberrations. Again, if there was fault to be found, it lay in the realm of PR: "Half-truths, distortions and outright lies were too often met with little or no rebuttal." Rumsfeld's conscience remains clear.

To disguise its failure to find weapons of mass destruction, the administration "changed the subject to democracy promotion"—a position Rumsfeld thought wrong-headed. In his own estimation, his views didn't carry that much weight. Although offering nothing but praise for Bush (and describing Dick Cheney as "uniquely influential" without ever explaining what the vice-president contributed), Rumsfeld describes the national security team on which he served as deeply dysfunctional. He is unsparing in his criticism of Colin Powell, portraying him as personally weak and captive to a cowardly, if not traitorous, State Department. "Powell tended not to speak out" at National Security Council meetings and seemed reluctant to express any disagreement with Bush.

Yet Rumsfeld reserves his most scathing attacks for Condoleezza Rice, depicted as out of her depth and given to twaddle. At one NSC meeting, in the presence of a cringing Rumsfeld, Rice announced that "human rights trump security." In interagency disputes, the national security adviser "studiously avoided forcing clear-cut decisions," preferring a "bridging approach" that maintained superficial harmony while papering over differences. Her shop became a black hole in which little if anything got done. Here lay the real explanation for why Iraq became something akin to a replay of Vietnam. In short, don't blame Rumsfeld: nobody was paying him any attention.

Above all, after Saddam's fall, Rumsfeld argued in vain for a prompt exit. He rejected comparisons of Iraq to Germany or Japan in 1945 — midwifing Arab democracy was never going to be easy. His own preferred model was France in 1944: liberate and quickly transfer sovereignty to someone qualified to exercise it. Although never venturing who he had in mind for the role of Charles de Gaulle, Rumsfeld wants it known that Ahmed Chalabi, the shifty Iraqi exile leader, was never his candidate.

Absolving himself of responsibility for the ensuing debacle finds Rumsfeld disowning the very people he chose to implement US policy in occupied Iraq. He describes as "inexplicable" the appointment of Lieutenant General Ricardo Sanchez, an officer of indifferent ability, to command all US forces in the theatre. (In his own memoir, Sanchez writes that Rumsfeld personally interviewed him for the post.) L. Paul Bremer, Rumsfeld's choice for the position of US pro-consul in Baghdad, turned out to be arrogant, insubordinate, and dishonest. In perhaps the book's most audacious passage, Rumsfeld summarizes his complaint with Bremer while simultaneously placing himself on the side of the angels: he found it difficult, he writes, to get Bremer to "accept the idea that Iraq belonged to Iraqis, and that Iraqis were entitled to their own culture and institutions."

Rumsfeld also had problems with pundits and retired generals who charged him with refusing to provide the numbers of troops needed for the mission. The charge was false; Rumsfeld insists that he was open to sending reinforcements if they were needed. Again and again he asked commanders in the field if they had any unfilled needs but never received "any responses that they wanted more forces or that they disagreed with the strategy." Granted, there was the odd slip of the tongue—it turns out that his "stuff happens" reaction to anarchy in Baghdad, interpreted as flippant, was his way of paying tribute to the transition "between the old order and the new." Yet, on balance, Rumsfeld judges his performance as largely without fault.

Anyway, in the end, it was all worth it. Venturing into the realm of unknown unknowns, Rumsfeld conjures lurid images of all that might have happened had the US not invaded Iraq, offering a veritable litany of apocalyptic possibilities. Above all, by conveying weakness, inaction would have paved the way for Islamists to erect a "single theocratic empire that imposes and enforces sharia." Instead, by toppling Saddam, Rumsfeld writes with characteristic certainty, the US "has created a more stable and secure world"—a judgment not sustained by recent and ongoing developments in Tunisia, Egypt, Yemen, Afghanistan and Pakistan.

"I don't spend a lot of time in recriminations, looking back or second-guessing decisions," Rumsfeld writes. Neither does he evidently devote much time to serious reflection. *Known and Unknown* is tendentious rather than instructive. The reader who wades in should expect a long, hard slog, with little likelihood of emerging on the far side appreciably enlightened. Rather than seriously contemplating the implications of the events in which he participated, Rumsfeld spends more than eight hundred pages dodging them.

That ham-handed and ill-advised US policies rather than perceived weakness might endanger American security; that weakness itself might be a self-inflicted wound, incurred as a result of embarking upon reckless or unnecessary wars; that self-restraint might preserve or even enhance genuine strength: even to suggest these possibilities is to call into question the pernicious known knowns to which Rumsfeld so desperately clings, even if doing so causes incalculable damage to the country he professes to love.

10

Albert and Roberta Wohlstetter

Tailors to the Emperor

(2011)

President Kennedy was categorical on the subject. Speaking at American University in Washington, DC, on June 10, 1963, he put it this way: "The United States, as the world knows, will never start a war." Twenty years later, President Reagan concurred. "The defense policy of the United States," he told Americans on March 23, 1983, "is based on a simple premise: the United States does not start fights. We will never be an aggressor." Given such authoritative (and bipartisan) assurances, how then can we explain the George W. Bush administration's promulgation of a doctrine of preventive war at the start of the twenty-first century? The simple answer, of course, is that 9/11 changed everything. Deputy Secretary of State Richard Armitage articulated a feeling that was widespread among Americans after the events of September 11: "History starts today." All bets were off. So too were the gloves. Deterrence and defense no longer sufficed. As President Bush himself put it, "the doctrine of containment just doesn't hold water." Self-protection was not good enough. In Secretary of Defense Rumsfeld's typically crisp formulation, "the best—and, in some cases, the only—defense is a good offense." This was one of those cases. In order to prevent another 9/11—or something even more nightmarish—the United States had no choice but to go permanently on the offensive. With the Bush Doctrine, Washington granted itself the authority to do just that. End of story.

But the truth is more complicated. In fact, the Bush Doctrine possesses a considerable provenance. Its gestation period coincided with the Age of Overkill—the years when authorities in Washington made nuclear-strike capacity the cornerstone of US national security policy and then, more or less as an afterthought, assessed the implications of having done so. The effort to wrestle with those implications, which turned out to be vast and troublesome, gave birth to a new tradition of strategic thought. Acknowledging the influence of its chief midwife, Albert Wohlstetter, that tradition can rightly be called the Wohlstetter School.

A filmmaker attempting a behind-the-scenes portrayal of US strategy in the nuclear age would surely give Albert Wohlstetter a place of prominence—although that place would likely be a bland faculty lounge instead of the Pentagon's bells-and-whistles War Room. Wohlstetter was the quintessential defense intellectual. From the 1950s through the 1990s, he wielded outsized influence in policy circles, without himself ever shouldering the burdens of personal responsibility—an outsider enjoying privileged inside access. Born in New York in 1913, he was a mathematician by training, who rose to prominence while an analyst at RAND, which he joined in 1951. (RAND also employed his wife, the historian Roberta Wohlstetter.) In 1964, Wohlstetter joined the political science faculty at the University of Chicago. There he remained for the rest of his career, training acolytes (among them Paul Wolfowitz) and mentoring protégés (among them Richard Perle), while engaging in classified research, advising government agencies and serving on blue-ribbon commissions—in general leaving his fingerprints all over the intellectual framework of US national security strategy.

"Paul thinks the way Albert thinks," Perle once remarked, referring to his friend Wolfowitz. This comment applied equally to more than a few others who rose to positions of prominence in Washington during the latter half of the twentieth century. In national security circles, Albert's way of thinking became pervasive. So too did the abiding theme of his work: the existing situation is bad; absent drastic action today, it is almost sure to get worse still tomorrow. To those who learned from, collaborated with, or drew inspiration from Albert Wohlstetter, therefore, any defensive posture by definition is either inadequate or soon will be. The defender forfeits the initiative, a defensive orientation too easily translating into passivity, inertia and even fatalism. In an age in which survival required constant alertness and continuing exertion to improve existing capabilities and devise new ones, to rely on defense alone as a basis for strategy was to incur great risk.

For members of the Wohlstetter School, the advent of the Bush Doctrine represented the culmination of a project that they had pursued over the course of decades. Long before the events of September 2001, ideas they had developed set the stage for the United States to embrace preventive war. For Wohlstetter's adherents, the proactive elimination of threats—thereby transcending concepts such as containment and deterrence—had long since acquired a tantalizing allure all of its own. Well before 9/11, they had persuaded themselves that preventive war was not only desirable but also feasible. All that was needed was an opportunity to put their theories into practice. On September 11, 2001, that opportunity presented itself.

Preemptive War

Commencement ceremonies for the graduating cadets at West Point on June 1, 2002, provided the occasion for Bush to unveil his doctrine of preventive war. Bush began by paying tribute to Presidents Kennedy and Reagan. Rather than recalling their assurances that the United States would never start a war, however, he praised them for refusing "to gloss over the brutality of tyrants" and giving "hope to prisoners and dissidents and exiles." In a difficult time, they had held high the torch of freedom. In some respects, the challenges now confronting the United States mirrored those that his Cold War predecessors had faced. "Now, as then," Bush declared, "our enemies are totalitarians. . . . Now, as then, they seek to impose a joyless conformity, to control every life and all of life." Yet in other crucial respects, the present situation was entirely new and fraught with unprecedented danger. Bush located the nexus of that danger "at the perilous crossroads of radicalism and technology." Against such a threat, Cold War strategies no longer sufficed. "Containment is not possible," the president continued, "when unbalanced dictators with weapons of mass destruction can deliver those weapons on missiles or secretly provide them to terrorist allies."

In such circumstances, defense alone was inadequate to provide security. Passivity was tantamount to courting suicide. "If we wait for threats to fully materialize, we will have waited too long." New conditions had rendered the promises of Kennedy and Reagan null and void. "We must take the battle to the enemy," Bush continued, "disrupt his plans, and confront the worst threats before they emerge. In the world we have entered, the only path to safety is the path of action. And this nation will act." Action necessarily implied military action, and the president emphasized the imperative of transforming the armed forces to create a military "ready to strike at a moment's notice in any dark corner of the world" and prepared "for preemptive action when necessary to defend our liberty and to defend our lives." Military forces in action would eliminate the terrorist threat; military might in itself would guarantee the peace: "America has, and intends to keep, military strength beyond challenge . . . thereby, making the destabilizing arms races of other eras pointless and limiting rivalries to trade and other pursuits of peace."

Lending this happy prospect a modicum of plausibility were newly emergent methods of waging war—precise, agile, flexible and discriminating—which Bush thought would endow US forces with hitherto unimagined levels of effectiveness. Released from the paralyzing effects of Hiroshima, war—undertaken by Americans for enlightened purposes—would acquire a new lease on life, the United States seizing the moment, in Bush's words, "to extend a just peace, by replacing poverty, repression and resentment around the world." The Bush Doctrine promised both to unharness American power and to invest it with renewed moral purpose. However unwittingly, Bush had thereby summarized and endorsed the several principles of the

Wohlstetter School. The implementation of the Bush Doctrine in the months and years that followed put those principles to the test.

Peril and Surprise

Four essential precepts define the Wohlstetter tradition. The theme of the first is looming peril. According to its adherents, America's enemies, strong and getting stronger, are implacably hostile and will, if given the chance, exploit any perceived US vulnerability; to make matters worse, US officials responsible for evaluating the threats bearing down on the country routinely underestimate the actual danger, lulling the American people into a false sense of security. In reality, crisis is a permanent condition, the threats facing the United States imminent and existential. The theme of the second precept is surprise, which greatly complicates the problem of how to gauge the danger. The prospect of the unforeseen is omnipresent and can never be entirely eliminated. Although efforts to guard against being caught unawares are essential, to assume that those efforts are succeeding is to invite disaster. Only those defenses that will work in the absence of warning can be deemed sufficient.

Minimizing the impact of surprise demands sustained and intensive attention to risk management: this is the Wohlstetter School's third precept. Conjuring up vulnerabilities that adversaries might exploit, crediting them with the ability and intent to do so, and devising remedies to prevent or reduce any resulting damage, thereby maintaining the ability to strike back and also raising the risks that adversaries will incur if choosing to attack: this, for Wohlstetter's followers, defines the very essence of risk management strategy. Effective risk management entails activism. To remain inert in the face of peril is to forfeit the initiative, thereby exacerbating the threat. To see some momentary advantage as a guarantee of safety, therefore, is to misapprehend the reality of strategic competition, which involves continuous interaction on ever-shifting terms.

In other words, the first precept of looming peril necessitates an anticipatory approach to self-defense. Yet the second precept of surprise means that an anticipatory self-defense that is strictly defensive in its orientation can never be fully satisfactory. Miscalculate just once—fail to see what lurks around the corner or over the horizon—and catastrophic failure ensues. The fourth precept looks beyond mere risk management—the third precept—to radical risk reduction—the Holy Grail of the Wohlstetter School. It posits the existence of capabilities that will confer upon the United States the ability not only to dispose of the perils it faces, but also to create a better world for all. To achieve this sort of risk reduction requires an offensively oriented approach. Rather than simply parrying, the US should thrust.

For a brief moment after 1945, some observers believed that the American nuclear monopoly had put the United States in a position to do just that. The founding members of the Wohlstetter School were among the first to recognize that this was a delusion and to see that far from enhancing US freedom of action, the advent of nuclear weapons created daunting complications and imposed constraints. Yet this insight, important in itself, did not dissuade them from seeking escape from those constraints. By the 1990s, leading Wohlstetterites believed they had discovered the means to do so.

NSC-68 and After

Just as McCarthyism predated Senator Joe McCarthy, so too ideas of the Wohlstetter School made their appearance even before Albert Wohlstetter signed on with RAND in 1951 to analyze nuclear strategy. Drafted early in 1950, National Security Council Report 68 remains a classic expression of the looming-threat precept. Emphasizing that the end of the nuclear monopoly had plunged the United States into deepest peril, with all of humanity now facing "the ever-present possibility of annihilation," freedom itself "mortally challenged," and the very survival "not only of this Republic but of civilization itself" hanging in the balance, NSC-68 may strike present-day readers as overwrought, if not altogether hysterical. With the Soviet Union having long since ceased to exist, the United States today finds itself more or less perpetually entangled in foreign wars, all the while professing a yearning for peace. Viewed from this perspective, NSC-68's attempted contrast between the "fanatic faith" inspiring the Kremlin's efforts to "impose its absolute authority over the rest of the world" and the "essential tolerance of our world outlook, our generous and constructive impulses, and the absence of covetousness in our international relations" might seem overdrawn.[1] Yet Paul Nitze, director of State Department policy planning and NSC-68's principal author—soon to emerge as a charter member of the Wohlstetter School—believed otherwise. By his own account, Nitze was simply looking facts in the face. A self-described hard-nosed pragmatist, he addressed questions of policy with "clear and rigorous logic, based upon a cold and unemotional assessment of the objective evidence."[2] If Nitze cried wolf, it was because a wolf (or perhaps a bear) was pawing at the door, even if others remained blind to the danger.

With a little help from the Korean War, NSC-68 demonstrated that in Cold War Washington crying wolf worked: Nitze won approval for his recommendation of a large-scale build-up of American military power, conventional as well as nuclear. At regular intervals thereafter, groups—some quasi-official, others unofficial, many including Nitze himself as a prominent participant—sought to replicate this achievement. Every couple of decades, the Committee on the Present Danger appeared on the scene, version 1.0 sounding the alarm in 1950, with 2.0 following in 1976 and 3.0 in 2004. Otherwise, even as the names varied, the refrain remained constant. The Gaither Committee (1957), the Committee to Maintain a Prudent Defense Policy (1969), "Team B" (1976), the Commission on Integrated Long-Term Strategy (1988), and the Rumsfeld Commission (1998) all subscribed to a common set of propositions: ignored or discounted by US intelligence agencies, the United States was falling behind; America's enemies were gaining an edge; absent prompt action to close the resulting capabilities gap, catastrophe beckoned.

An accommodating press routinely amplified the ominous warnings issued by the Wohlstetter School. When the classified findings of the Gaither Committee found their way into the hands of a *Washington Post* reporter, for example, the resulting story, appearing on December 20, 1958, carried the headline: "Secret Report Sees US in Great

---

1. NSC-68, "US Objectives and Programs for National Security" (April 14, 1950).

2. Paul Nitze, *From Hiroshima to Glasnost* (New York: Weidenfeld and Nicolson, 1989), ix.

Peril." Team B concluded its work as President Ford was preparing to leave office. In its January 10, 1977, issue, *Newsweek*'s coverage featured an essay called "The Russian Bear Redux?" The text of the article removed the question mark, describing the Team B report as "the most alarming forecast in years." Similarly, on July 17, 1998, the *Newark Star-Ledger* summarized the findings of the Rumsfeld Commission: "Experts See Missiles' Shadows Darkening Skies over US Cities."

The point here is not to contest the accuracy of these forecasts—although allegations of a "bomber gap" and later of a "missile gap" during the 1950s proved utterly fanciful—but to note their remarkable consistency. In this regard, the findings reported by Team B—convened by CIA director George H. W. Bush in response to charges by Wohlstetter (and others) that official estimates were understating the Soviet threat—are representative. As an exercise in intellectual inquiry, Team B's investigation was the equivalent of asking a group of senior academics to evaluate the pros and cons of tenure: the outcome was foreordained. Consisting of hardliners vociferously opposed to Soviet-American détente (Nitze and Wohlstetter protégé Paul Wolfowitz among them), Team B reached precisely the conclusions it would be expected to reach: US intelligence agencies had "substantially misperceived the motives behind Soviet strategic programs, and thereby tended consistently to underestimate their intensity, scope and implicit threat." With "all the evidence point[ing] to an undeviating Soviet commitment to what is euphemistically called the worldwide triumph of socialism but in fact connotes global Soviet hegemony," the Kremlin had no interest in settling for strategic equivalence. It was engaged in a single-minded pursuit of strategic supremacy. "Soviet leaders are first and foremost offensively rather than defensively minded," Team B reported. That statement applied in spades to Soviet thinking about nuclear weapons. The Soviets did not view nuclear conflict as tantamount to mutual suicide. Instead, they were expanding their arsenal in order to achieve a "war-fighting and war-winning capability." For the United States, the outlook was grim indeed.[3]

---

3. Report of Team B, "Intelligence Community Experiment in Competitive Analysis: Soviet Strategic Objectives, An Alternate View," undated.

Wohlstetter himself drafted the most beguiling and comprehensive articulation of the looming-peril hypothesis. Written under federal contract for RAND in 1958 and subsequently appearing in revised form in *Foreign Affairs*, "The Delicate Balance of Terror" qualifies in the estimation of one admirer as "probably the single most important article in the history of American strategic thought."[4] In late 1957 the USSR had launched Sputnik, the first Earth-orbiting artificial satellite. As Wohlstetter noted, the shock resulting from this demonstration of Soviet missile capabilities had "almost dissipated," however. American concern, momentarily bordering on panic, had subsided, with the prevailing assumption that a general thermonuclear war was "extremely unlikely" restored. Wohlstetter set out to demolish that assumption, "dispelling the nearly universal optimism about the stability of deterrence." The requirements for thwarting a Soviet nuclear attack, which in his view were stringent, made such optimism entirely unwarranted. To assume that the Kremlin leadership was "bumbling or, better, cooperative"—adhering to what he derisively referred to as "Western-preferred Soviet strategies"—was sheer folly. In fact, advances in Soviet strike capabilities had created prospects of *"an essentially warningless attack"* that the United States *"may not have the power to deter."*[5]

What followed was, in effect, a riff on Wohlstetter-preferred Soviet strategies. Elaborating on the difficulties of maintaining a viable second-strike capability, Wohlstetter found no reason to doubt that Soviet leaders possessed the cunning and ruthlessness to exploit those difficulties to their own advantage. The possibility of nuclear war causing considerable damage to the Soviet Union itself would not, in his view, dissuade the Kremlin from acting. After all, although World War II had killed more than 20 million Russians, the Soviet Union "had recovered extremely well." Under "several quite plausible circumstances,"

---

4. Marc Trachtenberg, *History and Strategy* (Princeton: Princeton University Press, 1991), 20.
5. Albert Wohlstetter, "The Delicate Balance of Terror," in *Nuclear Heuristics: Selected Writings of Albert and Roberta Wohlstetter* (Carlisle, PA: Strategic Studies Institute, 2009), 177–212 (emphasis in original).

he surmised, "the Russians might be confident of being able to limit damage to considerably *less* than this number," in which event, "striking first, by surprise, would be the sensible choice for them." In short, to imagine that "a carefully planned surprise attack can be checkmated almost effortlessly," with Americans thereby resuming "their deep pre-Sputnik sleep," was a recipe for disaster. On the contrary, shoring up the US deterrent required urgent, ongoing, and intensive effort: ensuring the survivability of retaliatory forces, thickening air defenses, protecting civilians, improving conventional capabilities, and exploring innovative non-nuclear modes of warfare, hitherto "financed by pitifully small budgets." Yet in outlining the minimum requirements for avoiding nuclear war in the 1960s—which he viewed as an iffy prospect at best—Wohlstetter was also describing "a new image of ourselves in a world of persistent danger." Responding to Wohlstetter-preferred Soviet strategies would oblige Americans to make hard choices entailing sacrifice and uncertainty. It also implied being kept in the dark about matters said to determine their chances of survival, while placing their fate in the hands of those claiming mastery of such matters—people like Albert Wohlstetter.

Anticipating Pearl Harbor

A treatise written by Roberta Wohlstetter has long served as the Wohlstetter School's urtext on the issue of surprise. *Pearl Harbor: Warning and Decision*, prepared under the auspices of RAND and published in 1962, won the prestigious Bancroft Prize for history, but this was history narrowly focused to serve—and privilege—a specific agenda. *Pearl Harbor* was written in order to answer the question "Why was the United States surprised on December 7, 1941?" In retrospect, indicators of an impending Japanese attack seemed blindingly obvious. How could Americans at all echelons of command—civilian and military alike, both in Washington and in Hawaii—have overlooked so many clues? Wohlstetter's answer emphasized the difficulty of distinguishing between the clues that mattered and those that did not: "we failed to anticipate Pearl Harbor not for want of the relevant materials, but because of the plethora of irrelevant ones."[6] What Roberta Wohlstetter described as noise—false or misleading information—obscured the signals that foretold an attack.

In "The Delicate Balance of Terror," her husband had identified six hurdles that the United States needed to overcome in order to achieve the assured second-strike capability required for effective deterrence, so as to demonstrate the enormous challenges involved.[7] In *Pearl Harbor*, Roberta Wohlstetter likewise identified six hurdles, factors increasing a nation's susceptibility to surprise attack: false alarms; alertness dulled by continuous tension; enemy efforts to conceal their true intent; spoofs, that is, enemy-generated noise designed to mislead; changes in the character of relevant intelligence, caused, for example, by technological advances; and bureaucratic barriers obstructing the sharing of relevant information. Roberta Wohlstetter's point reinforced her husband's: avoiding surprise, like creating an effective deterrent, was a difficult proposition indeed. The one major practical lesson of her study was that "we cannot *count* on strategic warning." In the two decades that had elapsed since Pearl Harbor, she concluded, "the balance of advantage" had clearly shifted "in favor of a surprise attacker. The benefits to be expected from achieving surprise have increased enormously and the penalties for losing the initiative in an all-out war have grown correspondingly." As a consequence, the United States needed to acknowledge the likelihood of being surprised. "We have to accept the fact of uncertainty and learn to live with it." Rather than expecting advance notice of an enemy attack, defenses "must be designed to function without it."

Events of 1962, the very year in which her book appeared, seemingly affirmed Roberta Wohlstetter's analysis. Soviet efforts to position a nuclear-strike force in Cuba caught the Kennedy administration completely unawares. Writing in *Foreign Affairs* three years after the

---

6. Roberta Wohlstetter, *Pearl Harbor: Warning and Decision* (Stanford: Stanford University Press, 1962).

7. These were attainment of "a stable, steady-state peacetime operation"; surviving an enemy first-strike; making and disseminating a decision to retaliate; reaching enemy territory with enough fuel to complete the mission; overcoming enemy defenses; and destroying assigned targets.

fact, she described it as a case of déjà vu. Once again, in October 1962 as in December 1941, there had been plenty of signals, but also an abundance of noise. Thanks to advances in aerial photography, notably from the U-2 spy plane, and the nuanced response of President Kennedy, the United States managed to recover from its initial surprise and avoid World War III. She found it "comforting to know that we do learn from one crisis to the next." Muting that comfort was her conviction that "the future doubtless holds many more shocks and attempts at surprise," with no reason to assume that next time the United States would be so lucky.[8]

Strategy Precluded

Wohlstetter's analysis of the Cuban Missile Crisis mirrors her analysis of the attack on Pearl Harbor in this additional respect: in both cases, she imputed strategic significance to actions that occur in the realm of tactics. Among adherents to the Wohlstetter School, this tendency is pervasive: a preoccupation with tactical matters—relabeled "strategic" to reflect the involvement of nuclear weapons or long-range delivery systems—supplants serious strategic analysis. So Wohlstetter begins her account of the Cuban Missile Crisis on August 31, 1962, when Senator Kenneth Keating of New York charged that the Soviets were installing missiles in Cuba, thereby posing a threat to the United States. (The Kennedy administration dismissed Keating's charge.) She evinces no interest in events occurring prior to that date. In her account, therefore, CIA-engineered efforts to overthrow Fidel Castro, collapsing the year before at the Bay of Pigs, go unmentioned. So too does the Cuban Revolution, its origins, and its purposes.

Implicitly, for Wohlstetter, the Cuban Missile Crisis came out of nowhere, making it unnecessary for her to ask if ill-advised US policies prior to 1962 might have laid the basis for the surprise that Castro and his allies in the Kremlin sprang in the autumn of that year. By extension,

---

8. Roberta Wohlstetter, "Cuba and Pearl Harbor: Hindsight and Foresight," *Foreign Affairs*, July 1965.

that same presumption foreclosed any need to consider whether Washington's vulnerability to surprise might stem less from lapses in US intelligence than from misguided US behavior toward Cuba. In framing the problem as a failure to distinguish between signals and noise, Wohlstetter disregarded the possibility that the problem might be one that the United States had brought upon itself—decades of meddling and manipulation producing unhappy consequences to which policymakers remained willfully blind. In short, for her, strategy as such—how Washington had defined US interests in Cuba and the prerogatives it had claimed in pursuing those interests—evaded serious scrutiny.

Much the same applies to her account of Pearl Harbor. Preoccupied with explaining the origins of the Japanese attack on December 7, Wohlstetter evinces no interest in assessing the origins of the Pacific War. She pays no attention whatsoever to developments prior to June 17, 1940, while focusing in detail only on events that occurred in November and December 1941. Again, strategy as such—how Washington defined its interests in the Asia-Pacific and the policies that put the United States on a collision course with Japan, beginning with the promulgation of the Open Door Notes in 1899–1900 and culminating in the summer of 1940 with the imposition of economic sanctions to punish Japan—simply does not qualify as relevant.[9]

To characterize the Pearl Harbor attack as a strategic failure—whether of "warning" or "decision," to cite the subtitle of Wohlstetter's book—is to abuse and misconstrue the word "strategy." Washington's actual strategic failure, its inability to persuade Japan to accept America's requirements for an Asian-Pacific order by means short of war, had become evident long before the first bombs fell on Oahu. When open hostilities finally erupted, the particulars of time and place

---

9. A partial list of the events creating the conditions for the Pacific War would necessarily include the following: US involvement in negotiating the treaty ending the Russo-Japanese War; blatant and widespread American discrimination against Japanese immigrants; Woodrow Wilson's rejection of a Japanese-proposed endorsement of racial equality in the Versailles Treaty; the 1921–22 Washington Naval Conference; US condemnation of Japan's invasion of Manchuria in 1931; the Stimson Doctrine refusing to recognize the legitimacy of Japanese conquests; and US support for China in its war against Japan.

may have come as a surprise; that the United States was already engaged in a winner-take-all contest with the Japanese did not. To impute strategic significance to the events of December 7, 1941, therefore, serves no purpose other than to insulate basic US policy from critical attention. This members of the Wohlstetter School consistently do— whether the issue at hand is the origins of the Pacific War, the Cold War, or the War on Terror, their fixation with the perils lying just ahead obviates any need to consider whether the United States itself may have had a hand in creating those dangers.

Rooting Out Risk

The Wohlstetter School's preoccupation with risk management derives in part from the conviction that passivity in the face of a building and evolving threat almost inevitably increases vulnerability, whereas well-conceived action can reduce it. "The problem of deterring a major power," wrote Albert Wohlstetter in 1961, "requires a continuing effort because the requirements for deterrence will change with the countermeasures taken by the major power." The imperative is to keep one step ahead in order to avoid falling a potentially fatal half-step behind. Staying ahead necessarily entails intensive, ongoing exertions, anticipating the adversary's next moves, and devising methods and capabilities from which to formulate a countermeasure.

Action undertaken to reduce risk necessarily entails a further element of risk, which is difficult to forecast (and easy to exaggerate). Yet members of the Wohlstetter School do not shrink from action, convinced that the risk of inaction could well be greater still. Persuading a skeptical public and skittish politicians to buy into this proposition can pose challenges. Writing in *Life* magazine in 1960, Albert Wohlstetter saw "no reason to believe that Americans would not make a greater effort for the major purposes which they share, if they understood that the risks of *not* making such an effort were large and the rewards for effort great." Americans seemed to think that by trying to stay that step ahead, they could forfeit all the benefits accruing from the country's advantageous postwar position. "I think this is wrong," Wohlstetter wrote. "They are threatened by the risks involved in failing to make an effort." Viewed from this perspective, the strategist's task is twofold: creating policy options to facilitate action, while nurturing a political environment conducive to the actual exercise of choice. Analysis was "about the invention of new solutions," wrote one admirer, describing Wohlstetter's *modus operandi*: "out of analysis emerged new choices."[10] Yet just as the absence of options could inhibit activism, so too could public unwillingness to defer to those at the center of power. Avoiding strategic paralysis required not only a rich menu of policy choices but also public willingness to let decision-makers choose.

With these twin tasks in mind, members of the Wohlstetter School have long specialized in concocting scenarios purporting to expose existing US defenses as grotesquely inadequate—according to Nitze, for example, the Gaither Committee "calculated that 90 per cent of our bomber force could be knocked out on the ground by a surprise Soviet bomber attack"—and then proposing ways to fix whatever problem they had conjured up.[11] Almost invariably, making things right imposes considerable demands on the US Treasury. But as Wohlstetter put it, "the initiation fee is merely a down payment on the expense of membership in the nuclear club." So during the Cold War, adopting Wohlstetter School recommendations on whether to disperse US bomber forces, harden missile launch sites, improve air defenses, or field new weapons—the list goes on—provided a continuing rationale for high levels of military spending, with implications not lost on the officer corps, members of Congress, corporate chieftains, or union bosses. Simply put, ideas generated by the Wohlstetter School produced lubricants that kept the wheels of the national security state turning, while also helping to fuel the military-industrial complex.

When it came to spotting (or inventing) flaws in US defenses, Albert Wohlstetter himself possessed a rare talent. His approach to framing and addressing problems was empirical, comprehensive, and uncompromising. Never content with generalities, Wohlstetter insisted that "actual details—missile accuracies, reliabilities and pay-

10. Alain Enthoven, "Commentary: *On Nuclear Deterrence*," in *Nuclear Heuristics*, 167.

11. Nitze, *From Hiroshima to Glasnost*, 167.

loads, bomb yields, bomber ranges," and the like mattered, indeed, were of central importance. Sloppy or lazy thinking—for example, expectations that the horrors implicit in thermonuclear war might suffice to preclude its occurrence—drew his particular ire. "Relentless questioning of everything and everyone" was Richard Perle's description. Wohlstetter demanded rigor and precision. He tested assumptions. He challenged conventional wisdom wherever he found it. "All this is familiar," he would say, when preparing to demolish the latest bit of comforting nonsense to which Washington had succumbed, "but is it true?"[12] In the eyes of his admirers, Wohlstetter was above all a disinterested seeker of truth.

In reality, Wohlstetter's reputed penchant for relentless probing extended only so far. For starters, he left untouched key assumptions undergirding Wohlstetter-preferred Soviet strategies. To him, the Soviet Union was a black box. While categorizing the Soviet regime as totalitarian, he never bothered to evaluate the validity of that label or to question whether any such abbreviated characterization could provide an adequate basis for gauging state behavior. Furthermore, neither he nor any other member of the Wohlstetter School ever paused to wonder what it was that made the United States itself tick. The "relentless questioning" so evident when probing contradictions in the US nuclear posture has never extended to US policy more broadly. Accepting at face value the prevailing American self-image of a nation whose purposes are benign and intentions peaceful, the Wohlstetter School does not trouble itself over how the United States got enmeshed in whatever predicament it happens to be facing.

Thus, while promoting stratagems to navigate through the perils of the moment, members of the Wohlstetter School remain oblivious to the role that ill-conceived US policies may have played in creating those dangers. As a consequence, an approach to strategy purporting to expand choice actually serves to circumscribe it, reducing strategy itself to a stylized process that Wohlstetter termed "opposed-systems analysis." Attributing supreme importance to matters such

12. Richard Perle, "Commentary: *Arms Race Myths vs. Strategic Competition's Reality*," in *Nuclear Heuristics,* 381, 384.

as "payloads, bomb yields and bomber ranges" obviates the need to examine the near-term benefits and long-term consequences of, say, plotting to overthrow the legitimately elected government of Iran, obstructing the non-violent unification of a divided Vietnam, or refusing to allow Cubans to determine their own destiny. Actually existing strategy—power expended in accordance with a discernible pattern—disappears behind a cloud of obfuscation.

Discriminate Deterrence?

The search for a Holy Grail derives its allure not simply from the value of the object sought, but from the challenges inherent in the quest. For the Wohlstetter School, the Holy Grail of radical risk reduction in lieu of mere risk management has proven elusive, with the pursuit itself not without disappointment. Early efforts to implement this fourth precept of the Wohlstetter School foundered in Indochina. There, variants of "opposed-systems analysis" found expression in US attempts to coerce the North Vietnamese into accepting the permanent division of their country. Active US participation in the Vietnam War, beginning in the 1950s and ending in the 1970s, spanned five presidential administrations. None of the five attempted to win the war outright. Rather, the United States relied on indirect means or calibrated violence, expecting Hanoi, either worn down or brought to its senses, eventually to concede the point. At issue was more than simply the fate of South Vietnam. Success in Vietnam would demonstrate that the United States possessed the ability to nip problems in the bud without exorbitant expenditures and without breaching the nuclear threshold. Such an outcome would notably enhance American power. To put it mildly, however, success was not forthcoming. For a time, Vietnam seemed, in the words of one keen observer, to be "the Waterloo for the entire enterprise of strategic analysis."[13]

---

13. Fred Kaplan, *The Wizards of Armageddon* (New York: Simon & Schuster, 1983), 336; A. Wohlstetter, "On Vietnam and Bureaucracy," RAND, 17 July 1968.

Albert Wohlstetter, for one, refused to accept this verdict. "Of all the disasters of Vietnam," he warned in 1968, "the worst may be the lessons that we'll draw from it." In his estimation, the worst lesson of all would be one persuading Americans that "we are better off reducing the choices available to us" rather than devising new ways "to use our power discriminately and for worthy ends." The reference to the discriminate use of power should be noted. So too should the reference to worthy ends. Among the various signatures of the Vietnam War—free-fire zones, napalm, Agent Orange, and carpet bombing by B-52 Stratofortresses—none were suggestive of power used discriminately or, indeed, worthily. Yet in that war Wohlstetter glimpsed the inkling of a vision for investing force with unprecedented efficacy, thereby reducing both moral and political inhibitions to its use.

The first generation of what we today call precision-guided munitions made their appearance on the battlefield during the latter stages of the Vietnam War. For the American military, the implications of this advance in weaponry were tactical—making possible, for example, the assured destruction of one North Vietnamese bridge by a single aircraft employing a single bomb, rather than numerous aircraft unleashing a hail of bombs with uncertain result. In Wohlstetter's eyes, the potential implications of precision weapons appeared much larger. In his view, advanced technology could expand the utility of force across a range of contingencies, even while reducing both risks and moral hazards. If Hiroshima had transformed the sword of military might into a sledgehammer possessing limited utility, Wohlstetter now saw the possibility of converting the sledgehammer into a scalpel with multiple applications. Here lay the possibility of escaping from the frustrations and uncertainties of deterrent strategies relying on nuclear weapons. To put it another way, it was an opportunity to impart to anticipatory self-defense an offensive orientation. During the 1970s and 1980s, Wohlstetter and like-minded figures such as Defense Department officials Andrew Marshall and Fred Iklé, along with Harvard's Samuel Huntington, closed in on their Holy Grail, now described as "discriminate deterrence." The central idea was this: by enabling the United States to make highly effective attacks with low collateral damage, the advent of near-zero-miss non-nuclear weapons promised to provide policymakers with a variety of strategic-response options as alternatives to massive nuclear destruction. By eliminating the unintended killing of noncombatants and the excessive physical destruction that made nuclear weapons essentially unusable, improvements in accuracy promised to make possible "the strategic use of non-nuclear weapons."[14]

As members of the Wohlstetter School explored the prospects of "discriminate deterrence" to check a Soviet Union that they described as on the march, the actually existing Soviet Union was entering its death spiral. Even before revolutionary technologies could supersede nuclear weapons, revolutionary change in the realm of politics brought the Cold War to an abrupt end, rendering "discriminate deterrence" obsolete even before it reached maturity. Yet in this moment of sudden technological and political change, the shackles hitherto limiting American freedom of action fell away. No sooner had discriminate deterrence become *passé* than discriminate attack began to emerge as an idea whose time had come. Back in 1958, Albert Wohlstetter had speculated about a situation in which "the risks of *not* striking might at some juncture appear very great to the Soviets," creating circumstances in which "striking first, by surprise, would be the sensible choice for them, and from their point of view the smaller risk." With the end of the Cold War and the advent of precision weapons, this might describe the situation facing the United States. For members of the Wohlstetter School, the appeal of striking first—fixing problems, rather than merely coping with them—glittered.

Targeting the Balkans

George W. Bush would refer, in his second inaugural address, to the interval between the end of the Cold War and the beginning of the War on Terror as "years of repose, years of sabbatical." Some repose, some sabbatical. The 1990s opened with war in the Persian Gulf, which, de-

---

14. Commission on Integrated Long-Term Strategy, *Discriminate Deterrence* (1988), excerpted in *Nuclear Heuristics*, 607.

spite the putative success of Operation Desert Storm, dragged on for years. A policy of coercive containment directed against the Saddam Hussein regime found expression in a never-ending sequence of feints, demonstrations, and punitive air strikes, reinforcements for draconian economic sanctions. The decade also included a host of lesser interventions, beginning in 1992 with Somalia and culminating in 1999 with Kosovo, all euphemistically referred to as "military operations other than war."

Meanwhile, Big Thinkers vied with one another to divine the implications of the Cold War's passing. They announced the end of history, proclaimed the arrival of a unipolar moment, worried about the coming anarchy, warned of a clash of civilizations, and found hope in the prospect of globalization creating a fast, flat, wide-open, and wealth-generating world. In Washington, consensus reigned on one point only: having gained unprecedented and unquestioned military supremacy, the United States needed to preserve it. How best to maximize the benefits of US military preeminence became a point of considerable disagreement. One view, found in a 1992 draft of the Defense Planning Guidance, advocated unambiguous and unapologetic US global dominion. A second view, styled as assertive multilateralism or humanitarian interventionism, sought to put American military might to work on behalf of others. The Wohlstetter School fashioned a third position bridging the differences between the two: activism on behalf of others to legitimate and sustain US global hegemony.

The long Balkan crisis, unfolding in fits and starts throughout the 1990s, provided the occasion for members of the Wohlstetter School to refine this third view. Here, it seemed, was a made-to-order chance to employ American power discriminately and for worthy ends. No one made the case for doing so with greater conviction and passion than Albert Wohlstetter himself. In the final years of his life, he published a string of scathing opinion pieces denouncing the West's fumbling reaction to horrific ethnic cleansing perpetrated by Europeans against Europeans in the former Yugoslavia. For decades, Wohlstetter had mocked anyone not sharing his view that nuclear deterrence was a complicated and problematic business. Now he mocked anyone who worried that using high-tech weapons might prove complicated and problematic.

The stakes, Wohlstetter insisted, could hardly be higher. The collapse of Communism had not eased the threats facing the United States; it had heightened them. To find reassurance in the fact that the "canonical attack"—a Warsaw Pact assault on NATO, escalating into all-out nuclear warfare—was not going to happen reflected a fundamental misunderstanding of what the Cold War had been about in the first place. That "apocalyptic danger—if it ever existed—had dwindled to a negligible likelihood more than three decades ago," Wohlstetter now announced. At the very moment when his "Delicate Balance" was winning acclaim as the latest in cutting-edge thinking, "threatening an unrestrained nuclear war against populations" had already become "plainly a loony alternative." The real concern even in the 1960s, it now turned out, had never been a nuclear holocaust; it was the prospect of disorder "in places like the flanks of Europe, the Middle East, the Persian Gulf, the trans-Caucasus, and Central and Northern Asia." With the disintegration of Yugoslavia, disorder was now in full flood, signifying in Wohlstetter's estimation "the total collapse of US policy in the critical Gulf region."

The US and European response to the Balkan crisis—which Wohlstetter described as "craven," "shameless," "a bloody farce," "a grim farce," "a grim charade," "gyrating indecisions," and "political apologetics for doing nothing"—had the effect of "spreading pan-nationalism and genocide," thereby allowing "brutal dictatorships [to] hide plans and programs for mass terror against countries near and far." Overall, Wohlstetter fulminated, it amounted to "the worst performance of the democracies since World War II," even "exceed-[ing] the nightmares of Vietnam." Furthermore, Washington's hand-wringing and hesitation were completely unnecessary since the United States had readily at hand the means required to settle the Balkan crisis forthwith—and, by extension, to dispatch any other ne'er-do-wells. Throughout history, war had been costly, hard, and fraught with uncertainty. No more. At the end of a career spent poking holes in erstwhile simple solutions, Albert Wohlstetter had latched onto his own simple solution: war remade—indeed perfected—by advanced information technology.

Legacies

By the time of Albert Wohlstetter's death in 1997, precepts he had promoted for decades permeated the ranks of the American national security establishment. Above all, his enthusiasm for precise, discriminate force as the basis of a new American way of war, imparting an expanded offensive potential to US defense policy, had come to enjoy wide circulation. Yet opening the ranks of the Wohlstetter School to include the riff-raff—the functionaries, elected and unelected, military and civilian, who translate theory into practice—came at a cost. Wohlstetter's ideas enjoyed wide dissemination but in a corrupt or vulgar form. The term that popularizers coined to describe this new way of war, touted as a sure-fire recipe for security, was Revolution in Military Affairs. During its brief heyday, the RMA gave birth to various offspring, almost all of them illegitimate. Two of these deserve attention here, since they played a significant role in creating the immediate climate from which the Bush Doctrine emerged. Both were products of the Clinton era. The first was "full-spectrum dominance," a concept unveiled in *Joint Vision 2010*, a Pentagon document drafted in the mid-1990s. *Joint Vision 2010* stands in relation to the RMA as Tom Friedman's *The Lexus and the Olive Tree* stands in relation to globalization: it is an infomercial—marketing disguised as elucidation. To read *JV 2010* is to learn how "dominant battlespace awareness" will enable US commanders to "sense dangers sooner" and "make better decisions more rapidly," while employing weapons possessing "an order of magnitude improvement in lethality," all of this making US forces "persuasive in peace, decisive in war, preeminent in any form of conflict."

Full-spectrum dominance was not some wild notion concocted by a technology-besotted general staff. It bore the imprimatur of official policy and won the full approval of senior civilian leaders. "The information revolution," a confident Secretary of Defense William Cohen declared in 1997, "is creating a revolution in military affairs that will fundamentally change the way US forces fight. We must exploit these and other technologies to dominate in battle. Our template for seizing on these technologies and ensuring military dominance is *Joint Vision 2010.*" The RMA, wrote Secretary Cohen, was providing US forces with "superior battlespace awareness, permitting them to dramatically reduce the fog of war." Or as the 1999 edition of the Clinton administration's national security strategy put it, "Exploiting the revolution in military affairs is fundamental if US forces are to retain their dominance in an uncertain world." Leveraging the RMA's "technological, doctrinal, operational and organizational innovations" promised to "give US forces greater capabilities and flexibility." Implicit in all of these references to dominance was an assumption about risk, that perennial bugaboo of the Wohlstetter School: the application of information technology to war was drastically curtailing it. As technology produced clarity, barriers to action were falling away; available options were increasing.

To what use would these dominant capabilities be put? Here we come to the RMA's second bastard child, captured in a single seemingly innocuous word: "shaping." Put simply, the RMA created expectations of sculpting the international order to suit American preferences. "Shape, respond, prepare": this was the slogan devised by the Clinton White House to describe the essence of post–Cold War US strategy. By limiting the actionable options available to would-be adversaries, American military preeminence would leave them with little alternative except to conform to Washington's wishes. If nothing else, "shaping" promised institutional relevance. In 1998, with major land wars nowhere to be seen, the US military was climbing aboard the bandwagon. "In support of our National Security Strategy," the secretary of the army wrote in his annual report, "America's Army shapes the international environment in ways favorable for our nation. By promoting democracy and stability around the world, the Army reduces threats the nation could face in the next century."

This concept found favor even among neoconservatives, who otherwise disdained Clinton's approach to policy. In its founding statement of principles, the soon-to-be-famous Project for the New American Century put it this way: "The history of the 20th century should have taught us that it is important to shape circumstances before crises emerge, and to meet threats before they become dire." Nor were civilians alone susceptible to these expectations. Senior military officers quickly bought in. "'Shaping' means creating a security setting such that it is unnecessary to fight to protect one's interests," General

Hugh Shelton, chairman of the Joint Chiefs of Staff, explained approvingly in a 1997 address at Harvard. "We shape the strategic environment," General John Shalikashvili, another JCS chairman, wrote "with forward presence, combined exercises, security assistance, and a host of other programs," thereby helping to "defuse potential conflict." Just as any cheap knock-off pays tribute to the original, Washington's enthusiasm for full-spectrum dominance and "shaping" in the interval between the Cold War and the War on Terror represented a sort of unacknowledged—perhaps even unconscious—homage to the Wohlstetter School during the Clinton era. Shaping offered a soft-power approach to anticipatory action specifically intended to reduce risk. If implying the exercise of quasi-imperial prerogatives, it also promised to avoid, or at least minimize, the unseemliness of bombs and bloodshed. After all, given the existence of full-spectrum dominance, resistance to Washington's dictates and desires would qualify as foolhardy in the extreme.

Yet during the 1990s US efforts to "shape" the Middle East yielded results other than those intended. Rather than reducing risk, forward presence, combined exercises, security assistance, and the related programs touted by General Shalikashvili enflamed anti-Americanism and played into the hands of those intent on waging violent jihad against the United States. A series of attacks on US forces and installations, targeting the US barracks at Khobar Towers in 1996, US embassies in Kenya and Tanzania in 1998, and the destroyer USS *Cole* in 2000, told the tale. Even before 9/11, the changing of the guard in Washington had brought to power men fully imbued with the tenets of the Wohlstetter School and persuaded that the Clinton approach to shaping had been too tentative and diffident. For Cheney, Rumsfeld, and Wolfowitz the events of September 11, showing that the United States was as vulnerable to surprise as it had been back in December 1941, elicited not second thoughts but a determination to up the ante.[15]

15. In explaining how the United States had been caught unawares on September 11, 2001, the 9/11 Commission made favorable allusions to Roberta Wohlstetter's book on Pearl Harbor. Once again, past US policies escaped examination.

The exercise of imperial prerogatives was going to entail bombs and bloodshed after all—precise, discriminate force actually employed, rather than merely held in reserve, with Washington seizing opportunities to eradicate danger, rather than merely trying to manage it, and also surprising others, rather than passively waiting to be surprised. In one form or another, these ideas had been circulating for decades. George W. Bush now invested them with the force of policy.

The sorry tale of all that subsequently ensued need not be retold here. Bush and his advisers wasted little time in identifying Saddam Hussein's Iraq as the venue in which to give America's new doctrine of preventive war a trial run. Those making the case for war did so by resurrecting old chestnuts lifted from the Wohlstetter tradition. The nation was once again in deepest peril, Saddam posing a threat that was both global and existential. Contemplating America's plight, the President and members of his inner circle assessed "the risk of action" to be "smaller than the risk of inaction," as Wolfowitz explained.[16] Benefiting from the close supervision of Donald Rumsfeld, planning for the invasion of Iraq put a premium on the use of precision force. Here was an occasion to use American power discriminately and for worthy ends.

The Iraq War began with high hopes of "shock and awe," as journalists and some enthusiastic analysts called it, producing an easy victory. Here, Richard Perle declared, "was the first war that's been fought in a way that would recognize Albert's vision of future wars." Operation Iraqi Freedom reflected "an implementation of his strategy and his vision." In many respects, the war's opening phases seemed to validate all that the Wohlstetter School as a whole stood for. Yet only briefly: the real Iraq War—the conflict that began when Baghdad fell—left the Wohlstetter vision in tatters. An admirer once described Albert Wohlstetter as "the tailor who sought to clothe the emperor."[17] In a case of history mimicking fable, the raiment adorning the Emperor Bush turned out to be a figment of imagination. Still, there remained this: the prior assurances of Kennedy and Reagan notwithstanding, starting wars now formed the very cornerstone of US policy.

---

16. Paul Wolfowitz, "Remarks at International Institute for Strategic Studies," December 2, 2002.

17. Stephen Lukasik, "Commentary: *Towards Discriminate Deterrence*," in *Nuclear Heuristics*, 514.

11

Fault Lines
Inside Rumsfeld's Pentagon

(2008)

Setting aside combat memoirs, of which there are a growing number, the literature of the Iraq War divides neatly into two categories. The first category, dominated by journalistic observers, indicts. The second category, accounts authored by insider participants, acquits. The two books reviewed here fall into the second category: They are exercises in self-exculpation.[1] Pretending to explain, their actual purpose is to deflect responsibility.

Douglas Feith and Ricardo Sanchez are not exactly marquee figures. Yet each for a time played an important role in America's Mesopotamian misadventure. From 2001 to 2005 Feith served in the Pentagon as the third-ranking figure in the Office of the Secretary of

---

1. Douglas J. Feith, *War and Decision: Inside the Pentagon at the Dawn of the War on Terrorism* (New York: Harper, 2008); Ricardo S. Sanchez, *Wiser in Battle: A Soldier's Story* (New York: Harper, 2008).

Defense (OSD) under Donald Rumsfeld and Paul Wolfowitz, Rumsfeld's deputy. From 2003 to 2004 Lieutenant General Sanchez, now retired, served in Baghdad, commanding all coalition forces in Iraq.

Of the two accounts, Feith's qualifies as the more sophisticated. It is also far and away the more dishonest. Feith trained as a lawyer, and *War and Decision* qualifies as a masterpiece of lawyerly, even Nixonian, obfuscation.

Like a shrewd defense attorney, Feith poses only those questions that will advance his case. As a result, his very long account confines itself to a very narrow range of issues. Although Feith styles himself a strategist, conscientious readers will learn nothing here about, say, the strategic significance of Persian Gulf oil. In *War and Decision*, oil just does not come up. Readers will be instructed in great detail about Saddam Hussein's record as a vile and cruel dictator. They will remain oblivious to the record of US support for the Iraqi tyrant during the Reagan era, despite the fact that Feith himself served in the Reagan administration. They will be reminded of the many intelligence failures attributable to the CIA. They will look in vain for any reference to allegations, substantiated at the highest level of the British government, that the Bush administration engaged in "fixing" intelligence to support precooked policy decisions. They will learn that Feith is Jewish and a self-described neoconservative, and that members of his extended family perished in the Holocaust. They will find no mention of Feith's involvement in right-wing Israeli politics, notably as a participant in the group responsible for "A Clean Break: A New Strategy for Securing the Realm," prepared in 1996 for Likud leader Benjamin Netanyahu. Among that study's recommendations was one identifying Saddam's overthrow as a key Israeli national security objective.

This careful discrimination between convenient and inconvenient facts enables Feith to craft a finely honed version of the Iraq War. The resulting narrative can be summarized in three sentences: Apart from the odd misstep or two, senior officials in OSD, to the man high-minded patriots and sophisticated thinkers, performed their duties brilliantly. Alas, their counterparts at the CIA and State Department, motivated by a combination of spite, prejudice, parochialism, and outright disloyalty to the president, conspired to frustrate or derail OSD's plans. Abetted by L. Paul Bremer, who headed the Coalition Provisional Authority that governed Iraq during the first year after Saddam's removal, they succeeded, with terrible consequences.

In mounting this defense of OSD, Feith concentrates on two themes. In the first, he offers a highly imaginative revisionist account of Operation Iraqi Freedom's rationale and justification. In the second, he absolves himself and his Pentagon colleagues of any responsibility for the invasion's catastrophic aftermath.

According to Feith, for all the emphasis that senior US officials prior to March 2003 placed on weapons of mass destruction and Saddam's alleged ties to al-Qaeda, those issues do not explain why the Bush administration *actually* opted for war. The truth is that the United States invaded Iraq as an act of self-defense. Saddam's regime, Feith explains, posed a direct, looming threat to America itself. To permit the Iraqi dictator to remain in power was to give him "a chance to intimidate and hurt the United States"—an intolerable prospect. Viewed from this perspective, the much-ballyhooed failure to find any nuclear or biological weapons or to establish any connection between Saddam and al-Qaeda is simply beside the point. Saddam's record of misbehavior and his persistent antagonism toward the United States provided more than ample justification for war. Indeed, Feith insists, after 9/11 force had become the only reasonable option. Invading Iraq was not only justified; it was a moral and strategic imperative.

Although Operation Iraqi Freedom opened on a promising note, President Bush's declaration of "Mission Accomplished," televised worldwide on May 1, 2003, proved a trifle premature. Hard on the heels of Saddam's removal came a protracted, costly, and deeply embarrassing insurgency. Feith's second theme is an attempt to claim credit for the successful drive on Baghdad while blaming everyone else for the ensuing quagmire. In effect, he constructs a variation on what we might call the Manstein Defense, mimicking German generals like Erich von Manstein who crowned themselves with laurels for the Wehrmacht's early victories while tagging Hitler with responsibility for the army's later defeats.

As Feith tells the tale, he and his Pentagon colleagues insisted from the outset on styling the American invasion as an act of liberation. The idea was to topple Saddam, quickly hand over the reins of government to friendly Iraqis, and get out. "Iraq belonged to the Iraqis," Feith writes, as if personally uncovering a profound truth. The model was to be Afghanistan, currently a narco-state riven with armed Islamic radicals, which Feith nonetheless depicts as a stupendous success. There, after the invasion of 2001, he observes, the United States "never became an occupying power." Mere weeks after the fall of Baghdad, however, the United States unwisely jettisoned its strategy of liberation. Largely as a consequence of a series of ill-advised decisions by Bremer, it opted instead to occupy and reconstruct Iraq. This, according to Feith, proved a fateful, yet utterly avoidable "self-inflicted wound."

Neither of these arguments stands up to even casual scrutiny. Yet however unwittingly, Feith tells a revealing story that demonstrates above all the astonishing combination of hubris and naiveté that pervaded Donald Rumsfeld's Pentagon.

History—US history included—is a chronicle of great powers waging wars of conquest in "self-defense." In 1846, for example, a "long-continued series of menaces" that culminated when enemy forces "invaded our territory and shed the blood of our fellow-citizens on our own soil" obliged the United States, ever so reluctantly, to take up arms against Mexico. So, at least, President James K. Polk explained in a message to Congress requesting a declaration of war. The amalgamation of California, Nevada, Utah, Arizona, and New Mexico territories into the Union followed in short order.

The case of Iraq after 9/11 is analogous. Small, distant, isolated, underdeveloped, crippled by sanctions, its airspace penetrated daily by Anglo-American combat patrols, its army a shell of the force that the United States and its allies handily defeated in 1991, Saddam's Iraq posed a negligible threat to the United States. Yet, as with the Polk administration in 1846, the Bush administration by 2003 (especially the upper echelons of OSD) had evolved large ambitions that could only be fulfilled by resorting to the sword.

The Mexican War worked out nicely for the American people, who soon gave up the pretense that the United States had invaded Mexico out of concern for self-defense. (For subsequent generations of Americans, Manifest Destiny became the preferred explanation for the war's origins.) Alas, President Bush demonstrated little of President Polk's acumen as a war manager. The Iraq War has benefited Americans not at all. With the failure to locate WMD or to establish direct Iraqi involvement in terrorism directed at the United States, the Bush administration's proximate rationale for the war collapsed. So Feith concocts "self-defense" as a last-ditch, *ex post facto* substitute. It won't wash.

What Feith will not acknowledge outright is that within OSD the prospect of a showdown with Iraq seemed inviting not because Saddam posed an imminent danger, but because he was so obviously weak. For those most keen to invade Iraq, the appeal of war lay in the expectation that an easy win there would give rise to an abundance of second-order benefits. In an appendix to *War and Decision*, Feith reprints a memo from Rumsfeld to national security adviser Condoleezza Rice dated July 27, 2001, in which the secretary of defense advocates ousting Saddam as a way to "enhance US credibility and influence throughout the region." Here we find an early hint of the Pentagon's post-9/11 views: eliminating a bona fide bad guy promised to endow the United States with additional leverage that it could then employ against other ne'er-do-wells, recalcitrants, and false friends. The idea, Feith wrote in a May 2004 memo to Rumsfeld, was to "transform the Middle East and the broader world of Islam politically." Employing American power to transform the Islamic world would "counter ideological support for terrorism," which, according to Feith, held "the key to defeating terrorism in the longer term."

In just about anyone's book, the political transformation of the Islamic world qualifies as a breathtakingly large project. How exactly did the Bush administration intend to achieve this goal? Although citing with considerable pride the "precision" and analytical rigor of OSD's work, Feith provides no evidence that the Pentagon ever addressed this fundamental question. Just days after 9/11, Rumsfeld was charging his subordinates to devise a plan of action that had "three, four, five moves behind it." In fact, OSD conjured a plan with exactly two moves: first Afghanistan, and then Iraq; once US forces made it to Baghdad, the other dominos were expected to topple.

This was not strategy; it was reckless opportunism, marinated in neoconservative ideology and further seasoned with OSD's spectacular insouciance when it came to considering resources. When the Bush administration set out to reorder the Islamic world after 9/11, no one even bothered to ask whether the United States possessed the means required to make good on such a bold ambition. Nor, apparently, did anyone in OSD pay much attention to exactly what "transformation" might entail. Did it require forswearing support for terror? Categorically rejecting WMD? Embracing liberal democracy? Making peace with Israel? All of the above? A memo to President Bush drafted by Feith in late September 2001 simply took "the vastness of [US] military and humanitarian resources" as a given. As the Pentagon's policy chief, Feith never bothered to question this assumption, which proved groundless in the face of events.

The key point is this: Feith's depiction of the Iraq War as a war of self-defense is a small lie concocted to camouflage a far more egregious transgression. The real crime lies not in dissembling about the war's origins — in politics, such fictions are a dime a dozen. Rather, the real crime lies in Feith's complicity in conceiving an ersatz strategy that failed to satisfy even the most rudimentary requirements of common sense. The Iraq War was always unnecessary. From the very moment of its conception, Feith and his colleagues in OSD contrived to make it profoundly stupid as well. Invading Iraq was never going to "transform" Islam. Nor was it ever going to "counter ideological support for terrorism." Indeed, war was almost guaranteed to produce precisely the opposite result — inflaming hostility toward the United States across the Islamic world.

Worse, this spurious Feith Doctrine of self-defense is at odds with existing American interests. To take but one example: If Saddam's past offenses and belligerent attitude constituted sufficient reason for the United States to wage a war of self-defense against Iraq, then surely Iran's nuclear program and its support for those resisting the US presence in Iraq can be justified on similar grounds; Washington's history of intervening in Iranian affairs and President Bush's inclusion of Iran in his "axis of evil" provide Tehran ample reason to fear US aggression. For those with a taste for irony, the massive infiltration of immigrants from south of the border into California and the Southwest might even qualify as an unconventional form of self-defense, Mexicans belatedly retrieving what was theirs in the first place.

Then there is Feith's charge that Bremer snatched defeat from the jaws of victory by abandoning "liberation" in favor of occupation. Here, too, what purports to be truth-telling is in reality little more than diversionary scapegoating.

A careful reading of Feith's account reveals that OSD's own plan for liberating Iraq amounted to occupation by another name. Under the terms of that plan, which Feith claims as his own handiwork, immediately upon removing Saddam Hussein from power, US officials in Baghdad were to constitute an Iraqi Interim Authority (IIA) consisting of Iraqi leaders who would manage Iraqi affairs while simultaneously devising the permanent political institutions for the post-Saddam era. From the outset, this project would have an Iraqi face and therefore, according to Feith, likely command broad Iraqi support. To put it another way, by its very existence, the IIA would remove any Iraqi inclination to oppose the United States.

Yet OSD never actually intended that Iraqis—other than those chosen in advance by the United States—would determine their own nation's fate. For Feith and his colleagues, "liberation" was a codeword that meant indirect control. OSD sought to exercise that control in three ways.

First, it established under Pentagon jurisdiction an agency designed to direct developments in Baghdad after Saddam's removal. This was the misleadingly named Office of Reconstruction and Humanitarian Assistance (ORHA), created by OSD in January 2003 and headed by retired army Lieutenant General Jay Garner, Rumsfeld's handpicked choice for the job.

Second, against bitter opposition from the CIA and State Department, Feith and his colleagues tried to ensure that OSD would have the final say in deciding exactly which Iraqis would occupy positions of influence in the IIA. Contemporary press reports identified neoconservative favorite Ahmad Chalabi as the Pentagon's preferred candidate to run the IIA. Feith denies that OSD was promoting Chalabi, but his relentless attacks on Chalabi's critics, professing bafflement at how others could malign someone of such manifest decency, belie those denials. (Subsequent charges that Chalabi was playing a double game, leaking sensitive intelligence to Iran, number among the matters that Feith ignores altogether.)

Third, even as it was touting the Iraqi Interim Authority as an embryonic government run by Iraqis, OSD established narrow limits on that government's prerogatives. For example, as Feith notes in passing, under the IIA, the United States would retain "the authority to appoint top officials for the ministries of Defense, Finance, Interior, and Oil." That authority provided the ultimate guarantee that the United States would continue to call the shots. The IIA would be a puppet regime, Feith and his colleagues apparently expecting Iraqis either not to notice or not to care who was actually pulling the strings.

The point here is not to defend L. Paul Bremer, whose tenure as head of the Coalition Provisional Authority produced an unmitigated disaster. Rather, the point is to recognize that as an alternative to Bremer's ham-handed policy of occupation, Feith's concept of liberation was really no alternative at all. It was the same policy with a different label attached.

There is a further problem with making Bremer the fall guy: he was, after all, Rumsfeld's man, doing Rumsfeld's bidding. With ORHA barely having set up shop in Baghdad, Rumsfeld decided that Garner had to go. Feith denies that Garner was fired, but to characterize his abrupt replacement in any other way is laughable. Rumsfeld then urged President Bush to install Bremer as head of the Coalition Provisional Authority, reporting directly to the secretary of defense.

Furthermore, by the summer of 2003 Rumsfeld himself did not want to speed up the process of creating a fully sovereign Iraqi government. Feith lets on that Rumsfeld was "unhappy that the Iraqis were pushing so hard for power." The secretary of defense needed more time to assess the political acceptability of the various Iraqis vying for positions of leadership. With that in mind, he "wanted to tap the brakes on the political process," slowing down efforts to transfer power. When Bremer scrapped the IIA, his decision was consistent with Rumsfeld's wishes. Indeed, Rumsfeld concurred in Bremer's decision.

Feith portrays the Iraqi Interim Authority as the war's great missed opportunity: If only Bremer had adhered to OSD's conception of liberation, all would have turned out well. The argument fails on two counts. First, the actual purpose of the IIA was not to empower Iraqis but to facilitate even while disguising the exercise of American control. Second, it was Rumsfeld himself who decided that indirect control did not suffice. The United States opted for a policy of outright occupation in large part because the Pentagon itself came to the conclusion that occupation was essential to achieving US objectives. If the occupation was a self-inflicted wound, Feith's boss pulled the trigger.

A memo drafted by Feith for Rumsfeld, reaching the desk of President Bush on September 30, 2001, declared, "If the war does not significantly change the world's political map, the U.S. will not achieve its aim." Considered in that light, the wars that Feith labored so mightily to promote, not only the war in Iraq but also the larger global war on terror, must be judged abject failures.

Feith wants his readers to believe that failure stemmed from errors in execution, most of them attributable to decisions made beyond the confines of OSD. The truth is that the principal explanation for failure is a conceptual one: pseudo-strategists within OSD misconstrued the threat, misread the Islamic world, and vastly overestimated American power. From day one, with Feith their willing accomplice, they got it wrong. This mendacious and self-serving book serves only to affirm Feith's complicity in the ensuing debacle.

Ricardo Sanchez is the highest-ranking Latino military officer in this nation's history, rising from grinding poverty to achieve the lofty rank of three-star general. *Wiser in Battle* is above all an expression of his anger and bitterness at not achieving four-star rank. He uses his memoir to lash out at those he holds responsible for denying him further promotion. The result can only be described as unseemly. It is never pretty to see a grown man whine.

General Sanchez depicts himself as a man of honor surrounded by careerists and connivers. During his thirty-three years as a serving officer, while "a greed for power" motivated others, he sought only to do the right thing. Long before he assumed command in Baghdad, Sanchez had reached certain conclusions about civilians back in Washington, not only politicians but also journalists: they tended to be largely clueless and were certainly not to be trusted.

Secretary of Defense Donald Rumsfeld confirmed this negative impression of anyone not wearing a uniform. Sanchez describes Rumsfeld as a meddler and a micromanager, intent on exercising not only civilian control but even "civilian command of the military." For a political appointee to claim such sweeping authority was, in Sanchez's eyes, "a recipe for disaster."

Without offering any substantiating evidence, Sanchez charges that Rumsfeld, shortly after 9/11, gave the green light for torture—according to Sanchez, a "colossal mistake." With his famously abrasive manner, Rumsfeld had also induced within the Pentagon "an environment of fear and retribution that made top military leaders hesitant to stand up to the administration's authoritarianism." In essence, after 9/11 an intimidated officer corps lost its moral compass. Embarking on its global war on terror, the Bush administration had "unleashed the hounds of hell." Even at the uppermost levels of the armed services, "no one seemed to have the moral courage to get the animals back in their cages."

Such qualms of conscience did not prevent Sanchez from interviewing with Rumsfeld for promotion to lieutenant general or from accepting an appointment to command all US and coalition forces in Iraq just weeks after President Bush's "Mission Accomplished" speech.

When Sanchez assumed command, evidence of a brewing insurgency was already mounting. While back in Washington Feith was lovingly perfecting his vision of an Iraqi Interim Authority, Baghdad was already coming apart at the seams. By the time Sanchez departed Baghdad a year later, chaos had engulfed Iraq, and US forces were caught in the middle of a civil war that Sanchez himself reports "our actions had undeniably ignited." Punctuating this deteriorating situation was the Abu Ghraib scandal, which seemed to affirm that something had gone fundamentally wrong.

In short, when the animals in Iraq escaped their cages, Ricardo Sanchez was the chief zookeeper. His mission was to secure Iraq. He failed egregiously. The results of his efforts were almost entirely negative. As measured by the number of American soldiers and Iraqi civilians killed and wounded, they were also costly. Yet none of this, Sanchez insists, was his fault.

According to a core value of the military professional ethic, commanders are responsible for everything that occurs on their watch. The whole point of *Wiser in Battle* is to suggest that in the case of Ricardo Sanchez the principle of command responsibility should not apply.

As a consequence, Sanchez's narrative of his year in Baghdad becomes essentially one long list of recriminations. Rumsfeld, who dangled the prospect of a fourth star only to reverse himself after Abu Ghraib, comes across as his principal nemesis. The secretary of defense, however, is but one target among many. Sanchez takes his own shots at the widely discredited Bremer, with whom he tangled repeatedly, and blasts the entire National Security Council mechanism as "incompetent." He professes shock at discovering that, for the White House, "ensuring the success of President Bush's reelection campaign" took precedence over all other considerations. Nor does Sanchez spare his fellow generals, especially those serving on the Joint Chiefs of Staff. When General Peter Pace, JCS vice-chairman, broke the news that the much-coveted promotion was not going to happen, Sanchez replied, "Well, sir, you all have betrayed me."

Sanchez refrains from criticizing the president directly, depicting him as well-intentioned yet utterly out of his depth. During a videoconference in the midst of the notorious first Fallujah offensive of April 2004, Bush offered the following guidance to his field commander: "Kick ass! If someone tries to stop the march to democracy, we will seek them out and kill them! We must be tougher than hell! . . . Stay strong! Stay the course! Kill them! Be confident! Prevail! We are going to wipe them out!" Two days later, orders from above directed Sanchez to suspend the offensive. "Politics"—Sanchez employs the term as shorthand for any intrusion by ignorant civilians with ulterior motives—had produced "a strategic defeat for the United States and a moral victory for the insurgents."

Sanchez's assessment of Bush applies to himself as well: no doubt meaning well, he was out of his depth. Unlike the execrable Feith, earnestly crafting memos back in the Pentagon, Sanchez knew better than to imagine that depicting Americans as "liberators" was going change the facts on the ground. "According to *any* definition," he writes, "we *were*, in fact, occupiers" (emphasis in original). Yet *Wiser in Battle* contains little to suggest that Sanchez understood the actual nature of the problem in Iraq any better than Feith did. The aggrieved general's distaste for politics, which is intrinsic to war and from the outset played a central role in this particular conflict, indicates that understanding lay beyond his ability. The book's title notwithstanding, wisdom—or even thoughtful reflection—is notable by its absence.

Sanchez was the wrong man for the job. That Feith's boss should have appointed Sanchez in the first place provides further confirmation—if any were needed—of OSD's monumental capacity for screwing up.

Apart from the finger-pointing and score-settling, these two accounts do agree at least implicitly on a single issue: taken as a whole, the national security apparatus is irredeemably broken. The so-called "interagency process" created to harmonize the efforts of national security institutions so that the president receives sound and timely advice and to ensure that presidential decisions are promptly implemented, whether in Baghdad or within the Beltway, actually produces the opposite effect. From quite different vantage points, Feith and Sanchez affirm that the principal product generated by the interagency process is disharmony, dishonesty, and dysfunction. Whether a different process employing the same people or recruiting different people while retaining the existing process would yield different results is difficult to say. To imagine, however, that simply electing a new chief executive in November will fix the problem is surely to succumb to an illusion.

12

Tommy Franks

A Modern Major General

(2004)

It is the flip side of the celebrity culture: prominent figures in various walks of life—entertainment, sports, big business, politics—bask in the adulation of the unwashed and inhabit a rarefied world of privilege and deference. But their entrée into that world is highly contingent, requiring that they continue to meet the capricious, even whimsical expectations of their adoring fans. Fail to deliver and the accounting can be as abrupt as it is brutal. Ask the movie star who bombs on successive pictures, the high-priced quarterback who somehow cannot win the big ones, the corporate executive who, for one too many quarters, falls short of "market expectations." Ask Al Gore.

But one highly visible segment of the American elite has been largely exempt from this rule. Ever since the Persian Gulf War of 1990–91, when by common consent the United States established itself as The Greatest Military Power The World Has Ever Seen, those entrusted with commanding US forces have enjoyed a protected status. As newspapers once treated the local archbishop with kid gloves lest they invite the charge of being insufficiently respectful of the Church, so in recent years otherwise free-swinging critics have generally given generals and admirals a pass lest they appear to violate that ultimate diktat of present-day political correctness: never do anything that might suggest less than wholehearted support for our men and women in uniform. As a consequence, those who occupy the uppermost ranks of the armed forces have become the least accountable members of the American elite. Or perhaps more accurately, members of this exclusive club are unique in being accountable only to their peers.

Consider: when Lieutenant General Ricardo Sanchez assumed command of coalition forces in Iraq in 2003, the first stirrings of an insurgency had begun to appear; his job was to snuff out that insurgency and establish a secure environment. When Sanchez gave up command a year later, Iraq was all but coming apart at the seams. Security had deteriorated appreciably. The general failed to accomplish his mission, egregiously so. Yet amidst all the endless commentary and chatter about Iraq, that failure of command has gone all but unnoted, as if for outsiders to evaluate senior officer performance qualifies as bad form. Had Sanchez been a head coach or a CEO, he would likely have been cashiered. But he is a general, so the Pentagon pins a medal on his chest and gives him a pat on the back. It is the dirty little secret to which the World's Only Superpower has yet to own up: as the United States has come to rely ever more heavily on armed force to prop up its position of global pre-eminence, the quality of senior American military leadership has seldom risen above the mediocre. The troops are ever willing, the technology remarkable, but first-rate generalship has been hard to come by.

Tommy Franks would dispute that charge. To rebut it, he would cite his own achievements as the senior field commander during the US-led incursion into Afghanistan in 2001 and the invasion of Iraq in 2003.[1] In each case, a brilliantly conceived plan—*his* plan, implemented under *his* direct control—resulted in decisive victory, gained with economy and dispatch. Indeed, the whole point of *American Soldier* is to stake out Franks's claim to being one of history's Great Captains.

---

1. Tommy Franks, *American Soldier* (HarperCollins: New York, 2004).

Readers predisposed to see Operations Enduring Freedom and Iraqi Freedom in glowing terms may well find the general's efforts to sustain his case persuasive. Those alive to the fact that Iraq has become a full-fledged quagmire and Afghanistan only slightly less so will find the general's claim to be ranked among the immortals less compelling. But even they will profit from reading *American Soldier*. For the account that Franks provides is as instructive as it is revealing. Given the vast pretensions and militarized nature of present-day US foreign policy, this is a document of genuine significance, as timely as it is troubling.

In terms of its overall composition, *American Soldier* adheres to, and therefore helps to legitimate, an emerging literary tradition: the military memoir as narrative of national redemption. As the wars, excursions and alarms of the post–Cold War era have piled up, so too have the published remembrances of senior American military leaders. In its latter-day form, this genre comes in two distinctive variants. Those falling into the first category are easily identified: in every instance, two-inch-tall letters on the dust jacket identify the author as Tom Clancy, who has actually never served a day in uniform. Underneath the author's name, almost as an afterthought in much smaller type, comes the acknowledgement that Clancy penned his account "with General Johnny So-and-So (ret.)."

For the better part of a decade Clancy, who achieved fame and fortune writing techno-thrillers, has been churning out these military chronicles with the same regularity that he produces best-selling novels. There are now four such volumes, the first three—*Into the Storm* (1997), *Every Man a Tiger* (1999), and *Shadow Warriors* (2002)— co-written, respectively, with Generals Fred Franks, Chuck Horner, and Carl Stiner, who all occupied senior command positions in Operation Desert Storm. The most recent was produced in conjunction with the marine officer who preceded Tommy Franks as head of United States Central Command, or CENTCOM, with an area of operations spanning East Africa, the Middle East, and Central Eurasia. This is *Battle Ready* (2004), by Tom Clancy with General Tony Zinni (ret.) and Tony Koltz—the addition of a third collaborator/ghost writer making it more difficult still to know exactly how much credence to give to these concoctions. The books give the impression of being not so much written as assembled—which is a shame: Zinni is, in fact, a thoughtful and interesting man who has emerged of late as an ardent critic of the Bush administration's conduct of its so-called global war on terror. But whether the critique expressed in *Battle Ready* actually qualifies as his own is anyone's guess.

The second category of the modern-day senior officer memoir is the one into which *American Soldier* blessedly falls. Although typically written with outside assistance, these books manage at least to retain a semblance of authenticity. The Norman Schwarzkopf of *It Doesn't Take a Hero* (1993) may be a somewhat sanitized version of the real Stormin' Norman. Certainly, the account of Operation Desert Storm forming the core of his narrative is self-serving. But the overall product bears at least some similarity to the genuine article. Much the same can be said about Colin Powell, who describes his military career in *My American Journey* (1995), or Wesley Clark, who in *Waging Modern War* (2001) recounts a journey to high command that culminates in the struggle for Kosovo.

Whether of the manufactured or handcrafted variety, virtually every one of these narratives conforms to a prescribed formula. The protagonist, after an upbringing spent acquiring a profound appreciation for American values, joins the armed forces and serves as a young officer in Vietnam. This war becomes the pivot around which all else turns — Franks, for example, titles the chapter describing his own Vietnam service "The Crucible." From his experience in a lost war, the protagonist derives certain essential truths that he vows to apply if ever called upon in some future crisis to serve in a position of authority. Upon returning home from battle, although dismayed to see his countrymen shunning those who served and sacrificed, he soldiers on, rising through the ranks during a lengthy apprenticeship. When his moment finally arrives, he orchestrates a great victory, by implication showing how Vietnam *ought* to have been fought. In vanquishing the enemy, he also helps heal old wounds at home, promoting both reconciliation and national renewal. Somewhat less loftily, in recounting this triumph the protagonist also makes use of every available opportunity to settle scores with old enemies and critics.

In *American Soldier*, the initial elements of this sequence stand out as clearly the best. The adopted only child of loving, working-class parents, Franks tells the story of his hardscrabble upbringing with wit and charm. Growing up in small town Oklahoma and Texas meant "living the American dream": exploring the outdoors and playing ball, rebuilding motorbikes and drag racers, chasing girls and drinking beer. When too much of the latter resulted in Franks flunking out of college, he enlisted in the army and in 1967 earned his commission through Officer Candidate School. Soon thereafter, the green-as-grass second lieutenant was off to Southeast Asia. Franks describes his year of combat as a field artilleryman in vivid detail. Cool-headed, courageous, and resourceful, he took to soldiering with the same alacrity as he had the carefree pursuits of boyhood. Although in joining up Franks had viewed the army as a detour eventually leading back to fraternity row, he found in military service a life that soon became a calling. When he returned from Vietnam in 1968 and contemplated the prospect of attending school alongside "guys who'd used student deferments to protest the war," he wasted little time in deciding to make the military a career. In the Cold War army of the 1970s and 1980s, he excelled. Franks sought out tough, demanding jobs and then delivered results. He was an ambitious officer who loved his family, but put his career first and steadily climbed the ladder of success. The Gulf War of 1990–91 found him a brigadier general. Ten years later, now wearing four stars, he assumed command of CENTCOM.

All the while Franks had cultivated a rough-around-the-edges, country-boy persona—the kid from west Texas professing amazement at how far he had come. "I had learned over the years that sometimes it's useful to operate behind a self-deprecating façade," he observes in an aside. Behind that façade, now Franks wants it known, was an erudite student of his profession and an original thinker. (Sensitive as well: Franks writes poetry, and *American Soldier* includes several unfortunate excerpts of his verse.) During his apprenticeship, he "had read about both war and peace: the accumulated wisdom of Sun Tzu and Clausewitz, Bertram [sic] Russell and Gandhi." Moreover, Franks insists, right from the outset he had been a "maverick" who found himself as a consequence "frequently on the outside of the Army's conservative mainstream."

In fact, Franks presents precious little evidence of free-thinking as he made his way to the top. Although he sprinkles his tale with quotations from long-deceased Chinese and German philosophers (none from the mysterious Mr. Russell), his observations about war and politics do not rise above the pedestrian. Franks writes knowingly of "a continuum of interaction between nations, factions and tribes." But he then translates that insight into his "Five Cs" theory of international politics, in which all interstate relationships fit into one of five categories: Conflict, Crisis, Co-existence, Collaboration, or Cooperation. And although as a junior commander or staff officer, Franks on occasion tinkered gingerly with military orthodoxy, he remained at all times comfortably within the system. In short, whether for good or for ill, by the time he ascended to command of CENTCOM in 2000, Franks had become the archetype of the Modern Major General.

That means among other things that Franks carried with him all the grudges that the officer corps had accumulated in Vietnam and has nursed ever since. In *American Soldier* these grudges emerge intact, with Franks piling on a few more of his own. Thus, several times in the course of this account, he lets fly at the media for what he describes as inaccurate, biased, and explicitly anti-military reporting. He takes swipes at "the intellectual arrogance" of civilian officials back in Washington, who imagine that air power alone "could kick open a door, through which exiled Iraqi opposition groups would march triumphantly to liberate their country." Such notions, writes Franks, were "absurd," as were expectations that Iraqi exile Ahmad Chalabi—a fraudulent "Gucci leader"—would be able to unite Iraq's various ethnic and religious factions.

Among the civilians that Franks scorches are Richard Clarke, the former White House anti-terrorism czar, dismissed as an impractical blowhard, and Douglas Feith, Undersecretary of Defense for policy and "the dumbest fucking guy on the planet." He likens these amateurs to "McNamara and his Whiz Kids [who] had repeatedly picked individual bombing targets and approved battalion-size maneuvers." Franks refuses to tolerate any such meddling. "My name is not Westmoreland," he growls during the Afghan campaign, "and I'm not going to go along with Washington giving tactics and targets to our kids in the cockpits and on the ground."

Nor does the general spare his own fellow professionals. He rails against the "ill-informed, disgruntled leakers finishing a dead-end career in some Pentagon cubicle" who presume to second-guess him. He derides the "motherfucking TV generals," many of whom "were much better TV analysts than they had been military officers." But he reserves his most ferocious salvo for the four-stars assigned as service chiefs. Advice proffered by the Joint Chiefs of Staff amounts to nothing more than "parochial bullshit." Franks expresses unmitigated contempt for the "Title Ten motherfuckers," who by law have no command authority and, hence, should refrain from nitpicking the plans of "warfighters" such as himself.

There is more here than histrionics. Sustaining the case for the general's induction into Valhalla requires that he demonstrate that he, and he alone, bears responsibility for the victories won in Afghanistan and especially Iraq. Franks wants to ensure that anyone finding fault with his performance does not get much of a hearing. But he also wants to make sure that no one horns in and claims laurels that he views as rightly his own. Yet in this regard, Clarke, Feith, the TV generals, and even the Joint Chiefs are comparative small fry. In imperial America, despite all the trappings of democracy, a relative handful of people exercise real power. (The imperial reference is not gratuitous: at one point Franks compares his role to that of "the Roman proconsul [Marcus Aemilius] Scaurus"; elsewhere he toys with the image of himself cloaked in "a purple-trimmed toga and a laurel wreath.") Depending on the issue, but especially in matters related to national security, decision-making at the summit involves as few as half a dozen serious players. To show that when it came to the wars in Afghanistan and Iraq he was really in charge, Franks must demonstrate that in the strategic interaction at the top *his* was the dominant voice. Franks must show, in short, that his role involved much more than simply following orders.

As Franks knows but does not acknowledge, contemporaneous reporting had suggested otherwise. The press had credited Secretary of Defense Donald Rumsfeld with devising the methods employed in Afghanistan and Iraq. In his own inimitable style, Rumsfeld had nudged, cajoled, and browbeaten a plodding theatre commander into embracing a novel approach to warfare that on successive occasions produced spectacular results—so at least the story went. Not so, Franks insists. From 9/11 on, he was the one driving the train: "CENTCOM 'pushed strategy up,' rather than waiting for Washington to 'push tactics down.'" At great length—this book gives substantially more attention to campaign planning than to fighting as such—Franks explains how he patiently educated the president and the defense secretary about contemporary warfare and brought them around to his own vision for how best to take down the Taliban and Saddam Hussein.

Although Franks professes to hold George W. Bush in the highest regard, the commander-in-chief emerges from this account as an affable, cliché-spouting airhead. Bush cheerfully presides over various briefings, offers a few random questions, and wraps things up with pithy admonitions like "Great job, Tommy. Keep it up. We will do what we have to do to protect America." Rumsfeld comes off as a more formidable interlocutor, repeatedly testing his field commander's patience and kept in line only through the most careful management. But Franks leaves no doubt that at the end of the day the twin invasions of 2001 and 2003 were fought his way.

The Franks vision, one that placed a premium on speed, surprise, deception, precision weapons, and the integration of all services into a fully unified fighting team, put him, he states categorically, "way outside the box of conventional doctrine." The upshot: two remarkable wins, the second of which Franks describes as "unequalled in its excellence by anything in the annals of war." But great as these accomplishments are, Franks wants it known that they possess a significance that continues to reverberate well beyond the battlefield. At home, victory triggered the revival of a "constant, deep patriotism by those who salute the flag, and by those who wave the flag"—Americans returning to those enduring values that young Tommy Franks had imbibed back in 1950s Texas. More substantively, the campaigns over which Franks presided constituted "a true revolution in warfare." The victories won in Afghanistan and Iraq thus provide assurances of US military supremacy as far as the eye can see.

Yet in making such specious assertions as both field commander and architect of a radically new American way of war, Franks puts himself in a fix not unlike that of Douglas MacArthur at the end of 1950. When, in September of that year, US forces at Inchon turned the tables on the North Koreans and instantly transformed the Korean War, MacArthur wanted no doubt left that the brilliance displayed was his and his alone. But in remarkably short order the masterstroke of

Inchon gave way to the shock of Chinese intervention, with the tables turning again. Try as he might, MacArthur could not claim ownership of the first without also being tagged with responsibility for the second.

Franks retired from active duty shortly after the well-televised toppling of Saddam Hussein's statue in Al Firdos Square, and thus cannot be held directly responsible for all that has transpired since in Iraq and Afghanistan; but neither can he ignore those developments. His efforts to explain them away, however, are feeble at best. With regard to the war against Saddam, Franks claims to have anticipated all along that the so-called Phase IV—the occupation and rehabilitation of Iraq—would be the most difficult and protracted. He states repeatedly that he expected the occupation to last several years and to require up to 250,000 coalition troops—although his own plan did not provide for anything close to that number. (Nowhere in *American Soldier* is there mention of the prescient pre-war estimate by one of Franks's Title Ten colleagues that the occupation might well consume several hundred thousand troops.)

Although Franks had speculated that "postwar Iraq might be modelled on post-World War II Japan or Germany," he shows little indication of having grasped the political or economic challenges that nation-building might entail. *After* the fall of Baghdad, Franks was on the phone to General Richard Myers, the JCS chairman, offering up bright ideas: "Dick, we need a major donor conference—hosted in Washington—to line up support, money and troops, as rapidly as possible." But by then it was too late; events were already outrunning the ability of the United States to control them.

Conditions have only worsened since. But for his part Franks remains stubbornly upbeat. Phase IV, he insists in surveying recent developments, is "actually going about as I had expected." Despite the "daily parade of negative headlines," Iraq is well on its way to success. Brushing aside the Abu Ghraib torture scandals as the work of a few bad apples and expressing confidence that the violence will soon taper off, he predicts that "a year from now, Iraq will be a different country." With US deaths climbing toward one thousand, with some US troops involuntarily extended in the combat zone and others returning for a second tour, and with the Washington-installed Iraqi government looking wobbly, it is difficult to share Franks's breezy optimism. One might even say that he is beginning to sound a bit like a TV general.

But forget all that and grant Franks his Inchon: his headlong thrust on Baghdad splintered Iraqi defenses and swiftly overturned the Ba'ath Party regime. No one can dispute that. Ironically, however, credit for this success is due at least in part to the fact that the principal rationale for the entire enterprise—Saddam Hussein's stock of chemical and biological weapons—turned out to be a chimera. Again and again, Franks emphasizes his certainty (and that of his bosses) that Saddam possessed weapons of mass destruction and thus posed a dire threat to the United States and its interests. In fact, of course, the Iraqi dictator had no such arsenal and posed no real threat other than to his own people. Franks shrugs off the error—as if it were simply an honest mistake—without bothering to consider the extent to which his reputation for military genius hangs on his having been so wildly wrong in estimating the enemy's capabilities. Had Saddam actually possessed usable WMD, it is reasonable to speculate that "major combat operations" would have gone less swimmingly. If so, the story that General Franks would be telling today would be considerably different.

Nor, it must be said, does Franks's effort to portray the Iraqi army of 2003 as a formidable force—at one point he compares the Republican Guard to Hitler's Waffen SS—stand up to close scrutiny. The fact is that Saddam's army never recovered from the drubbing that it endured in 1991. More than a decade of economic sanctions and diplomatic isolation, plus aerial bombardment from 1998 onwards, had made any such recovery impossible. Thus, although Franks does not mention the fact, by 2003 Iraq for all practical purposes did not possess an air force—no small matter in an age when air power has come to dominate conventional warfare.

Franks asserts that "there's never been a combat operation as successful as Iraqi Freedom." Only the narrowest definition of success makes that claim sustainable. In fact, the tangible benefits accruing from America's victory over Saddam Hussein have been few. In a sense, the US-led invasion of Iraq in 2003 bears comparison to Germany's invasion of Norway in 1940 or its lunge into Yugoslavia the following year. At the moment of execution, each seemed to affirm impressions that the German military juggernaut was unstoppable. But once the dust had settled, it became apparent that neither victory had brought the Nazi regime any closer to resolving the main issue. Each had saddled the Wehrmacht with burdens that it could ill afford to bear.

Then there is the almost forgotten matter of Afghanistan. The aim of Operation Enduring Freedom had been to "squeeze into extinction" the terrorists and terrorist-sympathizers present in that country. By the end of 2001, Franks declares, "we had accomplished our mission." But this is palpable nonsense. To be sure, the US intervention in Afghanistan damaged al-Qaeda and ousted the Taliban regime—hardly trivial accomplishments. But Operation Enduring Freedom came nowhere near to destroying either organization. Of equal moment— although the point receives scant attention in *American Soldier*—both Osama bin Laden and Taliban leader Mullah Omar managed to elude the forces that Franks commanded. Three years after they first arrived, US troops find themselves engaged in an arduous, open-ended effort to maintain even the most tenuous stability. They will not be going home anytime soon. In Afghanistan, General Franks no more accomplished his mission than did the younger von Moltke when he took the German army partway to Paris in 1914. Franks wrote *American Soldier* in hopes of securing his place in history. But in both Iraq and Afghanistan, history appears to be moving in directions not helpful to his cause.

Finally, no one even remotely familiar with recent trends in military affairs will find persuasive the general's efforts to portray himself as an out-of-the-box thinker. The belief that information technology is transforming force from a blunt to a precision instrument of unprecedented versatility—among other things, providing commanders, Franks writes, with "the kind of Olympian perspective that Homer had given his gods"—has been a shibboleth for the past quarter-century. At most, Franks appropriated the ideas of others and nudged US military doctrine further along the path down which it was already headed—completely oblivious to the possibility that this path, like any other, just might lead into an ambush.

As to denunciations of service parochialism and calls for greater "jointness," they are today about as fresh (and as brave) as politicians speaking out against racial bigotry. At least since the days of Eisenhower, senior Army commanders have been touting the imperative of inter-service cooperation. Over the past twenty years even Air Force generals and Navy admirals have climbed on the jointness bandwagon—though, as with old-school politicos from the Deep South proclaiming their devotion to racial harmony, the depth of Air Force and Navy conviction may on occasion be in doubt. In short, the author's claim to being a bold original is bogus.

Yet even if the victories that Franks won have lost some of their initial luster, and even if he was never quite the innovator he purports to be, *American Soldier* retains considerable value. Indeed, even if a decade from now the ambiguity that has come to surround General Schwarzkopf's once-famous liberation of Kuwait envelops the liberation of Afghanistan and the overthrow of Saddam Hussein, students of American globalism will still find in *American Soldier* a treasure trove of insight, if they read the book with the care it deserves. For these pages shed considerable light on one of the great unanswered questions of the day: How is it that over the past decade-and-a-half, as US forces have gone from one storied triumph to the next, the security of the United States has become ever more precarious? Why, when we flex our military muscles on behalf of freedom and peace, does the world beyond our borders become all the more cantankerous and disorderly? Madeleine Albright irritated Colin Powell by famously asking, "What's the point of having this great army you're always talking about if we can't use it?" From our present perspective, a better question might be: "What's the point of using this great army if the result is Fallujah, Najaf, and Karbala?"

Of course, these are perplexing matters for which there is no neat, tidy explanation. Greed, envy, miscalculation, sheer stupidity, ideological blinders, the nature of the international system, the sins of past generations coming home to roost, the hubris of militarized civilian elites, the iron law of unintended consequences: all of these deserve mention. But in *American Soldier* we see on vivid display one additional factor: the political naïveté and strategic ineptitude of military officers selected and presumably groomed for high command. Far from being a maverick marching to his own drummer, Franks embodies a set of convictions and prejudices common among officers of his generation. Ever since they returned from the jungles and rice paddies over thirty years ago, members of that generation have been engaged in a project that aims, as it were, to put right all that the luckless William Westmoreland got wrong. In essence, they want to reverse the verdict of Vietnam.

More specifically, they have sought to purge war of politics, reconstituting the conception of war as the exclusive province of military professionals. Throughout *American Soldier*, Franks makes it abundantly clear that he views political considerations as at best a distraction, if not an outright impediment. (Discussing the understanding he reached, "soldier-to-soldier," with Pakistan's Pervez Musharraf in the run-up to US operations in Afghanistan, Franks writes that such a partnership could have been forged long before, were it not for the "diplomatic envoys in business suits [who] had hectored soldier-politicians such as Musharraf about human rights and representative government.") Never having forgiven Robert McNamara, he and other members of his generation instinctively view civilians as troublemakers, constantly straying onto turf that rightly belongs to soldiers. Averting such unwelcome encroachments constitutes a categorical imperative.

Keeping civilians where they belong and reasserting a professional monopoly over the conduct of warfare requires drawing the clearest possible line to prevent politics and war from becoming tangled up with one another. Whereas Westmoreland, remembered today as too much the political general, allowed the Whiz Kids to intrude in matters that belonged under his purview, the subalterns who experienced the frustrations of defeat but then stayed on after Vietnam to revive American military power have vowed never to let that happen again. They insist that the conduct of war be recognized as *their* business and theirs alone. Hence, the general-in-chief who (like Franks) experiences combat vicariously in the comfort of an air-conditioned headquarters nonetheless insists on styling himself a chest-thumping "warfighter." He does so for more than merely symbolic reasons: asserting that identity permits him to advance prerogatives to which the officer corps lays absolute claim. This is *my* business; the suits—Franks would likely employ coarser language—should stay out.

It is the sort of sharp distinction between war and politics that Douglas Haig or Erich Ludendorff would have appreciated and understood. But what gets lost in drawing such distinctions—what Haig and

Ludendorff lost in World War I—is any possibility of strategic coherence. Fighting is, of course, integral to war. But, if in ways not always appreciated by or even agreeable to those who actually pull triggers and drop bombs, war is also and always profoundly political. Indeed, if war is to have any conceivable justification and prospect of utility, it must remain subordinated to politics. Effecting that subordination lies at the very heart of strategy. In the tradition of which Franks is an exponent there is a powerful tendency to resist this formulation. Thus, although the author of *American Soldier* mouths Clausewitzian slogans, when it comes to the relationship of war and politics, he rejects the core of what Clausewitz actually taught. And in that sense he typifies the post-Vietnam American officer.

Clausewitz sees the nature of war as complex and elusive; generalship requires not only intensive study and stalwart character, but also great intuitive powers. For Franks, war is a matter of engineering—and generalship the business of organizing and coordinating materiel. Thus, the Franks who reduces international politics to "five Cs" offers up a similarly schematic notion of strategy. When first directed by Rumsfeld to begin planning the invasion of Iraq, Franks sat down, legal pad in hand, and sketched out what he calls his "template" for decisive victory. The resulting matrix, which *American Soldier* proudly reprints in its original handwritten form, consists of seven horizontal "lines of operation"—enumerating US capabilities—intersecting with nine vertical "slices," each describing one source of Saddam Hussein's hold on power. At select points of intersection—thirty-six in all—Franks drew a "starburst." For purposes of further planning, these defined points of main effort.

There is nothing intrinsically wrong with generals sketching out 'lines and slices.' Commanders no longer wage war by pointing their swords at the enemy and hollering "Charge!" Campaign planning requires checklists and schedules, readily identifiable priorities and unambiguous lines of authority. If a seven-by-nine matrix can lend order to the process of gearing up a force for war, that is all to the good. But even a casual examination of Franks's sketch shows that it does not even remotely approximate a strategy. It is devoid of any political context. Narrowly focused on the upcoming fight, it pays no attention to the aftermath. Defining the problem as Iraq and Iraq alone, it ignores other power relationships and makes no provision for how war might alter those relationships, whether for good or ill. It is completely ahistorical and makes no reference to culture, religion, or ethnic identity. It has no moral dimension. It fails even to provide a statement of purpose. But according to Franks, it is an exquisitely designed example of what he terms "basic *grand strategy*" (emphasis in the original).

Here we come face to face with the essential dilemma with which the United States has wrestled ever since the Soviets had the temerity to deprive us of a stabilizing adversary—a dilemma that the events of 9/11 only served to exacerbate. The political elite that ought to bear the chief responsibility for formulating grand strategy instead nurses ideological fantasies of remaking the world in America's image, as the Bush administration's National Security Strategy of 2002 so vividly attests. Meanwhile, the military elite that could possibly puncture those fantasies and help restore a modicum of realism to US policy instead obsesses over operations. Reluctant to engage in any sort of political-military dialogue that might compromise their autonomy, the generals allow fundamental questions about the relationship between power and purpose to go unanswered and even unrecognized.

Into this void between the illusions of the political class and the fears of the generals disappears the possibility of establishing some equilibrium between ends and means. Instead, the United States careens ever closer to bankruptcy, exhaustion, and imperial overstretch. The US today has vast ambitions for how the world should operate, too vast to be practical. It wields great power, though not nearly so much as many imagine. But there exists nothing even approaching a meaningful strategy to meld the two together. In *American Soldier,* Tommy Franks helps us understand why.

13

Selling Our Souls

Of Idolatry and iPhones

(2011)

Confronting the twentieth century, Catholicism stood fast. This was its mission: church as bulwark against the disorders afflicting the age. The excitement of Vatican II (I was a teenager when the council convened) derived from the sense that the church possessed a hitherto unsuspected capacity to adapt its witness. Rather than merely standing in lonely opposition, the church intended to engage—and then redeem—modernity.

Catholics in the twenty-first century find it increasingly difficult—perhaps impossible—to sustain any such expectations. The problem is not simply that the institutional church today stands dishonored and discredited, but that it has misconstrued the problem. The ramparts it persists in defending—a moral order based on received, permanent truth—have long since been scaled, breached, and bypassed, and have fallen into ruin.

What went wrong? The great American historian Henry Adams— dead nearly a hundred years—offers a more cogent answer to that question than any we are likely to hear from Rome. Recalling his return to New York City after a lengthy stay in Europe in *The Education of Henry Adams*, the historian rendered this verdict: "The two-thousand-years failure of Christianity roared upward from Broadway," a panoply of false gods clattering in its wake. That failure had created a vacuum. The heresies that were filling that vacuum filled Adams with foreboding.

Worse, he could see no reason to consider Christianity's demise as anything other than definitive and irreversible. Yet a century later we remain largely oblivious to its implications. We still don't understand what hit us.

Not himself conventionally religious (watching his sister suffer an excruciatingly painful death, he had concluded that God might be "a Substance, but He could not be a Person"), Adams was referring to Christianity not as a belief system but as an organizing principle. Christianity as project—reference point, narrative, and source of authority—imparted to history a semblance of cohesion and purposefulness. So, for centuries, Europeans and Americans had believed, or at least pretended to believe.

For Adams, writing in the first decade of the twentieth century, even the pretense had become unsustainable. While attending the Chicago World's Fair of 1893 and then the Exposition Universelle seven years later in Paris—subjecting each to intense inspection—he found himself face-to-face with ominous new forces to which he took an instant dislike and from which he expected more ill to come than good. Subsequent events amply vindicated his low expectations.

The preeminent symbol of the Christian age (then in the final throes of disintegration, as he saw it) had been Mary, the Mother of God. The preeminent symbol of the age then dawning was the dynamo. If the Virgin embodied a conception of truth as fixed and singular, the dynamo implied the inverse: constant change and multiplicity. In place of coherence and unity, fragmentation and anarchy beckoned. "Power seemed to have outgrown its servitude," Adams wrote.

The cylinder had exploded and thrown great masses of stone and steam against the sky. Prosperity never before imagined, power never yet wielded by man, speed never reached by anything but a meteor, had made the world irritable, nervous, querulous, unreasonable, and afraid.

The machines providing the source of this never-before-seen power, prosperity, and speed (along with electrical generators, Adams cited locomotives and automobiles, "a nightmare at a hundred kilometers an hour") were displacing God, replacing him with objects more worthy of worship. Standing in a gallery at the Paris exhibition, he began to feel the forty-foot dynamos as a moral force, much as the early Christians felt the Cross. The planet itself seemed less impressive than this huge wheel. Before the end one began to pray to it; inherited instinct taught the natural expression of man before silent and infinite force.

Detached and sardonic, Adams was ideally suited to assess the implications of this emerging dystopia. He had no stake in the outcome. He merely observed, his interest reflecting his perpetual, if futile, quest for education.

For just that reason, Adams was quick to discern who profited from this transfer of divine attributes. The principal beneficiaries were the "Trusts and Corporations" with which his friend President Theodore Roosevelt was even then engaged in epic battle. "They were revolutionary," Adams wrote of these engines of enterprise, "troubling all the old conventions and values, as the screws of ocean steamers must trouble a school of herring. They tore society to pieces and trampled it underfoot," engineering a transformation of human existence rivaling that which Jesus had wrought through his death and resurrection. The great mechanisms of wealth creation were unscrupulous, obnoxious, and irreligious; but as TR and all his successors would learn, they were also wily, resourceful, and persistent. Trustbusting was a fruitless exercise.

When Adams composed these observations, of course, America itself embodied that ongoing transformation. In the United States, novelty and impermanence reigned. There factories and fortunes were bigger, machines faster, buildings taller. Yet Americans were oblivious to all that the onslaught portended. According to Adams, "They were wandering in a wilderness much more sandy than the Hebrews had ever trodden about Sinai; they had neither serpents nor golden calves to worship." Rejecting the commonplace charge of a country seduced and corrupted by Mammon, Adams leveled an even more severe indictment.

Worship of money was an old-world trait; a healthy appetite akin to worship of the gods, or to worship of power in any concrete shape; but the American wasted money more recklessly than anyone ever did before; he spent more to less purpose than any extravagant court aristocracy; he had no sense of relative values, and knew not what to do with his money when he got it, except use it to make more, or throw it away.

At best, money helped prop up the pretense that in America Christianity was alive and kicking. Were not pious plutocrats like Andrew Carnegie and John D. Rockefeller even then engaged in their mammoth philanthropies, endowing churches and concert halls, universities and libraries, hospitals and art museums? Meanwhile, at Sunday services from one week to the next, droves of ordinary citizens dutifully dropped their nickels into the collection basket. By such measures, fin de siècle Christianity seemed to be thriving.

Adams intuited that this was mostly hokum, a tacit collaboration of the powerful and the largely powerless distracting attention from the havoc then bearing down on the world. Christianity as a personal ethic or as a medium through which to seek individual salvation might survive, but Christianity as a formula for ordering human affairs had breathed its last.

Adams lived long enough to glimpse what was in store as a consequence. By the time of his death in March 1918, Christendom (as it had once been known) was tearing itself apart in a war that produced unspeakable carnage. At the various places that made the twentieth century such a horror Katyn, Auschwitz, Dresden, Hiroshima, and so on—worse was to come. The dynamo had been merely a portent. With World War II, the furies that Adams had presciently detected slipped their leash.

Scripture no longer provided an adequate explanation of these events—even to consider situating the Holocaust in what Christians called salvation history seemed obscene. Unwilling to own up to their own complicity in all that had gone awry—unwilling, that is, to acknowledge the implications of opting for dynamo over Virgin— nominally Christian Americans sought refuge in ideology. Framing the twentieth century as a contest between fascism, communism, and a third camp variously described as liberal, democratic, or simply free restored clear-cut boundaries between good and evil. That the Free World, alone among the three competitors, refrained from open hostility toward religion further clarified the apparent issue. The tattered remnants of Christendom found sanctuary under the protection of the Free World's acknowledged leader, the United States. Here, it seemed, was moral order restored.

Defining the issue in ideological terms allowed Cold War–era American statesmen to play dirty without compromising the righteousness of their cause. Of greater significance, however, was the way that ideology dulled sensibilities and narrowed choice, making it unnecessary (perhaps even unpatriotic) to assess critically the moral implications of the dynamo's offspring. Americans saw—or had been persuaded to see—flying machines, radio, motion pictures, television, nuclear power, guided missiles, computers, and all sorts of other gadgets and gewgaws as conducive to the exercise of authentic freedom.

In his all-but-forgotten "Kitchen Debate" with Nikita Khrushchev in 1959, Richard Nixon made the point with clumsy effectiveness: real freedom implied access to whatever was the latest in the material world. "American houses last for more than twenty years," Nixon told the Soviet leader, but "after twenty years, many Americans want a new house or a new kitchen. . . . The American system is designed to take advantage of new inventions and new techniques."

As long as the Cold War persisted, thinking critically about the freedom provided by this American system remained difficult. Giving credence to warnings that Adams had issued decades before was nearly impossible.

In 1989, the ideological twentieth century came to an abrupt and happy conclusion. Freedom had seemingly prevailed. The United States, freedom's chief exemplar, reigned supreme. Yet if Americans felt any sense of vindication, it proved surprisingly short-lived. Although much had seemed to hinge on the outcome of the Cold War, that outcome settled remarkably little.

The "end of history"—the triumph of liberal democratic capitalism—did not restore moral consensus. Adams for one would not have been surprised. The forces actually driving history—their power measured now not in kilowatts or megatons but in gigabytes—

were no closer to being harnessed than when he had taken their measure a hundred years earlier. Carnegie Steel and Standard Oil might not rule the roost, but Microsoft, Apple, and Google appeared in their place. In their pursuit of profit, corporate leviathans continued to call the tune.

As successor to the Machine Age, the so-called Information Age promises to empower humanity as never before and therefore to complete our liberation. Taking the form of a wireless handheld device, the dynamo of our time has truly become, as Adams wrote, "a symbol of infinity." Rather than spewing masses of stone and steam, it offers instant access to the Tree of the Knowledge of Good and Evil.

The Information Age does something else as well, however: it displays in stark terms our propensity to bow down before freedom's reputed source. Anyone who today works with or near young people cannot fail to see this: for members of the present generation, the smartphone has become an amulet. It is a sacred object to be held and caressed and constantly attended to. Previous generations fell in love with their cars or became addicted to TV, but this one elevates devotion to material objects to an altogether different level. In the guise of exercising freedom, its members engage in a form of idolatry. Small wonder that aficionados of Apple's iPhone call it the Jesus Phone.

So the frantic pursuit of self-liberation that Adams identified and warned against enters yet another cycle, with little sign of anything having been learned from past failures. If the God of the Hebrew Bible and the New Testament exists, then it must be that he wills this. Yet his purposes remain inscrutable.

Ever the cool observer, Adams might have posited two possible explanations: either humankind's quest for freedom in the here and now, achieved through human effort and ingenuity, represents the ultimate heresy and offense against God—in which case we invite his continuing punishment; or belief in God's existence represents the ultimate illusion—in which case the chaos humanity has inflicted on itself as it careens from one dynamo to the next may be merely a foretaste of what is to come.

14

Christopher Lasch

Family Man

(2010)

It is a recurring story of American politics: From the heartland, anger erupts, directed at Wall Street for fattening itself at the people's expense and at Washington for endemic corruption and endless shenanigans. Moneychangers have occupied the temple, comes the charge, and no alternative exists but to sweep the place clean.

Yet no sooner do the plain folk raise their pitchforks than a great tut-tutting is heard from on high. The problem, it turns out, lies not with Wall Street or Washington but with the people themselves. Populism—synonymous with bigotry and ignorance—has once again raised its ugly head. The good of the Republic requires that order be restored. The people must return to their places. If they have complaints to make, they should express them quietly and respectfully. Suggestions that the whole game is rigged against them are inappropriate and not to be entertained.

The popularity of Sarah Palin and other right-wing firebrands, the rise of the Tea Party, and perhaps above all, the temerity of voters in

Massachusetts who awarded the Kennedy family's Senate seat to a pickup truck–driving nonentity named Scott Brown have persuaded observers that populists are once again on the march. As if on cue, sophisticates unable to differentiate between a pitchfork and a honey spreader explain why this latest version of populism gets things all wrong and why it doesn't deserve to be treated seriously.

Here is David Brooks, peering down from his perch at the *New York Times*, offering a tutorial on why ordinary citizens, as opposed to well-heeled newspaper columnists living in the nation's capital, just don't understand what makes America tick. Populists, writes Brooks, mistakenly view the country through the lens of social class. Convinced that "economics is a struggle over finite spoils," they betray an "Us versus Them mentality." They see politics as a "struggle between the enlightened and the corrupt, the pure and the betrayers." Brooks wants it known that such heresies (which are, of course, daily fare within the Beltway) possess not even the slightest legitimacy when voiced by ordinary citizens from Indiana or Kansas.

Indeed, whatever slight problems the country may be facing—take the recession, for example—it's populist carping that prevents their solution. If the rubes "continue their random attacks on enterprise and capital," Brooks warns, "they will only increase the pervasive feeling of uncertainty, which is now the single biggest factor in holding back investment, job creation and growth." Still, Brooks finds consolation in knowing that uppitiness coming from the hinterland never really amounts to much. The verdict of history is clear: "dynamic optimism"— that's what real Americans believe in—"always wins," whereas "combative divisiveness"—that's what populism signifies "always loses."

Such condescension tells us less about populism than about the fears and prejudices of those who presume to police American political discourse lest it become tainted by unwelcome demands or expectations. The truth about American politics is this: disguised by the theatrics of squabbling Democrats and Republicans, Washington governs according to limits prescribed by a fixed and narrow consensus. The two main parties collaborate in preserving that consensus. Doing so requires declaring out-of-bounds anything even remotely resembling a fundamental critique of how power gets exercised or wealth distributed. Populism poses a challenge to that consensus—hence, the hostility with which it is treated by those purporting to express respectable opinion.

When it comes to political choice, devotees of the existing two-party system contend that Americans already have all they need or can handle. Folks inhabiting the middle of the country (while occupying the lower reaches of the socioeconomic ladder) don't necessarily see it that way. So radicalism persists. What Brooks and other enforcers of ideological discipline deride as populism is radicalism in the American grain, expressing itself in an authentically American, if less than genteel, voice.

Populism frightens the fat cats and the defenders of the status quo, and with good reason. Yet for observers who find the status quo intolerable, the populist critique contains elements worthy of empathy and respect.

One such observer was the late Christopher Lasch (1932–94), historian, cultural critic, contrarian, and wayfarer.[1] A son of the Middle Border, born and raised in Nebraska before his parents moved to Chicago, Lasch, writes Eric Miller, "was a surveyor, taking the measure of the wilderness." The wilderness was modern America. What Lasch discovered there were pathologies advertised as "progress," promoted by elites for their own benefit with little regard for the common good.

Miller, who teaches history at Geneva College, has written a biography of Lasch, with the evocative title *Hope in a Scattering Time*. A fine, thoughtful, and even moving book, its appearance could hardly be more opportune.

In our own day, the politics of progress have passed the point of exhaustion. Were there any lingering doubts on that score, the vast disparity between the expectations raised by President Obama's election and the dispiriting reality of the Obama Era has dispelled them once and for all. Only knaves and fools will look to Washington to devise solutions to the problems afflicting American society today. Indeed, further deference to established centers of power, on issues domestic or foreign, will surely perpetuate and even exacerbate those problems.

---

1. Eric Miller, *Hope in a Scattering Time: A Life of Christopher Lasch* (Grand Rapids, MI: Eerdmans, 2010).

So the times call for a searching reassessment of the American condition. Neither left nor right—especially in the adulterated form found in the actually existing Democratic and Republican parties—possesses the capacity to render such an assessment. To reconsider first principles requires an altogether different vantage point, firmly grounded in the American experience yet offering something other than the recitation of clichés and posturing in front of cameras.

Lasch occupied and speaks from such a vantage point. Through a series of books, chief among them *Haven in a Heartless World* (1977), *The Culture of Narcissism* (1979), and *The True and Only Heaven* (1991), he sought, in Miller's words, "to convince and persuade Americans of the true nature of their circumstance." Like some prophet from the Hebrew Bible transported to an America at the very height of its power, Lasch "moved in the spirit of reckoning, freely casting judgment on all." His countrymen could choose to listen or to turn a deaf ear: that was not his to decide. His calling was simply to speak the truth and offer it for their consideration. This he was determined to do, however harsh or unwelcome others might find the verdicts he handed down.

Begin with the issue of progress itself. Conservatives and liberals pretend to differ on how to define it and on how best to achieve it. Yet both camps subscribe to this common baseline: the progress they promote is quantitative. It entails amassing more choice, abundance, access, autonomy, and clout.

So defined, progress incrementally enhances American life, making it more democratic and enabling Americans in ever greater numbers to exercise freedom. Lasch rejected this proposition. Progress, he believed, was converting America into a spiritual wasteland. "The question for serious historians," he wrote in 1975, "is not whether progress exacts a price but whether the history of modern society can be considered progress in the first place." His own answer to that question was a resounding "No."

Where others saw progress, Lasch saw destruction. His own interpretation of the nation's past, according to Miller, "was centered not on grand, heroic movement from authoritarian control to freedom, as most Americans supposed, but rather on the shift from one form of overweening social control to another." A nefarious collaboration between market and state was transforming citizens into consumers, while intruding into the most intimate spheres of human existence. Rootlessness and chronic anxiety increasingly defined everyday American life, and individuals sought to fill the resulting void through compulsive efforts to satisfy unappeasable appetites. The marketplace proffered an array of solutions, usually chemical or technological, to "age-old discontents" such as "loneliness, sickness, weariness, [and] lack of sexual satisfaction." Others pursued a different route of escape, attaching themselves, however tenuously or even vicariously, "to those who radiate celebrity, power, and charisma."

Seeking relief, ordinary Americans instead purchased dependence. The "modern obsession with personal liberation" was, in Lasch's view, "itself a symptom of pervasive spiritual disorder."

A bit over the top? Watch some network TV tonight and don't leave the room when the commercials come on. Hang out awhile at your local Wal-Mart ("Save money. Live better."). Leaf through one of those glossy celebrity mags the next time you're stuck waiting in the checkout line. Consider how teenagers obsessively caress their cell phones and iPods as if cradling in their hands something sacred. Ask yourself why movies like George Clooney's recent *Up in the Air*— wherein a man defines fulfillment as gaining entry into American Airlines' "Ten Million Mile Club"—strike a chord.

This process of cultural debasement was not the product of spontaneous combustion. It occurred because it served the interests of large institutions and of individuals directing their fortunes. Writing in 1958, while still a graduate student, Lasch accurately discerned the implications: "The greatest rewards will fall to those whose job it is to keep consumers consuming." Those rewards included money, status, and power and were by no means restricted to the private sector. Once members of Congress figured out that the distribution of largesse held the key to perpetual incumbency, keeping consumers consuming— cash for clunkers!—became a key component of their job description as well.

As they accumulated cars, gadgets, and brand-name clothes, filled their bathroom cabinets with potions promising to make them look and feel good, and dragged their kids off to theme parks, Americans were told that life itself was getting better and better. Indeed, during the Cold War (and again, after September 11), government agencies promoted American-style freedom as the model to which the rest of the world was destined to conform. As interpreted by Washington, such was the will of Providence.

According to Lasch, however, all of this was bogus. Americans were being played for chumps. By defining progress as acquiring more stuff combined with the shedding of self-restraint, they were not gaining greater freedom. Instead, they were donning a straitjacket. "Beneath the appearance of contractual freedom, individual autonomy, and the rule of reason," he insisted, "domination still continued as the motor of history, class rule as the basis of wealth and economic power, and force as the basis of justice."

Individual Americans were forfeiting control over their own destinies. Lasch railed against "the pathology of domination, the growing influence of organizations (economic as well as military) that operate without regard to any rational objectives except their own aggrandizement." He decried "the powerlessness of individuals in the face of these giant agglomerations and the arrogance of those ostensibly in charge of them."

The upheaval of the 1960s briefly persuaded Lasch that a New Left might constitute the counterweight needed to reverse these trends. The antics of the counterculture soon disabused him of this expectation, however. "Hedonism, self-expression, doing your own thing, dancing in the streets, drugs, and sex are a formula for political impotence and a new despotism," he wrote with characteristic severity. The New Left contained its own elitist and authoritarian tendencies. "Mastery of the technological secrets of a modern society," Lasch believed, would enable the savvy few to "rule over an indolent population which has traded self-government for self-expression"—a prediction finding eventual fulfillment (of a sort) amidst the mindlessness of social networking and manufactured celebrity.

So the forces of revolution, such as they were, turned out to be fraudulent. Lasch soon forswore further political activism and thereafter remained apart, unleashing his thunderbolts, in Miller's words, "from a place well above, or below, the usual ideological perches." Lasch defied categorization. As a consequence, although his books and other writings commanded attention and attracted admirers, he had

few real allies. Lasch was his own drummer. His was a lonely movement of one.

Miller describes Lasch's quest as a search for "another way of
achieving America." With evidence of spiritual disarray piling up, that
search aimed to salvage and preserve as much as to create something
new. "The development of political freedom," Lasch wrote in 1973,
had proceeded "hand in hand with the growth of a system of private
enterprise that ravaged the land, eradicated the past, destroyed older
traditions of commercial life, and accentuated class conflict." How to
stem this malignant tide constituted the central problem of the age. So
Lasch, in Miller's words, began to articulate an altogether different vision of progress or freedom, one "rooted not in personal liberation but
in the dignity of privacy, kinship ties, moral order, and civic duty." He
sought to restore "joy in work, stable connections, family life, a sense
of place, and a sense of historical continuity."

In the context of American politics, of course, words like kinship,
duty, family, and place carry deeply conservative connotations. Indeed, over the course of his intellectual journey, Lasch moved toward
a cultural conservatism, which drew upon older Jeffersonian, agrarian,
and—above all—populist traditions. Conservatism in this sense was
less an ideology than an orientation, one that recognized, valued, and
sought to defend an inheritance assailed by the proponents of progress.
Once squandered, Lasch believed, that inheritance was likely to prove
irretrievable.

(A note to those for whom "conservative" conjures up images of
Karl Rove or Newt Gingrich: don't confuse the sham conservatism of
the Republican Party with the authentic article. Lasch expressed complete contempt for those styling themselves as conservative while wor-
shipping at the altar of capitalism, employing conservative-sounding
tropes to justify a worldview profoundly antagonistic to conservative
values. To understand this point, ask yourself, for example, what, if
anything, George W. Bush, an ostensible conservative, managed to
"conserve" during his eight years in the White House.)

For Lasch, only a genuinely conservative orientation was entirely
consistent with his radical self-identity. Indeed, in late-twentieth-
century America, only an anti-progressive sensibility could provide
the basis for serious radicalism.

Here lay the makings of a true counterculture, he believed, one that opposed excessive concentrations of wealth and power, rejected the notion that limitless economic growth held the key to human happiness, and stood for political decentralization, self-sufficiency, meaningful work, the closing of gaps between rich and poor, a decent respect for received wisdom, and modesty in claiming to interpret God's will or history's purpose.

This Tory radicalism, as Miller dubs it, placed Lasch at odds with other would-be radicals of his time. Nowhere was this more evident than on matters relating to gender. In Lasch's eyes, the chief accomplishment of contemporary feminism, with its emphasis on self-actualization and empowerment, was to deliver women into the maw of the marketplace. For the most part, the women's movement served as an adjunct to "the dominant culture of acquisitive individualism," rather than offering up a meaningful alternative. A small percentage of women benefited, as a result; the vast majority did not.

Although Lasch devoted the preponderance of his attention to domestic affairs, his critique has considerable implications for foreign policy. The progressive impulse to construct a secular utopia at home finds its counterpart in dreams of doing likewise in the great, wide world abroad: this has become an enduring theme of American statecraft. Do not mistake this rushing to the aid of others—Cubans in 1898, Afghans in 2010—for altruism, however. The impulse to do good remains bound inextricably to a determination to do well. Whether acknowledged or not, the exercise aims to sustain the existing American way of life, or, as Lasch put it, "to maintain our riotous standard of living, as it has been maintained in the past, at the expense of the rest the world."

Lasch declared progressivism, especially in its virulent Wilsonian form, to be "a messianic creed." In international politics, messianic tendencies foster illusions of omniscience and omnipotence. They also point ineluctably toward great crusades, since those standing in the path of righteousness necessarily represent the forces of darkness and put themselves beyond the pale.

The combination of conviction and power induces grandiosity reinforced by vast self-assurance, evident in Woodrow Wilson's "war to end all wars" and in the younger Bush's insistence that the time had come for Muslims everywhere to embrace American-style democracy, along with the American definition of human rights. For those of a messianic bent, inaction implies complicity with evil. Given such a mindset, prudential considerations need not apply: that which should be must be.

"The thirst for action, the craving for involvement, the longing to commit themselves to the onward march of events—these things dictated war." Lasch refers here to the progressives who threw their support behind Wilson's campaign to make the world safe for democracy. Yet the same might be said of the neoconservatives, faux conservatives, and militant liberals who formed the cheering section for Bush's preposterous "global war on terror." The most important thing was not to be left out or left behind. "Accordingly, they went to war and invented the reasons for it afterward." Written in connection to the events of 1917, Lasch's judgment applies just as neatly to the period following September 11.

The progressive mindset pervading *both* of the major American political parties refuses to acknowledge the existence of limits. An appreciation of limits—not simply of power, but also of understanding—infuses and distinguishes an authentically conservative sensibility.

Writing in 1983, Lasch located "the real promise of American life" in "the hope that a self-governing republic can serve as a source of moral and political inspiration to the rest of the world, not as the center of a new world empire." The record suggests that rather than erecting an empire—or fulfilling the obligations inherent in global leadership, as some would have it—the United States will serve as a moral and political exemplar only by keeping faith with the aspirations expressed in the nation's founding documents. In that regard, we have a long way to go.

Of at least equal importance, whereas the proponents of progress believe that the key to success is to entrust power to a corps of experts—a power elite, to use the classic formulation devised by C. Wright Mills—any serious conservative rightly sees this as mostly bunk. Do four-star generals, high-ranking government officials, insider journalists, corporate executives, and Wall Street financiers possess a demonstrably superior understanding of the way the world works? Are they any smarter, more sophisticated, or better intentioned than your Aunt Betty Lou or your Uncle Fred? Survey the various and sundry debacles of the past decade alone—the September 11 attacks, the invasion of Iraq, the collapse of Enron, Hurricane Katrina, the Madoff scandal, the Lehman Brothers downfall (the list goes on)—and the question answers itself.

"America in denial," writes Eric Miller, was "Lasch's perennial story." In our own day—still very much a scattering time—denial persists in spades, reinforced by a ruling class that throws money at problems in hopes of concealing them and by a national security apparatus that promotes an atmosphere of perpetual crisis in order to justify its existence. Washington attempts with one hand to buy people off and with the other to frighten them into acquiescence.

In 1962, the young Lasch observed that "progress is not enough." Sometimes progress isn't progress at all, especially in the cultural and spiritual realms. Instead, it's backsliding.

The record suggests that counting on large, distant, impersonal, and largely unaccountable institutions to make good on America's promise is misguided. This is the insight to which populists from the time of William Jennings Bryan to the present have returned again and again. The demonstrable truth of that insight explains why populism is not going away any time soon. It also explains why Christopher Lasch, the great exponent of democratic populism, deserves our respectful attention today.

15

Randolph Bourne
The Man in the Black Cape

(2009)

In his 1932 novel *Nineteen Nineteen*, John Dos Passos paid tribute to a "little sparrowlike man,"

> tiny twisted bit of flesh in a black cape,
> always in pain and ailing,
> [who] put a pebble in his sling
> and hit Goliath square in the forehead . . . .

The man in the black cape was Randolph Bourne, who in an unfinished essay shortly before his death in 1918 uttered one of the contemporary era's great truths: "War is the health of the State." Ninety years on, as Americans contemplate the implications of waging what the Pentagon is now calling "the Long War," Bourne's biting observation demands renewed attention.

Beset from birth by agonizing physical deformities, Bourne was an intellectual, a radical, and a patriot who cherished freedom and loved

America. His crucial contribution to political discourse was to draw a sharp distinction between Country — the people and their aspirations — and State, an apparatus that perverts those aspirations into a relentless quest for aggrandizement at the expense of others. "Country," Bourne wrote, "is a concept of peace, of tolerance, of living and letting live. But State is essentially a concept of power, of competition."

Bourne abhorred war, describing it as "a frenzied, mutual suicide," devoid of redeeming value. America's 1917 entry into the apocalyptic European conflict then known as "the Great War" appalled him, not least because, as he saw it, US intervention signified the triumph of State over Country. A war fought to make the world safe for democracy, as President Woodrow Wilson promised, was more likely to undermine authentic democracy at home.

As Wilson whipped up popular fervor for his great crusade (and as his administration relied on what Bourne described as "white terrorism" to punish anyone who opposed the war or questioned Wilson's policies), Bourne devoted himself to enumerating the perils of allowing State to eclipse Country. War, he warned, inevitably produces "a derangement of values," with the interests of the people taking a back seat to the purposes of the State. Prestige and authority shift from the periphery to the center, from the legislature to the executive, and from domestic concerns to foreign affairs. During times of war, the future is expected to take care of itself; only the present matters. The imperative of victory overrides all other considerations.

War imbues the State with an aura of sanctity. Those who purport to represent the State — the insiders, those who are in the know — expect deference and to a remarkable extent receive it. The more urgent the emergency, the more compliant the citizenry. A people at war, Bourne observed, become "obedient, respectful, trustful children again, full of that naive faith in the all-wisdom and all-power of the adult who takes care of them."

Above all, the sacralization of the State exalts the standing of the First Warrior, investing in the commander-in-chief something akin to blanket authority. "The President," wrote Bourne, "is an elected king, but the fact that he is elected has proved to be of far less significance . . . than the fact that he is pragmatically a king." As with the French monarchs in their heyday, so too with wartime American presidents:

L'État, c'est moi. In times of crisis, Bourne explained, the legislative branch effectively ceases to function "except as a wholly mechanical ratifier of the Executive's will."

The very concept of a democratic foreign policy, therefore, becomes "a contradiction in terms." Statecraft remains "the secret private possession of the executive branch." The deliberations that matter occur behind closed doors, with participants limited to those "able to get control of the machinery of the State" or the handful of outsiders with privileged access either conferred or purchased outright.

To those who most fully identify themselves with the State's interests—the king-president's inner circle—war signifies liberation, triggering, in Bourne's words, "a vast sense of rejuvenescence" that accompanies the full-throated exercise of power. The "State-obsessed" are drawn to war like moths are drawn to flame. Only through war and the quasi-war of recurrent crisis and confrontation can they express themselves fully.

When war erupts, it typically does so as a result of "steps taken secretly and announced to the public only after they had been consummated." Although Congress may issue a formal declaration, in Bourne's eyes this amounts to no more than "the merest technicality." Not infrequently, those dealing in secrets cross the line into deception and dissembling. Yet even when this occurs, Congress shies away from demanding accountability. After all, any legislator asserting that "the country had been grossly deceived by its own Government," with war the product of "almost criminal carelessness," would risk the charge of disloyalty, complicity, or sheer negligence. Better just to register a few complaints and quietly vote the money needed to fund the enterprise.

The architects and advocates of armed conflict broadcast "appealing harbingers of a cosmically efficacious and well-bred war." Such rosy predictions inevitably turn out to be illusory, but no matter: once thrust into the conflagration, the Country succumbs to "a spiritual compulsion which pushes it on, perhaps against all its interests, all its desires, and all its real sense of values." It's not that the people will war's perpetuation, but when told that no alternative exists except to persist, they acquiesce. Thus, according to Bourne, does the State have its way.

As it was in 1918, so it is in 2008. Granted, in its attempts to silence or discredit its critics, the Bush Administration's actions, however egregious, fall considerably short of constituting "white terrorism." On every other point, however, Bourne's critique of the State during the Age of Wilson describes with considerable precision State behavior during the Age of Bush and Cheney.

Since September 11, war has certainly enhanced the health of the State, which has grown in size, claimed new prerogatives, and expended resources with reckless abandon while accruing a host of new acolytes and retainers, a.k.a. "contractors." Once again, we have witnessed the compromise of democratic practices, as the imperatives of "keeping America safe" take precedence over due process and the rule of law. Once again, the maneuvering of insiders has produced war, cheerfully marketed as promising a clean, neat solution to messy and intractable problems. When that war went sour in Iraq, opponents in Congress solemnly promised to end it, but instead obligingly appropriated billions to ensure its continuation. Although the people profess unhappiness with all that the State has wrought, their confidence in the institutions of government all but exhausted, they remain reliably docile, if not apathetic. None of this, it seems fair to say, would have surprised Randolph Bourne.

By almost any measure, the Country has fared poorly of late, a point that presidential candidates John McCain and Barack Obama both explicitly endorsed. The State, meanwhile, has fattened itself on seven years of plenty. Unlike the biblical cycle, when abundance gave way to want, this pattern seems likely to continue. With the Long War projected to last for decades, if not generations, the ascendancy of the State bids fair to become a permanent condition.

When McCain and Obama competed with each other in promising to "change the way Washington works," they held out the prospect of re-subordinating State to Country. "Install me as king-president," each seemed to proclaim, "and I will employ the apparatus of the State to fulfill the people's fondest hopes and dreams. The State will do my bidding and therefore the Country's."

"Only in a world where irony was dead," as Bourne once mordantly observed, could such claims be taken seriously. Doing so requires us to ignore the extent to which the parties that the candidates represented, the advisers on whom they relied for counsel, and the moneyed interests to which they looked for support all share a vested interest in ensuring the State's continued primacy. This is as true of liberal Democrats as of conservative Republicans.

The reality is this: The election that so many saw as promising salvation was rigged. Its outcome was predetermined. Whichever candidate won in November and whichever party ended up governing, the State was guaranteed to come out on top. Barring the truly miraculous, our new President will continue to serve as primary agent of the State, privileging its well-being over that of the people. And the American penchant for war that Bourne decried and that has in our own day returned with a vengeance will persist. Piously wishing it were otherwise won't make it so.

Although ninety years ago the man in the black cape may have struck Goliath a sharp blow, the giant barely noticed and quickly recovered. Today Goliath is running the show.

16

William Appleman Williams
Tragedy Renewed

(2009)

Exactly fifty years ago, late in the Eisenhower era, if still early in the Cold War, William Appleman Williams, then a young historian teaching at the University of Wisconsin, started a revolution of sorts. With the publication of his book, *The Tragedy of American Diplomacy*, US foreign relations became as never before an exceedingly contentious subject. It has remained so ever since.

According to Williams, even in 1959 when *Tragedy* first made its appearance, US foreign policy was in the midst of a profound "crisis." An approach to statecraft that had once "worked brilliantly" had become "impossible to sustain." Revolutionary changes were sweeping the world. If the United States refused to adapt to those changes, it would soon find itself facing "literal isolation." Yet if they embraced the new order, Williams wrote, Americans could "help other peoples achieve their own aspirations in their own way" and "do much to sustain and extend man's creativity."

Soon thereafter things got worse—much worse. The counsel offered by Williams became less hopeful and more urgent.

By 1962, when a "new enlarged edition" of *Tragedy* appeared, John F. Kennedy was occupying the White House. Just a year prior, the Bay of Pigs fiasco had occurred, heightening Williams's sense of alarm. "American foreign policy must be changed fundamentally," he now declared categorically. Americans were facing the prospect not of isolation but of annihilation. If the United States persisted on its present course, Williams foresaw "a further acceleration of the already serious momentum toward thermonuclear war," leading ultimately to "the destruction of democracy."

A decade passed before a "second revised and enlarged" edition of *Tragedy*—by now a very influential, if controversial, book—found its way into print. By this time, during the Cuban missile crisis, the world had survived a near miss with nuclear holocaust. Kennedy (among other national leaders) had been assassinated and his successor, Lyndon Baines Johnson, had plunged the country into the costly and divisive Vietnam War. In 1968, America had all but come apart at the seams, paving the way for Richard Nixon's ascent to the presidency.

For Williams, the word "tragedy" no longer sufficed to describe the situation in which the United States found itself. Although his book's title remained unchanged, he now wrote of an "aura of terror" that was enveloping American statecraft. Proposing fundamental changes in foreign policy had become pointless absent a comparably fundamental reorientation of the country itself. To transform American diplomacy, Williams insisted, "existing American society had to be changed" first. Otherwise, he foresaw "more interventions" abroad and "more deterioration at home."

Previously, Williams had invited Americans to view with sympathy the revolutions through which other peoples were seeking to work out their destinies. Now, he insisted, the time had come for revolution at home, with the anti-war movement inspired by Vietnam potentially offering the vehicle for such a domestic transformation. Yet woe to the nation if it failed to seize this opportunity to save itself. "The final terror," Williams wrote, "would come to be if ending the war did not lead to fundamental changes in the American outlook, in American society, and hence in American foreign policy."

The anti-war movement and the New Left that it helped inspire proved a tremendous disappointment to Williams. Williams braced himself for the worst. If Americans persisted along the path that they were following—as they gave every indication of doing—they invited the gravest consequences. "We will suffer what we did unto Hamburg, Dresden, and Tokyo," he predicted in 1980. "We will suffocate, sizzle and fry." America had "run out of imperial games to play." Armageddon beckoned.

That same year, by a large majority, voters elected as president someone of a decidedly different view. Ronald Reagan found no fault with America apart from the fault-finders (like Williams) who did not share his own sunny confidence that the nation represented the world's best hope of salvation and that its best days were still to come. Once installed in the White House, Reagan promptly embarked upon a massive build-up of US military power, declared the Soviet Union an "Evil Empire," and set out to bring that empire to its knees. By the time he left office eight years later, the Cold War had all but ended. New York and Los Angeles had escaped the fate of Dresden and Tokyo. Instead, under American leadership, the West had emerged intact, and in the eyes of many, even triumphant.

Events had seemingly refuted Williams's dour expectations. Instead, they had validated the twentieth century as the American Century. The preeminence of the United States, now universally acknowledged, promised to continue indefinitely. The Unipolar Moment was at hand.

In fact, that moment—spanning the interval between the fall of the Berlin Wall in 1989 and the invasion of Iraq in 2003—proved fleeting. During the 1990s, commentary favorably comparing the United States to the Roman and British empires at the height of their glory was all the rage. America stood alone and unchallenged as the world's sole superpower. A decade later, with US forces bogged down in two middling-sized wars, the very real limits of American power had become embarrassingly evident. Debt-strapped and increasingly dependent on pricey foreign oil, the United States had begun to look less like the world's Indispensable Nation and more like a country with an incorrigible penchant for unfettered profligacy.

Williams himself did not live to witness this remarkable turn of events. When he died in March 1990, the Soviet empire had begun to vanish, but the long US military campaign to dominate (or transform) the Greater Middle East—what the Pentagon today calls The Long War—had yet to begin. That would await Saddam Hussein's invasion of Kuwait in August of that year.

Yet were Williams still with us today, surely he would be tempted to revise *Tragedy* yet again, adding a coda incorporating this latest chapter in the narrative of US foreign policy. Making that temptation all the greater is the fact that this chapter—Williams might have called it "The Liberation Theology of American Empire"—serves to verify the core findings contained in the very first edition of *Tragedy* published fifty years ago.

Williams's greatness lay as a historian, not as prophet or political philosopher. His frequently voiced predictions of doom, centered on visions of the world engulfed in a fiery inferno, have not (yet) come to pass. His proposed antidote to the pathologies afflicting his fellow citizens, centered on his own obsessive yearning for "community," inspired a series of proposals for political decentralization that were—to be charitable—wildly unrealistic, where not simply fanciful.

(At the time of the bicentennial, Williams was promoting a proposal to break up the Union into a "federation of democratic Socialist communities." Under this scheme the states of Washington, Oregon, Idaho, and Montana would join together into an independent nation to be called *Neahkahnie*. Williams, who was then living in Oregon, believed that the people of this region shared a common set of interests likely to foster a common approach to politics. "Which is to say that we are willing and able to confront the power of corporations . . . and have evolved a hierarchy of values to guide us in our life together." The proposal garnered no political traction.)

Even as a historian, his greatness was confined to a specific sphere. Although a graduate of the United States Naval Academy and a decorated veteran of the Pacific War, Williams proved an unreliable interpreter of contemporary military developments. Intensely preoccupied with the dangers posed by nuclear weapons, he missed a central truth of the post-war era: the invention of the ultimate weapon did not mark warfare's arrival at some ultimate destination. Instead, mankind's newly acquired capacity to destroy itself merely inspired imaginative efforts to reinvent war, with an eye toward preserving its utility.

This capacity to reinvent war imparted to the American expansionist impulse restorative powers that Williams failed to appreciate. Military defeat did not produce a reevaluation of first principles; it merely promoted efforts to devise new techniques for employment on the next battlefield. Writing in 1972, Williams felt certain that Vietnam had "set the outer limits of the American Empire." As a consequence of failure there, "American expansion had finally been brought to bay." In fact, the reverse was true. Defeat in Vietnam produced in short order a burst of military innovation that within two decades had revived the American appetite for expansionism. Viewed in retrospect, the "lessons" of Vietnam proved remarkably superficial and short-lived.

Likewise, as a practitioner of what scholars today refer to as international history or global history, Williams's contributions do not stand the test of time. Granted, for Williams, global history never qualified as a central concern. Still, there hovers in the background of his writings, especially when addressing the twentieth century, the image of "a world in revolution." For Williams, social revolution defined the central reality of the age. The point was one to which he returned time and again: in China, Cuba, the Soviet Union, and dozens of other countries, powerful movements on behalf of radical change, inspired by collectivist or Marxian ideals with which Williams himself sympathized, were having a transformative effect. Williams did not deny that revolutions not infrequently gave rise to bloody excesses. He did not mistake Lenin or Castro for Francis of Assisi. Yet on balance he viewed this global turn toward revolution as both positive and irresistible. The challenge facing Americans, as he saw it, was to get with the program or risk being left behind.

From our present vantage point, we can make two points about the social revolutions of the past century. First, without exception, they failed utterly to make good on the ideals and expectations that inspired them. Especially when it came to fostering sustainable economic development, they flopped. Promising bread, land, and peace, they produced want and brutal oppression by regimes that routinely violated human rights on a massive scale. Second, to suggest that social revolutions defined the twentieth century is to give short shrift to a myriad of other factors that shaped the warp and woof of that era: resources and technology, race and religion, culture and sexuality, and not least of all, the age-old competition for wealth and power. In short, Williams both misread the revolutions of his time and attributed to them greater significance than they deserved.

Yet however much Williams may have misconstrued the evolution of modern war and the changing nature of the global order, the fact remains that he got his own country and his own people exactly right. These were, after all, the subjects about which he cared most passionately.

His gifts were largely intuitive. His major works, beginning with *Tragedy*, derive their power not from the quality of craftsmanship—Williams himself admitted that his scholarship might have been "less cryptic and more polished"—but from their boldness and interpretive originality. He delighted in going against the grain, skewering sacred cows, and challenging the conventional wisdom. Carl Becker, a generation older than Williams, once observed that the historian's true purpose was to provoke readers "to think otherwise." This describes how Williams defined his responsibility, an undertaking as much civic as it was scholarly.

Expanding on the achievements of Frederick Jackson Turner and Charles A. Beard and incorporating insights drawn from other disciplines, Williams sought above all to explain the emergence of the United States as a global superpower, a breathtaking feat accomplished over a startlingly brief expanse of time. He dismissed out of hand the myth that "that the American Empire just grew like Topsy" or that providence had mystically bestowed greatness on a people who simply wanted to tend to their own affairs. The United States acquired power because Americans consciously sought it and relentlessly pursued it.

Williams's singular contribution was to lay bare the reciprocal relationship among freedom, abundance, and empire throughout US history. Sustaining American freedom required ever-increasing prosperity. Enhancing American prosperity required territory, resources, markets, and influence. The resulting American imperium—continental during the nineteenth century, global during the twentieth—derived its moral justification from the conviction that the United States had erected a uniquely righteous Empire of Liberty that expressed history's (or God's) intentions.

Here lay the real genius of William Appleman Williams. Typically classified as a diplomatic historian, he was actually, to use one of his favorite terms, the great interpreter of the American *Weltanschauung*—a "definition of the world combined with an explanation of how it works."

As depicted by Williams in *Tragedy* and other writings, this *Weltanschauung* consists of several elements, among them the following:

- *A tendency to equate anti-colonialism with opposition to empire as such*, thereby crediting the United States, a frequent opponent of formal empire, with a steadfastly anti-imperial outlook;
- *An insistence that American values are universal values*, leading to this corollary: "other peoples cannot really solve their problems and improve their lives unless they go about it in the same way as the United States";
- *A self-serving commitment to the principle of self-determination*, informed by the conviction that "all peoples must ultimately self-determine themselves in the American Way if America itself is to be secure and prosperous"; or to put it another way, only when "historic American principles were honored by all" would world peace become possible;
- *A penchant for externalizing evil*, fostering an inclination to believe that trials and tribulations at home have their roots abroad; "domestic problems [therefore] became international problems" and US foreign policy became the continuation of domestic politics by other means;
- *A reflexive predilection for demonizing adversaries*; opponents of the United States are not merely wrong or misguided—they are by definition "beyond the pale and almost, if not wholly, beyond redemption";
- *A belief that the American economy cannot function absent opportunities for external expansion* and that the American political system cannot function absent prosperity; stagnation fostered internal unrest which threatened stability and raised "the specter of chaos," while economic expansion, therefore, "provided the sine qua non of domestic prosperity and social peace";

- *A steady, if unacknowledged, drift toward militarization*, as poli-cymakers "increasingly defined safety in terms of conquest—or at any rate domination"; yet as Williams emphasizes, "it was the ci-vilians who defined the world in military terms, not the military who usurped civilian power";
- *An unshakable confidence in American Exceptionalism and American beneficence*; in the end "a unique combination of eco-nomic power, intellectual and practical genius, and moral rigor" will enable the United States "to check the enemies of peace and progress—and build a better world—without erecting an empire in the process."

At the end of the 1890s, a decade of severe economic crisis, this American *Weltanschauung* achieved an apotheosis of sorts. In the wake of the Spanish-American War—launched in a fever of anti-colonialism, culminating in conquest and annexations—a freshly em-boldened United States government promulgated the terms under which it expected all powers henceforth to conduct themselves in rela-tion to China, then very much the target of imperialist exploitation.

This announcement came in the form of the famous Open Door Notes, which Williams interpreted not simply as an expression of US policy toward China but as a sophisticated articulation of a novel grand strategy. Explicitly anti-colonial, seemingly equitable and be-nign, the strategy of the Open Door sought in fact to set the terms of international competition in ways that played to America's strong suit while also catering to America's self-image. Here, for Williams, was the master key, an approach to policy that aimed "to establish the con-ditions under which America's preponderant economic power would extend the American system throughout the world without the embar-rassment and inefficiency of traditional colonialism." Over the next several decades, despite many trials and tribulations, as measured by America's progress toward the summit of power and prosperity the strategy achieved spectacular results.

The strategy of the Open Door was not the handiwork of cyn-ics or hypocrites. "American leaders were not evil men," Williams wrote. "They did not conceive and execute some dreadful con-spiracy." Rather, "they believed deeply in the ideals they proclaimed."

Policymakers saw no contradiction between those ideals and the reality of US policy. On the contrary, they "had internalized, and had come to *believe*, the theory, the necessity, and the morality of open-door expansion."

Nor was US strategy a plot conceived by the few and imposed on the many. Williams took pains to emphasize that the Open Door and the *Weltanschauung* from which it derived both reflected a broad-based political and popular consensus. Those who formulated policy, he insisted, acted in accordance with "an outlook that had been created and accepted by the majority." A citizenry unhappy with the results, therefore, had "no elite or other scapegoat to blame." They had only themselves "to confront and change."

His own thinking about what that change ought to entail was nothing if not heterodox. Williams the self-styled radical was keen to see Americans shed their preoccupation with acquisitive individualism to join in what he saw as a worldwide march toward socialism. Williams the deeply closeted conservative wrote admiringly of the colonial-era advocates of a "Christian commonwealth"—here lay a distinctively American model of community. Williams the product of a small-town Midwestern upbringing wistfully hoped that his fellow citizens might resurrect the remembered values of rural Iowa during the Great Depression. Williams the populist who in retirement preferred "playing pool with loggers and truck drivers and gippo fisherman" to hanging out with the learned or the well-heeled found among working stiffs an authenticity absent from more sophisticated climes: in blue-collar enclaves remnants of what America might have become had it rejected the allure of empire survived.

In reality, Americans, including loggers and truck drivers, evinced only passing interest in any of these prescriptions. The great majority remained committed to acquisitive individualism, which defined their commonplace understanding of life, liberty, and the pursuit of happiness. As a consequence, most saw little need to change their country, much less to "confront" themselves. By the time Williams died, the successful resolution of the Cold War and the ignominious collapse of Communism had vanquished any lingering doubts about the superiority of liberal democratic capitalism. The narrative of US foreign policy had not ended in tragedy; it had produced a triumph.

In fact, post–Cold War triumphalism obscured a more complex reality. The stubborn unwillingness of Americans to change or confront themselves had even then set in motion a sequence of events that in our own day has validated *Tragedy*'s central thesis.

Call it variations on a theme. Instead of access to Asian markets, access to Persian Gulf oil had become the main issue. The Open Door Notes of 1899–1900 found their functional equivalent in the Carter Doctrine promulgated in 1980. In place of China, US policymakers were soon to fixate on Iraq. Reprising the role of Woodrow Wilson, the most eloquent exponent of America's liberation theology, came the unlikely figure of George W. Bush, who outdid Wilson himself in expounding on history's purpose and in identifying America as history's anointed agent.

President Bush came to believe—and there is little reason to question the sincerity of his belief—that providence had charged the United States with ensuring that the "untamed fire of freedom will reach the darkest corners of our world." Translated into specific geographic terms, the world's darkest corners coincided with the furthest reaches of the Islamic world, which not coincidentally contained the world's most significant reserves of fossil fuels.

Oil, Williams wrote with considerable prescience in 1980, "is not the primary cause of empire. It is not even the principal definition of contemporary empire. But it is the slickest way we now lie to ourselves about the nature of empire." In our own day, the lie finds expression in the global war on terror, justified as a defensive response to an unprovoked attack launched on September 11, 2001, by jihadists hell-bent on imposing sharia law on all humankind.

In fact, the conflict did not erupt without warning on 9/11, as Williams would surely have been among the first to point out. Historians will long argue about when to date the beginning of this war. The toppling of the Ottomans during World War I, allowing Great Britain and France to carve up the Middle East, certainly qualifies as one candidate. Franklin Roosevelt's deal with Saudi Arabia's King Ibn Saud in 1945—security guarantees for the royal family in exchange for privileged access to oil—might also vie for the honor, along with the creation of Israel in 1948. But to pretend that the conflict began with the attack on the World Trade Center is to indulge in pointless self-deception.

After several decades of jockeying, which at different times saw Washington alternately at odds with and cozying up to most of the region's significant players—Libya and Egypt, Jordan and Israel, Iran and Iraq—the United States had long since forfeited any claim to innocence. Although to cite any single moment when America forfeited its virtue would be to oversimplify, Williams might have pointed to the overthrow of Iran's Prime Minister Mohammad Mosaddeq and the restoration of the Shah to the Peacock Throne, engineered by the CIA in 1953, as illustrative.

Finally, to pretend that the aims of the United States in prosecuting its Long War are defensive is simply silly. As Williams certainly appreciated, the concept of defensive war is alien to the American military tradition. The conflict in which the United States finds itself currently embroiled—which since 2001 alone has seen US forces invade Afghanistan and Iraq, while also conducting operations in places as far afield as Somalia, Yemen, Pakistan, and the Philippines—by no means qualifies as an exception. The United States is engaging in its Long War not to avert the rise of a new caliphate—an exceedingly unlikely prospect—but for the same reason that it has gone to war so many times in the past: to assert dominion over a region that American political leaders view as strategically critical.

In short, the reasoning that once sent US troops into Texas and California, Cuba and the Philippines, or Western Europe and East Asia now makes it imperative for them to deploy to the Persian Gulf and Central Asia: we've persuaded ourselves that American prosperity (and therefore American freedom) demands that the United States must determine the fate of these energy-rich precincts.

There is an important distinction, however. As originally conceived, the Open Door strategy established rules of a contest that Americans were confident they could win. Given the economic preponderance (and self-sufficiency) enjoyed by the United States through the first half of the twentieth century, Americans welcomed the chance to engage in a global competition for markets: the game was rigged in our favor. This is no longer the case. Today Americans buy more than they sell and borrow to cover the difference. Today too, strategic self-sufficiency has given way to strategic dependence, notably so with regard to oil. To the extent that the economic game is rigged, the rules now favor others, ironically given the provenance of the Open Door, the Chinese above all.

Yet if economic competition is no longer America's strong suit, there remains one arena in which the United States still retains a distinct advantage: the global projection of armed force. In the manufacture of cars and televisions the United States may have lost its competitive edge, but when it comes to delivering precision-guided munitions or deploying combat-ready brigades, it remains the world leader.

As a consequence, the revised and updated strategy of the Open Door deemphasizes commerce in favor of coercion. The United States once sought to "change the way that they live"—where "they" were the inhabitants of Latin America, Asia, and Europe—by selling them the products of factories back in Detroit and Chicago. Today the United States is engaged in an effort to "change the way that they live"—where "they" are the inhabitants of the Islamic world—by relying on the United States Army and Marine Corps to do the job. A century ago, Americans professed disdain for military power—it was the sort of thing that excited the Germans and Japanese. Today Americans embrace military power—it is, after all, what we do best.

Now, setting moral issues aside—and moral considerations never figure more than marginally in the formulation of policy—little of this would matter if the refurbished and militarized strategy of the Open Door, now directed toward the Greater Middle East, produced the results promised by Rumsfeld and others. Unfortunately, it doesn't.

The originally conceived Open Door worked brilliantly, enhancing American power and abundance. The revised Open Door is squandering American power while exacerbating American problems with debt and dependence. Regardless of its final outcome, the Iraq War does not provide a model for how to "transform" the Greater Middle East. Inspired by a determination to avoid at all costs modifying our own way of life, the Long War is a fool's errand. However impressive, US military power turns out to be an inadequate substitute for America's lost economic preponderance. The longer Americans persist in their illusions that salvation lies in "supporting the troops," the more difficult it will be for them to put their economic house back in order.

The United States today faces a crisis at least as challenging as that which inspired Williams to write *Tragedy* in the first place. Were he alive today, Williams would surely counsel against blaming our predicament on George W. Bush and his lieutenants, on the neoconservatives, on Big Oil, or on the military-industrial complex. To search for scapegoats is to evade the larger truth. The actual imperative remains what it was in the 1960s: Americans need to "confront and change" themselves.

Unhappily, they wouldn't then and we won't now. We will instead cling to the *Weltanschauung* that has for so long kept us in its thrall. As a consequence, the tragedy of American diplomacy promises to continue, with the people of the United States even now oblivious to the fate that awaits them.

17

Reinhold Niebuhr

Illusions of Managing History

(2007)

As pastor, teacher, activist, moral theologian, and prolific author, Reinhold Niebuhr was a towering presence in American intellectual life from the 1930s through the 1960s. He was, at various points in his career, a Christian Socialist, a pacifist, an advocate of US intervention in World War II, a staunch anti-Communist, an architect of Cold War liberalism, and a sharp critic of the Vietnam War.

For contemporary Americans, inclined to believe that history began anew on September 11, 2001, the controversies that engaged Niebuhr's attention during his long career appear not only distant but also permanently settled and therefore largely irrelevant to the present day. At least among members of the general public, Niebuhr himself is today a forgotten figure.

Among elites, however, evidence suggests that interest in Niebuhr has begun to revive. When historian Arthur Schlesinger Jr., who knew Niebuhr well and admired him greatly, published an essay in 2005 lamenting that his friend had vanished from public consciousness, the first indications of this resurgent interest had already begun to appear. Today politicians like John McCain and Barack Obama cite Niebuhr as a major influence. Pundits like neoconservative David Brooks and neoliberal Peter Beinart embellish their writings with references to Niebuhr. A new edition of Niebuhr's classic 1952 meditation on US foreign policy, *The Irony of American History*, long out of print, is in the works. The political theorist William Galston has recently gone so far as to describe Niebuhr as "the man of the hour."

Many of those who are reincorporating Niebuhr into American public discourse are doing so at Niebuhr's expense. Cribbing from Niebuhr's works to bolster their own preconceived convictions, they mangle his meaning and distort his intentions. In his book *The Good Fight*, Peter Beinart transforms Niebuhr into a dues-paying neoliberal and enlists him in the cause of "making America great again." For Beinart, Niebuhr's "core insight" is that "America should not fall in love with the supposed purity of its intentions." Niebuhr "knew that it was not just other countries that should fear the corruption of American power; we ourselves should fear it most of all." Yet once aware of its imperfections, the United States becomes an unstoppable force. In Beinart's words, "only when America recognizes that it is not inherently good can it become great." By running Niebuhr through his own literary blender, Beinart contrives a rationale for American Exceptionalism and a justification for the global war on terrorism.

In *The Mighty and the Almighty*, Madeleine Albright throws in the occasional dollop of Niebuhr to lend weight to an otherwise insipid work. Sagely quoting Niebuhr with regard to the persistence of conflict in human history, the former secretary of state briskly skirts around the implications of that insight. For Albright, Niebuhr simply teaches that "the pursuit of peace will always be uphill." In no time at all, she is back to reciting clichés about "what the right kind of leadership" can do "to prevent wars, rebuild devastated societies, expand freedom, and assist the poor." The Albright who cheerfully glimpses the emergence of "a globe on which might and right are close companions and where dignity and freedom are shared by all" nods respectfully in Niebuhr's direction, but embodies the very antithesis of Niebuhr's own perspective.

John McCain also holds Niebuhr in high regard. In *Hard Call*, his latest best seller, McCain expounds at length on Niebuhr's writings, which, he says, teach that "there are worse things than war, and human beings have a moral responsibility to oppose those worse things." Soon enough, however, it becomes clear that McCain is less interested in learning from Niebuhr than in appropriating him to support his own views. Thus, McCain broadly hints that were Niebuhr alive today, he would surely share the senator's own hawkish stance on Iraq.

Writing in the *Atlantic Monthly*, Paul Elie observes that with his rediscovery, Niebuhr is fast becoming the "man for all reasons," his posthumous support insistently claimed by various interpreters who resemble one another in one respect only: they all profess to have divined the authentic Niebuhr. Yet pressing Niebuhr into service on behalf of any and all causes will make him irrelevant even as it makes him once again familiar. The predicaments in which the United States finds itself enmeshed today—particularly in the realm of foreign policy—demand that we let Niebuhr speak for himself. We need to let Niebuhr be Niebuhr. In particular, we need to heed his warning that "our dreams of managing history pose a large and potentially mortal threat to the United States."

Since the end of the Cold War, the management of history has emerged as the all but explicitly stated purpose of American statecraft. In Washington, politicians speak knowingly about history's clearly discerned purpose and about the responsibility of the United States, at the zenith of its power, to guide history to its intended destination.

None have advanced this proposition with greater fervor and, on occasion, with greater eloquence than George W. Bush. Here is the president in January 2005 at his second inaugural, alluding to the challenges posed by Iraq while defending his decision to invade that country.

[B]ecause we have acted in the great liberating tradition of this nation, tens of millions have achieved their freedom. And as hope kindles hope, millions more will find it. By our efforts, we have lit a fire as well—a fire in the minds of men. It warms those who feel its power, it burns those who fight its progress, and one day this untamed fire of freedom will reach the darkest corners of our world.

The temptation to dismiss such remarks, especially coming from this president, as so much hot air is strong. Yet better to view the passage as authentically American, President Bush expressing sentiments that could just as well have come from the lips of Thomas Jefferson or Abraham Lincoln, Woodrow Wilson or Franklin Roosevelt, John Kennedy or Ronald Reagan. In remarkably few words, the president affirms a narrative to which the majority of our fellow citizens subscribe, while also staking out for the United States claims that most of them endorse.

This narrative renders the past in ways that purport to reveal the future. Its defining features are simplicity, clarity, and conviction. The story it tells unfolds along predetermined lines, leaving no doubt or ambiguity. History, the president goes on to explain, "has a visible direction, set by liberty and the Author of Liberty." Furthermore, at least by implication, the "Author of Liberty" has specifically anointed the United States as the Agent of Liberty. Thus assured, and proclaiming that "America's vital interests and our deepest beliefs are now one," the president declares, "We go forward with complete confidence in the eventual triumph of freedom."

President Bush's depiction of the past is sanitized, selective, and self-serving where not simply false. The great liberating tradition to which he refers is, to a considerable extent, poppycock. The president celebrates freedom without defining it, and he dodges any serious engagement with the social, cultural, and moral incongruities arising from the pursuit of actually existing freedom. A believer for whom God remains dauntingly inscrutable might view the president's confident explication of the Creator's purpose to be at the very least presumptuous, if not altogether blasphemous.

Still, one must acknowledge that in his second inaugural address, as in other presentations he has made, President Bush succeeds quite masterfully in capturing something essential about the way Americans see themselves and their country. Here is a case where myths and delusions combine to yield perverse yet important truths.

Reinhold Niebuhr helps us appreciate the large hazards embedded in those myths and delusions. Four of those truths merit particular attention at present: the persistent sin of American Exceptionalism, the indecipherability of history, the false allure of simple solutions, and, finally, the imperative of appreciating the limits of power.

The first persistent theme of Niebuhr's writings on foreign policy concerns the difficulty that Americans have in seeing themselves as they really are. "Perhaps the most significant moral characteristic of a nation," he declared in 1932, "is its hypocrisy." Niebuhr did not exempt his own nation from that judgment. The chief distinguishing feature of American hypocrisy lies in the conviction that America's very founding was a providential act, both an expression of divine favor and a summons to serve as God's chosen instrument. The Anglo-American colonists settling these shores, writes Niebuhr, saw it as America's purpose "to make a new beginning in a corrupt world." They believed "that we had been called out by God to create a new humanity." They believed further—as it seems likely that George W. Bush believes today—that this covenant with God marked America as a new Israel.

As a chosen people possessing what Niebuhr refers to as a "Messianic consciousness," Americans came to see themselves as set apart, their motives irreproachable, their actions not to be judged by standards applied to others. "Every nation has its own form of spiritual pride," Niebuhr observes in *The Irony of American History*. "Our version is that our nation turned its back upon the vices of Europe and made a new beginning." Even after World War II, he writes, the United States remained "an adolescent nation, with illusions of childlike innocency." Indeed, the outcome of World War II, vaulting the United States to the apex of world power, seemed to affirm that the nation enjoyed God's favor and was doing God's work.

Such illusions have proven remarkably durable. We see them in the way that President Bush, certain of the purity of US intentions in Iraq, shrugs off responsibility for the calamitous consequences ensuing from his decision to invade that country. We see them also in the way that the administration insists that Abu Ghraib or the policy of secret rendition that delivers suspected terrorists into the hands of torturers in no way compromises US claims of support for human rights and the rule of law.

It follows that only cynics or scoundrels would dare suggest that more sordid considerations might have influenced the American choice for war or that incidents like Abu Ghraib signify something other than simply misconduct by a handful of aberrant soldiers. As Niebuhr writes, when we swathe ourselves in self-regard, it's but a short step to concluding that "only malice could prompt criticism of any of our actions"—an insight that goes far to explain the outrage expressed by senior US officials back in 2003 when "Old Europe" declined to endorse the war.

In Niebuhr's view, America's rise to power derived less from divine favor than from good fortune combined with a fierce determination to convert that good fortune into wealth and power. The good fortune—Niebuhr refers to it as "America, rocking in the cradle of its continental security"—came in the form of a vast landscape, rich in resources, ripe for exploitation, and insulated from the bloody cockpit of power politics. The determination found expression in a strategy of commercial and territorial expansionism that proved staggeringly successful, evidence not of superior virtue but of shrewdness punctuated with a considerable capacity for ruthlessness.

In describing America's rise to power Niebuhr does not shrink from using words like "hegemony" and "imperialism." His point is not to tag the United States with responsibility for the world's evils. Rather, it is to suggest that we do not differ from other great powers as much as we imagine. On precisely this point he cites John Adams with considerable effect. "Power," observes Adams, "always thinks it has a great soul and vast views beyond the comprehension of the weak; and that it is doing God's service when it is violating all His laws."

Niebuhr has little patience for those who portray the United States as acting on God's behalf. In that regard, the religiosity that seemingly forms such a durable element of the American national identity has a problematic dimension. "All men are naturally inclined to obscure the morally ambiguous element in their political cause by investing it with religious sanctity," observes Niebuhr in an article that appeared in the magazine *Christianity and Crisis*. "This is why religion is more frequently a source of confusion than of light in the political realm." In the United States, he continues, "The tendency to equate our political with our Christian convictions causes politics to generate idolatry." The emergence of evangelical conservatism as a force in American politics, which Niebuhr did not live to see, has only reinforced this tendency.

Niebuhr anticipated that the American veneration of liberty could itself degenerate into a form of idolatry. He cautions that "no society, not even a democratic one, is great enough or good enough to make itself the final end of human existence." Niebuhr's skepticism on this point does not imply that he was anti-democratic. However, Niebuhr evinced an instinctive aversion to anything that smacked of utopianism, and he saw in the American creed a susceptibility to the utopian temptation. In the early phases of the Cold War, he provocatively suggests that "the evils against which we contend are frequently the fruits of illusions which are similar to our own."

Although Niebuhr was referring to the evils of Communism, his comment applies equally to the present, when the United States contends against the evils of Islamic radicalism. Osama bin Laden is a genuinely evil figure; George W. Bush merely misguided. Yet each of these two protagonists subscribes to all-encompassing, albeit entirely opposite, illusions. Each is intent on radically changing the Middle East, the former by ejecting the West and imposing sharia law, the latter by defeating "the terrorists" and imprinting modernity. Neither will succeed, although in the meantime they engage in an unintended collaboration that does enormous mischief—a perfect illustration of what Niebuhr once referred to as the "hidden kinship between the vices of even the most vicious and the virtues of even the most upright."

For Niebuhr, the tendency to sanctify American political values and by extension US policy was anathema. Tossing aside what he calls "the garnish of sentiment and idealism" or "the halo of moral sanctity," he summons us today to disenthrall ourselves from the self-aggrandizing parable to which President Bush refers when he alludes to America's "great liberating tradition." To purport that this tradition either explains or justifies the US presence in Iraq is to engage in self-deception.

Although politics may not be exclusively or entirely a quest for power, considerations of power are never absent from politics. Niebuhr understood that. He cherished democracy, but saw it as "a method of finding proximate solutions for insoluble problems." Its purpose is as much to constrain as to liberate. "Man's capacity for justice makes democracy possible," he writes; "but man's inclination to injustice makes democracy necessary." Borrowing a phrase from John Dewey, he reminds us that "entrenched predatory self-interest" shapes the behavior of states. Even if unwilling to acknowledge that this axiom applies in full to the United States, Americans might as a first step achieve what Niebuhr referred to as "the honesty of knowing that we are not honest."

Why is this so important? Because self-awareness is an essential precondition to Americans acquiring a more mature appreciation of history generally. On this point, Niebuhr is scathing and relentless. Those who pretend to understand history's direction and ultimate destination are, in his view, charlatans or worse. Unfortunately, the times in which we live provide a plethora of opportunities for frauds and phonies to peddle such wares.

Despite an abundance of evidence to the contrary, modern man, Niebuhr writes, clings to the view "that history is the record of the progressive triumph of good over evil." In that regard, President Bush certainly fits the definition of a modern man. So too do those who announce that, with history having "ended," plausible alternatives to democratic capitalism cannot exist, who declare categorically that globalization will determine the future of the international system, or who prattle on about America's supposed "indispensability" as the sole remaining superpower. All of these deep thinkers fall prey to what Niebuhr describes as "the inclination of wise men to imagine that their wisdom has exhausted the infinite possibilities of God's power and wisdom." The limits of their own imagination define the putative limits of what lies ahead—a perspective that, as we learned on September 11, 2001, serves only to set the observer up for a nasty surprise.

In Niebuhr's view, although history may be purposeful, it is also opaque, a drama in which both the story line and the dénouement remain hidden from view. The twists and turns that the plot has already taken suggest the need for a certain modesty in forecasting what is still to come. Yet as Niebuhr writes, "modern man lacks the humility to accept the fact that the whole drama of history is enacted in a frame of meaning too large for human comprehension or management."

Such humility is in particularly short supply in present-day Washington. There, especially among neoconservatives and neoliberals, the conviction persists that Americans are called on to serve, in Niebuhr's most memorable phrase, "as tutors of mankind in its pilgrimage to perfection." For the past six years Americans have been engaged in one such tutorial. After 9/11, the Bush administration announced its intention of bringing freedom and democracy to the people of the Islamic world. Ideologues within the Bush administration, egged on by pundits and policy analysts, persuaded themselves that American power, adroitly employed, could transform the Greater Middle East, with the invasion of Iraq intended to jumpstart that process. The results speak for themselves. Indeed, events have now progressed far enough to permit us to say, with Niebuhr, that in Iraq "the paths of progress" have turned out "to be more devious and unpredictable than the putative managers of history could understand."

The collapse of the Bush administration's hubristic strategy for the Middle East would not have surprised our prophet. Nearly fifty years ago, he cautioned that "even the most powerful nations cannot master their own destiny." Like it or not, even great powers are subject to vast forces beyond their ability to control or even understand, "caught in a web of history in which many desires, hopes, wills, and ambitions, other than their own, are operative." The masterminds who conceived the Iraq War imagined that they could sweep away the old order and usher into existence a new Iraq expected to be liberal, democratic, and aligned with the United States. Their exertions have only demonstrated, in Niebuhr's words, that "the recalcitrant forces in the historical drama have a power and persistence beyond our reckoning."

The first of our four truths (the persistent sin of American Exceptionalism) intersects with our second (the indecipherability of history) to produce the third, namely, the false allure of simple solutions. Nations possessed of outsized confidence in their own military prowess are notably susceptible to the apparent prospect of simple solutions, as the examples of Germany in 1914, Japan in 1937, and the Soviet Union in 1979 suggest. Americans are by no means immune to such temptations.

What Niebuhr wrote back in 1958 remains true today: "the American nation has become strangely enamored with military might." In the aftermath of 9/11, an administration enamored with military might insisted on the necessity of using force to eliminate the putative threat represented by Saddam Hussein. The danger that he posed was growing day by day. A showdown had become unavoidable. To delay further was to place at risk the nation's very survival. Besides, as one Washington insider famously predicted, a war with Iraq was sure to be a "cakewalk." These were the arguments mustered in 2002 and 2003 to persuade Americans—and the rest of the world—that preventive war had become necessary, justifiable, and even inviting.

A half-century earlier, Reinhold Niebuhr had encountered similar arguments. The frustrations of the early Cold War combined with the knowledge of US nuclear superiority to produce calls for preventive war against the Soviet Union. In one fell swoop, advocates of attacking Russia argued, the United States could eliminate its rival and achieve permanent peace and security. In Niebuhr's judgment, the concept of preventive war fails both normatively and pragmatically. It is not only morally wrong; it is also stupid. "So long as war has not broken out, we still have the possibility of avoiding it," he said. "Those who think that there is little difference between a cold and a hot war are either knaves or fools."

Throughout the second half of the twentieth century, such cautionary views, shared by American presidents, helped avoid a nuclear conflagration. Between 2002 and 2003, they did not suffice to carry the day. The knaves and fools got their war, which has yielded not the neat and tidy outcome promised, but a host of new complications. Even so, the president has shown no inclination to reconsider his endorsement of preventive war. The Bush Doctrine remains on the books and Congress has not insisted on its abrogation. Given what the implementation of this doctrine has produced in Iraq, Niebuhr would certainly have viewed its survival as both remarkable and deeply troubling.

Finally, there is the imperative of appreciating the limits of power, for Niebuhr the very foundation of sound statecraft. Perhaps the most disconcerting passage Niebuhr ever wrote is this one, from 1937:

> One of the most pathetic aspects of human history is that every civilization expresses itself most pretentiously, compounds its partial and universal values most convincingly, and claims immortality for its finite existence at the very moment when the decay which leads to death has already begun.

We Americans certainly live in a time when our political leaders have made pretentious proclamations something of a specialty, despite mounting evidence of decay apparent everywhere from the national debt (now approaching $9 trillion), the trade imbalance (surpassing $800 billion last year), and the level of oil imports (exceeding 60 percent of daily requirements). A large gap is opening up between the professed aspirations of our political class—still all but unanimously committed to the United States asserting a role of what is euphemistically called "global leadership"—and the means available to fulfill those aspirations. Each of the last four presidential administrations has relied on military might to conceal or to minimize the significance of this gap. Unfortunately, with the Iraq War now having demonstrated that US military power has very real limits, our claim of possessing "the greatest military the world has ever seen" no longer carries quite the clout that it once did.

"The greater danger," Niebuhr worried a half-century ago, "is that we will rely too much on military strength in general and neglect all the other political, economic, and moral factors" that constitute the wellsprings of "unity, health, and strength." The time to confront this neglect is at hand. We do so by giving up our Messianic dreams and ceasing our efforts to coerce history in a particular direction. This does not imply a policy of isolationism. It does imply attending less to the world outside of our borders and more to the circumstances within. It means ratcheting down our expectations. Americans need what Niebuhr described as "a sense of modesty about the virtue, wisdom and power available to us for the resolution of [history's] perplexities."

Rather than engaging in vain attempts to remake places like Iraq in our own image, the United States would be better served if it focused on creating a stable global order, preferably one that avoids the chronic barbarism that characterized the previous century. During the run-up to the Iraq War, senior members of the Bush administration repeatedly expressed their disdain for mere stability. Since March 2003, they have acquired a renewed appreciation for its benefits. The education has come at considerable cost—more than 3,800 American lives and several hundred billion dollars so far.

Niebuhr did not disdain stability. Given the competitive nature of politics and the improbability (and undesirability) of any single nation achieving genuine global dominion, he posited "a tentative equilibrium of power" as the proper goal of US policy. Among other things, he wrote, nurturing that equilibrium might afford the United States with "an opportunity to make our wealth sufferable to our conscience and tolerable to our friends." Yet efforts to establish such an equilibrium by fiat would surely fail. Creating and maintaining a balance of power requires finesse and flexibility, locating "the point of concurrence between the parochial and the general interest, between the national and the international common good." This, in a nutshell, writes Niebuhr, composes "the art of statecraft."

During the Cold War, within the Western camp at least, the United States enjoyed considerable success in identifying this point of concurrence. The resulting strategy of containment, which sought equilibrium, not dominance, served the economic and security interests of both the United States and its allies. As a result, those allies tolerated and even endorsed American primacy. The United States was the unquestioned leader of the Free World. As long as Washington did not mistake leadership as implying a grant of arbitrary authority, the United States remained first among equals.

After 9/11, the Bush administration rejected mere equilibrium as a goal. Rather than searching for a mutually agreeable point of concurrence, which implies a willingness to give and take, President Bush insisted on calling the shots. He demanded unquestioning conformity, famously declaring, "You are either with us or against us." Niebuhr once observed that the wealth and power of the United States presented "special temptations to vanity and arrogance which militate against our moral prestige and authority." In formulating their strategy for the global war on terror, President Bush and his lieutenants succumbed to that temptation.

The results have not been pretty. Hitherto reliable allies have become unreliable. Washington's capacity to lead has eroded. The moral standing of the United States has all but collapsed. In many parts of the world, American wealth and power have come to seem intolerable. The Bush record represents the very inverse of what Niebuhr defined as successful statecraft.

This is not to suggest that restoring realism and effectiveness to US foreign policy is simply a matter of reviving the habits and routines to which Washington adhered from the late 1940s through the 1980s. The East-West dichotomies that defined that era have vanished and the United States today is not the country that it was in the days of Harry

Truman or Dwight Eisenhower. The difficult challenges facing the United States require us to go forward, not backward. Yet here, too, Niebuhr, speaking to us from the days of Truman and Eisenhower, offers some suggestive insights on how best to proceed.

By the time *The Irony of American History* appeared in 1952, Niebuhr had evolved a profound appreciation for the domestic roots of US foreign policy. He understood that the expansionist impulse central to the American diplomatic tradition derived in no small measure from a determination to manage the internal contradictions produced by the American way of life.

From the very founding of the Republic, American political leaders had counted on the promise and the reality of ever-greater material abundance to resolve or at least alleviate those contradictions. As Niebuhr wrote, "we seek a solution for practically every problem of life in quantitative terms," convinced that more is better. It has long been, he explained,

> the character of our particular democracy, founded on a vast continent, expanding as a culture with its expanding frontier and creating new frontiers of opportunity when the old geographic frontier ended, that every ethical and social problem of a just distribution of the privileges of life is solved by so enlarging the privileges that either an equitable distribution is made easier, or a lack of equity is rendered less noticeable.

No other national community, he continued, had "followed this technique of social adjustment more consistently than we. No other community had the resources to do so." Through a strategy of commercial and territorial expansion, the United States accrued power and fostered material abundance at home. Expectations of ever-increasing affluence—Niebuhr called it "the American cult of prosperity"—in turn ameliorated social tensions and (with the notable exception of the Civil War) kept internal dissent within bounds, thereby permitting individual Americans to pursue their disparate notions of life, liberty, and happiness.

Yet even in 1952, Niebuhr expressed doubts about this strategy's long-term viability. Acknowledging that "we have thus far sought to solve all our problems by the expansion of our economy," he went on to say that "this expansion cannot go on forever."

This brings us to the nub of the matter. Considering things strictly from the point of national self-interest and acknowledging various blunders made along the way, a strategy that relies on expansion abroad to facilitate the creation of a more perfect union at home has worked remarkably well. At least it did so through the 1960s and the Vietnam War. Since that time, the positive correlations between expansionism and prosperity, national power and individual freedom have begun to unravel. Since 2003 and the beginning of the Iraq War, this strategy has become almost entirely undone.

By no means least of all, our adherence to a strategy of expansionism is exacting a huge moral price. I refer here not simply to the morally dubious policies devised to prosecute the global war on terror. At least as troubling is the moral dissonance generated by sending soldiers off to fight for freedom in distant lands when freedom at home appears increasingly to have become a synonym for profligacy, conspicuous consumption, and frivolous self-absorption. While US troops are engaged in Baghdad, Babylon, and Samarra—place names redolent with ancient imperial connotations—their civilian counterparts back on the block preoccupy themselves with YouTube, reality TV, and the latest misadventures of Hollywood celebrities.

This defines the essential crisis we face today. The basic precepts that inform US national security policy are not making us safer and more prosperous while guaranteeing authentic freedom. They have multiplied our enemies and put us on the road to ruin while indulging notions of freedom that are shallow and spurious. The imperative of the moment is to change fundamentally our approach to the world. Yet this is unlikely to occur absent a serious and self-critical examination of the domestic arrangements and priorities that define what we loosely refer to as the American way of life.

"No one sings odes to liberty as the final end of life with greater fervor than Americans," Niebuhr once observed. Yet it might also be said that no one shows less interest in discerning the true meaning of liberty than do Americans. Although I would not want to sell my countrymen short—the United States has in the past demonstrated a remarkable ability to weather crises and recover from adversity—I see little evidence today of interest in undertaking a critical assessment of our way of life, which would necessarily entail something akin to a sweeping cultural reformation.

Certainly, President Bush will not promote such a self-assessment. Nor will any of the leading candidates vying to succeed him. The political elite, the governing class, the Washington party—call it what you will—there is little likelihood of a great awakening starting from the top. We can only hope that, before too many further catastrophes befall us, fortuitous circumstances will bring about what Niebuhr referred to as "the ironic triumph of the wisdom of common sense over the foolishness of its wise men."

In the meantime, we should recall the warning with which Niebuhr concludes *The Irony of American History*. Should the United States perish, the prophet writes,

> the ruthlessness of the foe would be only the secondary cause of the disaster. The primary cause would be that the strength of a giant nation was directed by eyes too blind to see all the hazards of the struggle; and the blindness would be induced not by some accident of nature or history but by hatred and vainglory.

Change each "would be" to "was," and you have an inscription well-suited for the memorial that will no doubt be erected one day in Washington honoring those who sacrificed their lives in Iraq.

PART 2

History and Myth

18

━━━━━━━━━━━━━━━━━━━━━━━━━

Saving "America First"

(2017)

One of the privileges of power that Americans routinely abuse is to remember selectively. It was not surprising, then, that this year's centennial of the United States' entry into World War I attracted barely any official attention. A House resolution commending "the brave members of the United States Armed Forces for their efforts in 'making the world safe for democracy'" never made it out of committee. And although the Senate did endorse a fatuous decree "expressing gratitude and appreciation" for the declaration of war passed back in April 1917, the White House ignored the anniversary altogether. As far as Washington is concerned, that conflict retains little or no political salience.

It was not always so, of course. For those who lived through it, the "war to end all wars" was a searing experience. In its wake came acute disillusionment, compounded by a sense of having been deceived about its origins and purposes. The horrific conflict seemed only to create new problems; President Woodrow Wilson's insistence in a 1919 speech that the 116,000 American soldiers lost in that war had "saved the liberty of the world" rang hollow.

So twenty years later, when another European conflict presented Americans with a fresh opportunity to rescue liberty, many balked. A second war against Germany on behalf of France and the United Kingdom, they believed, was unlikely to produce more satisfactory results than the first. Those intent on keeping the United States out of that war organized a nationwide, grass-roots campaign led by the America First Committee. During its brief existence, the movement enlisted more supporters than the Tea Party, was better organized than Occupy Wall Street or Black Lives Matter, and wielded more political clout than the "resistance" to President Donald Trump.

Yet despite drawing support from across the political spectrum, the movement failed. Well before the Pearl Harbor attack in December 1941, President Franklin Roosevelt had embarked on a program of incremental intervention aimed at bringing the United States into the war as a full-fledged belligerent. When it came to Nazi Germany, Roosevelt believed that the putative lessons of World War I—above all, that France and the United Kingdom had played the United States for a sucker—did not apply. He castigated those who disagreed as "enemies of democracy" aligned with fascists, communists, and "every group devoted to bigotry and racial and religious intolerance." In effect, Roosevelt painted anti-interventionism as anti-American, and the smear stuck. The phrase "America First" became a term of derision. To the extent that anti-interventionist sentiment survived, it did so as a fringe phenomenon, associated with the extreme right and the far left.

For decades, World War II remained at the forefront of the American historical consciousness, easily overshadowing World War I. Politicians and pundits regularly paid homage to World War II's canonical lessons, warning against the dangers of appeasement and emphasizing the need to confront evil. As for "America First," the slogan that had resonated with those reeling from World War I, it appeared irredeemable, retaining about as much political salience as the Free Silver and Prohibition movements. Then came Trump, and the irredeemable enjoyed sudden redemption.

The Myopia of Utopianism

As long as the Cold War persisted and, with it, the perceived imperative of confronting international communism, America First remained an emblem of American irresponsibility, a reminder of a narrowly averted catastrophe. When the fall of the Soviet Union triggered a brief flurry of speculation that the United States might claim a "peace dividend" and tend to its own garden, elite opinion wasted no time in denouncing that prospect. With history's future trajectory now readily apparent—the collapse of communism having cleared up any remaining confusion in that regard—it was incumbent on the United States to implement that future. American leadership was therefore more important than ever, a line of thought giving rise to what the writer R. R. Reno has aptly termed "utopian globalism."

Three large expectations informed this post–Cold War paradigm. According to the first, corporate capitalism of the type pioneered in the United States, exploiting advanced technology and implemented globally, held the potential of creating wealth on a once unimaginable scale. According to the second, the possession of vast military might—displayed for all to see in the 1990–91 Gulf War—endowed the United States with an unprecedented ability to establish (and enforce) the terms of world order. And according to the third, the White House, no longer merely the official residence of the country's chief executive, was now to serve as a de facto global command post, the commander in chief's mandate extending to the far corners of the earth.

In policy circles, it was taken as a given that American power—wielded by the president and informed by the collective wisdom of the political, military, and corporate elite—was sufficient for the task ahead. Although a few outsiders questioned that assumption, such concerns never gained traction. The careful weighing of means and ends suggested timidity. It also risked indulging popular inclinations toward isolationism, kept under tight rein ever since the America First campaign met its demise at the hands of the Imperial Japanese Navy and Adolf Hitler.

Again and again during the 1990s, US officials warned against the dangers of backsliding. The United States was "the indispensable nation," they declared, a quasi-theological claim pressed into service as a basis for statecraft. After 9/11, policymakers saw the attacks not as a warning about the consequences of overreach but as a rationale for redoubling US efforts to fulfill the imperatives of utopian globalism. Thus, in 2005, in the midst of stalemated wars in Afghanistan and Iraq,

President George W. Bush summoned the spirit of Wilson and assured his fellow citizens that "the expansion of freedom in all the world" had become "the calling of our time."

A decade later, with both of those wars still simmering and other emergencies erupting regularly, despite vast expenditures of blood and treasure, Trump denounced the entire post–Cold War project as a fraud. During his presidential campaign, he vowed to "make America great again" and recover the jobs lost to globalization. He pledged to avoid needless armed conflicts and to win promptly any that could not be avoided.

Yet although he rejected the first two components of utopian globalism, he affirmed the third. As president, he and he alone would set things right. Once in office, he pledged to use his authority to the fullest, protecting ordinary Americans from further assault by the forces of globalization and ending the misuse of military power. Instead of embracing globalism, Trump promised to put "America First."

Trump's appropriation of that loaded phrase, which formed a central theme of his campaign and his inaugural address, was an affront to political correctness. Yet it was much more. At least implicitly, Trump was suggesting that the anti-interventionists who opposed Roosevelt had been right after all. By extension, he was declaring obsolete the lessons of World War II and the tradition of American statecraft derived from them.

The policy implications seemed clear. In a single stroke, the columnist Charles Krauthammer wrote, Trump's inaugural "radically redefined the American national interest as understood since World War II." Instead of exercising global leadership, the United States was now opting for "insularity and smallness." Another columnist, William Kristol, lamented that hearing "an American president proclaim 'America First'" was "profoundly depressing and vulgar."

That Trump himself is not only vulgar but also narcissistic and dishonest is no doubt the case. Yet fears that his embrace of "America First" will lead the United States to turn its back on the world have already proved groundless. Ordering punitive air strikes against a regime that murders its own citizens while posing no threat to the United States, as Trump did in Syria, is not isolationism. Nor is sending more

US troops to fight the campaign in Afghanistan, the very epitome of the endless wars that Trump once disparaged. And whatever one makes of Trump's backing of the Sunnis in their regional struggle with the Shiites, his vow to broker an Israeli-Palestinian peace deal, his threats against North Korea, and his evolving views on trade and the viability of NATO, they do not suggest disengagement.

What they do suggest is something much worse: an ill-informed, impulsive, and capricious approach to foreign policy. In fact, if "policy" implies a predictable pattern of behavior, US foreign policy ceased to exist when Trump took office. The United States now acts or refrains from action according to presidential whim. Trump's critics have misread their man. Those who worry about the ghost of Charles Lindbergh, the aviator and America First backer, taking up residence in the Oval Office can rest easy. The real problem is that Trump is making his own decisions, and he thinks he has things under control.

Yet more important, unlike Trump himself, Trump's critics have misread the moment. However oblivious he was to the finer points of diplomacy, candidate Trump correctly intuited that establishment views about the United States' proper role in the world had not worked. In the eyes of ordinary citizens, policies conceived under the direction of George H. W. Bush or George W. Bush, Bill Clinton or Hillary Clinton, Condoleezza Rice or Susan Rice no longer command automatic assent. America *über alles* has proved to be a bust—hence, the appeal of "America First" as an alternative. That the phrase itself causes conniptions among elites in both political parties only adds to its allure in the eyes of the Trump supporters whom the Democratic candidate Hillary Clinton dismissed during the campaign as "deplorable."

Whatever the consequences of Trump's own fumbling, that allure is likely to persist. So, too, will the opportunity awaiting any would-be political leader with the gumption to articulate a foreign policy that promises to achieve the aim of the original America First movement— to ensure the safety and well-being of the United States without engaging in needless wars. The challenge is to do what Trump himself is almost certainly incapable of doing, converting "America First" from a slogan burdened with an ugly history—including the taint of anti-Semitism—into a concrete program of enlightened action. To put it another way, the challenge is to save "America First" from Trump.

The problem with utopian globalism, according to Reno, is that it "disenfranchises the vast majority and empowers a technocratic elite." This is good news for the elite, but not for the disenfranchised. True, since the end of the Cold War, globalization has created enormous wealth. But it has also exacerbated inequality. Much the same can be said of US military policy: those presiding over and equipping American wars have made out quite handsomely; those actually sent to fight have fared less well. The 2016 presidential election made plain to all the depth of the resulting divisions.

Reno's proposed solution to those divisions is to promote "patriotic solidarity, or a renewed national covenant." He's right. Yet the term "covenant," given its religious connotation, won't fly in secular quarters. What's needed is a statement of purpose capable of binding Americans together as Americans (as opposed to citizens of the world), while also providing a basis for engaging with the world as it is, not as it might once have been.

To fill this tall order, Americans should go back to their beginnings and consult the Constitution. Its concise, fifty-two-word preamble, summarizing the purpose of the union, concludes with a pledge to "secure the Blessings of Liberty to ourselves and our Posterity." Put the emphasis on "ourselves," and this passage suggests a narrow, even selfish orientation. Put the emphasis on "our Posterity," however, and it invites a more generous response. Here is the basis for a capacious and forward-looking alternative to utopian globalism.

Taking seriously an obligation to convey the blessings of liberty to Americans' posterity brings to the fore a different set of foreign policy questions. First, what do Americans owe future generations if they are to enjoy the freedoms to which they are entitled? At a minimum, posterity deserves a livable planet, reasonable assurances of security, and a national household in decent working order, the three together permitting both the individual and the collective pursuit of happiness.

Second, what are the threats to these prerequisites of liberty? Several loom large: the possibility of large-scale environmental collapse, the danger of global conflict brought about by the rapidly changing roster of great powers, and the prospect of a citizenry so divided and demoralized that it can neither identify nor effectively pursue the common good. Taken separately, each of these threats poses a serious danger to the American way of life. Should more than one materialize, that way of life will likely become unsustainable. The simultaneous realization of all three would jeopardize the very existence of the United States as an independent republic. Therefore, the overarching purpose of US policy should be to forestall these eventualities.

How best to respond to these threats? Proponents of utopian globalism will argue for the United States to keep doing what it has been doing, even though since the end of the Cold War, their approach has exacerbated, rather than alleviated, problems. A broad conception of "America First" offers an alternative more likely to produce positive results and command popular support.

An "America First" response to environmental deterioration should seek to retard global warming while emphasizing the preservation of the United States' own resources—its air, water, and soil; its flora and fauna; and its coastlines and inland waterways. The pursuit of mere economic growth should take a backseat to repairing the damage caused by reckless exploitation and industrial abuse. To effect those repairs, Congress should provide the requisite resources with the kind of openhandedness currently reserved for the Pentagon. On all matters related to safeguarding the planet, the United States would serve as an exemplar, benefiting future generations everywhere.

An "America First" response to ongoing changes in the international order should begin with a recognition that the unipolar moment has passed. Ours is a multipolar era. Some countries, such as China and India, are just now moving into the first rank. Others long accustomed to playing a leading role, such as France, Russia, and the United Kingdom, are in decline while still retaining residual importance. Occupying a third category are countries whose place in the emerging order remains to be determined, a group that includes Germany, Indonesia, Iran, Japan, and Turkey.

As for the United States, although it is likely to remain preeminent for the foreseeable future, preeminence does not imply hegemony. Washington's calling should be not to impose a Pax Americana but to promote mutual coexistence. Compared with perpetual peace and universal brotherhood, stability and the avoidance of cataclysmic war may seem like modest goals, but achieve that much and future generations will be grateful.

Similar reasoning applies to the question of nuclear weapons. Whatever advantage a ready-to-launch strike force once conferred on the United States will almost surely disappear in the coming years. As the Pentagon continues to develop ever more discriminate and exotic ways of killing people and disabling adversaries, strategic deterrence will no longer depend on maintaining a capability to retaliate with nuclear weapons. Even as the actual use of US nuclear weapons becomes increasingly unimaginable, however, the United States' own vulnerability to these weapons will persist. As a first step toward eliminating the scourge of nuclear weapons altogether, Washington should pay more than lip service to its obligations under the Nuclear Nonproliferation Treaty, which requires signatories "to pursue negotiations in good faith on effective measures" leading to the abolition of nuclear arms. Taking that obligation seriously would exemplify enlightened self-interest: the very essence of what it means to put America first.

As for the societal fissures that gave rise to Trump, Americans are likely to find that restoring a common understanding of the common good will be a long time coming. The era of utopian globalism coincided with a period of upheaval in which traditional norms related to gender, sexuality, family, and identity fell from favor among many. The resulting rifts run deep. In one camp are those waging a fierce rearguard action in favor of a social order now in tatters; in the other are those intent on mandating compliance with precepts such as diversity and multiculturalism. Both sides manifest intolerance. Neither gives much evidence of empathy or willingness to compromise.

A reimagined "America First" approach to statecraft would seek to insulate US foreign policy from this ongoing domestic *Kulturkampf* as much as possible. It would remain agnostic as to which blessings of liberty the United States views as ready for export until Americans themselves reach a consensus on what liberty should actually entail.

This need not imply turning a blind eye to human rights abuses. Yet an "America First" foreign policy would acknowledge that on an array of hot-button issues, as varied as gun ownership and the status of transgender people, the definition of rights is in a state of flux. In that regard, the warning against "passionate attachments" that President George Washington issued in his Farewell Address should apply not only to countries but also to causes. In either case, those responsible for the formulation of foreign policy should avoid taking positions that threaten to undermine the nation's fragile domestic cohesion. It may be naïve to expect politics to stop at the water's edge. That said, diplomacy is not an appropriate venue for scoring points on matters on which Americans themselves remain deeply at odds. That's what elections are for. What the present generation of Americans owes to posterity is the opportunity to sort these things out for themselves.

Something similar applies to US military policy. Future generations deserve their own chance to choose. Unfortunately, military actions undertaken under the auspices of utopian globalism have narrowed the range of available choices and squandered vast resources. The duration of the post-9/11 wars tells the tale: Afghanistan is the longest in US history, and Iraq is the second longest. The countless sums of money wasted—few in Washington evince interest in tallying up how much—have contributed to the exploding size of the US national debt. It stood at approximately $4 trillion when the Cold War ended, has risen to $20 trillion today, and is projected to exceed $25 trillion by the end of this decade. The United States has become a country that does not finish what it starts and then borrows exorbitantly to conceal its failures.

From an "America First" perspective, the antidote is twofold: first, curb Washington's appetite for armed intervention except when genuinely vital US interests are immediately at risk, and second, pay for wars as they occur, rather than saddling future generations with their cost. Posterity deserves books that balance.

Critics will contend that a nation that fights only when vital interests are at stake will become oblivious to the suffering of those unfortunate people living in such hellholes as Syria. Yet fighting is neither the sole nor necessarily the best way to respond to suffering. Indeed, Washington's scorecard when it comes to sending US troops to liberate or protect is mixed at best. Consider the present-day conditions in Somalia, Iraq, and Libya, each the subject of US military action justified entirely or in large part by humanitarian concerns. In all three countries, armed intervention only made life worse for ordinary people.

Does this mean that Americans should simply avert their eyes from horrors abroad? Not at all. But when it comes to aiding the distressed, they should not look to US bombs or troops to fix things. The armed forces of the United States may occasionally engage in charitable works, but that should not be their purpose. Far better to incentivize concerned citizens to open their own wallets, thereby expanding the capacity of relief organizations to help. In comparison to bureaucratically engineered programs, voluntary efforts are likely to be more effective, both in making a difference on the ground and in winning hearts and minds. In short, let marines be marines, and help do-gooders do good.

POTUS on Notice

All these suggestions amount to little more than common sense. Yet given the state of US politics, defined above all by the outsize role of the president, none of it is likely to happen. In that regard, the most immediate goal of an "America First" policy must be to restore some semblance of constitutional balance. That means curtailing presidential power, an aim that is all the more urgent with Trump in the White House.

In utopian globalist circles, however, the thought of constraining executive authority is anathema. The entire national security apparatus is invested in the proposition that the president should function as a sort of quasi deity, wielding life-and-death authority. Disagree, and you've rendered yourself ineligible for employment on the seventh floor of the State Department, in the E Ring of the Pentagon, at CIA headquarters, or anywhere within a half mile of the Oval Office.

This line of thinking dates back to the debate over whether to enter World War II. Roosevelt won that fight and, as a result, endowed his successors with extraordinary latitude on issues of national security. Ever since, in moments of uncertainty or perceived peril, Americans have deferred to presidents making the case, as Roosevelt did, that military action is necessary to keep them safe.

Yet Trump, to put it mildly, is no Roosevelt. More to the point, both the world and the United States have changed in innumerable ways. Although the lessons of World War II may still retain some legitimacy, in today's radically different circumstances, they do not suffice. So although the risks of ill-considered appeasement persist, other dangers are at least as worrisome—among them, recklessness, hubris, and self-deception. In 1940, the original America First movement warned against such tendencies, which had in recent memory produced the catastrophe of World War I and which would lay the basis for even worse things to come. Today, those warnings deserve attention, especially given the recklessness, hubris, and self-deception that Trump displays daily.

The point is not to relitigate the arguments over whether the United States should have entered World War II: in that instance, Roosevelt got it right and those who thought Nazi Germany posed no threat to the United States got it wrong. Yet the latter were not wrong to insist that the previous war against Germany and all that it had wreaked remained relevant. Nor were they wrong to decry the chicanery and demagoguery that Roosevelt was employing to maneuver the United States toward war.

Americans today need to do a better job of remembering. To remember with an open mind is to consider the possibility that those on the losing end of old arguments might be worth listening to. The imperative now, amid the wreckage created by utopian globalism and the follies of Trump, is to think creatively about the predicaments that the United States faces. Stripped of their unfortunate historical associations and understood properly, many of the concerns and convictions that animated the original America First movement provide a sound point of departure for doing just that.

19

Kissing the Specious Present Goodbye

(2017)

Forgive me for complaining, but recent decades have not been easy ones for my peeps. I am from birth a member of the WHAM tribe, that once proud but now embattled conglomeration of white, heterosexual American males. We have long been—there's no denying it—a privileged group. When the blessings of American freedom get parceled out, WHAMs are accustomed to standing at the head of the line. Those not enjoying the trifecta of being white, heterosexual, and male get what's left.

Fair? No, but from time immemorial those have been the rules. Anyway, no real American would carp. After all, the whole idea of America derives from the conviction that some people (us) deserve more than others (all those who are not us). It's God's will—so at least the great majority of Americans have believed since the Pilgrims set up shop just about four hundred years ago.

Lately, however, the rules have been changing in ways that many WHAMs find disconcerting. True, some of my brethren—let's call them 1 percenters—have adapted to those changes and continue to do very well indeed. Wherever corporate CEOs, hedge fund managers, investment bankers, tech gurus, university presidents, publishers, politicians, and generals congregate to pat each other on the back, you can count on WHAMs—reciting bromides about the importance of diversity!—being amply represented.

Yet beneath this upper crust, a different picture emerges. Further down the socioeconomic ladder, being a WHAM carries with it disadvantages. The good, steady jobs once implicitly reserved for us—lunch pail stuff, yes, but enough to keep food in the family larder—are increasingly hard to come by. As those jobs have disappeared, so too have the ancillary benefits they conferred, self-respect not least among them. Especially galling to some WHAMs is being exiled to the back of the cultural bus. When it comes to art, music, literature, and fashion, the doings of blacks, Hispanics, Asians, gays, and women generate buzz. By comparison, white heterosexual males seem bland, uncool, and passé, or worst of all simply boring.

The Mandate of Heaven, which members of my tribe once took as theirs by right, has been cruelly withdrawn. History itself has betrayed us.

All of which is nonsense, of course, except perhaps as a reason to reflect on whether history can help explain why, today, WHAMs have worked themselves into such a funk in Donald Trump's America. Can history provide answers? Or has history itself become part of the problem?

Paging Professor Becker

"For all practical purposes history is, for us and for the time being, what we know it to be." So remarked Carl Becker in 1931 at the annual meeting of the American Historical Association. Professor Becker, a towering figure among historians of his day, was president of the AHA that year. His message to his colleagues amounted to a warning of sorts: Don't think you're so smart. The study of the past may reveal truths, he allowed, but those truths are contingent, incomplete, and valid only "for the time being."

Put another way, historical perspectives conceived in what Becker termed "the specious present" have a sell-by date. Beyond their time, they become stale and outmoded, and so should be revised or discarded. This process of rejecting truths previously treated as authoritative is inexorable and essential. Yet it also tends to be fiercely contentious. The present may be specious, but it confers real privileges, which a particular reading of the past can sustain or undermine. Becker believed it inevitable that "our now valid versions" of history "will in due course be relegated to the category of discarded myths." It was no less inevitable that beneficiaries of the prevailing version of truth should fight to preserve it.

Who exercises the authority to relegate? Who gets to decide when a historical truth no longer qualifies as true? Here, Becker insisted that "Mr. Everyman" plays a crucial role. For Becker, Mr. Everyman was Joe Doakes, John Q. Public, or the man in the street. He was "every normal person," a phrase broad enough to include all manner of people. Yet nothing in Becker's presentation suggested that he had the slightest interest in race, sexuality, or gender. His Mr. Everyman belonged to the tribe of WHAM.

In order to "live in a world of semblance more spacious and satisfying than is to be found within the narrow confines of the fleeting present moment," Becker emphasized, Mr. Everyman needs a past larger than his own individual past. An awareness of things said and done long ago provides him with an "artificial extension of memory" and a direction.

Memories, whether directly or vicariously acquired, are "necessary to orient us in our little world of endeavor." Yet the specious present that we inhabit is inherently unstable and constantly in flux, which means that history itself must be pliable. Crafting history necessarily becomes an exercise in "imaginative creation" in which all participate. However unconsciously, Mr. Everyman adapts the past to serve his most pressing needs, thereby functioning as "his own historian."

Yet he does so in collaboration with others. Since time immemorial, purveyors of the past—the "ancient and honorable company of wise men of the tribe, of bards and story-tellers and minstrels, of soothsayers and priests, to whom in successive ages has been entrusted the keeping of the useful myths"—have enabled him to "hold in memory . . . those things only which can be related with some reasonable degree of relevance" to his own experience and aspirations. In Becker's lifetime it had become incumbent upon members of the professoriate, successors to the bards and minstrels of yesteryear, "to enlarge and enrich the specious present common to us all to the end that 'society' (the tribe, the nation, or all mankind) may judge of what it is doing in the light of what it has done and what it hopes to do."

Yet Becker took pains to emphasize that professional historians disdained Mr. Everyman at their peril:

> Berate him as we will for not reading our books, Mr. Everyman is stronger than we are, and sooner or later we must adapt our knowledge to his necessities. Otherwise he will leave us to our own devices. . . . The history that does work in the world, the history that influences the course of history, is living history. . . . It is for this reason that the history of history is a record of the 'new history' that in every age rises to confound and supplant the old.

Becker stressed that the process of formulating new history to supplant the old is organic rather than contrived; it comes from the bottom up, not the top down. "We, historians by profession, share in this necessary effort," he concluded. "But we do not impose our version of the human story on Mr. Everyman; in the end it is rather Mr. Everyman who imposes his version on us."

Donald Trump as Everyman's Champion?

Becker offered his reflections on "Everyman His Own Historian" in the midst of the Great Depression. Perhaps because that economic crisis found so many Americans burdened with deprivation and uncertainty, he implicitly attributed to his Mr. Everyman a unitary perspective, as if shared distress imbued members of the public with a common outlook. That was not, in fact, the case in 1931 and is, if anything, even less so in our own day.

Still, Becker's construct retains considerable utility. Today finds more than a few white heterosexual American males, our own equivalent of Mr. Everyman, in a state of high dudgeon. From their perspective, the specious present has not panned out as it was supposed to. As a consequence, they are pissed. In November 2016, to make clear just how pissed they were, they elected Donald Trump as president of the United States.

This was, to put it mildly, not supposed to happen. For months prior to the election, the custodians of the past in its "now valid version" had judged the prospect all but inconceivable. Yet WHAMs (with shocking support from other tribes) intervened to decide otherwise. Rarely has a single event so thoroughly confounded history's self-assigned proctors. One can imagine the shade of Professor Becker whispering, "I warned you, didn't I?"

Those deeply invested in drawing a straight line from the specious present into the indefinite future blame Trump himself for having knocked history off its prescribed course. Remove Trump from the scene, they appear to believe, and all will once again be well. The urgent imperative of doing just that—immediately, now, no later than this afternoon—has produced what *New York Times* columnist Charles Blow aptly calls a "throbbing anxiety" among those who (like Blow himself) find "the relentless onslaught of awfulness erupting from this White House" intolerable. They will not rest until Trump is gone.

This *idée fixe*, reinforced on a daily basis by ever more preposterous presidential antics, finds the nation trapped in a sort of bizarre do-loop. The media's obsession with Trump reinforces his obsession with the media and between them they simply crowd out all possibility of thoughtful reflection. Their fetish is his and his theirs. The result is a cycle of mutual contempt that only deepens the longer it persists.

Both sides agree on one point only: that history began anew last November 8, when (take your pick) America either took leave of its senses or chose greatness. How the United States got to November 8 qualifies, at best, as an afterthought or curiosity. It's almost as if the years and decades that had preceded Trump's election had all disappeared into some vast sinkhole.

Where, then, are we to turn for counsel? For my money, Charles Blow is no more reliable as a guide to the past or the future than is Donald Trump himself. Much the same could be said of most other newspaper columnists, talking heads, and online commentators. As for politicians of either party, they have as a class long since forfeited any right to expect a respectful hearing.

God knows Americans today do not lack for information or opinion. On screens, over the airways, and in print, the voices competing for our attention create a relentless cacophony. Yet the correlation between insight and noise is discouragingly low.

What would Carl Becker make of our predicament? He would, I think, see it as an opportunity to "enlarge and enrich the specious present" by recasting and reinvigorating history. Yet doing so, he would insist, requires taking seriously the complaints that led our latter-day Mr. Everyman to throw himself into the arms of Donald Trump in the first place. Doing *that* implies a willingness to engage with ordinary Americans on a respectful basis.

Unlike President Trump, I do not pretend to speak for Mr. Everyman or for his female counterpart. Yet my sense is that many Americans have an inkling that history of late has played them for suckers. This is notably true with respect to the post–Cold War era, in which the glories of openness, diversity, and neoliberal economics, of advanced technology and unparalleled US military power all promised in combination to produce something like a new utopia in which Americans would indisputably enjoy a privileged status globally.

In almost every respect, those expectations remain painfully unfulfilled. The history that "served for the time being" and was endlessly reiterated during the presidencies of Bush 41, Clinton, Bush 43, and Obama no longer serves. It has yielded a mess of pottage: grotesque inequality, worrisome insecurity, moral confusion, an epidemic of self-destructive behavior, endless wars, and basic institutions that work poorly if at all. Nor is it just WHAMs who have suffered the consequences. The history with which Americans are familiar cannot explain this outcome.

Alas, little reason exists to expect Becker's successors in the guild of professional historians to join with ordinary Americans in formulating an explanation. Few academic historians today see Mr. Everyman as a worthy interlocutor. Rather than berating him for not reading their books, they ignore him. Their preference is to address one another.

By and large, he returns the favor, endorsing the self-marginalization of the contemporary historical profession. Contrast the influence wielded by prominent historians in Becker's day—during the first third of the twentieth century, they included, along with Becker, such formidables as Henry Adams, Charles and Mary Beard, Alfred Thayer Mahan, and Frederick Jackson Turner—with the role played by historians today. The issue here is not erudition, which today's scholars possess in abundance, but impact. On that score, the disparity between then and now is immense.

In effect, professional historians have ceded the field to a new group of bards and minstrels. So the bestselling "historian" in the United States today is Bill O'Reilly, whose books routinely sell more than a million copies each. Were Donald Trump given to reading books, he would likely find O'Reilly's both accessible and agreeable. But O'Reilly is in the entertainment business. He has neither any interest nor the genuine ability to create what Becker called "history that does work in the world."

Still, history itself works in mysterious ways known only to God or to Providence. Only after the fact do its purposes become evident. It may yet surprise us.

Owing his election in large part to my fellow WHAMs, Donald Trump is now expected to repay that support by putting things right. Yet as events make it apparent that Trump is no more able to run a government than Bill O'Reilly is able to write history, they may well decide that he is not their friend after all. With that, their patience is likely to run short. It is hardly implausible that Trump's assigned role in history will be once and for all to ring down the curtain on our specious present, demonstrating definitively just how bankrupt all the triumphalist hokum of the past quarter-century—the history that served "for the time being"—has become.

When that happens, when promises of American greatness restored prove empty, there will be hell to pay. Joe Doakes, John Q. Public, and the man in the street will be even more pissed. Should that moment arrive, historians would do well to listen seriously to what Mr. Everyman has to say.

20

The Age of Great Expectations

(2017)

The fall of the Berlin Wall in October 1989 abruptly ended one historical era and inaugurated another. So, too, did the outcome of last year's US presidential election. What are we to make of the interval between those two watershed moments? Answering that question is essential to understanding how Donald Trump became president and where his ascendency leaves us.

Hardly had this period commenced before observers fell into the habit of referring to it as the "post–Cold War" era. Now that it's over, a more descriptive name might be in order. My suggestion: America's Age of Great Expectations.

Forgive and Forget

The end of the Cold War caught the United States completely by surprise. During the 1980s, even with Mikhail Gorbachev running the Kremlin, few in Washington questioned the prevailing conviction that the Soviet-American rivalry was and would remain a defining feature of international politics more or less in perpetuity. Indeed, endorsing such an assumption was among the prerequisites for gaining entrée to official circles. Virtually no one in the American establishment gave serious thought to the here-today, gone-tomorrow possibility that the Soviet threat, the Soviet empire, and the Soviet Union itself might someday vanish. Washington had plans aplenty for what to do should a Third World War erupt, but none for what to do if the prospect of such a climactic conflict simply disappeared.

Still, without missing a beat, when the Berlin Wall fell and two years later the Soviet Union imploded, leading members of that establishment wasted no time in explaining the implications of developments they had totally failed to anticipate. With something close to unanimity, politicians and policy-oriented intellectuals interpreted the unification of Berlin and the ensuing collapse of communism as an all-American victory of cosmic proportions. "We" had won, "they" had lost—with that outcome vindicating everything the United States represented as the archetype of freedom.

From within the confines of that establishment, one rising young intellectual audaciously suggested that the "end of history" itself might be at hand, with the "sole superpower" left standing now perfectly positioned to determine the future of all humankind. In Washington, various powers-that-be considered this hypothesis and concluded that it sounded just about right. The future took on the appearance of a blank slate upon which Destiny itself was inviting Americans to inscribe their intentions.

American elites might, of course, have assigned a far different, less celebratory meaning to the passing of the Cold War. They might have seen the outcome as a moment that called for regret, repentance, and making amends.

After all, the competition between the United States and the Soviet Union, or more broadly between what was then called the Free World and the Communist bloc, had yielded a host of baleful effects. An arms race between two superpowers had created monstrous nuclear arsenals and, on multiple occasions, brought the planet precariously close to Armageddon. Two singularly inglorious wars had claimed the lives of many tens of thousands of American soldiers and literally millions of

Asians. One, on the Korean peninsula, had ended in an unsatisfactory draw; the other, in Southeast Asia, in catastrophic defeat. Proxy fights in Asia, Africa, Latin America, and the Middle East killed so many more and laid waste to whole countries. Cold War obsessions led Washington to overthrow democratic governments, connive in assassinations, make common cause with corrupt dictators, and turn a blind eye to genocidal violence. On the home front, hysteria compromised civil liberties and fostered a sprawling, intrusive, and unaccountable national security apparatus. Meanwhile, the military-industrial complex and its beneficiaries conspired to spend vast sums on weapons purchases that somehow never seemed adequate to the putative dangers at hand.

Rather than reflecting on such somber and sordid matters, however, the American political establishment together with ambitious members of the country's intelligentsia found it so much more expedient simply to move on. As they saw it, the *annus mirabilis* of 1989 wiped away the sins of former years. Eager to make a fresh start, Washington granted itself a plenary indulgence. After all, why contemplate past unpleasantness when a future so stunningly rich in promise now beckoned?

Three Big Ideas and a Dubious Corollary

Soon enough, that promise found concrete expression. In remarkably short order, three themes emerged to define the new American age. Informing each of them was a sense of exuberant anticipation toward an era of almost unimaginable expectations. The twentieth century was ending on a high note. For the planet as a whole, but especially for the United States, great things lay ahead.

Focused on the world economy, the first of those themes emphasized the transformative potential of turbocharged globalization led by US-based financial institutions and transnational corporations. An "open world" would facilitate the movement of goods, capital, ideas, and people and thereby create wealth on an unprecedented scale. In the process, the rules governing American-style corporate capitalism would come to prevail everywhere on the planet. Everyone would benefit, but especially Americans who would continue to enjoy more than their fair share of material abundance.

Focused on statecraft, the second theme spelled out the implications of an international order dominated as never before—not even in the heydays of the Roman and British Empires—by a single nation. With the passing of the Cold War, the United States now stood apart as both supreme power and irreplaceable global leader, its status guaranteed by its unstoppable military might.

In the editorial offices of the *Wall Street Journal*, the *Washington Post*, the *New Republic*, and the *Weekly Standard*, such "truths" achieved a self-evident status. Although more muted in their public pronouncements than Washington's reigning pundits, officials enjoying access to the Oval Office, the State Department's seventh floor, and the E-ring of the Pentagon generally agreed. The assertive exercise of (benign!) global hegemony seemingly held the key to ensuring that Americans would enjoy safety and security, both at home and abroad, now and in perpetuity.

The third theme was all about rethinking the concept of personal freedom as commonly understood and pursued by most Americans. During the protracted emergency of the Cold War, reaching an accommodation between freedom and the putative imperatives of national security had not come easily. Cold War–style patriotism seemingly prioritized the interests of the state at the expense of the individual. Yet even as thrillingly expressed by John F. Kennedy—"Ask not what your country can do for you, ask what you can do for your country"—this was never an easy sell, especially if it meant wading through rice paddies and getting shot at.

Once the Cold War ended, however, the tension between individual freedom and national security momentarily dissipated. Reigning conceptions of what freedom could or should entail underwent a radical transformation. Emphasizing the removal of restraints and inhibitions, the shift made itself felt everywhere, from patterns of consumption and modes of cultural expression to sexuality and the definition of the family. Norms that had prevailed for decades if not generations—marriage as a union between a man and a woman, gender identity as fixed at birth—became passé. The concept of a transcendent common good, which during the Cold War had taken a backseat to national security, now took a backseat to maximizing individual choice and autonomy.

Finally, as a complement to these themes, in the realm of governance, the end of the Cold War cemented the status of the president as quasi-deity. In the Age of Great Expectations, the myth of the president as a deliverer from (or, in the eyes of critics, the ultimate perpetrator of) evil flourished. In the solar system of American politics, the man in the White House increasingly became the sun around which everything seemed to orbit. By comparison, nothing else much mattered.

From one administration to the next, of course, presidential efforts to deliver Americans to the Promised Land regularly came up short. Even so, the political establishment and the establishment media collaborated in sustaining the pretense that out of the next endlessly hyped "race for the White House," another Roosevelt or Kennedy or Reagan would magically emerge to save the nation. From one election cycle to the next, these campaigns became longer and more expensive, drearier and yet ever more circus-like. No matter. During the Age of Great Expectations, the reflexive tendency to see the president as the ultimate guarantor of American abundance, security, and freedom remained sacrosanct.

Blindsided

Meanwhile, between promise and reality, a yawning gap began to appear. During the concluding decade of the twentieth century and the first decade-and-a-half of the twenty-first, Americans endured a seemingly endless series of crises. Individually, none of these merit comparison with, say, the Civil War or World War II. Yet never in US history has a sequence of events occurring in such close proximity subjected American institutions and the American people to greater stress.

During the decade between 1998 and 2008, they came on with startling regularity: one president impeached and his successor chosen by the direct intervention of the Supreme Court; a massive terrorist attack on American soil that killed thousands, traumatized the nation, and left senior officials bereft of their senses; a mindless, needless, and unsuccessful war of choice launched on the basis of false claims and outright lies; a natural disaster (exacerbated by engineering folly) that all but destroyed a major American city, after which government agencies mounted a belated and half-hearted response; and finally, the worst economic downturn since the Great Depression, bringing ruin to millions of families.

For the sake of completeness, we should append to this roster of seismic occurrences one additional event: Barack Obama's election as the nation's first black president. He arrived at the zenith of American political life as a seemingly messianic figure called upon not only to undo the damage wrought by his predecessor, George W. Bush, but also somehow to absolve the nation of its original sins of slavery and racism.

Yet during the Obama presidency race relations, in fact, deteriorated. Whether prompted by cynical political calculations or a crass desire to boost ratings, race baiters came out of the woodwork—one of them, of course, infamously birthered in Trump Tower in mid-Manhattan—and poured their poisons into the body politic. Even so, as the end of Obama's term approached, the cult of the presidency itself remained remarkably intact.

Individually, the impact of these various crises ranged from disconcerting to debilitating to horrifying. Yet to treat them separately is to overlook their collective implications, which the election of Donald Trump only now enables us to appreciate. It was not one president's dalliance with an intern *or* "hanging chads" *or* 9/11 *or* "Mission Accomplished" *or* the inundation of the Lower Ninth Ward *or* the collapse of Lehman Brothers *or* the absurd birther movement that undermined the Age of Great Expectations. It was the way all these events together exposed those expectations as radically suspect.

In effect, the various crises that punctuated the post–Cold War era called into question key themes to which a fevered American triumphalism had given rise. Globalization, militarized hegemony, and a more expansive definition of freedom, guided by enlightened presidents in tune with the times, *should* have provided Americans with all the blessings that were rightly theirs as a consequence of having prevailed in the Cold War. Instead, between 1989 and 2016, things kept happening that weren't supposed to happen. A future marketed as all but foreordained proved elusive, if not illusory. As actually experienced, the Age of Great Expectations became an Age of Unwelcome Surprises.

A Candidate for Decline

True, globalization created wealth on a vast scale, just not for ordinary Americans. The already well-to-do did splendidly, in some cases unbelievably so. But middle-class incomes stagnated and good jobs became increasingly hard to find or keep. By the election of 2016, the United States looked increasingly like a society divided between haves and have-nots, the affluent and the left behind, the 1 perecnt and everyone else. Prospective voters were noticing.

Meanwhile, policies inspired by Washington's soaring hegemonic ambitions produced remarkably few happy outcomes. With US forces continuously engaged in combat operations, peace all but vanished as a policy objective (or even a word in Washington's political lexicon). The acknowledged standing of the country's military as the world's best-trained, best-equipped, and best-led force coexisted uneasily with the fact that it proved unable to win. Instead, the national security establishment became conditioned to the idea of permanent war, high-ranking officials taking it for granted that ordinary citizens would simply accommodate themselves to this new reality. Yet it soon became apparent that, instead of giving ordinary Americans a sense of security, this new paradigm induced an acute sense of vulnerability, which left many susceptible to demagogic fear mongering.

As for the revised definition of freedom, with autonomy emerging as the national *summmum bonum*, it left some satisfied but others adrift. During the Age of Great Expectations, distinctions between citizen and consumer blurred. Shopping became tantamount to a civic obligation, essential to keeping the economy afloat. Yet if all the hoopla surrounding Black Friday and Cyber Monday represented a celebration of American freedom, its satisfactions were transitory at best, rarely extending beyond the due date printed on a credit card statement. Meanwhile, as digital connections displaced personal ones, relationships, like jobs, became more contingent and temporary. Loneliness emerged as an abiding affliction. Meanwhile, for all the talk of empowering the marginalized—people of color, women, gays—elites reaped the lion's share of the benefits while ordinary people were left to make do. The atmosphere was rife with hypocrisy and even a whiff of nihilism.

To these various contradictions, the establishment itself remained stubbornly oblivious, with the 2016 presidential candidacy of Hillary Clinton offering a case in point. As her long record in public life made abundantly clear, Clinton embodied the establishment in the Age of Great Expectations. She believed in globalization, in the indispensability of American leadership backed by military power, and in the post–Cold War cultural project. And she certainly believed in the presidency as the mechanism to translate aspirations into outcomes.

Such commonplace convictions of the era, along with her vanguard role in pressing for the empowerment of women, imparted to her run an air of inevitability. That she deserved to win appeared self-evident. It was, after all, her turn. Largely overlooked were signs that the abiding themes of the Age of Great Expectations no longer commanded automatic allegiance.

Gasping for Air

Senator Bernie Sanders offered one of those signs. That a past-his-prime, self-professed socialist from Vermont with a negligible record of legislative achievement and tenuous links to the Democratic Party might mount a serious challenge to Clinton seemed, on the face of it, absurd. Yet by zeroing in on unfairness and inequality as inevitable byproducts of globalization, Sanders struck a chord.

Knocked briefly off balance, Clinton responded by modifying certain of her longstanding positions. By backing away from free trade, the *ne plus ultra* of globalization, she managed, though not without difficulty, to defeat the Sanders insurgency. Even so, he, in effect, served as the canary in the establishment coal mine, signaling that the Age of Great Expectations might be running out of oxygen.

A parallel and far stranger insurgency was simultaneously wreaking havoc in the Republican Party. That a narcissistic political neophyte stood the slightest chance of capturing the GOP nomination seemed even more improbable than Sanders taking a nomination that appeared Clinton's by right.

Coarse, vulgar, unprincipled, uninformed, erratic, and with little regard for truth, Trump was *sui generis* among presidential candidates. Yet he possessed a singular gift: a knack for riling up those who nurse gripes and are keen to pin the blame on someone or something. In post–Cold War America, among the millions that Hillary Clinton was famously dismissing as "deplorables," gripes had been ripening like cheese in a hothouse.

Through whatever combination of intuition and malice afore-thought, Trump demonstrated a genius for motivating those deplor-ables. He pushed their buttons. They responded by turning out in droves to attend his rallies. There they listened to a message that they found compelling.

In Trump's pledge to "make America great again" his followers heard a promise to restore everything they believed had been taken from them in the Age of Great Expectations. Globalization was neither beneficial nor inevitable, the candidate insisted, and he vowed, once elected, to curb its effects along with the excesses of corporate capi-talism, thereby bringing back millions of lost jobs from overseas. He would, he swore, fund a massive infrastructure program, cut taxes, keep a lid on the national debt, and generally champion the cause of working stiffs. The many complications and contradictions inherent in these various prescriptions would, he assured his fans, give way to his business savvy.

In considering America's role in the post–Cold War world, Trump exhibited a similar impatience with the status quo. Rather than allow-ing armed conflicts to drag on forever, he promised to win them (put-ting to work his mastery of military affairs) or, if not, to quit and get out, pausing just long enough to claim as a sort of consolation prize whatever spoils might be lying loose on the battlefield. At the very least, he would prevent so-called allies from treating the United States like some patsy. Henceforth, nations benefitting from American pro-tection were going to foot their share of the bill. What all of this added up to may not have been clear, but it did suggest a sharp departure from the usual post-1989 formula for exercising global leadership.

No less important than Trump's semi-coherent critique of globalization and American globalism, however, was his success in channeling the discontent of all those who nursed an inchoate sense that post–Cold War freedoms might be working for some, but not for them.

Not that Trump had anything to say about whether freedom confers obligations, or whether conspicuous consumption might not actually hold the key to human happiness, or any of the various controversies related to gender, sexuality, and family. He was indifferent to all such matters. He was, however, distinctly able to offer his followers a grimly persuasive explanation for how America had gone off course and how the blessings of liberties to which they were entitled had been stolen. He did that by fingering as scapegoats Muslims, Mexicans, and others "not-like-me."

Trump's political strategy reduced to this: as president, he would overturn the conventions that had governed right thinking since the end of the Cold War. To the amazement of an establishment grown smug and lazy, his approach worked. Even while disregarding all received wisdom when it came to organizing and conducting a presidential campaign in the Age of Great Expectations, Trump won. He did so by enchanting the disenchanted, all those who had lost faith in the promises that sprang from the bosom of the elites who had been taken by surprise with the end of the Cold War.

Adrift Without a Compass

Within hours of Trump's election, among progressives, expressing fear and trepidation at the prospect of what he might actually do on assuming office became *de rigueur*. Yet those who had actually voted for Trump were also left wondering what to expect. Both camps assign him the status of a transformative historical figure. However, premonitions of incipient fascism and hopes that he will engineer a new American Golden Age are likely to prove similarly misplaced. To focus on the man himself rather than on the circumstances that produced him is to miss the significance of what has occurred.

Note, for example, that his mandate is almost entirely negative. It centers on rejection—of globalization, of counterproductive military meddling, and of the post–Cold War cultural project. Yet neither Trump nor any of his surrogates has offered a coherent alternative to the triad of themes providing the through line for the last quarter-century of American history. Apart from a lingering conviction that forceful—in The Donald's case, blustering—presidential leadership can somehow turn things around, "Trumpism" is a dog's breakfast.

In all likelihood, his presidency will prove less transformative than transitional. As a result, concerns about what he may do, however worrisome, matter less than the larger question of where we go from here. The principles that enjoyed favor following the Cold War have been found wanting. What should replace them?

Efforts to identify those principles should begin with an honest accounting of the age we are now leaving behind, the history that happened after "the end of history." That accounting should, in turn, allow room for regret, repentance, and making amends—the very critical appraisal that ought to have occurred at the end of the Cold War but was preempted when American elites succumbed to their bout of victory disease.

Don't expect Donald Trump to undertake any such appraisal. Nor will the establishment that candidate Trump so roundly denounced, but which President-elect Trump, at least in his senior national security appointments, now shows signs of accommodating. Those expecting Trump's election to inject courage into members of the political class or imagination into inside-the-Beltway "thought leaders" are in for a disappointment. So the principles we need—an approach to political economy providing sustainable and equitable prosperity; a foreign policy that discards militarism in favor of prudence and pragmatism; and an enriched, inclusive concept of freedom—will have to come from somewhere else.

"Where there is no vision," the Book of Proverbs tells us, "the people perish." In the present day, there is no vision to which Americans collectively adhere. For proof, we need look no further than the election of Donald Trump.

The Age of Great Expectations has ended, leaving behind an ominous void. Yet Trump's own inability to explain what should fill that great void provides neither excuse for inaction nor cause for despair. Instead, Trump himself makes manifest the need to reflect on the nation's recent past and to think deeply about its future.

A decade before the Cold War ended, writing in *democracy*, a short-lived journal devoted to "political renewal and radical change," the historian and social critic Christopher Lasch sketched out a set of principles that might lead us out of our current crisis. Lasch called for a politics based on "the nurture of the soil against the exploitation of resources, the family against the factory, the romantic vision of the individual against the technological vision, [and] localism over democratic centralism." Nearly a half-century later, as a place to begin, his prescription remains apt.

21

American Imperium

(2016)

Republicans and Democrats disagree today on many issues, but they are united in their resolve that the United States must remain the world's greatest military power. This bipartisan commitment to maintaining American supremacy has become a political signature of our times. In its most benign form, the consensus finds expression in extravagant and unremitting displays of affection for those who wear the uniform. Considerably less benign is a pronounced enthusiasm for putting our soldiers to work "keeping America safe." This tendency finds the United States more or less permanently engaged in hostilities abroad, even as presidents from both parties take turns reiterating the nation's enduring commitment to peace.

To be sure, this penchant for military activism attracts its share of critics. Yet dissent does not imply influence. The trivializing din of what passes for news drowns out the antiwar critique. One consequence of remaining perpetually at war is that the political landscape in America does not include a peace party. Nor, during presidential-election cycles, does that landscape accommodate a peace candidate of consequence. The campaign now in progress has proved no exception. Candidates calculate that tough talk wins votes. They are no more likely to question the fundamentals of US military policy than to express skepticism about the existence of a deity. Principled opposition to war ranks as a disqualifying condition, akin to having once belonged to the Communist Party or the KKK. The American political scene allows no room for the intellectual progeny of Jane Addams, Eugene V. Debs, Dorothy Day, or Martin Luther King Jr.

So, this November, voters will choose between rival species of hawks. Each of the finalists will insist that freedom's survival hinges on having in the Oval Office a president ready and willing to employ force, even as each will dodge any substantive assessment of what acting on that impulse has produced of late. In this sense, the outcome of the general election has already been decided. As regards so-called national security, victory is assured. The status quo will prevail, largely unexamined and almost entirely intact.

Citizens convinced that US national security policies are generally working well can therefore rest easy. Those not sharing that view, meanwhile, might wonder how it is that military policies that are manifestly defective—the ongoing accumulation of unwon wars providing but one measure—avoid serious scrutiny, with critics of those policies consigned to the political margins.

History provides at least a partial answer to this puzzle. The constructed image of the past to which most Americans habitually subscribe prevents them from seeing other possibilities, a condition for which historians themselves bear some responsibility. Far from encouraging Americans to think otherwise, these historians have effectively collaborated with those interests that are intent on suppressing any popular inclination toward critical reflection. This tunnel vision affirms certain propositions that are dear to American hearts, preeminently the conviction that history itself has summoned the United States to create a global order based on its own self-image. The resulting metanarrative unfolds as a drama in four acts: in the first, Americans respond to but then back away from history's charge; in the second, they indulge in an interval of adolescent folly, with dire consequences; in the third, they reach maturity and shoulder their providentially assigned responsibilities; in the fourth, after briefly straying off course, they stage an extraordinary recovery. When the final curtain in this drama falls, somewhere around 1989, the United States is the last superpower standing.

For Americans, the events that established the twentieth century as their century occurred in the military realm: two misleadingly named "world wars" separated by an "interwar period" during which the United States ostensibly took a timeout, followed by a so-called Cold War that culminated in decisive victory despite being inexplicably marred by Vietnam. To believe in the lessons of this melodrama—which warn above all against the dangers of isolationism and appeasement—is to accept that the American Century should last in perpetuity. Among Washington insiders, this view enjoys a standing comparable to belief in the Second Coming among devout Christians.

Unfortunately, in the United States these lessons retain little relevance. Whatever the defects of current US policy, isolationism and appeasement do not number among them. With its military active in more than 150 countries, the United States today finds itself, if anything, overextended. Our principal security challenges—the risks to the planet posed by climate change, the turmoil enveloping much of the Islamic world and now spilling into the West, China's emergence as a potential rival to which Americans have mortgaged their prosperity—will not yield to any solution found in the standard Pentagon repertoire. Yet when it comes to conjuring up alternatives, the militarized history to which Americans look for instruction has little to offer.

Prospects for thinking otherwise require an altogether different historical frame. Shuffling the deck—reimagining our military past—just might produce lessons that speak more directly to our present predicament.

Consider an alternative take on the twentieth-century US military experience, with a post-9/11 codicil included for good measure. Like the established narrative, this one also consists of four episodes: a Hundred Years' War for the Hemisphere, launched in 1898; a War for Pacific Dominion, initiated in 1898, petering out in the 1970s but today showing signs of reviving; a War for the West, already under way when the United States entered it in 1917 and destined to continue for seven more decades; and a War for the Greater Middle East, dating from 1980 and ongoing still with no end in sight.

In contrast to the more familiar four-part narrative, these several military endeavors bear no more than an incidental relationship to one another. Even so, they resemble one another in this important sense: each found expression as an expansive yet geographically specific military enterprise destined to extend across several decades. Each involved the use (or threatened use) of violence against an identifiable adversary or set of adversaries.

Yet for historians inclined to think otherwise, the analytically pertinent question is not against whom US forces fought, but why. It's what the United States was seeking to accomplish that matters most. Here, briefly, is a revised account of the wars defining the (extended) American Century, placing purpose or motive at the forefront.

The Hundred Years War for the Hemisphere

In February 1898, the battleship USS *Maine*, at anchor in Havana Harbor, blew up and sank, killing 266 American sailors. Widely viewed at the time as an act of state-sponsored terrorism, this incident initiated what soon became a War for the Hemisphere.

Two months later, vowing to deliver Cubans from oppressive colonial rule, the United States Congress declared war on Spain. Within weeks, however, the enterprise evolved into something quite different. After ousting Cuba's Spanish overseers, the United States disregarded the claims of nationalists calling for independence, subjected the island to several years of military rule, and then converted it into a protectorate that was allowed limited autonomy. Under the banner of anti-imperialism, a project aimed at creating an informal empire had commenced.

America's intervention in Cuba triggered a bout of unprecedented expansionism. By the end of 1898, US forces had also seized Puerto Rico, along with various properties in the Pacific. These actions lacked a coherent rationale until Theodore Roosevelt, elevated to the presidency in 1901, took it on himself to fill that void. An American-instigated faux revolution that culminated with a newly founded Republic of Panama signing over to the United States its patrimony—the route for a transisthmian canal—clarified the hierarchy of US interests. Much as concern about Persian Gulf oil later induced the United States to assume responsibility for policing that region, so concern for securing the as-yet-unopened canal induced it to police the Caribbean.

In 1904, Roosevelt's famous "corollary" to the Monroe Doctrine, claiming for the United States authority to exercise "international police power" in the face of "flagrant . . . wrongdoing or impotence," provided a template for further action. Soon thereafter, US forces began to intervene at will throughout the Caribbean and Central America, typically under the guise of protecting American lives and property but in fact to position the United States as regional suzerain. Within a decade, Haiti, the Dominican Republic, and Nicaragua joined Cuba and Panama on the roster of American protectorates. Only in Mexico, too large to occupy and too much in the grip of revolutionary upheaval to tame, did US military efforts to impose order come up short.

"Yankee imperialism" incurred costs, however, not least of all by undermining America's preferred self-image as benevolent and peace-loving, and therefore unlike any other great power in history. To reduce those costs, beginning in the 1920s successive administrations sought to lower the American military profile in the Caribbean basin. The United States was now content to allow local elites to govern, so long as they respected parameters established in Washington. Here was a workable formula for exercising indirect authority, one that prioritized order over democracy, social justice, and the rule of law.

By 1933, when Franklin Roosevelt inaugurated his Good Neighbor policy with the announcement that "the definite policy of the United States from now on is one opposed to armed intervention," the War for the Hemisphere seemed largely won. Yet neighborliness did not mean that US military forces were leaving the scene. As insurance against backsliding, Roosevelt left intact the US bases in Cuba and Puerto Rico, and continued to garrison Panama.

So rather than ending, the Hundred Years' War for the Hemisphere had merely gone on hiatus. In the 1950s, the conflict resumed and even intensified, with Washington now defining threats to its authority in ideological terms. Leftist radicals rather than feckless caudillos posed the problem. During President Dwight D. Eisenhower's first term, a CIA-engineered coup in Guatemala tacitly revoked FDR's nonintervention pledge and appeared to offer a novel way to enforce regional discipline without actually committing US troops. Under President John F. Kennedy, the CIA tried again, in Cuba. That was just for starters.

Between 1964 and 1994, US forces intervened in the Dominican Republic, Grenada, Panama, and Haiti, in most cases for the second or third time. Nicaragua and El Salvador also received sustained American attention. In the former, Washington employed methods that were indistinguishable from terrorism to undermine a regime it viewed as illegitimate. In the latter, it supported an ugly counterinsurgency campaign to prevent leftist guerrillas from overthrowing right-wing oligarchs. Only in the mid-1990s did the Hundred Years' War for the Hemisphere once more begin to subside. With the United States having forfeited its claim to the Panama Canal and with US-Cuban relations now normalized, it may have ended for good.

Today the United States enjoys unquestioned regional primacy, gained at a total cost of fewer than a thousand US combat fatalities, even counting the luckless sailors who went down with the *Maine*. More difficult to say with certainty is whether a century of interventionism facilitated or complicated US efforts to assert primacy in its "own back yard." Was coercion necessary? Or might patience have produced a similar outcome? Still, in the end, Washington got what it wanted. Given the gaping imbalance of power between the Colossus of the North and its neighbors, we may wonder whether the final outcome was ever in doubt.

The War for Pacific Dominion

During its outward thrust of 1898, the United States seized the entire Philippine archipelago, along with smaller bits of territory such as Guam, Wake, and the Hawaiian Islands. By annexing the Philippines, US authorities enlisted in a high-stakes competition to determine the fate of the Western Pacific, with all parties involved viewing China as the ultimate prize. Along with traditional heavyweights such as France, Great Britain, and Russia, the ranks of the competitors included two emerging powers. One was the United States, the other imperial Japan. Within two decades, thanks in large part to the preliminary round of the War for the West, the roster had thinned considerably, putting the two recent arrivals on the path for a showdown.

The War for Pacific Dominion confronted the US military with important preliminary tasks. Obliging Filipinos to submit to a new set of colonial masters entailed years of bitter fighting. More American soldiers died pacifying the Philippines between 1899 and 1902 than were to lose their lives during the entire Hundred Years' War for the Hemisphere. Yet even as US forces were struggling in the Philippines, orders from Washington sent them venturing more deeply into Asia. In 1900, several thousand American troops deployed to China to join a broad coalition (including Japan) assembled to put down the so-called Boxer Rebellion. Although the expedition had a nominally humanitarian purpose—Boxers were murdering Chinese Christians while laying siege to legations in Peking's diplomatic quarter—its real aim was to preserve the privileged status accorded foreigners in China. In that regard, it succeeded, thereby giving a victory to imperialism.

Through its participation in this brief campaign, the United States signaled its own interest in China. A pair of diplomatic communiqués known as the Open Door Notes codified Washington's position by specifying two non-negotiable demands: first, to preserve China's territorial integrity; and second, to guarantee equal opportunity for all the foreign powers engaged in exploiting that country. Both of these demands would eventually put the United States and Japan at cross-purposes. To substantiate its claims, the United States established a modest military presence in China. At Tientsin, two days' march from Peking, the US Army stationed an infantry regiment. The US Navy ramped up its patrols on the Yangtze River between Shanghai and Chungking—more or less the equivalent of Chinese gunboats today traversing the Mississippi River between New Orleans and Minneapolis.

United States and Japanese interests in China proved to be irreconcilable. In hindsight, a violent collision between these two rising powers appears almost unavoidable. As wide as the Pacific might be, it was not wide enough to accommodate the ambitions of both countries. Although a set of arms-limiting treaties negotiated at the Washington Naval Conference of 1921–22 put a momentary brake on the rush toward war, that pause could not withstand the crisis of the Great

Depression. Once Japanese forces invaded Manchuria in 1931 and established the puppet state of Manchukuo, the options available to the United States had reduced to two: either allow the Japanese a free hand in China or muster sufficient power to prevent them from having their way. By the 1930s, the War for Pacific Dominion had become a zero-sum game.

To recurring acts of Japanese aggression in China Washington responded with condemnation and, eventually, punishing economic sanctions. What the United States did not do, however, was reinforce its Pacific outposts to the point where they could withstand serious assault. Indeed, the Navy and War Departments all but conceded that the Philippines, impulsively absorbed back in the heady days of 1898, were essentially indefensible. At odds with Washington over China, Japanese leaders concluded that the survival of their empire hinged on defeating the United States in a direct military confrontation. They could see no alternative to the sword. Nor, barring an unexpected Japanese capitulation to its demands, could the United States. So the December 7, 1941, attack on Pearl Harbor came as a surprise only in the narrow sense that US commanders underestimated the prowess of Japan's aviators.

That said, the ensuing conflict was from the outset a huge mismatch. Only in willingness to die for their country did the Japanese prove equal to the Americans. By every other measure—military-age population, raw materials, industrial capacity, access to technology—they trailed badly. Allies exacerbated the disparity, since Japan fought virtually alone. Once FDR persuaded his countrymen to go all out to win—after Pearl Harbor, not a difficult sell—the war's eventual outcome was not in doubt. When the incineration of Hiroshima and Nagasaki ended the fighting, the issue of Pacific dominion appeared settled. Having brought their principal foe to its knees, the Americans were now in a position to reap the rewards.

In the event, things were to prove more complicated. Although the United States had thwarted Japan's efforts to control China, developments within China itself soon dashed American expectations of enjoying an advantageous position there. The United States "lost" it to communist revolutionaries who ousted the regime that Washington had supported against the Japanese. In an instant, China went from ally to antagonist.

So US forces remained in Japan, first as occupiers and then as guarantors of Japanese security (and as a check on any Japanese temptation to rearm). That possible threats to Japan were more than theoretical became evident in the summer of 1950, when war erupted on the nearby Korean peninsula. A mere five years after the War for Pacific Dominion had seemingly ended, G.I.'s embarked on a new round of fighting.

The experience proved an unhappy one. Egregious errors of judgment by the Americans drew China into the hostilities, making the war longer and more costly than it might otherwise have been. When the end finally came, it did so in the form of a painfully unsatisfactory draw. Yet with the defense of South Korea now added to Washington's list of obligations, US forces stayed on there as well.

In the eyes of US policymakers, Red China now stood as America's principal antagonist in the Asia-Pacific region. Viewing the region through rose-tinted glasses, Washington saw communism everywhere on the march. So in American eyes a doomed campaign by France to retain its colonies in Indochina became part of a much larger crusade against communism on behalf of freedom. When France pulled the plug in Vietnam, in 1954, the United States effectively stepped into its role. An effort extending across several administrations to erect in Southeast Asia a bulwark of anticommunism aligned with the United States exacted a terrible toll on all parties involved and produced only one thing of value: machinations undertaken by President Richard Nixon to extricate the United States from a mess of its own making persuaded him to reclassify China not as an ideological antagonist but as a geopolitical collaborator.

As a consequence, the rationale for waging war in Vietnam in the first place—resisting the onslaught of the Red hordes—also faded. With it, so too did any further impetus for US military action in the region. The War for Pacific Dominion quieted down appreciably, though it didn't quite end. With China now pouring its energies into internal development, Americans found plentiful opportunities to invest and indulge their insatiable appetite for consumption. True, a possible renewal of fighting in Korea remained a perpetual concern. But when your biggest worry is a small, impoverished nation-state that is unable even to feed itself, you're doing pretty well.

As far as the Pacific is concerned, Americans may end up viewing the last two decades of the twentieth century and the first decade of the twenty-first as a sort of golden interlude. The end of that period may now be approaching. Uncertainty about China's intentions as a bona fide superpower is spooking other nearby nations, not least of all Japan. That another round of competition for the Pacific now looms qualifies at the very least as a real possibility.

The War for the West

For the United States, the War for the West began in 1917, when President Woodrow Wilson persuaded Congress to enter a stalemated European conflict that had been underway since 1914. The proximate cause of the US decision to intervene was the resumption of German U-boat attacks on American shipping. To that point, US policy had been one of formal neutrality, a posture that had not prevented the United States from providing Germany's enemies, principally Great Britain and France, with substantial assistance, both material and financial. The Germans had reason to be miffed.

For the war's European participants, the issue at hand was as stark as it was straightforward. Through force of arms, Germany was bidding for continental primacy; through force of arms, Great Britain, France, and Russia were intent on thwarting that bid. To the extent that ideals figured among the stated war aims, they served as mere window dressing. Calculations related to *Machtpolitik* overrode all other considerations.

President Wilson purported to believe that America's entry into the war, ensuring Germany's defeat, would vanquish war itself, with the world made safe for democracy—an argument that he advanced with greater passion and eloquence than logic. Here was the cause for which Americans sent their young men to fight in Europe: the New World was going to redeem the Old.

It didn't work out that way. The doughboys made it to the fight, but belatedly. Even with 116,000 dead, their contribution to the final outcome fell short of being decisive. When the Germans eventually quit, they appealed for a Wilsonian "peace without victory." The Allies had other ideas. Their conception of peace was to render Germany too weak to pose any further danger. Meanwhile, Great Britain and France wasted little time claiming the spoils, most notably by carving up the Ottoman Empire and thereby laying the groundwork for what would eventually become the War for the Greater Middle East.

When Wilson's grandiose expectations of a world transformed came to naught, Americans concluded—not without cause—that throwing in with the Allies had been a huge mistake. What observers today mischaracterize as "isolationism" was a conviction, firmly held by many Americans during the 1920s and 1930s, that the United States should never again repeat that mistake.

According to myth, that conviction itself produced an even more terrible conflagration, the European conflict of 1939–45, which occurred (at least in part) because Americans had second thoughts about their participation in the war of 1914–18 and thereby shirked their duty to intervene. Yet this is the equivalent of blaming a drunken brawl between rival street gangs on members of Alcoholics Anonymous meeting in a nearby church basement.

Although the second European war of the twentieth century differed from its predecessor in many ways, it remained at root a contest to decide the balance of power. Once again, Germany, now governed by nihilistic criminals, was making a bid for primacy. This time around, the Allies had a weaker hand, and during the war's opening stages they played it poorly. Fortunately, Adolf Hitler came to their rescue by committing two unforced errors. Even though Joseph Stalin was earnestly seeking to avoid a military confrontation with Germany, Hitler removed that option by invading the Soviet Union in June 1941. Franklin Roosevelt had by then come to view the elimination of the Nazi menace as a necessity, but only when Hitler obligingly declared war on the United States, days after Pearl Harbor, did the American public rally behind that proposition.

In terms of the war's actual conduct, only the United States was in a position to exercise any meaningful choice, whereas Great Britain and the Soviet Union responded to the dictates of circumstance. Exercising that choice, the Americans left the Red Army to bear the burden of fighting. In a decision that qualifies as shrewd or perfidious depending on your point of view, the United States waited until the German army was already on the ropes in the east before opening up a real second front.

The upshot was that the Americans (with Anglo-Canadian and French assistance) liberated the western half of Europe while conceding the eastern half to Soviet control. In effect, the prerogative of determining Europe's fate thereby passed into non-European hands. Although out of courtesy US officials continued to indulge the pretense that London and Paris remained centers of global power, this was no longer actually the case. By 1945 the decisions that mattered were made in Washington and Moscow.

So rather than ending with Germany's second defeat, the War for the West simply entered a new phase. Within months, the Grand Alliance collapsed and the prospect of renewed hostilities loomed, with the United States and the Soviet Union each determined to exclude the other from Europe. During the decades-long armed standoff that ensued, both sides engaged in bluff and bluster, accumulated vast arsenals that included tens of thousands of nuclear weapons, and mounted impressive displays of military might, all for the professed purpose of preventing a "cold" war from turning "hot."

Germany remained a source of potential instability, because that divided country represented such a coveted (or feared) prize. Only after 1961 did a semblance of stability emerge, as the erection of the Berlin Wall reduced the urgency of the crisis by emphasizing that it was not going to end anytime soon. All parties concerned concluded that a Germany split in two was something they could live with.

By the 1960s, armed conflict (other than through gross miscalculation) appeared increasingly improbable. Each side devoted itself to consolidating its holdings while attempting to undermine the other side's hold on its allies, puppets, satellites, and fraternal partners. For national security elites, managing this competition held the promise of a bountiful source of permanent employment. When Mikhail Gorbachev decided, in the late 1980s, to call the whole thing off, President Ronald Reagan numbered among the few people in Washington willing to take the offer seriously. Still, in 1989 the Soviet-American rivalry ended. So, too, if less remarked on, did the larger struggle dating from 1914 within which the so-called Cold War had formed the final chapter.

In what seemed, misleadingly, to be the defining event of the age, the United States had prevailed. The West was now ours.

War for the Greater Middle East

Among the bequests that Europeans handed off to the United States as they wearied of exercising power, none can surpass the Greater Middle East in its problematic consequences. After the European war of 1939–45, the imperial overlords of the Islamic world, above all Great Britain, retreated. In a naïve act of monumental folly, the United States filled the vacuum left by their departure.

For Americans, the War for the Greater Middle East kicked off in 1980, when President Jimmy Carter designated the Persian Gulf a vital US national security interest. The Carter Doctrine, as the president's declaration came to be known, initiated the militarizing of America's Middle East policy, with next to no appreciation for what might follow.

During the successive "oil shocks" of the previous decade, Americans had made clear their unwillingness to tolerate any disruption to their oil-dependent lifestyle, and, in an immediate sense, the purpose of the War for the Greater Middle East was to prevent the recurrence of such disagreeable events. Yet in its actual implementation, the ensuing military project became much more than simply a war for oil.

In the decades since Carter promulgated his eponymous doctrine, the list of countries in the Islamic world that US forces have invaded, occupied, garrisoned, bombed, or raided, or where American soldiers have killed or been killed, has grown very long indeed. Since 1980, that list has included Iraq and Afghanistan, of course, but also Iran, Lebanon, Libya, Turkey, Kuwait, Saudi Arabia, Qatar, Bahrain, the United Arab Emirates, Jordan, Bosnia, Kosovo, Yemen, Sudan, Somalia, Pakistan, and Syria. Of late, several West African nations with very large or predominantly Muslim populations have come in for attention. At times, US objectives in the region have been specific and concrete. At other times, they have been broad and preposterously gauzy.

Overall, however, Washington has found reasons aplenty to keep the troops busy. They arrived variously promising to keep the peace, punish evildoers, liberate the oppressed, shield the innocent, feed the starving, avert genocide or ethnic cleansing, spread democracy, and advance the cause of women's rights. Rarely have the results met announced expectations.

In sharp contrast with the Hundred Years' War for the Hemisphere, US military efforts in the Greater Middle East have not contributed to regional stability. If anything, the reverse is true. Hopes of achieving primacy comparable to what the United States gained by 1945 in its War for Pacific Dominion remain unfulfilled and appear increasingly unrealistic. As for "winning," in the sense that the United States ultimately prevailed in the War for the West, the absence of evident progress in the theaters that have received the most US military attention gives little cause for optimism.

To be fair, US troops have labored under handicaps. Among the most severe has been the absence of a common agreement regarding the mission. Apart from the brief period of 2002–2006 when George W. Bush fancied that what ailed the Greater Middle East was the absence of liberal democracy (with his Freedom Agenda the needed antidote), policymakers have struggled to define the mission that American troops are expected to fulfill. The recurring inclination to define the core issue as "terrorism," with expectations that killing "terrorists" in sufficient numbers should put things right, exemplifies this difficulty. Reliance on such generic terms amounts to a de facto admission of ignorance.

When contemplating the world beyond their own borders, many Americans—especially those in the midst of campaigning for high office—reflexively adhere to a dichotomous teleology of good versus evil and us versus them. The very "otherness" of the Greater Middle East itself qualifies the region in the eyes of most Americans as historically and culturally alien. United States military policy there has been inconsistent, episodic, and almost entirely reactive, with Washington cobbling together a response to whatever happens to be the crisis of the moment. Expediency and opportunism have seldom translated into effectiveness.

Consider America's involvement in four successive Gulf Wars over the past thirty-five years. In Gulf War I, which began in 1980, when

Iraq invaded Iran, and lasted until 1988, the United States provided both covert and overt support to Saddam Hussein, even while secretly supplying arms to Iran. In Gulf War II, which began in 1990, when Iraq invaded Kuwait, the United States turned on Saddam. Although the campaign to oust his forces from Kuwait ended in apparent victory, Washington decided to keep US troops in the region to "contain" Iraq. Without attracting serious public attention, Gulf War II thereby continued through the 1990s. In Gulf War III, the events of 9/11 having rendered Saddam's continued survival intolerable, the United States in 2003 finished him off and set about creating a new political order more to Washington's liking. United States forces then spent years vainly trying to curb the anarchy created by the invasion and subsequent occupation of Iraq.

Unfortunately, the eventual withdrawal of US troops at the end of 2011 marked little more than a brief pause. Within three years, Gulf War IV had commenced. To prop up a weak Iraqi state now besieged by a new enemy, one whose very existence was a direct result of previous US intervention, the armed forces of the United States once more returned to the fight. Although the specifics varied, US military actions since 1980 in Islamic countries as far afield as Afghanistan, Lebanon, Libya, and Somalia have produced similar results—at best they have been ambiguous, more commonly disastrous.

As for the current crop of presidential candidates vowing to "smash the would-be caliphate" (Hillary Clinton), "carpet bomb them into oblivion" (Ted Cruz), and "bomb the hell out of the oilfields" (Donald Trump), Americans would do well to view such promises with skepticism. If US military power offers a solution to all that ails the Greater Middle East, then why hasn't the problem long since been solved?

Learning

Lessons drawn from this alternative narrative of twentieth-century US military history have no small relevance to the present day. Among other things, the narrative demonstrates that the bugaboos of isolationism and appeasement are pure inventions.

If isolationism defined US foreign policy during the 1920s and 1930s, someone forgot to let the American officer corps in on the secret. In 1924, for example, Brigadier General Douglas MacArthur was commanding US troops in the Philippines. Lieutenant Colonel George C. Marshall was serving in China as the commander of the 15th Infantry. Major George S. Patton was preparing to set sail for Hawaii and a stint as a staff officer at Schofield Barracks. Dwight D. Eisenhower's assignment in the Pacific still lay in the future; in 1924, Major Eisenhower's duty station was Panama. The indifference of the American people may have allowed that army to stagnate intellectually and materially. But those who served had by no means turned their backs on the world.

As for appeasement, hang that tag on Neville Chamberlain and Édouard Daladier, if you like. But as a description of US military policy over the past century, it does not apply. Since 1898, apart from taking an occasional breather, the United States has shown a strong and consistent preference for activism over restraint and for projecting power abroad rather than husbanding it for self-defense. Only on rare occasions have American soldiers and sailors had reason to complain of being underemployed. So although the British may have acquired their empire "in a fit of absence of mind," as apologists once claimed, the same cannot be said of Americans in the twentieth century. Not only in the Western Hemisphere but also in the Pacific and Europe, the United States achieved preeminence because it sought preeminence.

In the Greater Middle East, the site of our most recent war, a similar quest for preeminence has now foundered, with the time for acknowledging the improbability of it ever succeeding now at hand. Such an admission just might enable Americans to see how much the global landscape has changed since the United States made its dramatic leap into the ranks of great powers more than a century ago, as well as to extract insights of greater relevance than hoary old warnings about isolationism and appeasement.

The first insight pertains to military hegemony, which turns out to be less than a panacea. In the Western Hemisphere, for example, the undoubted military supremacy enjoyed by the United States is today largely beside the point. The prospect of hostile outside powers intruding in the Americas, which US policymakers once cited as a justification for armed intervention, has all but disappeared.

Yet when it comes to actually existing security concerns, conventional military power possesses limited utility. Whatever the merits of gunboat diplomacy as practiced by Teddy Roosevelt and Wilson or by Eisenhower and JFK, such methods won't stem the flow of drugs, weapons, dirty money, and desperate migrants passing back and forth across porous borders. Even ordinary Americans have begun to notice that the existing paradigm for managing hemispheric relations isn't working—hence the popular appeal of Donald Trump's promise to "build a wall" that would remove a host of problems with a single stroke. However bizarre and impractical, Trump's proposal implicitly acknowledges that with the Hundred Years' War for the Hemisphere now a thing of the past, fresh thinking is in order. The management of hemispheric relations requires a new paradigm, in which security is defined chiefly in economic rather than in military terms and policing is assigned to the purview of police agencies rather than to conventional armed forces. In short, it requires the radical demilitarization of US policy. In the Western Hemisphere, apart from protecting the United States itself from armed attack, the Pentagon needs to stand down.

The second insight is that before signing up to fight for something, we ought to make sure that something is worth fighting for. When the United States has disregarded this axiom, it has paid dearly. In this regard, the annexation of the Philippines, acquired in a fever of imperial enthusiasm at the very outset of the War for Pacific Dominion, was a blunder of the first order. When the fever broke, the United States found itself saddled with a distant overseas possession for which it had little use and which it could not properly defend. Americans may, if they wish, enshrine the ensuing saga of Bataan and Corregidor as glorious chapters in US military history. But pointless sacrifice comes closer to the truth.

By committing itself to the survival of South Vietnam, the United States replicated the error of its Philippine commitment. The fate of the Vietnamese south of the seventeenth parallel did not constitute a vital interest of the United States. Yet once we entered the war, a reluctance to admit error convinced successive administrations that there was no choice but to press on. A debacle of epic proportions ensued.

Jingoists keen to insert the United States today into minor territorial disputes between China and its neighbors should take note. Leave it to the likes of John Bolton, a senior official during the George W. Bush Administration, to advocate "risky brinkmanship" as the way to put China in its place. Others will ask how much value the United States should assign to the question of what flag flies over tiny island chains such as the Paracels and Spratlys. The answer, measured in American blood, amounts to milliliters.

During the twentieth century, achieving even transitory dominion in the Pacific came at a very high price. In three big fights, the United States came away with one win, one draw, and one defeat. Seeing that one win as a template for the future would be a serious mistake. Few if any of the advantages that enabled the United States to defeat Japan seventy years ago will pertain to a potential confrontation with China today. So unless Washington is prepared to pay an even higher price to maintain Pacific dominion, it may be time to define US objectives there in more modest terms.

A third insight encourages terminating obligations that have become redundant. Here the War for the West is particularly instructive. When that war abruptly ended in 1989, what had the United States won? As it turned out, less than met the eye. Although the war's conclusion found Europe "whole and free," as US officials incessantly proclaimed, the epicenter of global politics had by then moved elsewhere. The prize for which the United States had paid so dearly had in the interim lost much of its value.

Americans drawn to the allure of European culture, food, and fashion have yet to figure this out. Hence the far greater attention given to the occasional terrorist attack in Paris than to comparably deadly and more frequent incidents in places such as Nigeria or Egypt or Pakistan. Yet events in those countries are likely to have as much bearing, if not more, on the fate of the planet than anything occurring in the ninth or eleventh arrondissement.

Furthermore, "whole and free" has not translated into "reliable and effective." Visions of a United States of Europe partnering with the United States of America to advance common interests and common values have proved illusory. The European Union actually resembles a loose confederation, with little of the cohesion that the word "union" implies. Especially in matters related to security, the E.U. combines ineptitude with irresolution, a point made abundantly clear during the Balkan crises of the 1990s and reiterated since.

Granted, Americans rightly prefer a pacified Europe to a totalitarian one. Yet rather than an asset, Europe today has become a net liability, with NATO having evolved into a mechanism for indulging European dependency. The Western alliance that was forged to deal with the old Soviet threat has survived and indeed expanded ever eastward, having increased from sixteen members in 1990 to twenty-eight today. As the alliance enlarges, however, it sheds capability. Allowing their own armies to waste away, Europeans count on the United States to pick up the slack. In effect, NATO provides European nations an excuse to dodge their most fundamental responsibility: self-defense.

Nearly a century after Americans hailed the kaiser's abdication, more than seventy years after they celebrated Hitler's suicide, and almost thirty years after they cheered the fall of the Berlin Wall, a thoroughly pacified Europe cannot muster the wherewithal to deal even with modest threats such as post-Soviet Russia. For the United States to indulge this European inclination to outsource its own security might make sense if Europe itself still mattered as much as it did when the War for the West began. But it does not. Indeed, having on three occasions over the course of eight decades helped prevent Europe from being dominated by a single hostile power, the United States has more than fulfilled its obligation to defend Western civilization. Europe's problems need no longer be America's.

Finally, there is this old lesson, evident in each of the four wars that make up our alternative narrative but acutely present in the ongoing War for the Greater Middle East. That is the danger of allowing moral self-delusion to compromise political judgment. Americans have a notable penchant for seeing US troops as agents of all that is good and holy pitted against the forces of evil. On rare occasions, and even then only loosely, the depiction has fit. Far more frequently, this inclination has obscured both the moral implications of American actions and the political complexities underlying the conflict to which the United States has made itself a party.

Indulging the notion that we live in a black-and white world inevitably produces military policies that are both misguided and morally dubious. In the Greater Middle East, the notion has done just that, exacting costs that continue to mount daily as the United States embroils itself more deeply in problems to which our military power cannot provide an antidote. Perseverance is not the answer; it's the definition of insanity. Thinking otherwise would be a first step toward restoring sanity. Reconfiguring the past so as to better decipher its meaning offers a first step toward doing just that.

22

History That Makes Us Stupid

(2015)

"History is now and England," the expatriate poet T. S. Eliot wrote back in 1942. Not any more. Today, as far as Americans are concerned, the History That Matters centers on the recent past—the period from 1914 to 1989, to be exact—and on the United States. My aim in this brief essay is to explain why that's a problem.

In Donald Rumsfeld's famous taxonomy of *known knowns*, *unknown knowns*, and *unknown unknowns*, the History That Matters— hereinafter the HTM—occupies a special niche of its own. That niche consists of *mythic knowns*.

All history is selective and interpretive. In the HTM, mythic knowns determine the process of selection and interpretation. Chief among the mythic knowns to which most Americans (academic historians excepted) subscribe are these:

- that history itself has an identifiable shape, direction, and endpoint;
- that history is purposeful, tending toward the universal embrace of values indistinguishable from American values;

- that in the interest of propagating those values, history confers on the United States unique responsibilities and prerogatives.

None of these propositions qualifies as empirically true. Yet pretending that they are facilitates the exercise of power, which describes the HTM's underlying, even if unacknowledged, purpose.

By no means does the HTM purport to tell the whole story. Rather, it reduces the past to its pith or essence. Like the Ten Commandments, it identifies specific shalts and shalt nots. Like the Sermon on the Mount, it prescribes a code of conduct. In doing so, the HTM makes the past usable and, by extension, suitable for exploitation.

This usable past, laced throughout with mythic knowns, finds expression in a simple and straightforward narrative. This narrative depicts the twentieth century—nothing occurring earlier possessing real importance—as the first American Century, shaped throughout by the actions (or inaction) of the United States. Although incorporating setbacks and disappointments, the narrative culminates in triumph, which signifies vindication and offers reassurance. On balance, things are headed in the right direction.

In this sense, the HTM concerns itself as much with the present and future as it does with the past. Endlessly reiterated in political speech and reinforced by popular culture, its "lessons" prescribe what the United States—the indispensable nation—is called upon to do and what it must refrain from doing. Paying homage to the HTM affirms and renews its validity.

That history consists of a drama in three acts, each centered on a large-scale military undertaking. Cast in the principal roles are politicians, generals, bankers, press barons, industrialists, and functionaries of various types acting in the capacity of warlords. Serving as a chorus of sorts are millions of ordinary soldiers sent into harm's way. The HTM is nothing if not bloody.

The first act in this drama, initially known as the Great War, subsequently renamed World War I, occurred between 1914 and 1918. When this conflict began, Americans were having none of it. Yet after considerable hesitation, urged on by a president who believed it incumbent upon the New World to save the Old, they took the plunge. The United States went off to fight, Woodrow Wilson declared, "for the ultimate peace of the world and for the liberation of its peoples."[1] That this uplifting vision was considerably at odds with the actual war aims of the several belligerents on both sides did not trouble the president.

Alas, before permanent peace was fully achieved and the liberation of peoples well and truly won, Americans began having second thoughts and reneged on Wilson's vow. Disaster ensued. World War I thereby set the stage for another even more horrific conflict just two decades later, widely attributed to the refusal of Americans to fulfill the duties to which destiny had summoned them.

In the interim, a group of historians had mounted an energetic challenge to this interpretation of World War I as a worthy enterprise prematurely abandoned. In effect, they launched a preemptive attack on the HTM even before it had fully formed. These so-called revisionists argued forcefully that US entry into the Great War had been a huge blunder. This became a rare occasion when scholarship both reflected and reinforced the popular mood of the moment. When the moment passed, however, revisionism fell out of fashion and the HTM's onward march resumed.

As an episode in the History That Matters, therefore, World War I derives its significance not from the baleful events that actually occurred—devastation and slaughter, starvation and revolution—but from what came next. Act One represents missed opportunity, warning of the consequences likely to result should the United States fail to lead.

Act Two began in 1939 or 1938 or 1936 or 1933—the date dependent on the "lesson" to which you're calling attention—but ended definitively in 1945. As an episode in the HTM, World War II offered Americans a "second chance" to get it right and redeem themselves. Largely remembered today as a Great Crusade to defeat Nazi Germany, the war pitted good against evil, freedom against slavery, civilization against barbarism, and democracy against dictatorship.

Not merely in myth but also in fact, World War II was all of these things. But it was much more as well. It was a winner-take-all contest between rival claimants to Pacific dominion, between competing

---

1. Woodrow Wilson, "War Message to Congress" (April 2, 1917). U.S. 65th Cong., 1st Sess., Senate Document 5.

conceptions of how to govern peoples deemed inferior, and between two decidedly different but overlapping brands of totalitarianism, one of them aligned with the United States. One thing World War II was emphatically not: it was not a war to avert genocide. At the time, the fate of European Jews facing extermination at the hands of Nazi Germany figured as an afterthought. By contrast, exterminating the inhabitants of large German and Japanese cities through strategic bombing claimed considerable attention.

Per Rumsfeld, we might categorize these several realities as *discomfiting knowns*. Americans intent on imparting moral clarity to the History That Matters generally prefer to ignore them. Crediting Europe's liberation to the Anglo-American alliance—forged by Franklin and Winston singing "Onward Christian Soldiers" onboard HMS *Prince of Wales* off Argentina in August 1941—makes for a suitably uplifting story. Acknowledging the Red Army's far larger contribution to defeating the Nazi menace—with Eastern Europeans paying a steep price for their "liberation" at Soviet hands—only serves to complicate things. The HTM has a decided aversion to complications.

Lasting considerably longer than the first two acts combined along with the interval between them, the third segment in this drama ran from roughly 1947 to 1989.

Act Three consisted of many scenes, some of which resisted easy incorporation into the HTM. Despite having ostensibly absorbed all of the wisdom offered by Acts One and Two, the warlords in Washington seemed at times to take leave of their senses. Nuclear arsenals containing tens of thousands of weapons; partnerships with various unsavory despots; coups and assassination plots by the bushel; not to mention Korea, the Bay of Pigs, the Missile Crisis, and Vietnam; all capped off with the astonishing course change that found the Leader of the Free World exchanging pleasantries in Beijing with Red China's murderous Great Helmsman: each of these made it difficult to cast Act Three as a virtuous sequel to Act Two.

Historians took note. A new generation of revisionists challenged the official line depicting the Cold War as another round of good against evil, freedom against slavery, civilization against barbarism, and democracy against dictatorship. Among HTM proponents, now aligned with the warlords, these revisionists provoked outrage. At least briefly, the History That Matters seemed up for grabs. For a time—the last time—a debate among American historians actually drew the attention of the general public.

The end of the Cold War deflected this challenge, with the HTM now emerging in mature form. To wide applause, a political scientist announced that history itself had ended. That ending validated the mythic knowns that had underpinned the HTM from the outset. History's trajectory and purpose now appeared self-evident, as did America's extraordinary singularity.

In 1992, an unproven presidential candidate keen to distance himself from the controversies that had roiled Act Three reduced the History That Matters to a homely parable. "I am literally a child of the Cold War," Bill Clinton began.

> My parents' generation wanted little more than to return from a world war and resume the blessedly ordinary joys of home and family and work. Yet . . . history would not let them rest. Overnight, an expansionist Soviet Union summoned them into a new struggle. Fortunately, America had farsighted and courageous leaders [who] roused our battle-weary nation to the challenge. Under their leadership, we rebuilt Europe and Japan, organized a great military coalition of free nations, and defended our democratic principles against yet another totalitarian threat.

In declaring his fealty to the HTM, Clinton hoped thereby to establish his credibility as a would-be statesman. Yet implicit in his succinct and sanitized account was a handy template for dealing with challenges to come.

When those challenges duly appeared and with the History That Matters now sacrosanct, Clinton's successor reflexively reverted to that very same template. "We have seen their kind before," George W. Bush reassured his badly shaken countrymen after 9/11.

> They're the heirs of all the murderous ideologies of the 20th century. By sacrificing human life to serve their radical visions, by abandoning every value except the will to power, they follow in the path of fascism, Nazism and totalitarianism. And they will

follow that path all the way to where it ends in history's un-marked grave of discarded lies.

For President Bush, the History That Matters mandated a large-scale military enterprise comparable to those that had made the twentieth century an American Century. The Global War on Terror, in effect, constituted an addendum to the HTM—a fourth act in history's on-ward march. To emphasize the continuities, some observers even pro-posed styling the US response to 9/11 World War IV, with the Cold War retroactively designated World War III.

Alas, by whatever name World War IV has proven a bust. Fifteen years after it began, victory is nowhere in sight. Indeed, it seems fair to say that no plausible conception of how exactly the United States might achieve victory exists, either in Washington or anywhere else. Muddling through has become the order of the day. In that regard, the ongoing military campaign against the Islamic State offers Exhibit A. For Exhibit B, see Washington's flaccid support for the "moderate rebels" in Syria's civil war.

Meanwhile, when it comes to devising an alternative to muddling, the ostensibly usable past has become a straitjacket. Finding solace and reassurance in its familiarity, Americans remain firmly moored to the HTM, although Acts One and Three have taken a backseat to Act Two. So the debate over the Iran nuclear deal during the summer of 2015, for example, inspired innumerable references to Iran as Nazi Germany and Barack Obama as Neville Chamberlain, while warning of Israelis being marched off to death camps.

For their part, members of the historical profession tend to view the HTM as a caricature or cartoon. Yet their very disdain provides one explanation for why it persists. In effect, the myths sustaining this fatuous narrative go unchallenged.

The prevailing version of the usable past is worse than unusable. In the United States, it obstructs serious debate over the use and misuse of power. So no less than was the case in the 1920s/30s and 1960s/70s, the times call for revisionism. The task this time is to reframe the en-tire twentieth century, seeing it for the unmitigated disaster that it was and recognizing its profound moral ambiguity without, however, suc-cumbing to moral equivalence.

To cling to the History That Matters is to make real learning impossible. Yet critically engaging the HTM with vigor sufficient to affect public understanding of the past implies a revival of fields that have become decidedly unhip. The present-day historical profession does not prioritize political, diplomatic, and military themes. Whether for good or for ill, race, class, gender, and sexuality claim pride of place.

So among Americans at least, count on the HTM to endure—history that lets us feel good, even as it makes us stupid.

23

![black bar]

Always and Everywhere

(2013)

The abiding defect of US foreign policy? It's isolationism, my friend. Purporting to steer clear of war, isolationism fosters it. Isolationism impedes the spread of democracy. It inhibits trade and therefore prosperity. It allows evildoers to get away with murder. Isolationists prevent the United States from accomplishing its providentially assigned global mission. Wean the American people from their persistent inclination to look inward and who knows what wonders our leaders will accomplish.

The United States has been at war for well over a decade now, with US attacks and excursions in distant lands having become as commonplace as floods and forest fires. Yet during the recent debate over Syria, the absence of popular enthusiasm for opening up another active front evoked expressions of concern in Washington that Americans were once more turning their backs on the world.

As he was proclaiming the imperative of punishing the government of Bashar al-Assad, Secretary of State John Kerry also chided skeptical members of the Senate Foreign Relations Committee that "this is not the time for armchair isolationism." Commentators keen to have a go at the Syrian autocrat wasted little time in expanding on Kerry's theme.

Reflecting on "where isolationism leads," Jennifer Rubin, the reliably bellicose *Washington Post* columnist, was quick to chime in, denouncing those hesitant to initiate another war as "infantile." American isolationists, she insisted, were giving a green light to aggression. Any nation that counted on the United States for protection had now become a "sitting duck," with "Eastern Europe [and] neighbors of Venezuela and Israel" among those left exposed and vulnerable. News reports of Venezuelan troop movements threatening Brazil, Colombia, or Guyana were notably absent from the *Post* or any other media outlet, but no matter—you get the idea.

Military analyst Frederick Kagan was equally troubled. Also writing in the *Post*, he worried that "the isolationist narrative is rapidly becoming dominant." His preferred narrative emphasized the need for ever greater military exertions, with Syria just the place to launch a new campaign. For Bret Stephens, a columnist with the *Wall Street Journal*, the problem was the Republican Party. Where had the hawks gone? The Syria debate, he lamented, was "exposing the isolationist worm eating its way through the GOP apple."

The *Journal*'s op-ed page also gave the redoubtable Norman Podhoretz, not only still alive but vigorously kicking, a chance to vent. Unmasking President Obama as "a left-wing radical" intent on "reduc[ing] the country's power and influence," the unrepentant neoconservative accused the president of exploiting the "war-weariness of the American people and the rise of isolationist sentiment . . . on the left and right" to bring about "a greater diminution of American power than he probably envisaged even in his wildest radical dreams."

Obama escalated the war in Afghanistan, "got" Osama bin Laden, toppled one Arab dictator in Libya, and bashed and bombed targets in Somalia, Yemen, Pakistan, and elsewhere. Even so, it turns out he is actually *part of the isolationist conspiracy to destroy America!*

Over at the *New York Times*, similar concerns, even if less hysterically expressed, prevailed. According to *Times* columnist Roger Cohen, President Obama's reluctance to pull the trigger showed that he had "deferred to a growing isolationism." Bill Keller concurred. "America is again in a deep isolationist mood." In a column entitled

"Our New Isolationism," he decried "the fears and defeatist slogans of knee-jerk isolationism" that were impeding military action. (For Keller, the proper antidote to isolationism is amnesia. As he put it, "Getting Syria right starts with getting over Iraq.")

For his part, *Times* staff writer Sam Tanenhaus contributed a bizarre two-minute exercise in video agitprop—complete with faked scenes of the Japanese attacking Pearl Harbor—that slapped the isolationist label on anyone opposing entry into any war whatsoever, or tiring of a war gone awry, or proposing that America go it alone.

When the "New Isolationism" Was New

Most of this, of course, qualifies as overheated malarkey. As a characterization of US policy at any time in memory, isolationism is a fiction. Never really a tendency, it qualifies at most as a moment, referring to that period in the 1930s when large numbers of Americans balked at the prospect of entering another European war, the previous one having fallen well short of its "War To End All Wars" advance billing.

In fact, from the day of its founding down to the present, the United States has never turned its back on the world. Isolationism owes its storied history to its value as a rhetorical device, deployed to discredit anyone opposing an action or commitment (usually involving military forces) that others happen to favor. If I, a grandson of Lithuanian immigrants, favor deploying US forces to Lithuania to keep that NATO ally out of Vladimir Putin's clutches and you oppose that proposition, then you, sir or madam, are an "isolationist." Presumably, Jennifer Rubin will see things my way and lend her support to shoring up Lithuania's vulnerable frontiers.

For this very reason, the term isolationism is not likely to disappear from American political discourse anytime soon. It's too useful. Indeed, employ this verbal cudgel to castigate your opponents and your chances of gaining entrée to the nation's most prestigious publications improve appreciably. Warn about the revival of isolationism and your prospects of making the grade as a pundit or candidate for high office suddenly brighten. This is the great thing about using isolationists as punching bags: it makes actual thought unnecessary. All that's required to posture as a font of wisdom is the brainless recycling of clichés, half-truths, and bromides.

No publication is more likely to welcome those clichés, half-truths, and bromides than the *New York Times*. There, isolationism always looms remarkably large and is just around the corner.

In July 1942, the *New York Times Magazine* opened its pages to Vice President Henry A. Wallace, who sounded the alarm about the looming threat of what he styled a "new isolationism." This was in the midst of World War II, mind you.

After the previous world war, the vice president wrote, the United States had turned inward. As summer follows spring, "the choice led up to this present war." Repeat the error, Wallace warned, and "the price will be more terrible and will be paid much sooner." The world was changing and it was long past time for Americans to get with the program. "The airplane, the radio, and modern technology have bound the planet so closely together that what happens anywhere on the planet has a direct effect everywhere else." In a world that had "suddenly become so small," he continued, "we cannot afford to resume the role of hermit."

The implications for policy were self-evident: "This time, then, we have only one real choice. We must play a responsible part in the world—leading the way in world progress, fostering a healthy world trade, helping to protect the world's peace."

One month later, it was Archibald MacLeish's turn. On August 16, 1942, the *Times* magazine published a long essay of his under the title of—wouldn't you know it—"The New Isolationism." For readers in need of coaching, *Times* editors inserted this seal of approval before the text: "There is great pertinence in the following article."

A well-known poet, playwright, and literary gadfly, MacLeish was at the time serving as Librarian of Congress. From this bully pulpit, he offered the reassuring news that "isolationism in America is dead." Unfortunately, like zombies, "old isolationists never really die: they merely dig in their toes in a new position. And the new position, whatever name is given it, is isolation still."

Fortunately, the American people were having none of it. They had "recaptured the current of history and they propose to move with it; they don't mean to be denied." MacLeish's fellow citizens knew what he knew: "that there is a stirring in our world . . . , a forward thrusting and overflowing human hope of the human will which must be given a channel or it will dig a channel itself." In effect, MacLeish was daring the isolationists, in whatever guise, to stand in the way of this forward thrusting and overflowing hopefulness. Presumably, they would either drown or be crushed.

The end of World War II found the United States donning the mantle of global leadership, much as Wallace, MacLeish, and the *Times* had counseled. World peace did not ensue. Instead, a host of problems continued to afflict the planet, with isolationists time and again fingered as the culprits impeding their solution.

The Gift That Never Stops Giving

In June 1948, with a notable absence of creativity in drafting headlines, the *Times* once again found evidence of "the new isolationism." In an unsigned editorial, the paper charged that an American penchant for hermit-like behavior was "asserting itself again in a manner that is both distressing and baffling." With the Cold War fully joined and US forces occupying Germany, Japan, and other countries, the *Times* worried that some Republicans in Congress appeared reluctant to fund the Marshall Plan.

From their offices in Manhattan, members of the *Times* editorial board detected in some quarters "a homesickness for the old days." It was incumbent upon Americans to understand that "the time is past when we could protect ourselves easily behind our barriers behind the seas." History was summoning the United States to lead the world: "The very success of our democracy has now imposed duties upon us which we must fulfill if that democracy is to survive." Those entertaining contrary views, the *Times* huffed, "do not speak for the American people."

That very month, Joseph Stalin announced that the Soviet Union was blockading Berlin. The United States responded not by heading for the exits but by initiating a dramatic airlift. Oh, and Congress fully funded the Marshall Plan.

Barely a year later, in August 1949, with Stalin having just lifted the Berlin Blockade, *Times* columnist Arthur Krock discerned another urge to disengage. In a piece called "Chickens Usually Come Home," he cited congressional reservations about the recently promulgated Truman Doctrine as evidence of, yes, a "new isolationism." As it happened, Congress duly appropriated the money President Truman was requesting to support Greece and Turkey against the threat of communism—as it would support similar requests to throw arms and money at other trouble spots like French Indochina.

Even so, in November of that year, the *Times* magazine published yet another warning about "the challenge of a new isolationism." The author was Illinois Governor Adlai Stevenson, then positioning himself for a White House run. Like many other would-be candidates before and since, Stevenson took the preliminary step of signaling his opposition to the I-word.

World War II, he wrote, had "not only destroyed fascism abroad, but a lot of isolationist notions here at home." War and technological advance had "buried the whole ostrich of isolation." At least it should have. Unfortunately, some Republicans hadn't gotten the word. They were "internationally minded in principle but not in practice." Stevenson feared that when the chips were down such head-in-the-sand inclinations might come roaring back. This he was determined to resist. "The eagle, not the ostrich," he proclaimed, "is our national emblem."

In August 1957, the *Times* magazine was at it once again, opening its pages to another Illinois Democrat, Senator Paul Douglas, for an essay familiarly entitled "A New Isolationism—Ripples or Tide?" Douglas claimed that "a new tide of isolationism is rising in the country." United States forces remained in Germany and Japan, along with Korea, where they had recently fought a major war. Even so, the senator worried that "the internationalists are tiring rapidly now."

Americans needed to fortify themselves by heeding the message of the Gospels: "Let the spirit of the Galilean enter our worldly and power-obsessed hearts." In other words, the senator's prescription for American statecraft was an early version of "What Would Jesus Do?" Was Jesus Christ an advocate of American global leadership? Senator Douglas apparently thought so.

Then came Vietnam. By May 1970, even *Times* men were showing a little of that fatigue. That month, star columnist James Reston pointed (yet again) to the "new isolationism." Yet in contrast to the paper's scribblings on the subject over the previous three decades, Reston didn't decry it as entirely irrational. The war had proven to be a bummer and "the longer it goes on," he wrote, "the harder it will be to get public support for American intervention." Washington, in other words, needed to end its misguided war if it had any hopes of repositioning itself to start the next one.

A Concept Growing Long in the Tooth

By 1980, the *Times* showed signs of recovering from its brief Vietnam funk. In a review of Norman Podhoretz's *The Present Danger*, for example, the noted critic Anatole Broyard extolled the author's argument as "dispassionate," "temperate," and "almost commonsensical."

The actual text was none of those things. What the pugnacious Podhoretz called—get ready for it—"the new isolationism" was, in his words, "hard to distinguish from simple anti-Americanism." Isolationists—anyone who had opposed the Vietnam War on whatever grounds—believed that the United States was "a force for evil, a menace, a terror." Podhoretz detected a "psychological connection" between "anti-Americanism, isolationism, and the tendency to explain away or even apologize for anything the Soviet Union does, no matter how menacing." It wasn't bad enough that isolationists hated their country; they were, it seems, commie symps to boot.

Fast forward a decade, and—less than three months after US troops invaded Panama—*Times* columnist Flora Lewis sensed a resurgence of you-know-what. In a February 1990 column, she described "a convergence of right and left" with both sides "arguing with increasing intensity that it's time for the U.S. to get off the world." Right-wingers saw the world as too nasty to save; left-wingers saw the United States as too nasty to save the world. "Both," she concluded (of course), were "moving toward a new isolationism."

Five months later, Saddam Hussein sent his troops into Kuwait. Instead of getting off the world, President George H. W. Bush deployed US combat forces to defend Saudi Arabia. For Joshua Muravchik, however, merely defending that oil-rich kingdom wasn't nearly good enough. Indeed, here was a prime example of the "New Isolationism, Same Old Mistake," as his *Times* op-ed was entitled.

The mistake was to flinch from instantly ejecting Saddam's forces. Although opponents of a war against Iraq did not "see themselves as isolationists, but as realists," he considered this a distinction without a difference. Muravchik, who made his living churning out foreign policy analysis for various Washington think tanks, favored "the principle of investing America's power in the effort to fashion an environment congenial to our long-term safety." War, he firmly believed, offered the means to fashion that congenial environment. Should America fail to act, he warned, "our abdication will encourage such threats to grow."

Of course, the United States did act and the threats grew anyway. In and around the Middle East, the environment continued to be thoroughly uncongenial. Still, in the *Times'* world, the American penchant for doing too little rather than too much remained the eternal problem, eternally "new." An op-ed by up-and-coming journalist James Traub appearing in the *Times* in December 1991, just months after a half-million US troops had liberated Kuwait, was typical. Assessing the contemporary political scene, Traub detected "a new wave of isolationism gathering force." Traub was undoubtedly establishing his bona fides. (Soon after, he landed a job working for the paper.)

This time, according to Traub, the problem was the Democrats. No longer "the party of Wilson or of John F. Kennedy," Democrats, he lamented, "aspire[d] to be the party of middle-class frustrations—and if that entails turning your back on the world, so be it." The following year Democrats nominated as their presidential candidate Bill Clinton, who insisted that he would never under any circumstances turn his back on the world. Even so, no sooner did Clinton win than *Times* columnist Leslie Gelb was predicting that the new president would "fall into the trap of isolationism and policy passivity."

Get Me Rewrite!

Arthur Schlesinger defined the problem in broader terms. The famous historian and Democratic Party insider had weighed in early on the matter with a much-noted essay that appeared in the *Atlantic Monthly* back in 1952. He called it—you guessed it—"The New Isolationism."

In June 1994, more than forty years later, with the Cold War now finally won, Schlesinger was back for more with a *Times* op-ed that sounded the usual alarm. "The Cold War produced the illusion that traditional isolationism was dead and buried," he wrote, but of course—this is, after all, the *Times*—it was actually alive and kicking. The passing of the Cold War had "weakened the incentives to internationalism" and was giving isolationists a new opening, even though in "a world of law requiring enforcement," it was incumbent upon the United States to be the lead enforcer.

The warning resonated. Although the *Times* does not normally give commencement addresses much attention, it made an exception for Madeleine Albright's remarks to graduating seniors at Barnard College in May 1995. The US ambassador to the United Nations had detected what she called "a trend toward isolationism that is running stronger in America than at any time since the period between the two world wars," and the American people were giving in to the temptation "to pull the covers up over our heads and pretend we do not notice, do not care, and are unaffected by events overseas." In other circumstances in another place, it might have seemed an odd claim, given that the United States had just wrapped up armed interventions in Somalia and Haiti and was on the verge of initiating a bombing campaign in the Balkans.

Still, Schlesinger had Albright's back. The July/August 1995 issue of *Foreign Affairs* prominently featured an article of his entitled "Back to the Womb? Isolationism's Renewed Threat," with *Times* editors having published a CliffsNotes version on the op-ed page a month earlier. "The isolationist impulse has risen from the grave," Schlesinger announced, "and it has taken the new form of unilateralism."

His complaint was no longer that the United States hesitated to act, but that it did not act in concert with others. This "neo-isolationism," he warned, by introducing a new note into the tradition of isolationism-bashing for the first time in decades, "promises to prevent the most powerful nation on the planet from playing any role in enforcing the peace system." The isolationists were winning—this time through pure international belligerence. Yet "as we return to the womb," Schlesinger warned his fellow citizens, "we are surrendering a magnificent dream."

Other *Times* contributors shared Schlesinger's concern. On January 30, 1996, the columnist Russell Baker chipped in with a piece called "The New Isolationism." For those slow on the uptake, Jessica Mathews, then a fellow at the Council on Foreign Relations, affirmed Baker's concerns by publishing an identically titled column in the *Washington Post* a mere six days later. Mathews reported "troubling signs that the turning inward that many feared would follow the Cold War's end is indeed happening." With both the *Times* and the *Post* concurring, "the new isolationism" had seemingly reached pandemic proportions (as a title, if nothing else).

Did the "new" isolationism then pave the way for 9/11? Was al-Qaeda inspired by an unwillingness on Washington's part to insert itself into the Islamic world?

Unintended and unanticipated consequences stemming from prior US interventions might have seemed to offer a better explanation. But this much is certain: as far as the *Times* was concerned, even in the midst of George W. Bush's Global War on Terror, the threat of isolationism persisted.

In January 2004, David M. Malone, president of the International Peace Academy, worried in a *Times* op-ed "that the United States is retracting into itself"—this despite the fact that US forces were engaged in simultaneous wars in Iraq and Afghanistan. Among Americans, a concern about terrorism, he insisted, was breeding "a sense of self-obsession and indifference to the plight of others." "When Terrorists Win: Beware America's New Isolationism," blared the headline of Malone's not-so-new piece.

Actually, Americans should beware those who conjure up phony warnings of a "new isolationism" to advance a particular agenda. The essence of that agenda, whatever the particulars and however packaged, is this: if the United States just tries a little bit harder—one more intervention, one more shipment of arms to a beleaguered "ally," one more line drawn in the sand—we will finally turn the corner and the bright uplands of peace and freedom will come into view.

This is a delusion, of course. But if you write a piece exposing that delusion, don't bother submitting it to the *Times*.

24

![black bar divider]

The Ugly American Telegram

(2013)

On August 24, 1963, the American ambassador to South Vietnam, Henry Cabot Lodge, received a top-secret message with the bureaucratically anodyne title Deptel 243. But the content of the message was anything but routine. Hastily drafted and cleared over the course of a single day, with most of official Washington on vacation, Deptel 243, also known as the Hilsman telegram, signaled a major shift in American policy. A few days later Mr. Lodge remarked, "We are launched on a course from which there is no respectable turning back."

For years the witticism "Sink or swim with Ngo Dinh Diem"—the South Vietnamese president—had captured the essence of America's position regarding the Southeast Asian country. Nearly a decade before, the United States had helped install Mr. Diem in power and had supported him ever since. On a trip to Southeast Asia in 1961, Vice President Lyndon B. Johnson affirmed Mr. Diem's standing in Washington's eyes, hailing him as the "Churchill of Asia." He was our guy.

Now, according to Deptel 243, he wasn't.

Mr. Diem's principal offense was his refusal to do America's bidding. Fiercely anti-Communist, he was also fiercely nationalistic, and

250

an autocrat to boot. He resented outsiders telling him how to run a country that was his, not theirs.

Unfortunately, his insistence on exercising power outstripped his aptitude for doing so. Internal opponents besieged his regime. Insurgents supported by Communist North Vietnam controlled large swaths of the countryside. The Army of the Republic of Vietnam, or A.R.V.N., built under American tutelage, was neither militarily effective nor politically reliable.

Things came to a head in the spring of 1963. In major South Vietnamese cities, Buddhist monks mounted large anti-Diem protests, culminating in dramatic acts of self-immolation. The American government pressed President Diem to calm troubled waters. His government responded by roiling them further.

His influential sister-in-law Tran Le Xuan, commonly known as Madame Nhu, mocked the ritual suicides as "barbecues." Her husband, Mr. Diem's brother and right-hand man Ngo Dinh Nhu, used the protests as a pretext to launch a violent crackdown—which he then blamed on the army, angering A.R.V.N. generals.

Worse still were rumors about Mr. Nhu secretly approaching North Vietnam to explore a possible peace deal. Any such deal would strike at the foundations of America's Cold War policy, based on the premise that the United States presided over a bloc of freedom-loving peoples devoted to preventing the spread of tyranny. Allowing lesser nations to opt out by reconciling with tyrants would leave the self-anointed "leader of the free world" looking foolish.

This was the situation facing the Kennedy administration on Saturday, August 24, 1963, when the White House received word of an A.R.V.N. plot to overthrow Mr. Diem. In Saigon, embassy officials sought guidance.

Seizing the moment, three second-tier officials—Michael V. Forrestal, W. Averell Harriman, and Roger Hilsman—set out to provide it. Within hours, the United States government had thrown in with the coup plotters. Mr. Diem had become expendable.

"No one made a decision," the historian Howard Jones later observed. More or less in a fit of exasperation, senior policy makers "merely signed off on one that they all thought someone else had made."

Released at 9:36 p.m. that night, Deptel 243 instructed American officials in Saigon to notify A.R.V.N. leaders that providing further military or economic support had become "impossible" unless "steps are taken immediately" by the South Vietnamese president to remove Mr. Nhu—in essence offering Mr. Diem a chance to come around. If, however, "Diem remains obdurate and refuses, then we must face the possibility that Diem himself cannot be preserved."

Although providing Mr. Lodge with no specifics on how to make all this happen, the cable assured him that "we will back you to the hilt on actions you take to achieve our objectives." The ambassador had a free hand.

The August plot came to nothing, but the change in American policy proved irreversible. Assured of Washington's backing, disgruntled A.R.V.N. generals eventually got their act together. On November 1, 1963, they overthrew—and murdered—Mr. Diem and his brother. The prospect of a reinvigorated war effort beckoned.

This, of course, was not to be. If anything, conditions grew worse. Inept generals proved unable to govern. In Saigon, political chaos reigned. Away from the capital, prosecution of the war flagged. Mr. Diem's departure from the scene had opened a Pandora's box, setting in motion the sequence of events that culminated in 1965 with the disastrous decision to Americanize the Vietnam War.

Reflecting on American complicity in Mr. Diem's overthrow a quarter-century after the fact, the diplomat Richard C. Holbrooke, who was in South Vietnam at the time of Mr. Diem's overthrow, expressed hope that the mistakes had at least left policy makers a bit wiser. Perhaps, he speculated, they "learned to ask themselves more searching questions about what kind of regime might follow the incumbents; about the real extent of American influence, and of its ability to control events."

They hadn't then. They haven't since. In Washington, the conviction that removing obstreperous leaders, whether adversaries like Saddam Hussein or "friends" like Hosni Mubarak, facilitates Washington's ability to steer events remains the most persistent—and dangerous—of illusions. Yet time and again, the effect has been to let loose the forces of anarchy.

25

The Revisionist Imperative

(2012)

Not long before his untimely death, the historian Tony Judt observed that "for many American commentators and policymakers the message of the twentieth century is that war works." Judt might have gone even further. Well beyond the circle of experts and insiders, many ordinary Americans at least tacitly share that view.

This reading of the twentieth century has had profound implications for US policy in the twenty-first century. With the possible exception of Israel, the United States today is the only developed nation in which belief in war's efficacy continues to enjoy widespread acceptance. Others—the citizens of Great Britain and France, of Germany and Japan—took from the twentieth century a different lesson: war devastates. It impoverishes. It coarsens. Even when seemingly necessary or justified, it entails brutality, barbarism, and the killing of innocents. To choose war is to leap into the dark, entrusting the nation's fate to forces beyond human control.

Americans persist in believing otherwise. That belief manifests itself in a number of ways, not least in a pronounced willingness to invest in, maintain, and employ military power. (The belief that war works has *not* made soldiering per se a popular vocation; Americans prefer war as a spectator sport rather than as a participatory one).

Why do Americans cling to a belief in war that other advanced nations have long since abandoned? The simple answer is that for a time, war *did* work, or seemed to anyway– at least for the United States, even if not for others.

After all, the vast conflagration we remember not altogether appropriately as "World War II" vaulted the United States to the very summit of global power. The onset of that conflict found Americans still struggling to cope with a decade-long economic crisis. Recall that the unemployment rate in 1939 was several percentage points above the highest point it has reached during our own Great Recession. Notwithstanding the palliative effects of Franklin Roosevelt's New Deal, the long-term viability of liberal democratic capitalism remained an open question. Other ideological claimants, on the far left and far right, were advancing a strong case that *they* defined the future.

By 1945, when the conflict ended, almost all of that had changed. At home, war restored economic prosperity and set the stage for a decades-long boom. At least as important, the war reinvigorated confidence in American institutions. The challenges of war management had prodded Washington to get its act together. Prodigious feats of production in places like Cleveland, Detroit, and Pittsburgh had enabled the United States to raise vast air, sea, and land forces, which it then employed on a global scale with considerable effectiveness.

The American *way of war* implied a remarkable knack for doing big things in a big way, sweeping aside whatever obstacles might stand in the way. The bumptious wartime motto of the Army Corps of Engineers testified to this approach: "The difficult we do at once; the impossible takes a little longer." This wasn't empty bluster: the Manhattan Project, culminating in the development of the atomic bomb, testified to American technical prowess, but also implied broader claims of superiority. The United States was once again a country that did things — really big things — that no other country could do.

Meanwhile, with the gross domestic product *doubling* in barely half a decade, the American *way of life* once again signified levels of material abundance that made its citizens the envy of the world.

Thanks in considerable part to war, in other words, the United States had become an economic, technological, political, military, and cultural juggernaut without peer.

This was the America into which I was born in 1947. I breathed in the war's vapors, which lingered long after the war itself had ended. Both of my parents had served, my father a signalman on a destroyer escort in the Atlantic, my mother an army nurse in the Pacific. For them, as for countless others, the war shaped perceptions of past and present. It shaped as well their expectations for the future and their understanding of the dangers and opportunities that lay ahead.

How well I remember as a very young boy watching *Victory at Sea* on television, with that stirring score by Richard Rodgers, the documentary series narrated by Leonard Graves, who as the theme music faded began each episode by announcing in a stentorian voice, "And now . . ."

Here was history: gripping, heroic, immediate, and filled with high drama. Here too was the cornerstone of a grand narrative, constructed around the momentous events of 1939–45, with special emphasis on those in which the United States had played a notable hand. I couldn't get enough of it.

The history I absorbed then and carried into adulthood—the story that really mattered—divided neatly into three distinctive chapters. The tale commenced with a prelude recounting the events of a *prewar* era, a period of fecklessness and folly, even if for a youngster the details tended to be a bit vague. It concluded with what Americans were calling the *postwar* era, unfolding in the war's shadow, its course to be determined by how well the nation had absorbed the war's self-evident lessons.

But constituting the heart of the story was the war itself: a slumbering America brutally awakened, rising up in righteous anger, smiting evildoers, and thereby saving the world. One might say that the account I imbibed adhered closely to Winston Churchill's, albeit shorn of any British accent. Thanks in no small part to Churchill (though not he alone), the war became in Judt's words "a moral memory palace," a source of compelling, instantly recognizable parables. Compressed into just a word or two—Munich, Pearl Harbor, Normandy, Auschwitz, Yalta, Hiroshima—each parable expressed permanent, self-contained, and universally valid truths. Here was instruction that demanded careful attention.

With millions of others I accepted this instruction as unquestioningly as I accepted the proposition that major league baseball should consist of two leagues with eight teams each, none of them situated in cities west of the Missouri River. In the decades since, of course, baseball has changed dramatically—and not necessarily for the better, one might add. Meanwhile, our commonplace understanding of World War II has remained largely fixed. So too has the historical narrative within which that conflict occupies so prominent a place.

I submit that this poses a problem. For history to serve more than an ornamental function, it must speak to the present. The version of past formed by World War II and perpetuated since—the version persuading Americans that war works—has increasingly little to say. Yet even as the utility of that account dissipates, its grip on the American collective consciousness persists.

The times, therefore, are ripe for revisionism. Replacing the canonical account of the twentieth century with something more germane to the actually existing problems of the twenty-first century has become an imperative. And that requires rethinking the role of war in contemporary history. In any such revisionist project, military historians should play a prominent part. Let me emphasize two preliminary points as strongly as I can.

First, when I speak of history I am not referring to the ongoing scholarly conversation promoted by organizations such as the American Historical Association, a conversation that only obliquely and intermittently affects our civic life. I refer instead to history as a commonplace understanding of the past, fashioned less by academics than by politicians and purveyors of popular culture—an interpretation shaped in Washington and Hollywood rather than in Cambridge or Berkeley.

Second, I want to acknowledge that revisionism can be a morally hazardous undertaking. To overturn received wisdom is to create opportunities for mischief makers as well as for truth seekers. When the subject is World War II, the opportunities to make mischief are legion.

Yet the clout wielded by the Washington-Hollywood Axis of Illusions should not deter historians from accepting the revisionist challenge. Nor should the prospect of sharing a dais with someone (like me) who, while conceding that the so-called isolationists of the 1930s got some things wrong, will insist that they also got a whole lot right, much of it deserving respectful consideration even today. If Charles Beard may not merit three lusty cheers, he deserves at least one and perhaps two.

To illustrate the possibilities of revisionist inquiry, let me advance the following broad proposition for your consideration: For citizens of the twenty-first century, the twentieth century actually has two quite different stories to tell. The first story is familiar, although imperfectly understood. The second is little known, with large implications that have gone almost entirely ignored.

Enshrined today as a story of freedom besieged, but ultimately triumphant, the familiar story began back in 1914 and continued until its (apparently) definitive conclusion in 1989. Call this the Short Twentieth Century.

The less familiar alternative recounts a story in which freedom as such has figured only intermittently. It has centered on the question of who will dominate the region that we today call the Greater Middle East. Also kicking into high gear in 1914, this story continues to unfold in the present day, with no end in sight. Call this the story of the Long Twentieth Century.

The Short Twentieth Century, geographically centered on Eurasia, pitted great powers against one another. Although alignments shifted depending on circumstance, the roster of major players remained fairly constant. That roster consisted of Great Britain, France, Germany, Russia, and Japan, with the United States biding its time before eventually picking up most of the marbles.

From time to time, the Long Twentieth Century has also pitted great powers against one another. Yet that struggle has always had a second element. It has been a contest between outsiders and insiders. Western intruders with large ambitions, preeminently Great Britain until succeeded by the United States, pursued their dreams of empire or hegemony, typically cloaked in professions of uplift or "benevolent assimilation." The beneficiaries of imperial ministrations—from Arabs in North Africa to Moros in the southern Philippines—seldom proved grateful and frequently resisted.

The Short Twentieth Century had a moral and ideological aspect. If not especially evident at first, this became clearer over time. Viewed in retrospect, President Woodrow Wilson's effort to portray the cataclysm of 1914–18 as a struggle of democracy vs. militarism appears more than a little strained. The problem is not that Germany was innocent of the charge of militarism. It is, rather, that Western theories of democracy in those days left more than a little to be desired. After all, those who labored under the yoke of Western rule across large swathes of Africa, Asia, and the Middle East enjoyed precious little freedom.

Yet the advent of the Third German Reich produced a moral clarity hitherto more theoretical than real. The war against Nazi Germany *was* indubitably a war on behalf of liberal democracy against vile, murderous totalitarianism. Of course, sustaining that construct is easier if you keep one eye covered.

The central event of the Short Twentieth Century loses some of its moral luster once you acknowledge the following:

- concern for the fate of European Jewry exercised no discernible influence on Allied conduct of the war, Allied forces failing to make any serious attempt to avert, halt, or even retard the Final Solution;
- in both Europe and the Pacific, Allied strategic bombing campaigns killed noncombatants indiscriminately on a scale dwarfing, say, the atrocity of 9/11;
- the price of liberating western Europe included the enslavement of eastern Europeans, a direct consequence of allocating to Uncle Joe Stalin's Red Army primary responsibility for defeating the *Wehrmacht*;
- at war's end, the victors sanctioned campaigns of ethnic cleansing on a scale not seen before or since;
- on the American home front, the war fought for freedom and democracy left intact a well-entrenched system of de facto apartheid, racial equality not numbering among Franklin Roosevelt's Four Freedoms.

None of these disturbing facts, it need hardly be said, made any significant impact on the way World War II became enshrined in

American memory. I do not recall encountering any of them while watching *Victory at Sea*.

Yet they matter. They remind us that if the Short American Century was *sometimes* about values, it was *always* about politics and power. The Allies who joined together to defeat the Axis (a righteous cause) simultaneously jockeyed against one another for relative advantage. They also showed a willingness to employ means that were anything but righteous.

Whether out of conscience or expediency, the onset of the postwar era soon enough prompted Americans to rethink some of the morally dubious practices that made it necessary to sanitize the narrative of World War II. So after 1945, liberal democracies, the United States now in the vanguard, turned on the left-wing totalitarianism that had played such a crucial role in the fight against right-wing totalitarianism. Rather than a valued ally, Stalin became the new Hitler. However haltingly, the United States also began to amend the pronounced defects in its own approach to democratic practice. For example, the modern civil rights movement commenced.

Both of these facilitated efforts by Cold Warriors to infuse the anti-communist crusade with a moral clarity that in their minds approximated that of World War II. As with World War II so too with the Cold War: American leaders framed the ongoing contest in ideological rather than in geopolitical terms. The Free World ostensibly asked nothing more than that freedom itself should survive. This served to camouflage the real stakes: rival powers, previous wars having reduced their ranks to two, were vying for primacy in Eurasia.

This framing device had important implications when the era of bipolarity came to its abrupt and surprising end. I don't know about you, but recalling the events that unfolded between 1978 when John Paul II became pope and 1989 when the Berlin Wall came down still makes me dizzy. Right before our very eyes, history had seemingly handed down a conclusive verdict. The search for alternatives to liberal democratic capitalism had failed. That failure was definitive. The Short Twentieth Century was kaput. Born 1914. Died 1989. Finis.

During what turned out to be a very abbreviated post–Cold War era, American politicians and commentators vied with one another to construct a suitably grandiose conception of what the passing of the Short Twentieth Century signified. Whatever the specifics, the results were sure to be very good and very long lasting. As the "sole superpower," America stood in solitary splendor, recognized by all as the "indispensable nation," able to discern even as it simultaneously embodied "the right side of history."

My text encloses those phrases in quotes. But during the 1990s, ostensibly serious people making such claims did not intend to be ironic. They were merely reciting what had become the conventional wisdom. As well they might. Expanding on or embroidering such themes got your books on best-seller lists, your columns in all the best newspapers, and your smiling face on the Sunday talk shows.

My favorite artifact of this era remains the *New York Times Magazine* dated March 28, 1999. The cover story excerpted *The Lexus and the Olive Tree*, Tom Friedman's just-released celebration of globalization-as-Americanization. The cover itself purported to illustrate "What the World Needs Now." Alongside a photograph of a clenched fist adorned with the Stars and Stripes in brilliant red, white, and blue appeared this text: "For globalism to work, America can't be afraid to act like the almighty superpower that it is."

This was the *New York Times*, mind you, not the *Weekly Standard* or the editorial pages of the *Wall Street Journal*. More or less overlooked amidst all this triumphalism was the fact that the other twentieth century—the one in which promoting freedom had never figured as a priority—continued without interruption.

In Egypt, Saudi Arabia, the West Bank, Iraq, Iran, and Afghanistan, the collapse of communism did not qualify as a cosmic event. In such places, the competition to dominate Eurasia had been a sideshow, not the main event. So the *anus mirabilis* of 1989 notwithstanding, the Long Twentieth Century continued apace, drawing the almighty superpower ever more deeply into what was fast becoming one helluva mess.

For those with a taste for irony try this one: 1991 was the year in which the USSR finally gave up the ghost; it was also the year of the Persian Gulf War. One headache went away; another was about to become a migraine.

In making the case for war against Iraq, George H. W. Bush depicted Saddam Hussein as a Hitler-like menace—neither the first nor the last time the infamous führer would play a walk-on role in climes far removed from Germany. Indeed, Adolf Hitler has enjoyed an impressive second career as a sort of stunt-double for Middle Eastern villains.

Recall that back in 1956, to justify the reckless Anglo-French-Israeli assault on Egypt, Prime Minister Anthony Eden had fingered Colonel Nasser as another Hitler. Just a few months ago, Lindsey Graham, the reflexively hawkish Republican senator from South Carolina, likened Libya's Muammar Gaddafi to the Nazi leader. More recently still, the journalist Max Boot, who has made a career out of promoting wars, found Hitler's spirit lurking in present-day Iran.

However absurd such comparisons, the Nazi dictator's periodic guest appearances make an important point. They illustrate the persistent Western disinclination to see the struggle for the Greater Middle East on its own terms. Instead, to explain developments there, Western leaders import clichés or stock figures ripped from the more familiar and, from their perspective, more reassuring Short Twentieth Century. In doing so, they confuse themselves and us.

Alas, the elder Bush's effort to eliminate his Hitler came up short. Celebrated in its day as a great victory, Operation Desert Storm turned out to be anything but. The Persian Gulf War deserves to be remembered chiefly as a source of wildly inflated and pernicious illusions. More than any other event, this brief conflict persuaded Washington, now freed of constraints imposed by the Cold War, that the application of US military power held the key to reordering the Greater Middle East in ways likely to serve American interests. Here, it seemed, was evidence that war still worked and worked handsomely indeed.

Flexing US military muscle on the battlefields of Europe and the Pacific had once made America stronger and the world a better place. Why not count on American power to achieve similar results in the Persian Gulf and Central Asia? Why not take the means that had seemingly brought the Short Twentieth Century to such a happy conclusion and apply them to the problems of the Greater Middle East?

Throughout the 1990s, neoconservatives and other jingoists vigorously promoted this view. After 9/11, George W. Bush made it his own. So in explaining what had happened on September 11, 2001, and what needed to happen next, President Bush appropriated precepts from the Short Twentieth Century. It was going to be World War II and the Cold War all over again.

"We have seen their kind before," the president said of the terrorists who had assaulted America. The occasion was an address before a joint session of Congress barely more than a week after the attack on the World Trade Center. "They're the heirs of all the murderous ideologies of the 20th century," he continued.

> By sacrificing human life to serve their radical visions, by abandoning every value except the will to power, they follow in the path of fascism, Nazism and totalitarianism. And they will follow that path all the way to where it ends in history's unmarked grave of discarded lies.

Lest there be any doubt of where Bush was situating himself historically, he made a point of warmly welcoming the British prime minister to the proceedings. "America has no truer friend than Great Britain," the president declared, adding that "once again, we are joined together in a great cause." The implications were clear: the partnership of Tony and George revived the tradition of Winston and Franklin and of Maggie and Ron. Good once again stood firm against evil.

From his vantage point in the great beyond, Churchill must have lit a cigar and poured himself a brandy. Imagine his gratitude to President Bush for overlooking the role that he and his countrymen had played in bollixing up the Greater Middle East in the first place. In reality, during the Long Twentieth Century, the United States had only intermittently viewed Great Britain as a friend. "Perfidious Albion" had instead been a recurring source of rapacious tomfoolery—making a mess of things and then walking away once staying on had become inconvenient, the former British Mandate for Palestine offering one notable example.

Even so, many gullible (or cynical) observers endorsed President Bush's interpretation. September 2001 became December 1941 all over again. Once again World War II—unwelcome or inconvenient details excluded, as always—was pressed into service as "a moral memory palace." As the bellicose authors of a great agitprop classic published in 2004 put it, "There is no middle way for Americans: it is victory or holocaust." And so a new crusade—preposterously dubbed World War IV in some quarters—commenced.

We gather here more than a decade later. Although President Bush is gone, the war he declared continues. Once commonly referred to as the Global War on Terror (World War IV never really caught on), today we hardly know what to call the enterprise. Bush's attempt to graft the putative rationale for war during the Short Twentieth Century onto the new wars in the Greater Middle East didn't take. His Freedom Agenda withered and died. Even so, with Bush's successor closing down some fronts, ratcheting up others, and opening up new ones in places like Pakistan, Yemen, and Libya, the conflict itself persists. It's become the Long War—a collection of nominally related "overseas contingency operations," defined chiefly by their duration. Once begun, campaigns continue indefinitely.

What then of the American conviction, drawn from the remembered experience of the Short Twentieth Century, that "war works"? What evidence exists to suggest that this proposition retains any validity?

Others may differ, but I see little to indicate that our affinity for war is making the country more powerful or more prosperous. If anything, a plethora of socio-economic indicators suggest that the reverse is true. Whatever the United States is experiencing today, it's not a reprise of World War II. Newsmagazines may enthuse over today's Iraq and Afghanistan veterans as our "New Greatest Generation," but they overlook a rather large distinction. In contrast to the opportunities that awaited the previous "Greatest Generation" when its members came home, the wars fought by today's veterans point toward a bleaker rather than a brighter future.

History—the version that privileges the Short Twentieth Century above all other possibilities—makes it difficult to grasp the quandary in which we find ourselves as a consequence of our penchant for using force. After all, that account instructs us that "war works" or at least ought to if we simply try hard enough.

Yet it's just possible that a more expansive and less self-congratulatory accounting of the recent past—one that treats the Long Twentieth Century with the respect it deserves—could potentially provide a way out. To put it another way, we need to kick down the doors of the moral memory palace. We need to let in some fresh air.

I am not thereby suggesting that the classic lessons of the Short Twentieth Century have lost all relevance. Far from it. Yet it's past time to restock our storehouse of policy-relevant parables. This means according to Sykes-Picot, Hussein-McMahon, Deir Yassin, TPAJAX, Suez, Iran-Contra, and, yes, Operation Iraqi Freedom pedagogical weight equal to that habitually accorded to Munich, Pearl Harbor, and Auschwitz. We need a bit less of the Churchill who stood defiantly alone against Hitler and a bit more of the Churchill who, in seeking to police the Middle East on the cheap, proposed shortly after World War I "experimental work on gas bombs, especially mustard gas" as a way to "inflict punishment on recalcitrant natives."

Implicit in the standard American account of the Short Twentieth Century is the conviction that history is purposeful, with the vigorous deployment of US power the best way to hasten history's arrival at its intended destination. A sober appreciation of the surprises, miscalculations, and disappointments permeating the Long Twentieth Century, beginning with Great Britain's cavalier decision to dismember the Ottoman Empire and running all the way to George W. Bush's ill-fated attempt to transform the Greater Middle East, should temper any such expectations. What the Long Twentieth Century teaches above all is humility.

"Ideas are not mirrors, they are weapons." The words are George Santayana's, written back when the twentieth century was young. "[T]heir function," he continued, "is to prepare us to meet events, as future experience may unroll them. Those ideas that disappoint us are false ideas; those to which events are true are true themselves."

The ideas, assumptions, and expectations embedded in the received account of the Short Twentieth Century may not be entirely false. But they are supremely inadequate to the present.

As historians, our obligation to the students who pass through our classrooms includes this one: to provide them with a *usable* past, preparing them as best we can to meet events as they unfold. Measured by that standard, military historians are falling short.

William Faulkner famously said of the past, "It's not dead. It's not even past." As a general proposition, there's something to be said for that view. Not in this case, however. The past that Americans know is worse than dead; it's become a cause of self-inflicted wounds. As historians, we need to do better. The means to do so are readily at hand.

26

The End of (Military) History?

(2010)

"In watching the flow of events over the past decade or so, it is hard to avoid the feeling that something very fundamental has happened in world history." This sentiment, introducing the essay that made Francis Fukuyama a household name, commands renewed attention today, albeit from a different perspective.

Developments during the 1980s, above all the winding down of the Cold War, had convinced Fukuyama that the "end of history" was at hand. "The triumph of the West, of the Western *idea*," he wrote in 1989, "is evident . . . in the total exhaustion of viable systematic alternatives to Western liberalism."

Today the West no longer looks quite so triumphant. Yet events during the first decade of the present century have delivered history to another endpoint of sorts. Although Western liberalism may retain considerable appeal, the Western way of war has run its course.

For Fukuyama, history implied ideological competition, a contest pitting democratic capitalism against fascism and communism. When he wrote his famous essay, that contest was reaching an apparently definitive conclusion.

Yet from start to finish, military might had determined that competition's course as much as ideology. Throughout much of the twentieth century, great powers had vied with one another to create new, or more effective, instruments of coercion. Military innovation assumed many forms. Most obviously, there were the weapons: dreadnoughts and aircraft carriers, rockets and missiles, poison gas and atomic bombs—the list is a long one. In their effort to gain an edge, however, nations devoted equal attention to other factors: doctrine and organization, training systems and mobilization schemes, intelligence collection and war plans.

All of this furious activity, whether undertaken by France or Great Britain, Russia or Germany, Japan or the United States, derived from a common belief in the plausibility of victory. Expressed in the simplest terms, the Western military tradition could be reduced to this proposition: war remains a viable instrument of statecraft, the accoutrements of modernity serving, if anything, to enhance its utility.

Grand Illusions

That was theory. Reality, above all the two world wars of the last century, told a decidedly different story. Armed conflict in the industrial age reached new heights of lethality and destructiveness. Once begun, wars devoured everything, inflicting staggering material, psychological, and moral damage. Pain vastly exceeded gain. In that regard, the war of 1914–18 became emblematic: even the winners ended up losers. When fighting eventually stopped, the victors were left not to celebrate but to mourn. As a consequence, well before Fukuyama penned his essay, faith in war's problem-solving capacity had begun to erode. As early as 1945, among several great powers—thanks to war, now great in name only—that faith disappeared altogether.

Among nations classified as liberal democracies, only two resisted this trend. One was the United States, the sole major belligerent to emerge from the Second World War stronger, richer, and more confident. The second was Israel, created as a direct consequence of the horrors unleashed by that cataclysm. By the 1950s, both countries subscribed to this common conviction: national security (and, arguably, national survival) demanded unambiguous military superiority. In the lexicon of American and Israeli politics, "peace" was a code word. The essential prerequisite for peace was for any and all adversaries, real or potential, to accept a condition of permanent inferiority. In this regard, the two nations—not yet intimate allies—stood apart from the rest of the Western world.

So even as they professed their devotion to peace, civilian and military elites in the United States and Israel prepared obsessively for war. They saw no contradiction between rhetoric and reality.

Yet belief in the efficacy of military power almost inevitably breeds the temptation to put that power to work. "Peace through strength" easily enough becomes "peace through war." Israel succumbed to this temptation in 1967. For Israelis, the Six Day War proved a turning point. Plucky David defeated, and then became, Goliath. Even as the United States was flailing about in Vietnam, Israel had evidently succeeded in definitively mastering war.

A quarter-century later, US forces seemingly caught up. In 1991, Operation Desert Storm, George H. W. Bush's war against Iraqi dictator Saddam Hussein, showed that American troops, like Israeli soldiers, knew how to win quickly, cheaply, and humanely. Generals like H. Norman Schwarzkopf persuaded themselves that their brief desert campaign against Iraq had replicated—even eclipsed—the battlefield exploits of such famous Israeli warriors as Moshe Dayan and Yitzhak Rabin. Vietnam faded into irrelevance.

For both Israel and the United States, however, appearances proved deceptive. Apart from fostering grand illusions, the splendid wars of 1967 and 1991 decided little. In both cases, victory turned out to be more apparent than real. Worse, triumphalism fostered massive future miscalculation.

On the Golan Heights, in Gaza, and throughout the West Bank, proponents of a Greater Israel—disregarding Washington's objections—set out to assert permanent control over territory that Israel had seized. Yet "facts on the ground" created by successive waves of Jewish settlers did little to enhance Israeli security. They succeeded chiefly in shackling Israel to a rapidly growing and resentful Palestinian population that it could neither pacify nor assimilate.

In the Persian Gulf, the benefits reaped by the United States after 1991 likewise turned out to be ephemeral. Saddam Hussein survived and became in the eyes of successive American administrations an imminent threat to regional stability. This perception prompted (or provided a pretext for) a radical reorientation of strategy in Washington. No longer content to prevent an unfriendly outside power from controlling the oil-rich Persian Gulf, Washington now sought to dominate the entire Greater Middle East. Hegemony became the aim. Yet the United States proved no more successful than Israel in imposing its writ.

During the 1990s, the Pentagon embarked willy-nilly upon what became its own variant of a settlement policy. Yet US bases dotting the Islamic world and US forces operating in the region proved hardly more welcome than the Israeli settlements dotting the occupied territories and the soldiers of the Israeli Defense Forces (IDF) assigned to protect them. In both cases, presence provoked (or provided a pretext for) resistance. Just as Palestinians vented their anger at the Zionists in their midst, radical Islamists targeted Americans whom they regarded as neo-colonial infidels.

Stuck

No one doubted that Israelis (regionally) and Americans (globally) enjoyed unquestioned military dominance. Throughout Israel's near abroad, its tanks, fighter-bombers, and warships operated at will. So, too, did American tanks, fighter-bombers, and warships wherever they were sent.

So what? Events made it increasingly evident that military dominance did not translate into concrete political advantage. Rather than enhancing the prospects for peace, coercion produced ever more complications. No matter how badly battered and beaten, the "terrorists" (a catch-all term applied to anyone resisting Israeli or American authority) weren't intimidated, remained unrepentant, and kept coming back for more.

Israel ran smack into this problem during Operation Peace for Galilee, its 1982 intervention in Lebanon. United States forces encountered it a decade later during Operation Restore Hope, the West's gloriously titled foray into Somalia. Lebanon possessed a puny army;

Somalia had none at all. Rather than producing peace or restoring hope, however, both operations ended in frustration, embarrassment, and failure.

And those operations proved but harbingers of worse to come. By the 1980s, the IDF's glory days were past. Rather than lightning strikes deep into the enemy rear, the narrative of Israeli military history became a cheerless recital of dirty wars — unconventional conflicts against irregular forces yielding problematic results. The First Intifada (1987–93), the Second Intifada (2000–2005), a second Lebanon War (2006), and Operation Cast Lead, the notorious 2008–9 incursion into Gaza, all conformed to this pattern.

Meanwhile, the differential between Palestinian and Jewish Israeli birth rates emerged as a looming threat that military forces, unless employed pursuant to a policy of ethnic cleansing, could do little to redress. Even as the IDF tried repeatedly and futilely to bludgeon Hamas and Hezbollah into submission, demographic trends continued to suggest that within a generation a majority of the population within Israel and the occupied territories would be Arab.

Trailing a decade or so behind Israel, the United States military nonetheless succeeded in duplicating the IDF's experience. Moments of glory remained, but they would prove fleeting indeed. After 9/11, Washington's efforts to transform (or "liberate") the Greater Middle East kicked into high gear. In Afghanistan and Iraq, George W. Bush's Global War on Terror began impressively enough, as US forces operated with a speed and élan that had once been an Israeli trademark. Thanks to "shock and awe," Kabul fell, followed less than a year and a half later by Baghdad. As one senior Army general explained to Congress in 2004, the Pentagon had war all figured out:

> We are now able to create decision superiority that is enabled by networked systems, new sensors and command and control capabilities that are producing unprecedented near real time situational awareness, increased information availability, and an ability to deliver precision munitions throughout the breadth and depth of the battlespace. . . . Combined, these capabilities of the future networked force will leverage information dominance, speed and precision, and result in decision superiority.

The key phrase in this mass of techno-blather was the one that occurred twice: "decision superiority." At that moment, the officer corps,
like the Bush administration, was still convinced that it knew how
to win.

Such claims of success, however, proved obscenely premature.
Campaigns advertised as being wrapped up in weeks dragged on for
years, while American troops struggled with their own *intifadas*. When
it came to achieving decisions that actually stuck, the Pentagon (like
the IDF) remained clueless.

Winless

If any overarching conclusion emerges from the Afghan and Iraq Wars
(and from their Israeli equivalents), it's this: victory is a chimera.
Counting on today's enemy to yield in the face of superior force makes
about as much sense as buying lottery tickets to pay the mortgage: you
better be really lucky.

Meanwhile, as the US economy went into a tailspin, Americans
contemplated their equivalent of Israel's "demographic bomb"—a "fiscal bomb." Ingrained habits of profligacy, both individual and collective, held out the prospect of long-term stagnation: no growth, no
jobs, no fun. Out-of-control spending on endless wars exacerbated
that threat.

By 2007, the American officer corps itself gave up on victory, although without giving up on war. First in Iraq, then in Afghanistan,
priorities shifted. High-ranking generals shelved their expectations of
winning—at least as a Rabin or Schwarzkopf would have understood
that term. They sought instead to not lose. In Washington as in US
military command posts, the avoidance of outright defeat emerged as
the new gold standard of success.

As a consequence, US troops today sally forth from their base
camps not to defeat the enemy, but to "protect the people," consistent
with the latest doctrinal fashion. Meanwhile, tea-sipping US commanders cut deals with warlords and tribal chieftains in hopes of persuading guerrillas to lay down their arms.

A new conventional wisdom has taken hold, endorsed by everyone from new Afghan War commander General David Petraeus, the most celebrated soldier of this American age, to Barack Obama, commander-in-chief and Nobel Peace Prize laureate. For the conflicts in which the United States finds itself enmeshed, "military solutions" do not exist. As Petraeus himself has emphasized, "we can't kill our way out of" the fix we're in. In this way, he also pronounced a eulogy on the Western conception of warfare for the last two centuries.

The Unasked Question

What, then, are the implications of arriving at the end of Western military history? In his famous essay, Fukuyama cautioned against thinking that the end of ideological history heralded the arrival of global peace and harmony. Peoples and nations, he predicted, would still find plenty to squabble about.

With the end of military history, a similar expectation applies. Politically motivated violence will persist and may in specific instances even retain marginal utility. Yet the prospect of Big Wars solving Big Problems is probably gone for good. Certainly, no one in their right mind, Israeli or American, can believe that a continued resort to force will remedy whatever it is that fuels anti-Israeli or anti-American antagonism throughout much of the Islamic world. To expect persistence to produce something different or better is moonshine.

It remains to be seen whether Israel and the United States can come to terms with the end of military history. Other nations have long since done so, accommodating themselves to the changing rhythms of international politics. That they do so is evidence not of virtue, but of shrewdness. China, for example, shows little eagerness to disarm. Yet as Beijing expands its reach and influence, it emphasizes trade, investment, and development assistance. Meanwhile, the People's Liberation Army stays home. China has stolen a page from an old American playbook, having become today the preeminent practitioner of "dollar diplomacy."

The collapse of the Western military tradition confronts Israel with limited choices, none of them attractive. Given the history of Judaism and the history of Israel itself, the reluctance of Israeli Jews to entrust their safety and security to the good will of their neighbors or the warm regard of the international community is understandable. In a mere six decades, the Zionist project has produced a vibrant, flourishing state. Why put all that at risk? Although the demographic bomb may be ticking, no one really knows how much time remains on the clock. If Israelis are inclined to continue putting their trust in (American-supplied) Israeli arms while hoping for the best, who can blame them?

In theory, the United States, sharing none of Israel's demographic or geographic constraints and far more richly endowed, should enjoy far greater freedom of action. Unfortunately, Washington has a vested interest in preserving the status quo, no matter how much it costs or where it leads. For the military-industrial complex, there are contracts to win and buckets of money to be made. For those who dwell in the bowels of the national security state, there are prerogatives to protect. For elected officials, there are campaign contributors to satisfy. For appointed officials, civilian and military, there are ambitions to be pursued.

And always there is a chattering claque of militarists, calling for jihad and insisting on ever greater exertions, while remaining alert to any hint of backsliding. In Washington, members of this militarist camp, by no means coincidentally including many of the voices that most insistently defend Israeli bellicosity, tacitly collaborate in excluding or marginalizing views that they deem heretical. As a consequence, what passes for debate on matters relating to national security is a sham. Thus are we invited to believe, for example, that General Petraeus's appointment as the umpteenth US commander in Afghanistan constitutes a milestone on the way to ultimate success.

Nearly twenty years ago, a querulous Madeleine Albright demanded to know: "What's the point of having this superb military you're always talking about if we can't use it?" Today, an altogether different question deserves our attention: What's the point of constantly using our superb military if doing so doesn't actually work?

Washington's refusal to pose that question provides a measure of the corruption and dishonesty permeating our politics.

27

Twilight of the Republic?

(2006)

In his 2005 inaugural address, President George W. Bush declared the promulgation of freedom to be "the mission that created our nation." Fulfilling what he described as America's "great liberating tradition" now requires that the United States devote itself to "ending tyranny in our world." Many Americans find such sentiments compelling. Yet to credit the United States with possessing a "liberating tradition" is like saying that Hollywood has a "tradition of artistic excellence." The movie business is just that—a business. Its purpose is to make money. If once in a while the studios produce a film of aesthetic value, that may be cause for celebration, but profit, not revealing truth and beauty, defines the purpose of the enterprise. Something of the same can be said of the enterprise launched on July 4, 1776. The hard-headed lawyers, merchants, farmers, and slaveholding plantation owners gathered in Philadelphia that summer did not set out to create a church. They founded a republic. Their purpose was not to save mankind. It was to guarantee for people like themselves "life, liberty, and the pursuit of happiness."

In the years and decades that followed, the United States achieved remarkable success in making good on those aims. Yet never during America's rise to power did the United States exert itself to liberate others absent an overriding perception that the nation itself had large security or economic interests at stake. From time to time, although not nearly as frequently as we like to imagine, some of the world's unfortunates managed as a consequence to escape from bondage. The Civil War did produce emancipation. Yet to explain the conflagration of 1861–65 as a response to the plight of enslaved African Americans is to engage in vast oversimplification. Near the end of World War II, GIs did liberate the surviving inmates of Nazi death camps. Yet for those who directed the American war effort of 1941–45, the fate of European Jews never figured as more than an afterthought. Crediting America with a "great liberating tradition" sanitizes the past and obscures the actual motive behind American politics and US foreign policy. It transforms history into a morality tale and thereby provides a rationale for dodging serious moral analysis. To insist that the liberation of others has never been more than an ancillary motive of US policy is not cynicism; it is a prerequisite to self-understanding.

America Ascendant

If the young United States had a mission, it was not to liberate but to expand. "Of course," declared Theodore Roosevelt in 1899, as if explaining the self-evident to the obtuse, "our whole national history has been one of expansion." He spoke truthfully. The Founders viewed stasis as tantamount to suicide. From the outset, Americans evinced a compulsion to acquire territory and to extend their commercial reach abroad. How was expansion achieved? On this point, the historical record leaves no room for debate: by any means necessary. Depending on the circumstances, the United States relied on diplomacy, hard bargaining, bluster, chicanery, intimidation, or naked coercion. We infiltrated land belonging to our neighbors and then brazenly proclaimed it our own. We harassed, filibustered, and, when the situation called for it, launched full-scale invasions. We engaged in ethnic cleansing. At times, we insisted that treaties be considered sacrosanct. On other occasions, we blithely jettisoned agreements that had outlived their usefulness.

As the methods employed varied, so did the rationale offered to justify action. We touted our status as God's new Chosen People, erecting a "city upon a hill" destined to illuminate the world. We acted at the behest of providential guidance and responded to the urgings of our "manifest destiny." We declared our obligation to spread the gospel of Jesus Christ and to uplift Little Brown Brother. With Woodrow Wilson as our tutor, we shouldered our responsibility to "show the way to the nations of the world how they shall walk in the paths of liberty." Critics who derided these claims as bunkum—the young Lincoln during the war with Mexico, Mark Twain after 1898, Robert LaFollette in 1917—scored points but lost the argument.

Periodically revised and refurbished, the concept of American Exceptionalism (which implied exceptional American prerogatives) persisted. Meanwhile, when it came to action rather than talk, the architects of US policy, even the most idealistic, remained fixated on one overriding aim: enhancing American influence, wealth, and power. The narrative of American foreign relations from the earliest colonial encounters with Native Americans until, say, the end of the Cold War reveals a record that is neither uniquely high-minded nor uniquely hypocritical and exploitive. In this sense, the interpretations of America's past offered by George W. Bush and by Osama bin Laden fall equally wide of the mark. As a rising power, the United States adhered to the iron laws of international politics, which allow little space for altruism. If the tale contains a moral theme, that theme is necessarily one of ambiguity.

To be sure, America's ascent did not occur without missteps: opéra bouffe incursions into Canada; William McKinley's ill-advised annexation of the Philippines; complicity in China's "century of humiliation"; disastrous interwar economic policies that paved the way for the Depression; and Harry Truman's decision in 1950 to send US forces north of Korea's Thirty-Eighth Parallel, to name only some. Most of these mistakes Americans have long since shrugged off. A few, like Vietnam, we find impossible to forget even as we persistently disregard their implications. Yet however embarrassing, these missteps pale in significance when compared to the masterstrokes of American statecraft. In purchasing Louisiana from the French, Thomas Jefferson may have overstepped the bounds of his authority and in seizing California from Mexico, James Polk may have perpetrated a war of conquest, but their actions ensured that the United States would one day become a great power. To secure the isthmus of Panama, Theodore Roosevelt orchestrated an outrageous swindle. The result affirmed America's hemispheric dominion. In collaborating with Joseph Stalin, FDR made common cause with an indisputably evil figure. But in doing so he destroyed the murderous Hitler while simultaneously vaulting the United States to a position of unquestioned economic supremacy. A similar collaboration forged by Richard Nixon with the murderous Mao Zedong helped bring down the Soviet empire, thereby elevating the United States to the self-proclaimed position of sole superpower.

The achievements of these preeminent American statesmen derived not from their common devotion to a liberating tradition but from boldness unburdened by excessive scruples. Notwithstanding the high-sounding pronouncements that routinely emit from the White House and the State Department, the defining characteristic of US foreign policy is not idealism. It is pragmatism, sometimes laced with pragmatism's first cousin, opportunism. This remains true today even when President Bush has declared without qualification that "America's vital interests and our deepest beliefs are now one." In practice, this dictum allows the Bush administration to hector Iran or North Korea about their undemocratic ways while giving a pass to Egypt and Pakistan. It provides a rationale for military intervention in energy-rich Iraq, but finds no application in Darfur, Burma, and Zimbabwe. (On a flight, shortly after the US invasion of Iraq, I sat beside a retired Zimbabwean supreme court justice. Lamenting the dire situation in his country, he remarked, "Ah, if only we had oil. Then you would come rescue us.") Bush's critics charge him with abandoning principles that long governed American statecraft. A fairer judgment would credit him with having seized on 9/11 to reinterpret those principles, thereby claiming for the United States new prerogatives (such as waging preventive war) while shedding constraints (such as respect for the sensibilities of key allies) that had seemingly lost their utility. In this regard, the president was adhering to a well-established tradition. In the annals of history, the rise of the United States to the pinnacle of world power is an epic story worthy of Thucydides or Tacitus. It represents a stunning achievement. Yet those who see America's ascent as an affirmation of virtue are indulging in self-deluding sentimentality. Although sentimentality may sell greeting cards, it ill becomes a great nation that, having reached that pinnacle, now finds itself beset with challenges.

Land of the Free

For those fortunate enough to be Americans, this rise to global power yielded rich rewards. Expansion made the United States the land of opportunity. From expansion came abundance. Out of abundance came substantive freedom. Documents drafted in Philadelphia promised liberty. Making good on those promises required a political economy that facilitated the creation of wealth on an enormous scale. Writing over a century ago, Frederick Jackson Turner made the essential point. "Not the Constitution, but free land and an abundance of natural resources open to a fit people," he argued, made American democracy possible. A half-century later, the historian David Potter discovered a similar symbiosis between affluence and liberty. Potter credited "a politics of abundance" with creating the American way of life, "a politics which smiled both on those who valued abundance as a means to safeguard freedom and those who valued freedom as an aid in securing abundance." In short, American prosperity underwrote American freedom. The relationship between the two was reciprocal. Especially as the Industrial Revolution took hold, Americans looked to material abundance to ameliorate domestic tensions and anesthetize the unruly. Money became the preferred lubricant for keeping social and political friction within tolerable limits. As Reinhold Niebuhr once observed, "we seek a solution for practically every problem of life in quantitative terms," certain that more is better. Over time, prosperity also recast freedom, modifying the criteria for eligibility and broadening its claims. Running in tandem with the chronicle of American expansion abroad is a second narrative of expansion, relating to the transformation of freedom at home. It too is a story of epic achievement overlaid with ambiguity.

Who merits the privileges of citizenship? The answer prevailing in 1776—white male freeholders—was never satisfactory. By the stroke of a Jeffersonian pen, the Declaration of Independence had rendered such a definition untenable. Pressures to amend that restricted conception of citizenship emerged almost immediately. Until World War II, progress achieved on this front was real but fitful. During the years of the postwar economic boom, and especially during the 1960s, the floodgates opened. Barriers fell. The circle of freedom widened appreciably. The percentage of Americans marginalized as "second-class citizens" dwindled. Political credit for this achievement lies squarely with the Left. Abundance sustained in no small measure by a postwar presumption of American "global leadership" made possible the expansion of freedom at home. Possibility became reality thanks to progressive political activism. Pick the group: blacks, Jews, women, Asians, Hispanics, working stiffs, gays, the handicapped—in every case, the impetus for providing equal access to the rights guaranteed by the Constitution originated among radicals, pinks, liberals, and bleeding-heart fellow-travelers. When it comes to ensuring that every American should get a fair shake, the contribution of modern conservatism has been essentially nil. Had Martin Luther King in the 1950s and 1960s counted on William F. Buckley and the *National Review* to take up the fight against racial segregation, Jim Crow would still be alive and well.

Granting the traditionally marginalized access to freedom constitutes the central theme of American politics since World War II. It does not diminish the credit due to those who engineered this achievement to note that their success stemmed in part from the fact that the United States was simultaneously asserting its claim to unquestioned global leadership. The reformers who pushed and prodded for racial equality and women's rights did so in tacit alliance with the officials presiding over the postwar rehabilitation of Germany and Japan, with oil executives pressing to bring the Persian Gulf into America's sphere of influence, and with defense contractors promoting expensive new weapons programs. The creation of what became by the 1950s an informal American empire of global proportions was not a conspiracy designed to benefit the few. Postwar foreign policy derived its legitimacy from the widely shared perception that the exercise of power abroad was making possible a more perfect union at home. In this sense, a proper understanding of contemporary history requires that we acknowledge an ironic kinship linking Cold Warriors like Curtis LeMay to feminists like Betty Friedan. General LeMay's Strategic Air Command—both as manifestation of American might and as central component of the postwar military-industrial complex—helped to foster the conditions from which Friedan's National Organization for Women emerged.

Cultural Revolution

During the same postwar period, but especially since the 1960s, the nation's abiding cultural preoccupation focused on reassessing what freedom actually means. The political project was long the exclusive preserve of the Left (although belatedly endorsed by the Right). From the outset, the cultural project has been a collaborative one to which both Left and Right contributed, albeit in different ways. The very real success of the political project lies at the heart of the Bush administration's insistence that the United States today offers a proper model for other nations—notably those in the Islamic world—to follow. The largely catastrophic results of the cultural project belie that claim. The postwar political project sought to end discrimination. The postwar cultural project focused on dismantling constraints, especially on matters touching, however remotely, on sexuality and self-gratification. "Men are qualified for civil liberty," Edmund Burke once observed, "in exact proportion to their disposition to put moral chains upon their appetites." In the aftermath of World War II, Americans rejected that counsel and set out to throw off their manacles.

Freedom came increasingly to imply unfettered self-indulgence. The Left contributed to this effort by promoting a radical new ethic of human sexuality. Removing chains in this regard meant normalizing behavior once viewed as immoral, unnatural, or inconsistent with the common good. On the cutting edge of American culture, removing impediments to the satisfaction of sexual desire emerged as an imperative. Laws, traditions, and social arrangements impeding the fulfillment of this imperative became obsolete. As a direct consequence, homo-sexuality, abortion, divorce, out-of-wedlock pregnancies, and children raised in single-parent homes—all once viewed as problematic—lost much of their stigma. Pornography—including child pornography—reached epidemic proportions. Pop culture became a titillating arena for promoting sexual license and celebrating sexual perversity. And popular music became, in the words of cultural critic Martha Bayles, a "masturbatory fantasy." Some Americans lament this revolution. Many others view it as inevitable or necessary or positively swell. Regardless, the foreign policy implications of the sexual revolution loom large. The ideals that President Bush eagerly hopes to propagate throughout the Islamic world—those contained in Jefferson's Declaration and in the Bill of Rights—today come packaged with the vulgar exhibitionism of Madonna and the debased sensibility of Robert Mapplethorpe. Note, however, that the metamorphosis of freedom has had a second aspect, one that has proceeded in harmony with—and even reinforced—the sexual revolution. Here the effect has been to foster a radical new conception of freedom's economic dimension. Increasingly, during the decades of the postwar boom, citizens came to see personal liberty as linked inextricably to the accumulation of "stuff."

Enthusiasm for throwing off moral chains came from the Right. The forces of corporate capitalism relentlessly promoted the notion that liberty correlates with choice and that the key to human fulfillment (not to mention sexual allure and sexual opportunity) is to be found in conspicuous consumption—acquiring a bigger house, a fancier car, the latest fashions, the niftiest gadgets. By the end of the twentieth century, many Americans had concluded, in the words of the historian Gary Cross, that "to consume was to be free." The events of 9/11 did not dislodge that perception. In early 2006—with the nation locked in what President Bush insisted was an epic confrontation with "Islamofascism"—an article in the *New York Times Magazine* posed the question "Is Freedom Just Another Word for Many Things to Buy?" In the conduct their daily affairs, countless Americans, most of them oblivious to Bush's war, answer that question in the affirmative. Along the way, consumption eclipsed voting or military service as the nearest thing to an acknowledged civic obligation. If citizenship today endows "the sovereign shopper with the right to select from store shelves," Cross comments, it also imposes "the duty to spend for the 'good of the economy.'"

Americans once assessed the nation's economic health by tallying up the output of the nation's steel mills or the tons of bullion locked away in Fort Knox. Today, consumer demand has emerged as the favored metric of overall economic well-being. In recent years "Black Friday" has taken its place among notable dates on the national calendar—the willingness of consumers to open their pocketbooks on the day after Thanksgiving having become a key indicator of economic vigor. Woe betide the nation should holiday shoppers spend less this year than last.

American globalism did little to foster this radical change in American culture. But the cultural revolution—both the sexual liberation demanded by the Left and the conspicuous consumption promoted by the Right—massively complicates our relations with those beyond our borders, who see our reigning conceptions of freedom as shallow and corrosive.

Empire of Red Ink

Still, this consumer's paradise retains considerable appeal for outsiders looking in. The many millions from south of the border or across the seas seeking entry testify to this fact. In the eyes of the typical Third Worlder, to be American is to be rich, pampered, and profligate. Entrance into the United States implies the prospect of being well-fed, well-housed, and well-clothed—to walk where streets are paved with gold. But how real are our riches? In the recent book *Among Empires*, Charles Maier, professor of history at Harvard, has chronicled the shift from what he calls America's postwar Empire of Production, when we made the steel, the cars, and the TVs, to today's Empire of Consumption, when goods pour in from Japan and China. The implications of this shift for foreign policy are profound. If we are still paving our streets with gold, we're doing so with someone else's money. In paradise, it turns out, the books don't balance. The federal budget is perpetually in the red. The current account deficit mounts from one year to the next, now topping $800 billion per annum. The national debt is closing in on $9 trillion. The Republican-controlled Congress of the past decade has dealt with this troubling problem precisely as Congress did back when Democrats called the shots: it has routinely raised the ceiling to allow the debt to balloon ever upward.

Despite these alarming trends, we Americans refuse to live within our means. We have discarded old-fashioned notions of thrift, deferred gratification, and putting up for a rainy day. We have forgotten how to save. We won't trim entitlements. We adamantly ignore what President Bush himself refers to as our "addiction" to foreign oil. To sustain the Empire of Consumption we are acquiring a mountain of debt, increasingly owed to foreign countries. The unspoken assumption is that our credit line is endless and that the bills won't ever come due. Once upon a time, Americans would have dismissed such thinking as twaddle. No more. Having made a fetish of freedom-as-consumption, we have become beholden to others. Dependence, wrote Jefferson two centuries ago, "begets subservience and venality, suffocates the germ of virtue and prepares fit tools for the design of ambition." As our dependence has deepened, the autonomy that from 1776 through the 1950s ranked as the nation's greatest strategic asset has withered away. Although periodically bemoaning this slide toward dependence, the nation's political leaders have done little to restore our economic house to order. In practice, ensuring the uninterrupted flow of foreign oil and borrowing from abroad to feed the consumer's insatiable appetite for cheap imports have become categorical imperatives.

Back in 1992, when the immediate issue related to curbing greenhouse gases, President George H. W. Bush cut to the heart of the matter: "The American way of life is not up for negotiation." Compromise, accommodation, trimming back the expectations implied by that way of life—none of these are to be countenanced. Dependence has large foreign-policy consequences. It circumscribes freedom of action. A week after 9/11, Donald Rumsfeld spelled out the implications. In formulating a response to the terrorist attack, the United States had only two options. "We have a choice," Rumsfeld remarked, "either to change the way we live, which is unacceptable, or to change the way that they live, and we chose the latter."

The global "war on terror" represents the Bush administration's effort to do just that—to change the way that they live. "They," of course, are the 1.4 billion Muslims who inhabit an arc stretching from North Africa to Southeast Asia. The overarching strategic aim of that war is to eliminate the Islamist threat by pacifying the Islamic world, with particular attention given to the energy-rich Persian Gulf. Pacification implies not only bringing Muslims into compliance with American norms. It also requires the establishment of unassailable American hegemony, affirming the superiority of US power beyond the shadow of doubt and thereby deterring attempts to defy those norms. Hegemony means presence, evidenced by the proliferation of US military bases throughout strategically critical regions of the Islamic world. Seen in relation to our own history, the global "war on terror" signifies the latest phase in an expansionist project that is now three centuries old. This effort to pacify Islam has foundered in Iraq. The Bush administration's determination to change the way Iraqis live has landed us in a quagmire. Today the debate over how to salvage something positive from the Iraq debacle consumes the foreign-policy apparatus.

Just beyond lie concerns about how events in Iraq are affecting the overall "war on terror." Expressing confidence that all will come out well, President Bush insists that historians will eventually see the controversies surrounding his Iraq policy as little more than a comma. Rather than seeing Iraq as a comma, we ought to view it as a question mark. The question posed, incorporating but also transcending the larger "war on terror," is this: Are ongoing efforts to "change the way that they live" securing or further distorting the American way of life? To put it another way, will the further expansion of American dominion abroad enhance the freedom we profess to value? Or have we now reached a point where expansion merely postpones and even exacerbates an inevitable reckoning with the cultural and economic contradictions to which our pursuit of freedom has given rise?

If the survival of American freedom requires pacification of the Islamic world, as adherents of the old expansionist tradition believe, then this must be said: exertions made up to this point have been laughably inadequate. Changing the way they live presumes a seriousness hitherto lacking on the part of the American people or their elected representatives, including the president himself. If we intend to transform not only Iraq but also Syria, Iran, Pakistan, Egypt, and Saudi Arabia, prudence dictates that we stop kidding ourselves that the intended beneficiaries of our ministrations will welcome us with open arms.

Why bamboozle ourselves with claims of righteousness that few others believe? Better to acknowledge, as the hawkish military analyst Ralph Peters has done, that we are actually engaged "in an effort to keep the world safe for our economy and open to our cultural assault." Doing so will prevent us from being surprised by the intensity of resistance that awaits us as we enforce President Bush's so-called Freedom Agenda across the broad expanse of Islam. Mounting such a campaign implies mobilization, commitment, sacrifice, and reordering national priorities with the prerequisites of victory rising to first place. It will necessarily require the allocation of additional resources to satisfy the mushrooming requirements of "national security." We will have to hire many more soldiers. A serious attempt to pacify the Islamic world means the permanent militarization of US policy. Almost inevitably, it will further concentrate authority in the hands of an imperial presidency. This describes the program of the "faster, please" ideologues keen to enlarge the scope of US military action. To paraphrase Che Guevara, it is a program that calls for "one, two, many Iraqs," ignoring the verdict already rendered by the actually existing Iraq. The fact is that events there have definitively exposed the very real limits of American hard power, financial reserves, and will. Leviathan has shot his wad.

Seeking an escape from our predicament through further expansion points toward bankruptcy and the dismantling of what remains of the American republic. Genuine pragmatism—and the beginning of wisdom—lies in paying less attention to "the way that they live" and more attention to the way we do. Ultimately, conditions within American society determine the prospects of American liberty. As early multiculturalist Randolph Bourne observed nearly a century ago, ensuring that authentic freedom will flourish at home demands that we attend in the first instance to "cultivating our own garden." This does not imply assuming a posture of isolationism, although neoconservative and neoliberal proponents of the global "war on terror" will be quick to level that charge. Let us spare no effort to track down those who attacked us on 9/11, beginning with Osama bin Laden, still at large more than five years later. But let us give up once and for all any pretensions about an "indispensable nation" summoned to exercise "benign global hegemony" in the midst of a uniquely opportune "unipolar moment." For too long now these narcissistic and fallacious claims, the source of the pretensions expressed by President Bush since September 2001, have polluted our discussion of foreign policy and thereby prevented us from seeing ourselves as we are.

Cultivating our own garden begins with taking stock of ourselves. Thoughtful critics have for decades been calling for just such a critical self-examination. Among the very first canaries to venture into the deteriorating mineshaft of postwar American culture was the writer Flannery O'Connor. "If you live today," she observed with characteristic bluntness a half-century ago, "you breathe in nihilism." O'Connor correctly diagnosed the disease and other observers bore witness to its implications. Her fellow Southerner Walker Percy wondered if freedom American-style was not simply becoming the "last and inalienable possession in a sick society." The social critic Christopher Lasch derided "the ideology of progress" manipulated by elites contemptuous of the ethnic, social, and religious traditions to which ordinary folk subscribed. Lasch foresaw an impending "dark night of the soul." From his vantage point, Robert Nisbet detected the onset of what he called "a twilight age," marked by "a sense of cultural decay, erosion of institutions . . . and constantly increasing centralization— and militarization—of power." In such an age, he warned, "representative and liberal institutions of government slip into patterns ever more imperial in character. . . . Over everything hangs the specter of war." Towering above them all was Pope John Paul II who, in a message clearly directed toward Americans, pointedly cautioned that a democracy bereft of values "easily turns into a thinly disguised totalitarianism." Our own self-induced confusion about freedom, reflected in our debased culture and our disordered economy, increases our susceptibility to this totalitarian temptation even as it deadens our awareness of the danger it poses. Escaping its clutches will require something more than presidents intoning clichés about America's historic mission while launching crusades against oil-rich tyrants on the other side of the globe.

We are in difficult straits and neither arms (already fully committed) nor treasure (just about used up) will get us out. Our corrupt age requires reformation. Shedding or at least discrediting the spurious conceptions of freedom to which Americans have lately fallen prey qualifies as a large task. Still, when compared to the megalomania of those who, under the guise of "eliminating tyranny," are intent on remaking the entire Islamic world, the restoration of our own culture appears to be a positively modest goal. At the end of the day, as William Pfaff has observed, "The only thing we can remake is ourselves." And who knows? Should we, as a consequence of such a reformation, actually live up to our professed ideals—restoring to American freedom something of the respect that it once commanded—we may yet become, in some small way, a model worthy of emulation.

28

![black bar]

What Happened at Bud Dajo

(2006)

One hundred years ago this past week, on March 7, 1906, the American military's first sustained incursion into the Islamic world reached a climax of sorts. At Bud Dajo, on an island in the southern Philippines, US troops massacred as many as a thousand Filipino Muslims.

In the conventional narrative of America's rise to greatness, Bud Dajo hardly qualifies for a footnote. Yet the events that occurred there a century ago deserve their own chapter. For those hankering today to use American power to transform the Islamic world, Bud Dajo offers a cautionary tale.

The US troops had arrived on a mission of liberation, promising to uplift the oppressed. But the subjects of American beneficence, holding views of their own, proved recalcitrant. Doing good required first that the liberators pacify resistance and establish order. Before it was over, the Americans' honor had been lost, and uplift had given way to savagery.

Although it had seized the Philippines in 1898 during the course of its war with Spain, the United States made little immediate attempt to impose its authority over the Muslim minority—known as Moros—concentrated in the southern reaches of the archipelago. Under the terms of the 1899 Bates Agreement, American colonial administrators had promised the Moros autonomy in return for acknowledging nominal US sovereignty. But after the US suppressed the so-called Philippine Insurrection of 1899–1902, during which US forces defeated Filipino nationalists led by Emilio Aguinaldo, authorities in Manila turned their attention to the Moros. In 1903, they abrogated the Bates Agreement and ordered Major General Leonard Wood to assert unambiguous jurisdiction over what the Americans were now calling the Moro Province.

The imperious Wood, President Theodore Roosevelt's favorite general, viewed his new charges as "nothing more nor less than an unimportant collection of pirates and highwaymen." He did not bother to disguise his intentions: the Moros would either submit or suffer harsh consequences. As one of Wood's subordinates noted approvingly, "We are going after Mr. Moro with a rough hand, we are holding him up to all the high ideals of civilization."

A rough hand it proved to be. Personally offended by the Moro propensity for blood feuds, polygamy, and human trafficking, Wood set out to render Moro culture compatible with prevailing Western values. Doing so meant first creating a new political order.

Certain that a generous dose of American firepower would make the Moros amenable to his program of reform, he arrived at his new headquarters in Zamboanga hankering for a fight. As he assured the president, "one clean-cut lesson will be quite sufficient for them."

Wood miscalculated. Neither one, nor a dozen, nor several dozen such lessons did the trick. His efforts to root out offending Moro customs—issuing edicts that declared ancient Moro practices illegal, demanding that Moro tribal chiefs profess their fealty to Washington, and visiting reprisals on those who refused—triggered a fierce backlash.

An ugly war ensued, pitting poorly armed Moro warriors against seasoned US Army regulars. The Moro weapon of choice was the kris, a short sword with a wavy blade; the Americans toted Springfield rifles and field guns. As in present-day Iraq, the Americans never lost an engagement. Yet even as they demolished one Moro stronghold after another and wracked up an impressive body count, the fighting persisted. The Moros remained incorrigible.

At Bud Dajo, a volcanic crater on the island of Jolo, things came to a head. In late 1905, hundreds of Moros—determined to avoid paying a US-imposed head tax, which they considered blasphemous—began taking refuge on the peak. Refusing orders to disperse, they posed, at least in the eyes of nervous American officials, an intolerable threat. In "open defiance of the American authority," the district governor on Jolo complained, the Moros of Bud Dajo were setting themselves up as "patriots and semi-liberators."

These would-be revolutionaries had to be crushed. So Wood dispatched several battalions of infantry to Bud Dajo with orders to "clean it up." On March 5, 1906, the reinforcements arrived and laid siege to the heights. The next day, they began shelling the crater with artillery. At daybreak on March 7, the final assault commenced, the Americans working deliberately along the rim of the crater and firing into the pit. Periodically, "a rush of shrieking men and women would come cutting the air and dash amongst the soldiers like mad dogs," one eyewitness reported, but the results were foreordained. When the action finally ended some twenty-four hours later, the extermination of the Bud Dajo Moros had been accomplished. Among the dead lay several hundred women and children.

Differing in scope but not in character from countless prior "battles," the incident at Bud Dajo would have gone entirely unnoticed had word of it not leaked to the press. When reports of the slaughter reached Washington, a minor flap ensued. Indignant members of Congress—chiefly Democrats hoping to embarrass the Republican Roosevelt—demanded an explanation. Perhaps predictably, an official inquiry found the conduct of US troops beyond reproach. When the War Department cleared Wood of any wrongdoing, the scandal faded as quickly as it had begun. For his part, Wood remained chillingly unrepentant. "Work of this kind," he wrote privately to Roosevelt, "has its disagreeable side, which is the unavoidable killing of women and children; but it must be done."

The president concurred. And yet the bloodletting at Bud Dajo accomplished next to nothing. The nameless dead were soon forgotten. Wood moved onward and upward, soon thereafter becoming Army chief of staff and eventually returning to the Philippines as governor-general. The American self-image as upholder of civilization's high ideals emerged a bit the worse for wear, but still intact, at least as far as most Americans were concerned.

In the Moro Province, the US campaign of pacification ground on, lasting several more years. Other atrocities followed. In short order, the incident at Bud Dajo and soon thereafter the entire American encounter with the Moros slipped down the hole of vanished memories, eclipsed by other, bigger, less ambiguous wars.

With the United States engaged today in an ambitious effort to transform large swathes of the Muslim world, the campaign against the Moros warns against the dangers of misreading the subjects of one's kindly intentions. Viewing the Moros as weak and malleable, Wood underestimated their determination and capacity to resist. This history also reminds us of how easily righteousness can kindle contempt. Wood's soldiers saw themselves as bearers of civilization, but when their exertions met with hostility rather than gratitude, they came to see the Moros as beyond saving and hence as disposable.

Above all, however, the results of the campaign to pacify the Moros suggest that pacifying Afghans, Iraqis, or others in the Muslim world today will require extraordinary persistence. The Moros never did submit. A full century after Leonard Wood confidently predicted that "one clean-cut lesson" would bring the Moros to heel, their resistance to outside rule continues: the present-day Moro Islamic Liberation Front, classified by the Bush administration as an al-Qaeda affiliate, carries on the fight for Moro independence. For advocates of today's "long war," eager to confer on Muslims everywhere the blessings of freedom and democracy, while preserving the honor of the US military, the sheer doggedness of Moro resistance ought to give pause.

29

The Folly of Albion

(2005)

One of the more bizarre notions currently finding favor in jingoistic quarters is a conviction that the United States in the twenty-first century ought to model itself after the British Empire in its nineteenth- and early-twentieth-century heyday. According to modish historians such as Niall Ferguson, the record of imperial Britain contains a trove of wisdom that imperial America can put to good use keeping order, fostering prosperity, and spreading the blessings of civilization. All that's needed is for the sole superpower of the present day—according to Ferguson, an "empire in denial"—to step up to the plate and overcome its refusal "to acknowledge the full extent of its responsibilities." With that in mind, Ferguson counsels the people of the United States "to get over the American inhibition about learning from non-American history."

There is something to be said for this advice: when it comes to tapping the lessons of history, Americans do tend to rely on a meager stock of familiar analogies of sometimes questionable relevance. To appreciate our current predicament, we ought to cast our net more broadly. So let us refrain from further references to quagmires and Tet Offensives. Enough already with the uncharitable comparisons of Donald Rumsfeld to Robert McNamara. As we consider the fate awaiting us as the Bush administration wades ever more deeply into the region that it grandly refers to as the Broader Middle East, let us profit from the experience of Great Britain.

Yet on that score, the lessons that history has to teach are almost entirely negative. British ambitions in the Middle East nearly a century ago, as grandiose in their way as the Bush administration's in our own day, produced disastrous results and cost Britain its empire.

"Our armies do not come into your cities and lands as conquerors or enemies, but as liberators." So proclaimed Lt. Gen. Sir Frederick Stanley Maude, the British equivalent of Gen. Tommy Franks and the commander of the British forces that entered Baghdad in March 1917. As with the rhetoric employed to justify the invasion of March 2003, Sir Frederick's statement was at best a half-truth. London's actual purpose—like Washington's some eighty-six years later—was hegemony. Freeing the people of Mesopotamia from Turkish oppression was a means to a larger end. The real aim was to institute a new political order, not only along the Tigris and Euphrates but across the region, thereby securing British control over the Persian Gulf oil that appeared crucial to the preservation of British power.

Granted, Britain could count on a homegrown variant of our own neoconservatives to camouflage the true nature of the enterprise. These ideologues, close to and sometimes within the British government, insisted that the motive force for British actions in the Middle East and elsewhere was to be found in British ideals. Thus, according to Arthur Hirtzel, an official of the India Office, "The Empire . . . has been given to us as a means to that great end for which Christ came into the world, the redemption of the human race. That is to say, it has been given to us to make it Christian. This is to be Britain's contribution to the redemption of mankind." In its way, Hirtzel's book *The Church, The Empire, and The World*, published in 1919, stands as a precursor to Richard Perle and David Frum's *An End to Evil*, published in 2003. The former summons Britain to redeem mankind by converting nonbelievers; the latter calls on the United States to redeem mankind by spreading democratic values. Both provide handy moral justifications for employing the sword, and both neatly disguise more sordid *raison d'etat.*

As in the Global War on Terror and in the so-called Great War, the incursion into Iraq was merely Step One in what was intended to be a multi-phased campaign. Employing a combination of its own army and surrogates to peel off portions of the ramshackle Ottoman Empire, Great Britain sought to maneuver itself into a position where it could redraw the map of the entire region. American soldiers who in 1918 rallied to assist hard-pressed British troops on the Western Front may have believed that they were fighting to make the world safe for democracy and to enshrine a new right of "self-determination." But British officials knew better: the war to defeat German militarism was also an opportunity for imperial expansion and for keeping competitors—not least of all the United States—from horning in on the strategically vital Persian Gulf.

The upshot: in the aftermath of World War I, British statesmen engineered a peace settlement that brought the empire to its high-water mark. Out of an Anglo-French system of mandates and protectorates, of puppet monarchs and compliant sheiks, there emerged the modern Middle East. By 1920, with luckless France obliged to content itself with Lebanon and Syria, Britain controlled directly or indirectly the territory encompassing the present-day countries of Egypt, Israel, Jordan, Saudi Arabia, Kuwait, the United Arab Emirates, Iraq, and Iran.

But British statesmen wanted to do more than simply rearrange boundaries and install local sycophants onto thrones of doubtful provenance. To ensure the permanent incorporation of the Middle East into Britain's sphere of influence, they sought to Anglicize the region. Local elites thoroughly imbued with British values could be counted on to defer willingly to London on matters large and small.

With this in mind, the British government devised what the Bush administration in our own day describes as a "strategy of transformation." Here Britain's imperial ambitions appeared to converge with the interests of Zionists lobbying to create a Jewish homeland. Even before the war and prior to the issuance of the Balfour Declaration, British statesmen fancied that the creation of a Zionist state in Palestine could serve as a beachhead of British values and culture in the region. Winston Churchill, for one, believed, "The establishment of a strong, free Jewish state astride the bridge between Europe and Africa . . . would not only be an immense advantage to the British Empire, but a notable step towards the harmonious disposition of the world among its peoples." The idea, according to Leo Amery, a member of Prime Minister Lloyd George's wartime inner circle, was quite simple: "using the Jews as we have used the Scots, to carry the English ideal through the Middle East," Britain could "make Palestine the centre of western influence."

It all seemed so logical and so straightforward. Yet even before the various elements of this bold design were in place, it all began to unravel. The new British order for the Middle East became, to cite the title of David Fromkin's brilliant book on the topic, *A Peace to End All Peace.*

Notably, among the first places in which trouble appeared was Iraq, which Britain in a spurious exercise in nation-building had cobbled together out of disparate tribal groups. Beginning in June 1920, a series of seemingly unrelated anti-British uprisings occurred, which the liberators attempted to suppress by relying on Britain's strong suit—not, as it turned out, Christian ideals, but superior firepower. Appreciating that Britain had too few ground troops to meet all of its far-flung responsibilities, Churchill, then serving as Secretary of State for War and Air, assigned the chief responsibility for pacifying Iraq to the Royal Air Force. Eager to prove its worth as an imperial police force, the fledgling RAF seized upon this mission with considerable eagerness. In the campaign of aerial intimidation that ensued, avoiding noncombatant casualties did not figure as a priority. As one RAF squadron leader noted, "if the tribespeople were doing something they ought not to be doing then you shot them."

Bringing recalcitrant Iraqis to heel was essential if Britain was to consolidate the winnings it had scooped up as a consequence of World War I. But in Iraq, firepower could win battles but not hearts and minds. Indeed, it was in Iraq that the long, mournful process of British imperial decline began.

In fact, the anticipated "transformation" of the new Middle East into a bastion of British influence never took hold. Instead, there ensued a delaying action that played itself out over several decades as London struggled to stanch the gradual erosion of its position in the region. The effort led Britain to overextend itself economically and to compromise itself morally—not least of all in its cynical response to the sensitive issue of Jewish immigration into Palestine.

Worse, resources frittered away in trying to maintain some semblance of a foothold in the Middle East were unavailable to counter the rising Nazi threat of the 1930s. Rather than contributing to British security, the Middle East served only to complicate it further. Indeed, when war erupted once again in Europe, most Arabs in the lands nominally controlled by Great Britain tilted toward Germany. In mid-1941, the RAF was once again bombing Iraqis—this time to put down a coup mounted by rabidly pro-Nazi (and anti-Semitic) fanatics.

By the time World War II ended, the jig was up. A series of humiliating setbacks ensued. In Palestine, London simply threw up its hands and left. (Not surprisingly, fostering the spread of British values did not appear on the agenda of the Jewish state that emerged shortly thereafter; Israelis did not see themselves as Scots.) Egypt and Iraq gave Britain the boot. Elsewhere, especially where oil profits were to be had, the rich Americans elbowed their impoverished ally aside. The low point came in the Suez Crisis of 1956 when President Dwight D. Eisenhower threatened to bring Britain to its knees economically if it did not call off its ill-advised invasion of Egypt. Prime Minister Anthony Eden meekly complied. The British lion was well on its way to becoming what present-day Britons themselves deride as an American poodle.

What does this record of miscalculation and misadventure have to teach the United States today? Viewed in retrospect, when it comes to pursuing its aims in the Middle East, Albion comes across not so much as perfidious as reckless and foolish. The schemes that Britain devised and the messianic claims offered up to justify those schemes seem silly. The lack of realism—the refusal to consider whether Britain possessed the reserves of power to fulfill its ambitions—appears simply stupefying. Above all, the assumption that the peoples of the Middle East would necessarily buy into British notions of what is right and good was utterly misguided. In short, the expectation that Great Britain in the 1920s might manipulate events so as to suit its own purposes was a pipe dream, doomed from the start.

To state the matter plainly, Great Britain botched the Middle East and forfeited its position as a world power as a consequence. Today British politicians like Tony Blair, with his neo-Churchillian posturing, and British imperial apologists like Niall Ferguson, with his neo-Kiplingesque call to shoulder the White Man's Burden, are asking the United States to clean up the mess created in no small measure as a direct result of British folly.

So let us learn from our cousins across the pond. If that's what empire has on offer, then thanks but no thanks.

30

The Real World War IV

(2005)

In the eyes of its most impassioned supporters, the Global War on Terror constitutes a de facto fourth world war. The conflict that erupted with the attacks on the World Trade Center and the Pentagon is really a sequel to three previous conflicts that, however different from one another in terms of scope and duration, have defined contemporary history.

According to this interpretation, most clearly articulated by the neoconservative thinker Norman Podhoretz in the pages of *Commentary* magazine, the long twilight struggle between communism and democratic capitalism qualifies as the functional equivalent of World War I (1914–18) and World War II (1939–45). In retrospect, we can see that the East-West rivalry commonly referred to as the Cold War was actually World War III (1947–89). After a brief interval of relative peace, corresponding roughly to the 1990s, a fourth conflict, comparable in magnitude to the previous three, erupted on September 11, 2001. This fourth world war promises to continue indefinitely.

Classifying the Global War on Terror as World War IV offers important benefits. It fits the events of September 11 and thereafter into a historical trope familiar to almost all Americans, and thereby offers a reassuring sense of continuity: we've been here before; we know what we need to do; we know how it ends. By extension, the World War IV construct facilitates efforts to mobilize popular support for US military actions undertaken in pursuit of final victory. It also ratifies the claims of federal authorities, especially those in the executive branch, who insist on exercising "wartime" prerogatives by expanding the police powers of the state and circumscribing constitutional guarantees of due process. Further, it makes available a stock of plausible analogies to help explain the otherwise inexplicable—the dastardly events of September 11, 2001, for example, are a reprise of the dastardly surprise of December 7, 1941. Thus, the construct helps to preclude awkward questions. It disciplines.

But it also misleads. Lumping US actions since 9/11 under the rubric of World War IV can too easily become an exercise in sleight of hand. According to hawks such as Podhoretz, the chief defect of US policy before 9/11 was an excess of timidity. America's actual problem has been quite the reverse.

The key point is this. At the end of the Cold War, Americans said "yes" to military power. Indeed, ever since Vietnam, Americans have evinced a deepening infatuation with armed force, soldiers, and military values. By the end of the twentieth century, the skepticism about arms and armies that informed the American experiment from its founding had vanished. Political leaders, liberal and conservative alike, became enamored of military might. Militarism insinuated itself into American life.

The ensuing affair has had a heedless, Gatsby-like aspect, a passion pursued in utter disregard of any likely consequences. Few in power have openly considered whether valuing military power for its own sake or cultivating permanent global military superiority might be at odds with American principles.

To the extent that some Americans are cognizant of a drift toward militarism by their country, the declaration of World War IV permits them to suppress any latent anxiety about that tendency. After all, according to precedent, a world war—by definition, a conflict thrust upon the United States—changes everything. Responsibility for world wars lies with someone else: with Germany in 1917, Japan in 1941, or the Soviet Union after 1945. Designating the several US military campaigns initiated in the aftermath of 9/11 as World War IV effectively absolves the United States of accountability for anything that went before. Blame lies elsewhere: with Osama bin Laden and al-Qaeda, with Saddam Hussein and his Baath Party thugs, with radical Islam. America's responsibility is to finish what others started.

But this militaristic predisposition, evident in the transformation of American thinking about soldiers, the armed services, and war itself since Vietnam, cannot of itself explain the rising tide of American bellicosity that culminated in March 2003 with the invasion of Iraq. We must look as well to national interests and, indeed, to the ultimate US interest, which is the removal of any obstacles or encumbrances that might hinder the American people in their pursuit of happiness ever more expansively defined. Rather than timidity or trepidation, it is unabashed confidence in the strength of American arms, combined with an unswerving determination to perfect American freedom, that has landed us in our present fix.

During the 1980s and 1990s, this combustible mix produced a shift in the US strategic center of gravity, overturning geopolitical priorities that had long appeared sacrosanct. A set of revised strategic priorities emerged, centered geographically in the energy-rich Persian Gulf but linked inextricably to the assumed prerequisites for sustaining American freedom at home. A succession of administrations, Republican and Democratic, opted for armed force as the preferred means to satisfy those new priorities. In other words, a new set of strategic imperatives, seemingly conducive to a military solution, and a predisposition toward militarism together produced the full-blown militarization of US policy so much in evidence since 9/11.

The convergence between preconditions and interests suggests an altogether different definition of World War IV—a war that did not begin on 9/11, does not have as its founding purpose the elimination of terror, and does not cast the United States as an innocent party. This alternative conception of a fourth world war constitutes not a persuasive rationale for the exercise of US military power in the manner pursued by the administration of George W. Bush, but the definitive expression of the dangers posed by the new American militarism. Waiting in the wings are World Wars V and VI, to be justified, inevitably, by the ostensible demands of freedom.

Providing a true account of World War IV requires that it first be placed in its correct relationship to World War III, the Cold War. As the great competition between the United States and the Soviet Union slips further into the past, scholars work their way toward an ever more fine-grained interpretation of its origins, conduct, and implications. Yet as far as public perceptions of the Cold War are concerned, these scholars' diligence goes largely unrewarded. When it comes to making sense of recent history, the American people, encouraged by their political leaders, have shown a demonstrable preference for clarity rather than nuance. Even as the central events of the Cold War recede into the distance, the popular image of the larger drama in which these events figured paradoxically sharpens.

"Cold War" serves as a sort of self-explanatory, all-purpose label, encompassing the entire period from the mid-1940s through the late 1980s. And since what is past is prologue, this self-contained, internally coherent, authoritative rendering of the recent past is ideally suited to serve as a template for making sense of events unfolding before our eyes.

From a vantage point midway through the first decade of the twenty-first century, the commonly accepted metanarrative of our time consists of three distinct chapters. The first, beginning where World War II leaves off, recounts a period of trial and tribulation lasting several decades but ending in an unambiguous triumph for the United States. The next describes a short-lived "post–Cold War era," a brief, dreamy interlude abruptly terminated by 9/11. The second chapter gives way to a third, still in the process of being written but expected to replicate in broad outlines the first—if only the United States will once again rise to the occasion. This three-part narrative possesses the virtues of simplicity and neatness, but it is fundamentally flawed. Perhaps worst of all, it does not alert Americans to the full dimensions of their present-day predicament. Instead, the narrative deceives them. It would be far more useful to admit to a different and messier parsing of the recent past.

For starters, we should recognize that, far from being a unitary event, the Cold War occurred in two distinct phases. The first, defined as the period of Soviet-American competition that could have produced an actual World War III, essentially ended by 1963. In 1961, by acquiescing in the erection of the Berlin Wall, Washington affirmed its acceptance of a divided Europe. In 1962, during the Cuban Missile Crisis, Washington and Moscow contemplated the real prospect of mutual annihilation, blinked more or less simultaneously, and tacitly agreed to preclude any recurrence of that frightening moment. A more predictable, more stable relationship ensued, incorporating a certain amount of ritualistic saber rattling but characterized by careful adherence to a well-established set of routines and procedures.

Out of stability came opportunities for massive stupidity. During the Cold War's second phase, from 1963 to 1989, both the major protagonists availed themselves of these opportunities by pursuing inane adventures on the periphery. In the 1960s, of course, Americans plunged into Vietnam, with catastrophic results. Beginning in 1979, the Soviets impaled themselves on Afghanistan, with results that proved altogether fatal. Whereas the inherent resilience of democratic capitalism enabled the United States to repair the wounds it had inflicted on itself, the Soviet political economy lacked recuperative powers. During the course of the 1980s, an already ailing Soviet empire became sick unto death.

The crucial developments hastening the demise of the Soviet empire emerged from within. When the whole ramshackle structure came tumbling down, Andrei Sakharov, Václav Havel, and Karol Wojtyla, the Polish prelate who became Pope John Paul II, could claim as much credit for the result as Ronald Reagan, if not more. The most persuasive explanation for the final outcome of the Cold War is to be found in Soviet ineptitude, in the internal contradictions of the Soviet system, and in the courage of the dissidents who dared to challenge Soviet authority.

In this telling of the tale, the Cold War remains a drama of compelling moral significance. But shorn of its triumphal trappings, the tale has next to nothing to say about the present-day state of world affairs. In a post-9/11 world, it possesses little capacity either to illuminate or to instruct. To find in the recent past an explanation of use to the present requires an altogether different narrative, one that resurrects the largely forgotten or ignored story of America's use of military power for purposes unrelated to the Soviet-American rivalry.

The fact is that, even as the Cold War was slowly reaching its denouement, World War IV was already under way—indeed, had begun two full decades before September 2001. So World Wars III and IV consist of parallel rather than sequential episodes. They evolved more or less in tandem, with the former overlaid on, and therefore obscuring, the latter.

The real World War IV began in 1980, and Jimmy Carter, of all people, declared it. To be sure, Carter acted only under extreme duress, prompted by the irrevocable collapse of a policy to which he and his seven immediate predecessors had adhered—specifically, the arrangements designed to guarantee the United States a privileged position in the Persian Gulf. For Cold War–era US policymakers, preoccupied with Europe and East Asia as the main theaters of action, the Persian Gulf had figured as something of a sideshow before 1980. Jimmy Carter changed all that, thrusting it into the uppermost tier of US geopolitical priorities.

From 1945 through 1979, the aim of US policy in the gulf region had been to ensure stability and American access, but to do so in a way that minimized overt US military involvement. Franklin Roosevelt had laid down the basic lines of this policy in February 1945 at a now-famous meeting with King Abd al-Aziz Ibn Saud of Saudi Arabia. Henceforth, Saudi Arabia could count on the United States to guarantee its security, and the United States could count on Saudi Arabia to provide it preferential treatment in exploiting the kingdom's vast, untapped reserves of oil.

From the 1940s through the 1970s, US strategy in the Middle East adhered to the military principle known as economy of force. Rather than establish a large presence in the region, Roosevelt's successors sought to achieve their objectives in ways that entailed a minimal expenditure of American resources and, especially, US military power. From time to time, when absolutely necessary, Washington might organize a brief show of force—in 1946, for example, when Harry Truman ordered the USS *Missouri* to the eastern Mediterranean to warn the Soviets to cease meddling in Turkey, or in 1958, when Dwight

Eisenhower sent US Marines into Lebanon for a short-lived, bloodless occupation—but these modest gestures proved the exception rather than the rule.

The clear preference was for a low profile and a hidden hand. Although by no means averse to engineering "regime change" when necessary, the United States preferred covert action to the direct use of force. To police the region, Washington looked to surrogates—British imperial forces through the 1960s, and, once Britain withdrew from "east of Suez," the shah of Iran. To build up the indigenous self-defense (or regime defense) capabilities of select nations, it arranged for private contractors to provide weapons, training, and advice. The Vinnell Corporation's ongoing "modernization" of the Saudi Arabian National Guard (SANG), a project now well over a quarter-century old, remains a prime example.

By the end of 1979, however, two events had left this approach in a shambles. The first was the Iranian Revolution, which sent the shah into exile and installed in Tehran an Islamist regime adamantly hostile to the United States. The second was the Soviet invasion of Afghanistan, which put the Red Army in a position where it appeared to pose a direct threat to the entire Persian Gulf—and hence to the West's oil supply.

Faced with these twin crises, Jimmy Carter concluded that treating the Middle East as a secondary theater, ancillary to the Cold War, no longer made sense. A great contest for control of the region had been joined. Rejecting out of hand any possibility that the United States might accommodate itself to the changes afoot in the Persian Gulf, Carter claimed for the United States a central role in determining exactly what those changes would be. In January 1980, to forestall any further deterioration of the US position in the gulf, he threw the weight of American military power into the balance. In his State of the Union address, the president enunciated what became known as the Carter Doctrine. "An attempt by any outside force to gain control of the Persian Gulf region," he declared, "will be regarded as an assault on the vital interests of the United States of America, and such an assault will be repelled by any means necessary, including military force."

From Carter's time down to the present day, the doctrine bearing his name has remained sacrosanct. As a consequence, each of Carter's successors has expanded the level of US military involvement and operations in the region. Even today, American political leaders cling to the belief that skillful application of military power will enable the United States to decide the fate not simply of the Persian Gulf proper but of the entire greater Middle East. This gigantic project, begun in 1980 and now well into its third decade, is the true World War IV.

What prompted Jimmy Carter, the least warlike of all recent US presidents, to take this portentous step? The Pentagon's first Persian Gulf commander, Lieutenant General Robert Kingston, offered a simple answer when he said that his basic mission was "to assure the unimpeded flow of oil from the Arabian Gulf." But General Kingston was selling his president and his country short. What was true of the three other presidents who had committed the United States to world wars—Woodrow Wilson, FDR, and Truman—remained true in the case of Carter and World War IV as well. The overarching motive for action was preservation of the American way of life.

By the beginning of 1980, a chastened Jimmy Carter had learned a hard lesson: It was not the prospect of making do with less that sustained American-style liberal democracy, but the promise of more. Carter had come to realize that what Americans demanded from their government was freedom, defined as more choice, more opportunity, and, above all, greater abundance, measured in material terms. That abundance depended on assured access to cheap oil—and lots of it.

In enunciating the Carter Doctrine, the president was reversing course, effectively renouncing his prior vision of a less materialistic, more self-reliant democracy. Just six months earlier, this vision had been the theme of a prescient, but politically misconceived, address to the nation, instantly dubbed by pundits the "Crisis of Confidence" speech, though, in retrospect, perhaps better called "The Road Not Taken."

Carter's short-lived vision emerged from a troubled context. By the third year of his presidency, economic conditions as measured by postwar standards had become dire. The rates of inflation and unemployment were both high. The prime lending rate was 15 percent and rising. Trends in both the federal deficit and the trade balance were sharply negative. Conventional analysis attributed US economic woes to the nation's growing dependence on increasingly expensive foreign oil.

In July 1979, Carter already anticipated that a continuing and unchecked thirst for imported oil was sure to distort US strategic priorities, with unforeseen but adverse consequences. (When Carter spoke, the United States was importing approximately 43 percent of its annual oil requirement; today it imports 56 percent.) He feared the impact of that distortion on an American democracy still reeling from the effects of the 1960s. So on July 15 he summoned his fellow citizens to change course, to choose self-sufficiency and self-reliance—and therefore true independence. But the independence was to come at the cost of collective sacrifice and lowered expectations.

Carter spoke that night of a nation facing problems "deeper than gasoline lines or energy shortages, deeper even than inflation or depression." The fundamental issue, in Carter's view, was that Americans had turned away from all that really mattered. In a nation once proud of hard work among strong, religious families and close-knit communities, too many Americans had come to worship self-indulgence and consumption. What you owned rather than what you did had come to define human identity. But according to Carter, owning things and consuming things did not satisfy our longing for meaning. Americans were learning that piling up goods could fill the emptiness of lives devoid of real purpose.

This moral crisis had brought the United States to a historic turning point. Either Americans could persist in pursuing "a mistaken idea of freedom" based on "fragmentation and self-interest" and inevitably "ending in chaos and immobility," or they could opt for "true freedom," which Carter described as "the path of common purpose and the restoration of American values."

How the United States chose to deal with its growing reliance on foreign oil would determine which of the two paths it followed. Energy dependence, according to the president, posed "a clear and present danger" to the nation, threatening the nation's security as well as its economic well-being. Dealing with this threat was "the standard around which we can rally." "On the battlefield of energy," declared Carter, "we can seize control again of our common destiny."

How to achieve this aim? In part, by restricting oil imports, investing in alternative sources, limiting the use of oil by the nation's utilities, and promoting public transportation. But Carter placed the larger burden squarely in the lap of the American people. The hollowing out of American democracy required a genuinely democratic response. "There is simply no way to avoid sacrifice," he insisted, calling on citizens as "an act of patriotism" to lower thermostats, observe the highway speed limit, use carpools, and "park your car one extra day per week."

Although Carter's stance was relentlessly inward looking, his analysis had important strategic implications. To the extent that "foreign oil" refers implicitly to the Persian Gulf—as it did then and does today—Carter was in essence proposing to annul the growing strategic importance attributed to that region. He sensed intuitively that a failure to reverse the nation's energy dependence was sure to draw the United States ever more deeply into the vortex of Persian Gulf politics, which, at best, would distract attention from the internal crisis that was his central concern, but was even more likely to exacerbate it.

But if Carter was prophetic when it came to the strategic implications of growing US energy dependence, his policy prescription reflected a fundamental misreading of his fellow countrymen. Indeed, as Garry Wills has observed, given the country's propensity to define itself in terms of growth, it triggered "a subtle panic [and] claustrophobia" that Carter's political adversaries wasted no time in exploiting. By January 1980, it had become evident that any program summoning Americans to make do with less was a political nonstarter. The president accepted this verdict. The promulgation of the Carter Doctrine signaled his capitulation.

Carter's about-face did not achieve its intended political purpose of preserving his hold on the White House—Ronald Reagan had already tagged Carter as a pessimist, whose temperament was at odds with that of the rest of the country—but it did set in motion a huge shift in US military policy, the implications of which gradually appeared over the course of the next two decades. Critics might cavil that the militarization of US policy in the Persian Gulf amounted to a devil's bargain, trading blood for oil. Carter saw things differently. On the surface the exchange might entail blood for oil, but beneath the surface the aim was to guarantee the ever-increasing affluence that underwrites the modern American conception of liberty. Without exception, every one of Carter's successors has tacitly endorsed this formulation.

Although the result was not fully apparent until the 1990s, changes in US military posture and priorities gradually converted the Persian Gulf into the epicenter of American grand strategy and World War IV's principal theater of operations.

"Even if there were no Soviet Union," wrote the authors of NSC-68, the spring 1950 US National Security Council document that became the definitive statement of America's Cold War grand strategy, "we would face the great problem of the free society, accentuated many fold in this industrial age, of reconciling order, security, the need for participation, with the requirement of freedom. We would face the fact that in a shrinking world the absence of order among nations is becoming less and less tolerable." Some three decades later, with the Soviet Union headed toward oblivion, the great problem of the free society to which NSC-68 alluded had become, if anything, more acute. But conceiving the principles to guide US policy turned out to be a more daunting proposition in World War IV than it had been during any of the three previous world wars. Throughout the 1980s and 1990s, US policymakers grappled with this challenge, reacting to crises as they occurred and then insisting after the fact that their actions conformed to some larger design. In fact, only after 9/11 did a fully articulated grand strategy take shape. George W. Bush saw the antidote to intolerable disorder as the transformation of the greater Middle East through the sustained use of military power.

Further complicating the challenge of devising a strategy for World War IV was the fundamental incompatibility of two competing US interests in the region. The first was a steadily increasing dependence on oil from the Middle East. Dependence meant vulnerability, as the crippling oil shocks of the 1970s, administered by the Organization of Petroleum Exporting Countries (OPEC), amply demonstrated. As late as World War II, the United States had been the world's Saudi Arabia, producing enough oil to meet its own needs and those of its friends and allies. By the end of the twentieth century, with Americans consuming one out of every four barrels of oil produced worldwide, the remaining US reserves accounted for less than two percent of the world's total. Projections showed the leverage of Persian Gulf producers mushrooming in the years to come, with oil exports from the region expected to account for between 54 and 67 percent of world totals by 2020.

The second US interest in the region, juxtaposed against Arab oil, was Israel. America's commitment to the security of the Jewish state complicated US efforts to maintain cordial relations with oil-exporting states in the Persian Gulf. Before the Six-Day War (1967), the United States had tried to manage this problem by supporting Israel's right to exist but resisting Israeli entreaties to forge a strategic partnership. After 1967, that changed dramatically. The United States became Israel's preeminent international supporter and a generous supplier of economic and military assistance.

The Arab-Israeli conflict could not be separated from World War IV, but figuring out exactly where Israel fit in the larger struggle proved a perplexing problem for US policymakers. Was World War IV a war of blood-for-oil-for-freedom in which Israel figured, at best, as a distraction and, at worst, as an impediment? Or was it a war of blood-for-oil-for-freedom in which the United States and Israel stood shoulder to shoulder in a common enterprise? For the first twenty years of World War IV, the American response to these questions produced a muddle.

During his final year in office, then, Carter initiated America's new world war. Through his typically hapless and ineffectual effort to rescue the Americans held hostage in Iran, he sprinkled the first few driblets of American military power onto the surface of the desert, where they vanished without a trace. The rescue effort, dubbed Desert One, remained thereafter the gold standard for how not to use force, but it by no means curbed America's appetite for further armed intervention in the region. Ronald Reagan gave the spigot labeled "military power" a further twist—and in so doing, he opened the floodgates. Although Carter declared World War IV, the war was fully, if somewhat haphazardly, engaged only on Reagan's watch.

Reagan himself professed to be oblivious to the war's existence. After all, his immediate preoccupation was with World War III. For public consumption, the president was always careful to justify the US military buildup of the 1980s as a benign and defensive response to Cold War imperatives. All that the United States sought was to be at peace. "Our country has never started a war," Reagan told the annual Veterans of Foreign Wars convention in 1983. "Our sole objective is deterrence, the strength and capability it takes to prevent war." "We Americans don't want war and we don't start fights," he insisted on another occasion. "We don't maintain a strong military force to conquer or coerce others."

This was, of course, at least 50 percent bunkum. During the Reagan era, with the first stirrings of revived American militancy, defense and deterrence seldom figured as the operative principles. In fact, the American military tradition has never viewed defense as anything other than a pause before seizing the initiative and taking the fight to the enemy.

Partisan critics saw Reagan's muscle flexing as the actions of a reckless ideologue unnecessarily stoking old Cold War tensions. Viewing events in relation to Vietnam and the Cuban Missile Crisis, they forecast dreadful consequences. Reagan's defenders, then and later, told a different story: having intuitively grasped that the Soviet system was in an advanced state of decay, Reagan proceeded with skill and dexterity to exploit the system's economic, technological, and moral vulnerabilities; the ensuing collapse of the Soviet empire proved conclusively that Reagan had gotten things right. Today neither interpretation, Reagan as trigger-happy cold warrior or Reagan as master strategist, is especially persuasive. Assessing the military record of the Reagan years from a post-9/11 perspective yields a set of different and arguably more relevant insights.

Looking back, we can see that the entire Reagan era was situated on the seam between a world war that was winding down and another that had begun but was not yet fully comprehended. Although preoccupied with waging the Cold War, Reagan and his chief advisers, almost as an afterthought, launched four forays into the Islamic world, with mixed results: the insertion of US Marine "peacekeepers" into Lebanon, culminating in the Beirut bombing of October 1983; clashes with Libya, culminating in punitive US strikes against targets in Tripoli and Benghazi in April 1986; the so-called tanker war of 1984–88, culminating in the commitment of US forces to protect the flow of oil from the Persian Gulf; and American assistance throughout the 1980s to Afghan "freedom fighters," culminating in the Soviet army's ouster from Afghanistan. These actions greatly enhanced the ability of the United States to project military power into the region, but they also emboldened the enemy and contributed to the instability that drew Reagan's successors more deeply into the region.

The nominal stimulus for action in each case varied. In Lebanon, the murkiest of the four, Reagan ordered marines ashore at the end of September 1982 "to establish an environment which will permit the Lebanese Armed Forces to carry out their responsibilities in the Beirut area." This was a daunting proposition, given that Lebanon, divided by a civil war and variously occupied by the Syrian army, the Israeli Defense Forces, and (until its recent eviction) the Palestinian Liberation Organization, possessed neither an effective military nor an effective government and had little prospect of acquiring either. Vague expectations that a modest contingent of US peacekeepers camped in Beirut might help restore stability to Lebanon motivated Reagan to undertake this risky intervention, which ended disastrously when a suicide bomber drove into the marine compound, killing 241 Americans.

In the case of Libya, Muammar al-Qaddafi's declared intention of denying the US Sixth Fleet access to the Gulf of Sidra, off Libya's coast, had led to preliminary skirmishing in 1981 and again in March 1986. But it was Qaddafi's support for terrorism and, especially, alleged Libyan involvement in the bombing of a Berlin disco frequented by GIs that prompted Reagan to order retaliation.

In the tanker war, Reagan was reacting to attacks perpetrated by both Iran and Iraq against neutral shipping in the Persian Gulf. Since 1980, the two nations had been locked in an inconclusive conflict. As that struggle spilled over into the adjacent waters of the gulf, it reduced the availability of oil for export, drove up insurance rates, and crippled merchant shipping. An Iraqi missile attack on the USS *Stark* on May 17, 1987, brought things to a head. Iraq claimed that the incident, which killed thirty-seven sailors, had been an accident, and offered compensation. The Reagan administration used the *Stark* episode to blame Iran for the escalating violence. In short order, Kuwaiti supertankers were flying the Stars and Stripes, and US forces were conducting a brisk campaign to sweep Iranian air and naval units out of the gulf.

In the case of Afghanistan, Reagan built on a program already in existence but hidden from public view. In July 1979, the Carter administration had agreed to provide covert assistance to Afghans resisting the pro-Soviet regime in Kabul. According to Zbigniew Brzezinski, Carter's national security adviser, the aim was to induce a Soviet military response, thereby "drawing the Russians into the Afghan trap." When the Soviets did invade, in December 1979, they became bogged down in a guerrilla war against the US-backed mujahideen. Reagan inherited this project, initially sustained it, and then, in 1985, greatly stepped up the level of US support for the Afghan resistance.

At first glance, these four episodes seem to be all over the map, literally and in terms of purpose, means, and outcome. Contemporaneous assessments tended to treat each in isolation from the others and to focus on near-term outcomes. "After the attack on Tripoli," Reagan bragged, "we didn't hear much more from Qaddafi's terrorists." Nonsense, replied critics, pointing to the suspected Libyan involvement (since confirmed) in the bombing of Pan American Flight 103 in December 1988 and in the midair destruction of a French DC-10 nine months later. When a ceasefire in 1988 ended the fighting between Iran and Iraq, Secretary of Defense Caspar Weinberger assessed US involvement in the tanker war as a major achievement. "We had now clearly won," he wrote in 1990. With several hundred thousand US troops deploying to the Persian Gulf that very same year to prepare for large-scale war, Weinberger's claims of victory seemed, at best, premature.

To be sure, Reagan himself labored to weave together a comprehensive rationale for the various military actions he ordered, but the result amounted to an exercise in mythmaking. To listen to him, all these disparate threats—Soviet leaders pursuing global revolution, fundamentalists bent on propagating Islamic theocracies, Arab fascists such as Libya's Qaddafi and Syria's Hafez al-Assad, fanatical terrorists such as Abu Nidal—morphed into a single conspiracy. To give way to one element of that conspiracy was to give way to all, so the essential thing was to hold firm everywhere for peace.

Further muddying the waters were administration initiatives seemingly predicated on an assumption that no such overarching conspiracy against peace actually existed, or at least that selective US collaboration with evildoers was permissible. The Reagan administration's notorious "tilt" toward Saddam Hussein in the Iran-Iraq War, offering intelligence and commercial credits to the region's foremost troublemaker—perhaps the final US effort to enlist a proxy to secure its Persian Gulf interests—provides one example. Such opportunism made a mockery of Reagan's windy pronouncements regarding America's role as peacemaker and fed suspicions that the president's rhetoric was actually intended to divert attention from his administration's apparent strategic disarray.

Considered from a post-9/11 vantage point, however, Reagan-era uses of force in Lebanon, Libya, Afghanistan, and the tanker war do cohere, at least in a loose sort of way. First, and most notably, all four initiatives occurred in the Greater Middle East, hitherto not the site of frequent US military activity. Second, none of the four episodes can be fully understood except in relation to America's growing dependence on imported oil. Although energy considerations did not drive US actions in every instance, they always loomed in the background. Lebanon, for example, was not itself an oil exporter, but its woes mattered to the United States because instability there threatened to undermine the precarious stability of the region as a whole.

The four episodes constituting Reagan's Islamic quartet were alike in one other way. Although each yielded a near-term outcome that the administration touted as conclusive, the actual results turned out to be anything but. Rather, each of the four pointed toward ever-deepening American military engagement.

The true significance of Reagan's several interventions in the Islamic world lies not in the events themselves but in the response they evoked from the US national security apparatus. A consensus emerged that, in the list of pressing US geopolitical concerns, the challenges posed by the politically volatile, energy-rich world of Islam were eclipsing all others, including the size of the Soviet nuclear arsenal and the putative ambitions of the Soviet politburo. Given the imperative of meeting popular expectations for ever-greater abundance (which meant importing ever-larger quantities of oil)—Jimmy Carter's one-term presidency having demonstrated the political consequences of suggesting a different course—the necessary response was to put the

United States in a position to determine the fate of the Middle East. That meant forces, bases, and infrastructure. Only by enjoying unquestioned primacy in the region could the government of the United States guarantee American prosperity—and thus American freedom.

From the outset, dominance was the aim and the driving force behind US actions in World War IV—not preventing the spread of weapons of mass destruction, not stemming the spread of terror, certainly not liberating oppressed peoples or advancing the cause of women's rights. The prize was mastery over a region that leading members of the American foreign-policy elite, of whatever political persuasion, had concluded was critically important to the well-being of the United States. The problem, at its very core, demanded a military solution.

In March 1984, Donald Rumsfeld, out of power but serving as a Reagan administration troubleshooter, told Secretary of State George Shultz that Lebanon was a mere "sideshow." The main show was the Persian Gulf; instability there "could make Lebanon look like a taffy pull." According to Shultz's memoir, *Turmoil and Triumph* (1993), Rumsfeld worried that "we are neither organized nor ready to face a crisis there." In fact, the effort to reorganize was already under way. And here is where Reagan made his most lasting contribution to the struggle to which Jimmy Carter had committed the United States.

Seven specific initiatives figured prominently in the Reagan administration's comprehensive effort to ramp up America's ability to wage World War IV:

- The upgrading in 1983 of the Rapid Deployment Joint Task Force, the Persian Gulf intervention force created by Carter after the Soviet incursion into Afghanistan, to the status of a full-fledged regional headquarters, US Central Command.
- The accelerated conversion of Diego Garcia, a tiny British-owned island in the Indian Ocean, from a minor US communications facility into a major US forward support base.
- The establishment of large stocks of supplies and equipment, preloaded on ships and positioned to facilitate the rapid movement of US combat forces to the Persian Gulf.
- The construction or expansion of air bases, ports, and other fixed locations required to receive and sustain large-scale US expedi-

tionary forces in Egypt, Saudi Arabia, Oman, Kenya, Somalia, and other compliant states.

- The negotiation of overflight rights and agreements to permit US military access to airports and other facilities in Morocco, Egypt, and elsewhere in the region to support the large-scale introduction of US troops.

- The refinement of war plans and the development of exercise programs to acclimate US forces to the unfamiliar and demanding desert environment.

- The redoubling of efforts to cultivate client states through arms sales and training programs, the latter administered either by the US military or by American-controlled private contractors employing large numbers of former US military personnel.

By the time Ronald Reagan retired from office, the skids had been greased. The national security bureaucracy was well on its way to embracing a highly militarized conception of how to deal with the challenges posed by the Middle East. Giving Reagan his due requires an appreciation of the extent to which he advanced the reordering of US national security priorities that Jimmy Carter had barely begun. Reagan's seemingly slapdash Islamic pudding turned out to have a theme after all.

Those who adjudge the present World War IV to be necessary and winnable will see in Reagan's record much to commend, and may well accord him a share of the credit even for Operations Enduring Freedom and Iraqi Freedom. It was Reagan who restored the sinews of American military might after Vietnam, refashioned American attitudes about military power, and began reorienting the Pentagon toward the Islamic world, thereby making possible the far-flung campaigns to overthrow the Taliban and remove Saddam Hussein. George W. Bush pulled the trigger, but Ronald Reagan had cocked the weapon.

Those who view World War IV as either sinister in its motivation or misguided in its conception will include Reagan in their bill of indictment. From their perspective, it was he who seduced his fellow citizens with promises of material abundance without limit. It was Reagan who made the fusion of military strength with American exceptionalism the centerpiece of his efforts to revive national self-confidence. It was Reagan's enthusiastic support of Afghan "freedom fighters"—an eminently defensible position in the context of World War III—that produced not freedom but a Central Asian power vacuum, Afghanistan becoming a cesspool of Islamic radicalism and a safe haven for America's chief adversary in World War IV. Finally, it was Reagan's inconclusive forays in and around the Persian Gulf that paved the way for still-larger, if equally inconclusive, interventions to come.

Throughout the first phase of World War IV, from 1980 to 1990, the United States viewed Iran as its main problem and even toyed with the idea that Iraq might be part of a solution. Washington saw Saddam Hussein as someone with whom it might make common cause against the mullahs in Tehran. During the second phase of World War IV, extending through the 1990s, Iraq supplanted Iran as the main US adversary, and policymakers came to see the Iraqi dictator as their chief nemesis.

Various and sundry exertions ensued, but as the US military profile in the region became ever more prominent, the difficulties with which the United States felt obliged to contend also multiplied. Indeed, instead of eliminating Saddam, the growing reliance on military power served only to rouse greater antagonism toward the United States. Actions taken to enhance Persian Gulf stability—more or less synonymous with guaranteeing the safety and survival of the Saudi royal family—instead produced instability.

Phase two of the war began in August 1990, when Saddam Hussein's army overran Kuwait. From the US perspective, Saddam's aim was clear. He sought to achieve regional hegemony and to control, either directly or indirectly, the preponderant part of the Persian Gulf's oil wealth. Were Saddam to achieve those objectives, there was every likelihood that in due course he would turn on Israel.

So after only the briefest hesitation, the administration of George H. W. Bush mounted a forthright response. At the head of a large international coalition, the nation marched off to war, and US forces handily ejected the Iraqi occupiers and restored the Al-Sabah family to its throne. (Bowing to American pressure, Israel stayed on the sidelines.) Its assigned mission accomplished, the officer corps, led by Colin Powell, had little interest in pressing its luck. The American army was eager to scoop up its winnings and go home.

The elder President Bush dearly hoped that Operation Desert Storm might become a great historical watershed, laying the basis for a more law-abiding international system. In fact, the war turned out to be both less and more than he had anticipated. No new world order emerged from the demonstration of American military prowess, but the war saddled the United States with new obligations from which came yet more headaches and complications.

Saddam survived in power by brutally suppressing those whom the Bush administration had urged to rise up in opposition to the dictator. After first averting its eyes from the fate of the Iraqi Shiites and Kurds, the administration eventually found itself shamed into action. To protect the Kurds (and to prevent Kurdish refugees from triggering a military response by neighboring Turkey, a key US ally), Bush sent US forces into northern Iraq. To limit Saddam's ability to use his army as an instrument of repression, the Bush administration, with British support, declared the existence of "no-fly zones" across much of northern and southern Iraq. In April 1991, Anglo-American air forces began routine combat patrols of Iraqi airspace, a mission that continued without interruption for the next twelve years. During his final weeks in office, Bush initiated the practice of launching punitive air strikes against Iraqi military targets.

Thus, in the year that followed what had appeared to be a decisive victory in Operation Desert Storm, the United States transitioned willy-nilly to a policy that seemed anything but decisive. As a result of that policy, which the Bush administration called "containment," the presence of substantial US forces in Saudi Arabia and elsewhere in the Persian Gulf, initially conceived as temporary, became permanent. A contingent of approximately 25,000 US troops remained after Desert Storm as a Persian Gulf constabulary—or, from the perspective of many Arabs, as an occupying army of infidels. As a second result of the policy, the United States fell into the habit of routinely employing force to punish the Iraqi regime. What US policymakers called containment was really an open-ended quasi-war.

This new policy of containment-with-bombs formed just one part of the legacy that President Bush bequeathed to his successor,

Bill Clinton. That legacy had two additional elements. The first was Somalia, the impoverished, chaotic, famine-stricken Islamic "failed state" into which Bush sent US forces after his defeat in the November 1992 elections. Bush described the US mission as humanitarian, and promised to have American troops out of the country by the time he left office. But when Clinton became president, the troops remained in place. The second element of the legacy Clinton inherited was the so-called peace process, Bush's post–Desert Storm initiative aimed at persuading the Arab world once and for all to accept Israel.

President Clinton was unable to extract from this ambiguous legacy much of tangible value, though not for want of trying. During his eight years in office, he clung to the Bush policy of containing Iraq while ratcheting up the frequency with which the United States used violence to enforce that policy. Indeed, during the two final years of his presidency, the United States bombed Iraq on almost a daily basis. The campaign was largely ignored by the media, and thus aptly dubbed by one observer "Operation Desert Yawn."

In the summer of 1993, Clinton had also ratcheted up the US military commitment in Somalia. The results proved disastrous. After the famous Mogadishu firefight of October 1993, Clinton quickly threw in the towel, tacitly accepting defeat at the hands of Islamic fighters. Somalia per se mattered little. Somalia as a battlefield of World War IV mattered quite a bit. The speedy US withdrawal after Mogadishu affirmed to many the apparent lesson of Beirut a decade earlier: Americans lacked the stomach for real fighting; if seriously challenged, they would fold. That was certainly the lesson Osama bin Laden drew. In his August 1996 fatwa against the United States, he cited the failure of US policy in Lebanon as evidence of America's "false courage," and he found in Somalia proof of US "impotence and weaknesses." When "tens of your soldiers were killed in minor battles and one American pilot was dragged in the streets of Mogadishu," crowed the leader of al-Qaeda, "you left the area, carrying disappointment, humiliation, defeat, and your dead with you."

From Mogadishu onward, the momentum shifted inexorably in favor of those contesting American efforts to dominate the Persian Gulf. For the balance of the Clinton era, the United States found itself in a reactive posture, and it sustained a series of minor but painful and painfully embarrassing setbacks: the bombing of SANG headquarters in Riyadh in November 1995; an attack on the US military barracks at Khobar Towers in Dhahran in June 1996; simultaneous attacks on US embassies in Kenya and Tanzania in August 1998; and the near-sinking of an American warship, the USS *Cole*, during a port call at Aden in August 2000.

To each of these in turn, the Clinton administration promised a prompt, decisive response, but such responses as actually materialized proved innocuous. The low point came in late August 1998, after the African embassy bombings. With the United States combating what Bill Clinton referred to as "the bin Laden network," the president ordered cruise missile strikes against a handful of primitive training camps in Afghanistan. For good measure, he included as an additional target a Sudanese pharmaceutical factory allegedly involved in the production of chemical weapons. Unfortunately for Clinton, the training camps turned out to be mostly empty, while subsequent investigation cast doubt on whether the factory in Khartoum had ever housed any nefarious activity. Although the president spoke grimly of a "long, ongoing struggle between freedom and fanaticism," and vowed that the United States was "prepared to do all that we can for as long as we must," the operation, given the code name Infinite Reach, accomplished next to nothing, and was over almost as soon as it began. The disparity between words and actions—between the operation's grandiose name and its trivial impact—spoke volumes. In truth, no one in the Clinton White House had a clear conception of what the United States needed to do—or to whom.

Finally, despite Clinton's energetic and admirable contributions, the peace process failed to yield peace. Instead, the collapse of that process at Camp David in 2000 gave rise to a new cycle of Palestinian terrorist attacks and Israeli reprisals. An alienated Arab world convinced itself that the United States and Israel were conspiring to humiliate and oppress Muslims. Just as the Israeli Defense Forces occupied Gaza and the West Bank, so too did the US military seemingly intend to occupy the Middle East as a whole. In Arab eyes, the presence of US troops amounted to "a new American colonialism," an expression of a larger effort to "seek control over Arab political and economic affairs." And just as Israel appeared callous in its treatment of the Palestinians, so too did the United States seem callous in its attitude toward Iraqis by persisting in a policy of sanctions that put the burden of punishment not on Saddam Hussein but on the Iraqi people.

The end of the 1980s had found the Reagan administration engaged in a far-reaching contest for control of the Middle East, a de facto war whose existence Reagan himself either could not see or was unwilling to acknowledge. Ten years later, events ought to have removed any doubt as to whether the circumstances facing the United States qualified as a war, but the Clinton administration's insistence on describing the adversary as disembodied "terrorists" robbed those events of any coherent political context. In the manner of his immediate predecessors, Clinton refused to concede that the violence directed against the United States might stem from some plausible (which is not to imply justifiable) motivation—even as Osama bin Laden outlined his intentions with impressive clarity. In his 1996 declaration of jihad, for example, bin Laden identified his objectives: to overthrow the corrupt Saudi regime that had become a tool of the "Zionist-Crusader alliance," to expel the infidels from the land of the Two Holy Places, and to ensure the worldwide triumph of Islam. But his immediate aim was more limited: to destroy the compact forged by President Roosevelt and King Ibn Saud. A perfectly logical first step toward that end was to orchestrate a campaign of terror against the United States.

For Clinton to acknowledge bin Laden's agenda was to acknowledge as well that opposition to the US presence in and around the Persian Gulf had a history, and that, like all history, it was fraught with ambiguity. In the Persian Gulf, the United States had behaved just like any other nation, even as it proclaimed itself democracy's greatest friend. For decades it had single-mindedly pursued its own interests, with only occasional regard for how its actions affected others. Expediency dictated that American policymakers avert their eyes from the fact that throughout much of the Islamic world the United States had aligned itself with regimes that were arbitrary, corrupt, and oppressive. The underside of American exceptionalism lay exposed.

In the annals of statecraft, US policy in the Persian Gulf from Franklin Roosevelt through Clinton did not qualify as having been notably harsh or irresponsible, but neither had it been particularly wise or enlightened. Bin Laden's campaign, however contemptible, and more general opposition to US ambitions in the Greater Middle East, developed at least in part as a response to earlier US policies and actions, in which lofty ideals and high moral purpose seldom figured. The United States cannot be held culpable for the maladies that today find expression in violent Islamic radicalism. But neither can the United States absolve itself of any and all responsibility for the conditions that have exacerbated those maladies. After several decades of acting as the preeminent power in the Persian Gulf, America did not arrive at the end of the twentieth century with clean hands.

Years before 9/11, bin Laden understood that World War IV had been fully joined, and he seems to have rejoiced in the prospect of a fight to the finish. Even as they engaged in an array of military activities intended to deflect threats to US control of the Persian Gulf and its environs, a succession of American presidents persisted in pretending otherwise. For them, World War IV remained a furtive enterprise.

Unlike Franklin Roosevelt, who had deceived the American people but who understood long before December 7, 1941, that he was steadily moving the United States toward direct engagement in a monumental struggle, the lesser statesmen who inhabited the Oval Office during the 1980s and 1990s, in weaving their deceptions, managed only to confuse themselves. Despite endless assertions that the United States sought only peace, Presidents Reagan, Bush, and Clinton were each in fact waging war. But a coherent strategy for bringing the war to a successful conclusion eluded them.

Even as it flung about bombs and missiles with abandon, the United States seemed to dither throughout the 1990s, whereas bin Laden, playing a weak hand, played it with considerable skill. In the course of the decade, World War IV became bigger and the costs mounted, but its resolution was more distant than ever. The Bush and Clinton administrations used force in the Middle East not so much as an extension of policy but as a way of distracting attention from the contradictions that riddled US policy. Bombing something—at times, almost anything—became a convenient way of keeping up appearances. Thus, despite (or perhaps because of) the military hyperactivity of the two administrations, the overall US position deteriorated even further during World War IV's second phase.

George W. Bush inherited this deteriorating situation when he became president in January 2001. Bush may or may not have brought into office a determination to finish off Saddam Hussein at the first available opportunity, but he most assuredly did not bring with him a comprehensive, ready-made conception of how to deal with the incongruities that plagued US policy in the Greater Middle East. For its first eight months in office, the second Bush administration essentially marked time. Apart from some politically inspired grandstanding—shunning an international agreement to slow global warming, talking tough on North Korea, accelerating plans to field ballistic missile defenses—Bush's foreign policy before 9/11 hewed closely to the lines laid down by his predecessor. Although Republicans had spent the previous eight years lambasting Clinton for being weak and feckless, their own approach to World War IV, initially at least, amounted to more of the same.

Osama bin Laden chose this moment to begin the war's third phase. His direct assault on the United States left thousands dead, wreaked havoc with the American economy, and exposed the acute vulnerabilities of the world's sole superpower.

President Bush's spontaneous response to the events of 9/11 was to see them not as vile crimes but as acts of war. In so doing, he openly acknowledged the existence of the conflict in which the United States had been engaged for the previous twenty years. World War IV became the centerpiece of the Bush presidency, although the formulation preferred by members of his administration was "the Global War on Terror."

When committing the United States to large-scale armed conflict, presidents have traditionally evinced a strong preference for explaining the stakes in terms of ideology, thereby distracting attention from geopolitics. Americans ostensibly fight for universal values rather than sordid self-interest. Thus, Franklin Roosevelt cast the war against Japan as a contest that pitted democracy against imperialism. The Pacific war was indeed that, but it was also a war fought to determine the future of East Asia, with both Japan and the United States seeing China as the main prize. Harry Truman and his successors characterized the Cold War as a struggle between a free world and a totalitarian one. Again, the war was that, but it was also a competition to determine which of two superpowers would enjoy preponderant influence in Western Europe, with both the Soviet Union and the United States viewing Germany as the nexus of conflict.

During its preliminary phases—from January 1980 to September 2001—World War IV departed from this pattern. Regardless of who happened to be occupying the Oval Office, universal values did not figure prominently in the formulation and articulation of US policy in the Persian Gulf. Geopolitics routinely trumped values in the war. Everyone knew that the dominant issue was oil, with Saudi Arabia understood to be the crown jewel. Only after 9/11 did values emerge as the ostensible driving force behind US efforts in the region—indeed, throughout the Greater Middle East. On September 11, 2001, World War IV became, like each of its predecessors, a war for "freedom." To this theme President George W. Bush returned time and again.

In fact, President Bush's epiphany was itself a smoke screen. His conversion to the church of Woodrow Wilson left substantive US objectives in World War IV unaltered. Using armed might to secure American preeminence across the region, especially in the oil-rich Persian Gulf, remained the essence of US policy. What changed after 9/11 was that the Bush administration was willing to pull out all the stops in its determination to impose America's will on the Greater Middle East.

In that regard, the administration's invasion of Iraq in March 2003 can be said to possess a certain bizarre logic. As part of a larger campaign to bring the perpetrators of 9/11 to justice, Operation Iraqi Freedom made no sense at all and was probably counterproductive. Yet as the initial gambit of an effort to transform the entire region through the use of superior military power, it not only made sense but also held out the prospect of finally resolving the incongruities bedeviling US policy. Iraq was the "tactical pivot"—not an end in itself but a way station. "With Saddam gone," former counter-terrorism official Richard Clarke has written in *Against All Enemies* (2004), "the U.S. could reduce its dependence on Saudi Arabia, could pull its forces out of the Kingdom, and could open up an alternative source of oil."

Pulling US forces out of Saudi Arabia did not imply removing them from the region; a continuing American troop presence was necessary to guarantee US access to energy reserves. But having demonstrated its ability to oust recalcitrants, having established a mighty striking force in the center of the Persian Gulf, and having reduced its susceptibility to the oil weapon, the United States would be well positioned to create a new political order in the region, incorporating values such as freedom, democracy, and equality for women. A Middle East pacified, brought into compliance with American ideological norms, and policed by American soldiers could be counted on to produce plentiful supplies of oil and to accept the presence of a Jewish state in its midst. "In transforming Iraq," one senior Bush administration official confidently predicted, "we will take a significant step in the direction of the longer-term need to transform the region as a whole."

Bush and his inner circle conceived of this as a great crusade, and, at its unveiling, a clear majority of citizens also judged the preposterous enterprise to be justifiable, feasible, and indeed necessary. At least two factors help to explain their apparent gullibility.

The first is self-induced historical amnesia. Shortly after 9/11, Deputy Secretary of State Richard Armitage growled that "history starts today." His sentiment suffused the Bush administration and was widely shared among the American people. The grievous losses suffered in the attacks on the World Trade Center and the Pentagon had rendered irrelevant all that went before—hence the notable absence of interest among Americans in how the modern Middle East had come into existence, or in the role the United States had played since World War II in its evolution. The events of 9/11 wiped the slate clean, and on this clean slate the Bush administration, in quintessential American fashion, fancied that it could begin the history of the Greater Middle East all over again.

There is a second explanation for this extraordinary confidence in America's ability to reorder nations according to its own preferences. The progressive militarization of US policy since Vietnam—especially US policy as it related to the Middle East—had acquired a momentum to which the events of 9/11 only added. The aura that by 2001 had come to suffuse American attitudes toward war, soldiers, and military institutions had dulled the capacity of the American people to think critically about the actual limits of military power. And nowhere had those attitudes gained a deeper lodgment than in the upper echelons of the younger Bush's administration. The experiences of the previous thirty years had thoroughly militarized the individuals to whom the president turned in shaping his Global War on Terror, formulating grand statements, such as his National Security Strategy of the United States of America, and planning campaigns, such as the invasions of Afghanistan and Iraq. Theirs was a vision, writes James Mann in *The Rise of the Vulcans* (2004), of "a United States whose military power was so awesome that it no longer needed to make compromises or accommodations (unless it chose to do so) with any other nation or groups of countries."

As the epigraph to his book *Why We Were in Vietnam* (1982), Norman Podhoretz chose a quotation from Bismarck: "Woe to the statesman whose reasons for entering a war do not appear so plausible at its end as at its beginning." For the architects of the Global War on Terror—George W. Bush, Dick Cheney, Donald Rumsfeld, Condoleezza Rice, and Paul Wolfowitz—it's too late to heed the Iron Chancellor's warning. But the outsized conflict that is their principal handiwork continues.

As this is written, the outcome of World War IV hangs very much in the balance. American shortsightedness played a large role in creating this war, and American hubris has complicated it unnecessarily, emboldening the enemy, alienating old allies, and bringing US forces close to exhaustion. Yet like it or not, Americans are now stuck with their misbegotten crusade. God forbid that the United States should fail, allowing the likes of Osama bin Laden and his henchmen to decide the future of the Islamic world.

But even if the United States ultimately prevails, the prospects for the future will be no less discouraging. On the far side of World War IV, a time we are not now given to see, there wait others who will not readily concede to the United States the prerogatives and the dominion that Americans have come to expect as their due. The ensuing collision between American requirements and a noncompliant world will provide the impetus for more crusades. Each will be justified in terms of ideals rather than interests, but the sum of them may well doom the United States to fight perpetual wars in a vain effort to satisfy our craving for limitless freedom.

PART 3

War and Empire

31

Save Us From Washington's Visionaries

(2015)

En route back to Washington at the tail end of his most recent overseas trip, John Kerry, America's peripatetic secretary of state, stopped off in France "to share a hug with all of Paris." Whether Paris reciprocated the secretary's embrace went unrecorded.

Despite the requisite reference to General Pershing ("Lafayette, we are here!") and flying James Taylor in from the 1960s to assure Parisians that "You've Got a Friend," in the annals of American diplomacy Kerry's hug will likely rank with President Eisenhower's award of the Legion of Merit to Nicaraguan dictator Anastasio Somoza for "exceptionally meritorious conduct" and Jimmy Carter's acknowledgment of the "admiration and love" said to define the relationship between the Iranian people and their Shah. In short, it was a moment best forgotten.

Alas, this vapid, profoundly silly event is all too emblematic of statecraft in the Obama era. Seldom have well-credentialed and well-meaning people worked so hard to produce so little of substance.

Not one of the signature foreign policy initiatives conceived in Obama's first term has borne fruit. When it came to making a fresh start with the Islamic world, responsibly ending the "dumb" war in Iraq (while winning the "necessary" one in Afghanistan), "resetting" US-Russian relations, and "pivoting" toward Asia, mark your scorecard 0 for 4.

There's no doubt that when Kerry arrived at the State Department he brought with him some much-needed energy. That he is giving it his all—the department's website reports that the secretary has already clocked over 682,000 miles of travel—is doubtless true as well. The problem is the absence of results. Remember when *his* signature initiative was going to be an Israeli-Palestinian peace deal? Sadly, that quixotic plan, too, has come to naught.

Yes, Team Obama "got" bin Laden. And, yes, it deserves credit for abandoning a self-evidently counterproductive fifty-plus-year-old policy toward Cuba and for signing a promising agreement with China on climate change. That said, the administration's overall record of accomplishment is beyond thin, starting with that first-day-in-the-Oval-Office symbol that things were truly going to be different: Obama's order to close Guantanamo. That, of course, remains a work in progress (despite regular reassurances of light glimmering at the end of what has become a very long tunnel).

In fact, taking the president's record as a whole, noting that on his watch occasional US drone strikes have become routine, the Nobel Committee might want to consider revoking its Peace Prize.

Nor should we expect much in the time that Obama has remaining. Perhaps there is a deal with Iran waiting in the wings (along with the depth charge of ever-fiercer congressionally mandated sanctions), but signs of intellectual exhaustion are distinctly in evidence.

"Where there is no vision," the Hebrew Bible tells us, "the people perish." There's no use pretending: if there's one thing the Obama administration most definitely has not got and has never had, it's a foreign policy vision.

In Search of Truly Wise (White) Men—Only Those Eighty-Four or Older Need Apply

All of this evokes a sense of unease, even consternation bordering on panic, in circles where members of the foreign policy elite congregate.

Absent visionary leadership in Washington, they have persuaded themselves, we're all going down. So the world's sole superpower and self-anointed global leader needs to get game—and fast.

Leslie Gelb, former president of the Council on Foreign Relations, recently weighed in with a proposal for fixing the problem: clean house. Obama has surrounded himself with fumbling incompetents, Gelb charges. Get rid of them and bring in the visionaries.

Writing at the *Daily Beast*, Gelb urges the president to fire his entire national security team and replace them with "strong and strategic people of proven foreign policy experience." Translation: the sort of people who sip sherry and nibble on brie in the august precincts of the Council of Foreign Relations. In addition to offering his own slate of nominees, including several veterans of the storied George W. Bush administration, Gelb suggests that Obama consult regularly with Henry Kissinger, Brent Scowcroft, Zbigniew Brzezinski, and James Baker. These distinguished war-horses range in age from eighty-four to ninety-one. By implication, only white males born prior to World War II are eligible for induction into the ranks of the Truly Wise Men.

Anyway, Gelb emphasizes, Obama needs to get on with it. With the planet awash in challenges that "imperil our very survival," there is simply no time to waste.

At best, Gelb's got it half right. When it comes to foreign policy, this president has indeed demonstrated a knack for surrounding himself with lackluster lieutenants. That statement applies equally to national security adviser Susan Rice (and her predecessor), to Secretary of State Kerry (and his predecessor), and to outgoing Pentagon chief Chuck Hagel. Ashton Carter, the technocrat slated to replace Hagel as defense secretary, comes from the same mold.

They are all "seasoned"—in Washington, a euphemism for bland, conventional, and utterly unimaginative—charter members of the Rogers-Christopher school of American statecraft. (That may require some unpacking, so pretend you're on *Jeopardy*. Alex Trebek: "Two eminently forgettable and completely forgotten twentieth-century secretaries of state." You, hitting the buzzer: "Who were William Rogers and Warren Christopher?" "Correct!")

Members of Obama's national security team worked long and hard to get where they are. Yet along the way—perhaps from absorbing too many position papers, PowerPoint briefings, and platitudes about "American global leadership"—they lost whatever creative spark once endowed them with the appearance of talent and promise. Ambition, unquestioned patriotism, and a capacity for putting in endless hours (and enduring endless travel)—all these remain. But a serious conception of where the world is heading and what that implies for basic US foreign policy? Individually and collectively, they are without a clue.

I submit that maybe that's okay, that plodding mediocrity can be a boon if, as at present, the alternatives on offer look even worse.

A Hug for Obama

You want vision? Obama's predecessor surrounded himself with visionaries. Dick Cheney, Condoleezza Rice, Donald Rumsfeld, and Paul Wolfowitz, products of the Cold War one and all, certainly fancied themselves large-bore strategic thinkers. Busily positioning the United States to run (just another "i" and you have "ruin") the world, they were blindsided by 9/11. Unembarrassed and unchastened by this disaster, they initiated a series of morally dubious, strategically boneheaded moves that were either (take your pick) going to spread freedom and democracy or position the United States to exercise permanent dominion. The ensuing Global War on Terror did neither, of course, while adding trillions to the national debt and helping fracture great expanses of the planet. Obama is still, however ineffectually, trying to clean up the mess they created.

If that's what handing the keys to big thinkers gets you, give me Susan Rice any day. Although Obama's "don't do stupid shit" may never rank with Washington's Farewell Address or the Monroe Doctrine in the history books, George W. Bush might have profited from having some comparable axiom taped to his laptop.

Big ideas have their place—indeed, are essential—when the issues at hand are clearly defined. The Fall of France in 1940 was one such moment, which President Franklin Roosevelt recognized. So too, arguably, was the period immediately after World War II. The defeat of Nazi Germany and Imperial Japan had left a dangerous power vacuum in both Europe and the Pacific to which George Marshall,

Dean Acheson, and their compatriots forged a necessary response. Perhaps the period 1968–69 falls into that same category, the debacle of Vietnam requiring a major adjustment in US Cold War strategy. This Richard Nixon and Henry Kissinger undertook with their opening to China.

Yet despite the overwrought claims of Gelb (and others) that America's very survival is today at risk, the present historical moment lacks comparable clarity. Ours is not a time when we face a single overarching threat. Instead, on several different fronts, worrisome developments are brewing. Environmental degradation, the rise of China and other emerging powers, the spread of radical Islam, the precarious state of the global economy, vulnerabilities that are an inevitable byproduct of our pursuit of a cyber-utopia: all of these require very careful watching. Each one today should entail a defensive response, the United States protecting itself (and its allies) against worst-case outcomes. But at the present moment, none of these justifies embarking upon a let-out-all-the-stops offensive. Chasing after one problem would necessarily divert attention from the rest.

The immediate future remains too opaque to say with certainty which threat will turn out to pose the greatest danger, whether in the next year or the next decade—and which might even end up not being a threat at all but an unexpected opportunity. Conditions are not ripe for boldness. The abiding imperative of the moment is to discern, which requires careful observation and patience. In short, forget about strategy.

And there's a further matter. Correct discernment assumes a proper vantage point. What you see depends on where you sit and which way you're facing. Those who inhabit the upper ranks of the Obama administration (and those whom Leslie Gelb offers as replacements) sit somewhere back in the twentieth century, their worldview shaped by memories of Munich and Yalta, Korea and Vietnam, the Cuban Missile Crisis and the Berlin Wall, none of which retain more than tangential relevance to the present day.

You want vision? That will require a new crop of visionaries. Instead of sitting down with ancients like Kissinger, Scowcroft, Brzezinski, or Baker, this president (or his successor) would be better served to pick the brain of the army captain back from multiple combat tours in Iraq and Afghanistan, the moral theologian specializing in inter-religious dialog, the Peace Corps volunteer who spent the last two years in West Africa, and the Silicon Valley entrepreneur best able to spell out the political implications of the next big thing.

In short, a post-twentieth century vision requires a post-twentieth century generation, able to free itself from old shibboleths to which Leslie Gelb and most of official Washington today remain stubbornly dedicated. That generation waits in the wings and after another presidential election or two may indeed wield some influence. We should hope so. In the meantime, we should bide our time, amending the words of the prophet to something like this: "Where there is no vision, the people muddle along and await salvation."

So as Obama and his team muddle toward their finish line, their achievements negligible, we might even express a modicum of gratitude. When they depart the scene, we will forget the lot of them. Yet at least they managed to steer clear of truly epic disasters. When muddling was the best Washington had on offer, they delivered. They may even deserve a hug.

32

A War of Ambition

(2014)

History, wrote T. S. Eliot in 1920, "deceives with whispering ambitions" and "guides us by vanities." Over the past decade, ambitions and vanities have led the United States badly astray, nowhere more than in the Islamic world. Let us tally up the damage.

Among most Americans, the terrorist attacks of September 11, 2001, prompted a response combining fear, anger, and mourning. Yet in Washington, in circles where ambition and vanity held sway, those events also represented a signal opportunity. In a twinkling, action had become the order of the day. Existing restraints on the use of US power suddenly fell away. A radical reorientation of American statecraft suddenly appeared possible. Overnight, the previously implausible had become not only necessary, but also alluring.

For decades, US policy in the Middle East had sought to shore up that region's precarious stability. In a part of the world always teetering on the brink of chaos, averting war had formed the centerpiece of US policy.

Now, however, the administration of George W. Bush contrived a different approach. Through war, the United States would destabilize the region and then remake it to the benefit of all. "The United States may not be able to lead countries through the door of democracy," Deputy Secretary of Defense Paul Wolfowitz remarked, "but where that door is locked shut by a totalitarian deadbolt, American power may be the only way to open it up."

The "Democratic Domino Theory"

Where then to begin this process of creative destruction? On the first weekend after September 11, at a war council meeting at Camp David, according to the 9/11 Commission Report, Mr. Wolfowitz made the case for striking Iraq. Then, in late November 2001, a small study group of Washington insiders convened at Wolfowitz's behest. Christopher DeMuth, then president of the American Enterprise Institute, recruited the group's members and later shared its conclusions with Bob Woodward. The group identified Saddam Hussein's Iraq as the best place for blowing that door off its hinges. Although most of the 9/11 hijackers had come from Saudi Arabia and Egypt, "the problems there [were] intractable." Iraq was seen as "different, weaker, more vulnerable," Mr. Woodward reported in his book *State of Denial* (2006). Here was the place to implement America's new "democratic domino theory." As President Bush himself proclaimed, toppling Saddam "would serve as a dramatic and inspiring example for freedom for other nations in the region."

The point is crucial. Only by appreciating the magnitude of the Bush administration's post-9/11, vanity-saturated ambitions does it become possible to gauge their unforeseen consequences. Only then can we fully appreciate the deeply ironic outcome that those ambitions yielded.

Put simply, invading Iraq was never itself the end. Doing so pointed toward a much larger objective. Writing months before the United States launched Operation Iraqi Freedom, the journalist Mark Danner accurately characterized President Bush's post-9/11 strategy as "comprehensive, prophetic, [and] evangelical." That strategy was nothing if not bold and brazen.

Washington, Mr. Danner observed, had jettisoned "the ideology of a status quo power" that had largely shaped US policy since World War II. Containing evil no longer sufficed. "The transformation of the Middle East," insisted Condoleezza Rice, Mr. Bush's national security advisor, offered "the only guarantee that it will no longer produce ideologies of hatred that lead men to fly airplanes into buildings in New York or Washington."

Transformation—there was a word redolent with ambition and vanity. By invading Iraq and overthrowing a dictator, an administration disdainful of mere stability would make a start at transforming the entire Islamic world. In the first decade of the twenty-first century, the United States intended to reprise the role it credited itself with playing during the second half of the twentieth century. Across the Middle East, ideologies of hatred would give way to the ideology of freedom.

Unfortunately, this preening liberation narrative, that hardy perennial of American political discourse, did not describe the twentieth century that the peoples of the Middle East had actually experienced. Arabs, Iranians, and other Muslims had little reason to look to the United States (or any other Western nation) for liberation. Nor did the freedom to which they aspired necessarily accord with Washington's tacit understanding of the term: "friendly" governments that on matters ranging from oil to Israel to terrorism obligingly deferred to US policy preferences.

Much to its chagrin, the Bush administration soon learned that the dyad pitting hatred against freedom did not exhaust the full range of possible outcomes. The United States dispatched Saddam Hussein, but the results confidently predicted by the war's architects failed to materialize. The blown-open door admitted not democracy, but endemic violence. Even today, a decade into the post-Saddam era and two years after the last American soldier departed, the Iraq War continues. In October 2013 alone, that war claimed the lives of nearly one thousand Iraqis.

Nor did that violence confine itself to Iraq. Following in the wake of the US invasion of Iraq came not transformation, but disorder that enveloped large swaths of the Middle East. In Tunisia, Libya and Egypt popular uprisings overthrew dictators. Nowhere, however, did this so-called Arab Spring yield effective governments, much less liberal democracy. Nowhere did upheaval enhance American stature, standing or influence.

Intervention's End?

Then came Syria. There indigenous efforts to overthrow another dictator led to an immensely bloody civil war. Declaring that Syria's President Bashar al-Assad "must go," while drawing never-to-be-crossed "red lines," President Barack Obama still nursed the fancy that it was incumbent upon the United States to sort matters out.

Only on the eve of ordering another armed intervention did Mr. Obama pause long enough to notice that he was pretty much on his own. In the White House, illusions that US bombs and rockets could deliver Syrians from evil still lingered. Others—including a clear majority of the American people, both chambers of Congress and even the British Parliament—had concluded otherwise. With the stores of 9/11-induced vanity and ambition (not to mention the US Treasury) now depleted, faith in the transformative power of American military might had waned. The president prudently pulled back from the brink.

Whether Mr. Obama's about-face in Syria marks a decisive turn in overall US policy in the Middle East remains to be seen. Senior officials like National Security Advisor Susan E. Rice have hinted that the administration would like to turn its attention elsewhere. Even if it does, this much seems certain: The instability that US policymakers a decade ago so heedlessly sought will persist.

Scholars will long debate whether the misuse of American power caused or merely catalyzed this instability—or indeed whether the disorder roiling the Middle East derives from factors to which decisions made in Washington are largely irrelevant. What they will not debate is the outcome, best captured in the words of another poet, Robert Lowell. "Pity the planet," he wrote, "all joy gone." And "peace to our children when they fall/ in small war on the heels of small/ war—until the end of time."

Of course, the vast majority of those felled by the violence rippling through the Islamic world are not the offspring of Americans. They are someone else's children. Although this makes their fate that much easier for present-day Americans to stomach—and even ignore—it is unlikely to affect the judgment that history will render. Mindless policies conceived by an arrogant and ignorant elite have produced shameful results.

33

Naming Our Nameless War

(2013)

For well over a decade now the United States has been "a nation at war." Does that war have a name?

It did at the outset. After 9/11, George W. Bush's administration wasted no time in announcing that the United States was engaged in a *Global War on Terror*, or GWOT. With few dissenters, the media quickly embraced the term. The GWOT promised to be a gargantuan, transformative enterprise. The conflict begun on 9/11 would define the age. In neoconservative circles, it was known as *World War IV*.

Upon succeeding to the presidency in 2009, however, Barack Obama without fanfare junked Bush's formulation. Yet if the appellation went away, the conflict itself, shorn of identifying marks, continued.

Does it matter that ours has become and remains a nameless war? Very much so.

Names bestow meaning. When it comes to war, a name attached to a date can shape our understanding of what the conflict was all about.

To specify when a war began and when it ended is to privilege certain explanations of its significance while discrediting others. Let me provide a few illustrations.

With rare exceptions, Americans today characterize the horrendous fraternal bloodletting of 1861–65 as the *Civil War*. Yet not many decades ago, diehard supporters of the Lost Cause insisted on referring to that conflict as the *War Between the States* or the *War for Southern Independence* (or even the *War of Northern Aggression*). The South may have gone down in defeat, but the purposes for which Southerners had fought—preserving a distinctive way of life and the principle of states' rights—had been worthy, even noble. So at least they professed to believe, with their preferred names for the war reflecting that belief.

Schoolbooks tell us that the *Spanish-American War* began in April 1898 and ended in August of that same year. The name and dates fit nicely with a widespread inclination from President William McKinley's day to our own to frame US intervention in Cuba as an altruistic effort to liberate that island from Spanish oppression.

Yet the Cubans were not exactly bystanders in that drama. By 1898, they had been fighting for years to oust their colonial overlords. And although hostilities in Cuba itself ended on August 12, they dragged on in the Philippines, another Spanish colony that the United States had seized for reasons only remotely related to liberating Cubans. Notably, US troops occupying the Philippines waged a brutal war not against Spaniards but against Filipino nationalists no more inclined to accept colonial rule by Washington than by Madrid. So widen the aperture to include this Cuban prelude and the Filipino postlude and you end up with something like this: The *Spanish-American-Cuban-Philippines War of 1895–1902*. Too clunky? How about the *War for the American Empire*? This much is for sure: rather than illuminating, the commonplace textbook descriptor serves chiefly to conceal.

Strange as it may seem, Europeans once referred to the calamitous events of 1914–18 as the *Great War*. When Woodrow Wilson decided in 1917 to send an army of doughboys to fight alongside the Allies, he went beyond "Great." According to the president, the *Great War* was going to be the *War To End All Wars*. Alas, things did not pan out as he expected. Perhaps anticipating the demise of his vision of permanent peace, War Department General Order 115, issued on October 7, 1919, formally declared that, at least as far as the United States was concerned, the recently concluded hostilities would be known simply as the *World War*.

In September 1939—presto chango!—the *World War* suddenly became the *First World War*, the Nazi invasion of Poland having inaugurated a *Second World War*, also known as *World War II* or more cryptically *WWII*. To be sure, Soviet dictator Joseph Stalin preferred the *Great Patriotic War*. Although this found instant—almost unanimous—favor among Soviet citizens, it did not catch on elsewhere.

Does *World War II* accurately capture the events it purports to encompass? With the crusade against the Axis now ranking alongside the crusade against slavery as a myth-enshrouded chapter in US history to which all must pay homage, Americans are no more inclined to consider that question than to consider why a playoff to determine the professional baseball championship of North America constitutes a "World Series."

In fact, however convenient and familiar, *World War II* is misleading and not especially useful. The period in question saw at least two wars, each only tenuously connected to the other, each having distinctive origins, each yielding a different outcome. To separate them is to transform the historical landscape.

On the one hand, there was the *Pacific War*, pitting the United States against Japan. Formally initiated by the December 7, 1941, attack on Pearl Harbor, it had in fact begun a decade earlier when Japan embarked upon a policy of armed conquest in Manchuria. At stake was the question of who would dominate East Asia. Japan's crushing defeat at the hands of the United States, sealed by two atomic bombs in 1945, answered that question (at least for a time).

Then there was the *European War*, pitting Nazi Germany first against Great Britain and France, but ultimately against a grand alliance led by the United States, the Soviet Union, and a fast-fading British Empire. At stake was the question of who would dominate Europe. Germany's defeat resolved that issue (at least for a time): no one would. To prevent any single power from controlling Europe, two outside powers divided it.

This division served as the basis for the ensuing *Cold War*, which wasn't actually cold, but also (thankfully) wasn't *World War III*, the retrospective insistence of bellicose neoconservatives notwithstanding. But when did the *Cold War* begin? Was it in early 1947, when President Harry Truman decided that Stalin's Russia posed a looming threat and committed the United States to a strategy of containment? Or was it in 1919, when Vladimir Lenin decided that Winston Churchill's vow to "strangle Bolshevism in its cradle" posed a looming threat to the Russian Revolution, with an ongoing Anglo-American military intervention evincing a determination to make good on that vow?

Separating the war against Nazi Germany from the war against Imperial Japan opens up another interpretive possibility. If you incorporate the European conflict of 1914–18 and the European conflict of 1939–45 into a single narrative, you get a *Second Thirty Years War* (the first having occurred from 1618–48)—not so much a contest of good against evil as a mindless exercise in self-destruction that represented the ultimate expression of European folly.

So, yes, it matters what we choose to call the military enterprise we've been waging not only in Iraq and Afghanistan, but also in any number of other countries scattered hither and yon across the Islamic world. Although the Obama administration appears no more interested than the Bush administration in saying when that enterprise will actually end, the date we choose as its starting point also matters.

Although Washington seems in no hurry to name its nameless war—and will no doubt settle on something self-serving or anodyne if it ever finally addresses the issue—perhaps we should jump-start the process. Let's consider some possible options, names that might actually explain what's going on.

The Long War

Coined not long after 9/11 by senior officers in the Pentagon, this formulation never gained traction with either civilian officials or the general public. Yet the *Long War* deserves consideration, even though—or perhaps because—it has lost its luster with the passage of time.

At the outset, it connoted grand ambitions buoyed by extreme confidence in the efficacy of American military might. This was going to be one for the ages, a multi-generational conflict yielding sweeping results.

The *Long War* did begin on a hopeful note. The initial entry into Afghanistan and then into Iraq seemed to herald "home by Christmas" triumphal parades. Yet this soon proved an illusion as victory slipped from Washington's grasp. By 2005 at the latest, events in the field had dashed the neo-Wilsonian expectations nurtured back home.

With the conflicts in Iraq and Afghanistan dragging on, "long" lost its original connotation. Instead of "really important," it became a synonym for "interminable." Today, the *Long War* does succinctly capture the experience of American soldiers who have endured multiple combat deployments to Iraq and Afghanistan.

For *Long War* combatants, the object of the exercise has become to persist. As for winning, it's not in the cards. The *Long War* just might conclude by the end of 2014 if President Obama keeps his pledge to end the US combat role in Afghanistan and if he avoids getting sucked into Syria's civil war. So the troops may hope.

The War Against al-Qaeda

It began in August 1996 when Osama bin Laden issued a "Declaration of War against the Americans Occupying the Land of the Two Holy Places," that is, Saudi Arabia. In February 1998, a second bin Laden manifesto announced that killing Americans, military and civilian alike, had become "an individual duty for every Muslim who can do it in any country in which it is possible to do it."

Although President Bill Clinton took notice, the US response to bin Laden's provocations was limited and ineffectual. Only after 9/11 did Washington take this threat seriously. Since then, apart from a pointless excursion into Iraq (where, in Saddam Hussein's day, al-Qaeda did not exist), US attention has been focused on Afghanistan, where US troops have waged the longest war in American history, and on Pakistan's tribal borderlands, where a CIA drone campaign is ongoing. By the end of President Obama's first term, US intelligence agencies were reporting that a combined CIA/military campaign had largely destroyed bin Laden's organization. Bin Laden himself, of course, was dead.

Could the United States have declared victory in its unnamed war at this point? Perhaps, but it gave little thought to doing so. Instead, the national security apparatus had already trained its sights on various al-Qaeda "franchises" and wannabes, militant groups claiming the bin Laden brand and waging their own version of jihad. These offshoots emerged in the Maghreb, Yemen, Somalia, Nigeria, and—wouldn't you know it—post-Saddam Iraq, among other places. The question as to whether they actually posed a danger to the United States got, at best, passing attention—the label "al-Qaeda" eliciting the same sort of Pavlovian response that the word "communist" once did.

Americans should not expect this war to end anytime soon. Indeed, the Pentagon's impresario of special operations recently speculated— by no means unhappily—that it would continue globally for "at least ten to twenty years." Freely translated, his statement undoubtedly means this: "No one really knows, but we're planning to keep at it for one helluva long time."

The War For/Against/About Israel

It began in 1948. For many Jews, the founding of the state of Israel signified an ancient hope fulfilled. For many Christians, conscious of the sin of anti-Semitism that had culminated in the Holocaust, it offered a way to ease guilty consciences, albeit mostly at others' expense. For many Muslims, especially Arabs, and most acutely Arabs who had been living in Palestine, the founding of the Jewish state represented a grave injustice. It was yet another unwelcome intrusion engineered by the West—colonialism by another name.

Recounting the ensuing struggle without appearing to take sides is almost impossible. Yet one thing seems clear: in terms of military involvement, the United States attempted in the late 1940s and 1950s to keep its distance. Over the course of the 1960s, this changed. The

United States became Israel's principal patron, committed to maintaining (and indeed increasing) its military superiority over its neighbors.

In the decades that followed, the two countries forged a multifaceted "strategic relationship." A compliant Congress provided Israel with weapons and other assistance worth many billions of dollars, testifying to what has become an unambiguous and irrevocable US commitment to the safety and well-being of the Jewish state. The two countries share technology and intelligence. Meanwhile, just as Israel had disregarded US concerns when it came to developing nuclear weapons, it ignored persistent US requests that it refrain from colonizing territory that it has conquered.

When it comes to identifying the minimal essential requirements of Israeli security and the terms that will define any Palestinian-Israeli peace deal, the United States defers to Israel. That may qualify as an overstatement, but only slightly. Given the Israeli perspective on those requirements and those terms—permanent military supremacy and a permanently demilitarized Palestine allowed limited sovereignty—the *War For/Against/About Israel* is unlikely to end anytime soon either. Whether the United States benefits from the perpetuation of this war is difficult to say, but we are in it for the long haul.

The War for the Greater Middle East

I confess that this is the name I would choose for Washington's unnamed war and is, in fact, the title of a course I teach. (A tempting alternative is the *Second Hundred Years War*, the "first" having begun in 1337 and ended in 1453.)

This war is about to hit the century mark, its opening chapter coinciding with the onset of World War I. Not long after the fighting on the western front in Europe had settled into a stalemate, the British government, looking for ways to gain the upper hand, set out to dismantle the Ottoman Empire, whose rulers had foolishly thrown in their lot with the German Reich against the Allies.

By the time the war ended with Germany and the Turks on the losing side, Great Britain had already begun to draw up new boundaries, invent states, and install rulers to suit its predilections, while also issuing mutually contradictory promises to groups inhabiting these new precincts of its empire. Toward what end? Simply put, the British were intent on calling the shots from Egypt to India, whether by governing through intermediaries or ruling directly. The result was a new Middle East and a total mess.

London presided over this mess, albeit with considerable difficulty, until the end of World War II. At this point, by abandoning efforts to keep Arabs and Zionists from one another's throats in Palestine and by accepting the partition of India, they signaled their intention to throw in the towel. Alas, Washington proved more than willing to assume Britain's role. The lure of oil was strong. So too were the fears, however overwrought, of the Soviets extending their influence into the region.

Unfortunately, the Americans enjoyed no more success in promoting long-term, pro-Western stability than had the British. In some respects, they only made things worse, with the joint CIA-MI6 overthrow of a democratically elected government in Iran in 1953 offering a prime example of a "success" that, to this day, has never stopped breeding disaster.

Only after 1980 did things get really interesting, however. The Carter Doctrine promulgated that year designated the Persian Gulf a vital national security interest and opened the door to greatly increased US military activity not just in the Gulf, but also throughout the Greater Middle East (GME). Between 1945 and 1980, considerable numbers of American soldiers lost their lives fighting in Asia and elsewhere. During that period, virtually none were killed fighting in the GME. Since 1990, in contrast, virtually none have been killed fighting anywhere except in the GME.

What does the United States hope to achieve in its inherited and unending *War for the Greater Middle East*? To pacify the region? To remake it in our image? To drain its stocks of petroleum? Or to just keep the lid on? However you define the war's aims, things have not gone well, which once again suggests that, in some form, it will continue for some time to come. If there's any good news here, it's the prospect of having ever more material for my seminar, which may soon expand into a two-semester course.

The War Against Islam

This war began nearly a thousand years ago and continued for centuries, a storied collision between Christendom and the Muslim *ummah*. For a couple of hundred years, periodic eruptions of large-scale violence occurred until the conflict finally petered out with the last crusade sometime in the fourteenth century.

In those days, many people had deemed religion something worth fighting for, a proposition to which the more sophisticated present-day inhabitants of Christendom no longer subscribe. Yet could that religious war have resumed in our own day? Professor Samuel Huntington thought so, although he styled the conflict a "clash of civilizations." Some militant radical Islamists agree with Professor Huntington, citing as evidence the unwelcome meddling of "infidels," mostly wearing American uniforms, in various parts of the Muslim world. Some militant evangelical Christians endorse this proposition, even if they take a more favorable view of US troops occupying and drones targeting Muslim countries.

In explaining the position of the United States government, religious scholars like George W. Bush and Barack (Hussein!) Obama have consistently expressed a contrary view. Islam is a religion of peace, they declare, part of the great Abrahamic triad. That the other elements of that triad are likewise committed to peace is a proposition that Bush, Obama, and most Americans take for granted, evidence not required. There should be no reason why Christians, Jews, and Muslims can't live together in harmony.

Still, remember back in 2001 when, in an unscripted moment, President Bush described the war barely begun as a "crusade"? That was just a slip of the tongue, right? If not, we just might end up calling this one the *Eternal War*.

34

How We Became Israel

(2012)

Peace means different things to different governments and different countries. To some it suggests harmony based on tolerance and mutual respect. To others it serves as a euphemism for dominance, peace defining the relationship between the strong and the supine.

In the absence of actually existing peace, a nation's reigning *definition* of peace shapes its proclivity to use force. A nation committed to peace-as-harmony will tend to employ force as a last resort. The United States once subscribed to this view. Or beyond the confines of the Western Hemisphere, it at least pretended to do so.

A nation seeking peace-as-dominion will use force more freely. This has long been an Israeli predilection. Since the end of the Cold War and especially since 9/11, however, it has become America's as well. As a consequence, US national security policy increasingly conforms to patterns of behavior pioneered by the Jewish state. This "Israelification" of US policy may prove beneficial for Israel. Based on the available evidence, it's not likely to be good for the United States.

Here is Israeli Prime Minister Benjamin Netanyahu describing what he calls his "vision of peace" in June 2009: "If we get a guarantee of demilitarization . . . we are ready to agree to a real peace agreement, a demilitarized Palestinian state side by side with the Jewish state." The inhabitants of Gaza and the West Bank, if armed and sufficiently angry, can certainly annoy Israel. But they cannot destroy it or do it serious harm. By any measure, the Israel Defense Forces (IDF) wield vastly greater power than the Palestinians can possibly muster. Still, from Netanyahu's perspective, "real peace" becomes possible only if Palestinians guarantee that their putative state will forego even the most meager military capabilities. Your side disarms, our side stays armed to the teeth: that's Netanyahu's vision of peace in a nutshell.

Netanyahu asks a lot of Palestinians. Yet however baldly stated, his demands reflect longstanding Israeli thinking. For Israel, peace derives from security, which must be absolute and assured. Security thus defined requires not simply military advantage but *military supremacy*.

From Israel's perspective, threats to supremacy require *anticipatory action*, the earlier the better. The IDF attack on Iraq's Osirak nuclear reactor in 1981 provides one especially instructive example. Israel's destruction of a suspected Syrian nuclear facility in 2007 provides a second.

Yet alongside perceived threats, perceived opportunity can provide sufficient motive for anticipatory action. In 1956 and again in 1967, Israel attacked Egypt not because the blustering Colonel Gamal Abdel Nasser possessed the capability (even if he proclaimed the intention) of destroying the hated Zionists, but because preventive war seemingly promised a big Israeli pay-off. In the first instance, the Israelis came away empty-handed. In the second, they hit the jackpot operationally, albeit with problematic strategic consequences.

For decades, Israel relied on a powerful combination of tanks and fighter-bombers as its preferred instrument of preemption. In more recent times, however, it has deemphasized its swift sword in favor of the shiv between the ribs. Why deploy lumbering armored columns when a missile launched from an Apache attack helicopter or a bomb fixed to an Iranian scientist's car can do the job more cheaply and with less risk? Thus has *targeted assassination* eclipsed conventional military methods as the hallmark of the Israeli way of war.

Whether using tanks to conquer or assassins to liquidate, adherence to this knee-to-the-groin paradigm has won Israel few friends in the region and few admirers around the world (Americans notably excepted). The likelihood of this approach eliminating or even diminishing Arab or Iranian hostility toward Israel appears less than promising. That said, the approach has thus far succeeded in preserving and even expanding the Jewish state: more than sixty years after its founding, Israel persists and even prospers. By this rough but not inconsequential measure, the Israeli security concept has succeeded. Okay, it's nasty, but so far at least, it's worked.

What's hard to figure out is why the United States would choose to follow Israel's path. Yet over the course of the Bush/Clinton/Bush/Obama quarter-century, that's precisely what we've done. The pursuit of global military dominance, a proclivity for preemption, a growing taste for assassination—all are justified as essential to self-defense. That pretty much describes our present-day MO.

Israel is a small country with a small population and no shortage of hostile neighbors. Ours is a huge country with an enormous population and no enemy within several thousand miles, unless you count the Cuban-Venezuelan Axis of Ailing Dictators. We have choices that Israel does not. Yet in disregarding those choices, the United States has stumbled willy-nilly into an Israeli-like condition of perpetual war, with peace increasingly tied to unrealistic expectations of adversaries and would-be adversaries acquiescing in Washington's will.

Israelification got its kick-start with George H. W. Bush's Operation Desert Storm, a triumphal Hundred-Hour War likened at the time to Israel's triumphal Six-Day War. Victory over the "fourth largest army in the world" fostered illusions of the United States exercising perpetually and on a global scale military primacy akin to what Israel has exercised regionally. Soon thereafter, the Pentagon announced that henceforth it would settle for nothing less than "Full Spectrum Dominance."

Bill Clinton's contribution to the process was to normalize the use of force. During the several decades of the Cold War, the US had resorted to overt armed intervention only occasionally. Although difficult today to recall, back then whole years might pass without US troops being sent into harm's way. Over the course of Clinton's two terms in office, however, intervention became commonplace.

The average Israeli had long since become inured to reports of IDF incursions into southern Lebanon or Gaza. Now the average American has become accustomed to reports of US troops battling Somali warlords, supervising regime change in Haiti, or occupying the Balkans. Yet the real signature of the Clinton years came in the form of airstrikes. Blasting targets in Afghanistan, Bosnia, Serbia, and Sudan, but above all in Iraq, became the functional equivalent of Israel's reliance on airpower to punish "terrorists" from standoff ranges.

In the wake of 9/11, George W. Bush, a true believer in Full Spectrum Dominance, set out to liberate or pacify (take your pick) the Islamic world. The United States followed Israel in assigning itself the prerogative of waging preventive war. Although it depicted Saddam Hussein as an existential threat, the Bush administration also viewed Iraq as an opportunity: here the United States would signal to other recalcitrants the fate awaiting them should they mess with Uncle Sam.

More subtly, in going after Saddam, Bush was tacitly embracing a longstanding Israeli conception of deterrence. During the Cold War, deterrence had meant conveying a credible threat to dissuade your opponent from hostile action. Israel had never subscribed to that view. Influencing the behavior of potential adversaries required more than signaling what Israel *might* do if sufficiently aggravated; influence was exerted by punitive action, ideally delivered on a disproportionate scale. Hit the other guy first, if possible; failing that, whack him several times harder than he hit you — not the biblical injunction of an eye for an eye, but both eyes, an ear, and several teeth, with a kick in the nuts thrown in for good measure. The aim was to send a message: screw with us and this will happen to you. This is the message Bush intended to convey when he ordered the invasion of Iraq in 2003.

Unfortunately, Operation Iraqi Freedom, launched with all the confidence that had informed Operation Peace for Galilee, Israel's equally ill-advised 1982 incursion into Lebanon, landed the United States in an equivalent mess. Or perhaps a different comparison applies: the US occupation of Iraq triggered violent resistance akin to what the IDF faced as a consequence of Israel occupying the West Bank. Two successive Intifadas had given the Israeli army fits. The insurgency in Iraq (along with its Afghan sibling) gave the American army fits. Neither the Israeli nor the American reputation for martial invincibility survived the encounter.

By the time Barack Obama succeeded Bush in 2009, most Americans—like most Israelis—had lost their appetite for invading and occupying countries. Obama's response? Hew ever more closely to the evolving Israeli way of doing things. "Obama wants to be known for winding down long wars," writes Michael Gerson in the *Washington Post*. "But he has shown no hesitance when it comes to shorter, Israel-style operations. He is a special ops hawk, a drone militarist."

With his affinity for missile-firing drones, Obama has established targeted assassination as the very centerpiece of US national security policy. With his affinity for commandos, he has expanded the size and mandate of US Special Operations Command, which now maintains an active presence in more than seventy countries. In Yemen, Somalia, the Philippines, and the frontier regions of Pakistan—and who knows how many other far-flung places—Obama seemingly shares Prime Minister Netanyahu's expectations: keep whacking and a positive outcome will eventually ensue.

The government of Israel, along with ardently pro-Israel Americans like Michael Gerson, may view the convergence of US and Israeli national security practices with some satisfaction. The prevailing US definition of self-defense—a self-assigned mandate to target anyone anywhere thought to endanger US security—is exceedingly elastic. As such, it provides a certain cover for equivalent Israeli inclinations. And to the extent that our roster of enemies overlaps with theirs—did someone say Iran?—military action ordered by Washington just might shorten Jerusalem's "to do" list.

Yet where does this all lead? "We don't have enough drones," writes the columnist David Ignatius, "to kill all the enemies we will make if we turn the world into a free-fire zone." And if Delta Force, the Green Berets, Army Rangers, Navy SEALs, and the like constitute (in the words of one SEAL) "the dark matter . . . the force that orders the universe but can't be seen," we probably don't have enough of them either. Unfortunately, the Obama administration seems willing to test both propositions.

The process of aligning US national security practice with Israeli precedents is now essentially complete. Their habits are ours. Reversing that process would require stores of courage and imagination that may no longer exist in Washington. Given the reigning domestic political climate, those holding or seeking positions of power find it easier—and less risky—to stay the course, vainly nursing the hope that by killing enough "terrorists," peace on terms of our choosing will result. Here too the United States has succumbed to Israeli illusions.

35

Breaking Washington's Rules

(2011)

As a boy growing up in the Midwest during the early years of the Cold War, I developed a clear understanding of what differentiated Americans from their communist adversaries. Simply put, we were pragmatists and they were ideologues. On our side flexibility and common sense prevailed; whatever worked, we were for it. In contrast, the people on the other side were rigid and dogmatic; bombast and posturing mattered more than results. The newsreels of the time told the tale: communist leaders barked ridiculous demands; the docile masses chanted prescribed slogans. It was impossible to imagine Americans tolerating such nonsense.

However belatedly, learning has overturned these youthful impressions. "Whatever works" no longer seems to guide everyday American behavior, if it ever did. Americans view it as their birthright that reality should satisfy desire. Forget *e pluribus unum*. "Whatever I want" has become the operative national motto. In the meantime, when it comes to politics, Americans do put up with nonsense. Week in and week out, members of a jaded governing class, purporting to speak for "the

American people," mouth tired clichés that would have caused members of the Soviet Politburo to blush with embarrassment.

The world—we are incessantly told—is becoming ever smaller, more complex, and more dangerous. Therefore, it becomes necessary for the nation to intensify the efforts undertaken to "keep America safe" while also, of course, advancing the cause of world peace. Achieving these aims—it is said—requires the United States to funnel ever greater sums of money to the Pentagon to develop new means of projecting power, and to hold itself in readiness for new expeditions deemed essential to pacify (or liberate) some dark and troubled quarter of the globe.

At one level, we can with little difficulty calculate the cost of these efforts: the untold billions of dollars added annually to the national debt and the mounting toll of dead and wounded US troops provide one gauge.

At a deeper level, the costs of adhering to the Washington Consensus defy measurement: families shattered by loss; veterans bearing the physical and psychological scars of combat; the perpetuation of ponderous bureaucracies subsisting in a climate of secrecy, dissembling, and outright deception; the distortion of national priorities as the military-industrial complex siphons off scarce resources; environmental devastation produced as a by-product of war and the preparation for war; and the evisceration of civic culture that results when a small praetorian guard shoulders the burden of waging perpetual war, while the great majority of citizens purport to revere its members, even as they ignore or profit from their service.

Furthermore, there is no end in sight, even though the conditions that first gave rise to the Washington rules have ceased to exist. United States allies in Western Europe and East Asia, weak and vulnerable in the immediate wake of World War II, are today stable, prosperous, and perfectly capable of defending themselves. The totalitarian ideologies that challenged liberalism in the twentieth century have definitively and irrevocably failed. Joseph Stalin is long gone, as is the Soviet Empire. Red China has become simply China, valued by Americans as a bountiful source of credit and consumer goods. Although communists still call the shots in Beijing, promoting exports ranks well above promoting Mao's teachings in the party's list of priorities. In the Islamic

Republic of Iran, once thought to be the incubator of powerful revolutionary forces, the mullahs find themselves hard-pressed just to maintain order in the streets. Washington's quasi-official enemies list now consists mostly of pygmies: North Korea, a nation unable to feed its own population; Syria, an Israeli punching bag; Venezuela, governed by a clown; and, for old times' sake, Cuba.

The world has by no means entered an era of peace and harmony. Far from it. Yet the threats demanding attention today—terrorism, climate change, drug cartels, Third World underdevelopment and instability, and perhaps above all, the proliferation of genocidal weapons invented and first employed by the West—have changed, while the solutions proffered by Washington remain largely the same. The conviction that the obligations of leadership require the United States to maintain a global military presence, configure its armed forces for power projection, and employ them to impose change abroad forms the enduring leitmotif of US national security policy. Washington clings to its credo not out of necessity, but out of parochial self-interest laced with inertia.

Dwight D. Eisenhower, for one, would have been appalled. Early in his first term as president, Ike contemplated the awful predicament wrought by the Cold War during its first decade. "What can the world, or any nation in it, hope for," he asked, "if no turning is found on this dread road?" The president proceeded to answer his own question. The worst to be feared would be a ruinous nuclear war.

> The best would be this: a life of perpetual fear and tension; a burden of arms draining the wealth and the labor of all peoples; a wasting of strength that defies the American system or the Soviet system or any system to achieve true abundance and happiness for the peoples of this earth.
> Every gun that is made, every warship launched, every rocket fired signified, in the final sense, a theft from those who hunger and are not fed, those who are cold and are not clothed.

Today, for most Americans, the Cold War has become a distant memory. Yet the "life of perpetual fear and tension" that Eisenhower described in 1953, the "burden of arms" that he decried, and "the wasting of strength" that undercuts the prospect of Americans achieving "true abundance and happiness" all persist. In Washington, practices that Eisenhower viewed as temporary expedients are now etched in stone.

Contemplate these three examples: the size of the Pentagon budget, the dimensions of the nuclear arsenal, and the extent of the US overseas military presence. If, rather than exceeding the military spending of the rest of the planet, Pentagon outlays merely equaled the combined defense budgets of, say, Russian, China, Iran, North Korea, Syria, Venezuela, and Cuba, would the United States face great peril? If the US nuclear stockpile consisted of several hundred weapons rather than several thousand, would the United States find itself appreciably more vulnerable to nuclear blackmail or attack? Were the United States, sixty-plus years after the end of World War II, finally to withdraw its forces from Germany, Italy, and the rest of Europe, would Americans sleep less easily in their beds at night?

Consider these questions pragmatically and the answer to each is self-evidently *no*. Consider them from a vantage point within the Washington consensus and you'll reach a different conclusion.

Adherents of that consensus categorically reject the notion that the defense spending of would-be adversaries could provide a gauge for our own military budget. They argue instead that America's unique responsibilities require extraordinary capabilities, rendering external constraints unacceptable. Even as US officials condemn others for merely contemplating the acquisition of nuclear weapons, they reject unilateral action to reduce America's own arsenal—the fancied risks of doing so being too great to contemplate. As for withdrawing US troops from Europe, doing so might—so the argument goes—call into question America's commitment to its allies and could therefore send the wrong "signal" to unnamed potential enemies. Thus do the Washington rules enforce discipline, precluding the intrusion of aberrant thinking that might engender an actual policy debate in our nation's capital.

Cui bono? Who benefits from the perpetuation of the Washington rules? The answer to that question helps explain why the national security consensus persists.

The answer, needless to say, is that Washington itself benefits. The Washington rules deliver profit, power, and privilege to a long list of beneficiaries: elected and appointed officials, corporate executives and corporate lobbyists, admirals and generals, functionaries staffing the national security apparatus, media personalities, and policy intellectuals from universities and research organizations.

Each year the Pentagon expends hundreds of billions of dollars to raise and support US military forces. This money lubricates American politics, filling campaign coffers and providing the source of largesse—jobs and contracts—for distribution to constituents. It provides lucrative "second careers" for retired US military officers hired by weapons manufacturers or by consulting firms appropriately known as "Beltway Bandits." It funds the activities of think tanks that relentlessly advocate policies guaranteed to fend off challenges to established conventions. "Military-industrial complex" no longer suffices to describe the congeries of interests profiting from and committed to preserving the national security status quo.

Nor are the benefits simply measurable in cold cash or political influence. The appeal of the Washington rules is psychic as well as substantive. For many, the payoff includes the added, if largely illusory, attraction of occupying a seat within or near what is imagined to be the very cockpit of contemporary history. Before power corrupts it attracts and then seduces.

Challenging the Washington consensus requires establishing the proposition that viable alternatives to permanent war do exist—that a different credo might offer a better way of ensuring the safety and well-being of the American people and even perhaps of fulfilling the mission that Americans persist in believing God or Providence has bestowed upon the United States.

The existing American credo assumes that the world is plastic, that American leaders are uniquely capable of divining whatever God or Providence intends, and that with its unequaled reserves of power the United States is uniquely positioned to fulfill those intentions. Experience since the dawn of the American Century in 1941, and especially over the course of the last decade, offers little support for these propositions.

The record of American statecraft during the era that began with the US entry into World War II and that culminates today with the

Long War does not easily reduce to a simple report card. Overall that record is mixed, combining wisdom with folly, generosity with short-sightedness, moments of insight with periods of profound blindness, admirable achievements with reckless misjudgments. The president who devised the Marshall Plan also ordered the bombing of Hiroshima. The president who created the Peace Corps also dabbled in assassination plots. The president who vowed to eliminate evil secretly authorized torture and then either could not bring himself to acknowledge the fact or simply lied about it.

Critics fasten on these contradictions as evidence of Washington's hypocrisy. What they actually reveal is the intractability of the human condition. Even the self-assigned agent of salvation persistently strays from the path of righteousness. No wonder the world at large remains stubbornly resistant to redemption. Notwithstanding prophetic pronouncements issued by American leaders, when it comes to discerning the future they, like other statesmen, fly blind. The leader of the Free World, surrounded by his impressively credentialed advisers, is hardly more capable of divining the global future than is a roomful of reasonably well-informed high-school students.

As with American clairvoyance, so too with American power: events have exposed its limits. Especially in economic terms, it is today a wasting asset.

Any new credo must take into account these lessons of the era now drawing to a close, acknowledging the recalcitrance of humankind, the difficulty of deciphering history's purposes, and the importance of husbanding American power.

These very insights formed the basis of an earlier credo, nurtured across many generations until swept aside by the conceits of the American Century. Proponents of this earlier credo did not question the existence of an American mission. Embracing John Winthrop's charge, issued to his followers on the eve of founding Massachusetts Bay Colony in 1630, they too sought to create a "city upon a hill." This defined America's obligation. Yet in discharging that obligation, in their view, the city's inhabitants should seek not to compel or enforce, but to exemplify and illuminate.

For the Founders, and for the generations that followed them, here was the basis of a distinctively American approach to leadership, informed by a conviction that self-mastery should take precedence over mastering others. This Founders' credo was neither liberal nor conservative. It transcended partisanship, blending both idealism and realism, emphasizing patience rather than immediacy, preferring influence to coercion. Until the end of the nineteenth century, this conception of America as exemplar, endorsed by figures as varied in outlook and disposition as George Washington and John Quincy Adams, commanded widespread assent.

With the advent of World War II, the tradition of America as exemplar—now widely and erroneously characterized as isolationism—stood almost completely discredited. In Washington after 1945, it carried no weight at all. In official circles, fixing the world now took precedence over remedying whatever ailments afflicted the United States.

Outside of such circles, an awareness of America's own imperfections—social, political, cultural, and moral—survived. The advent of the postwar American credo, with all of the costly undertakings that trailed in its wake, fostered for a minority a renewed appreciation of the all-but-forgotten Founders' credo. Among critics of US foreign policy, the old tradition of America as exemplar enjoyed a quiet renaissance.

Those critics questioned the wisdom and the feasibility of forcibly attempting to remake the world in America's image. They believed that even to make the attempt was to court corruption in the form of imperialism and militarism, thereby compromising republican institutions at home. Representing no one party but instead a great diversity of perspective, they insisted that, if America has a mission, that mission is to model freedom rather than to impose it.

The proper aim of American statecraft is not to redeem humankind or to prescribe some specific world order, nor to police the planet by force of arms. Its purpose is to permit Americans to avail themselves of the right of self-determination as they seek to create at home a "more perfect union." Any policy impeding that enterprise—as open-ended war surely does—is misguided and pernicious.

Come home and resurrecting the nation's true vocation becomes a possibility. Cling to the existing American credo and the betrayal of that vocation is assured. For anyone genuinely interested in education—a category that necessarily excludes partisans and ideologues—surely this stands out as a conclusion that the events of the post-9/11 era, and indeed the entire American Century, have made manifest.

Even if self-determination qualifies as a right, it is certainly not a gift. As with any right, it requires safeguards. To ensure that others will refrain from interfering with its efforts to create a more perfect union, the United States requires power. Yet in light of the credo described above, how precisely should the United States formulate and wield that power?

Here, too, there exists an alternative tradition to which Americans today could repair, should they choose to do so. This tradition harks back to the nearly forgotten anti-imperial origins of the Republic. Succinctly captured in the motto "Don't Tread on Me," this tradition is one that does not seek trouble but insists that others will accord the United States respect. Updated for our own time, it might translate into the following:

First, the purpose of the US military is not to combat evil or remake the world, but to defend the United States and its most vital interests. However necessary, military power itself is neither good nor inherently desirable. Any nation defining itself in terms of military might is well down the road to perdition, as earlier generations of Americans instinctively understood. As for military supremacy, the lessons of the past are quite clear. It is an illusion and its pursuit an invitation to mischief, if not disaster. Therefore, the United States should maintain only those forces required to accomplish the defense establishment's core mission.

Second, the primary duty station of the American soldier is in America. Just as the US military should not be a global police force, so too should it not be a global occupation force. Specific circumstances may from time to time require the United States to establish a military presence abroad on a temporary basis. Yet rather than defining the norm, Americans should view this prospect as a sharp departure, entailing public debate and prior congressional authorization. Dismantling the Pentagon's sprawling network of existing bases promises to be a lengthy process. Priority should be given to those regions where the

American presence costs the most while accomplishing the least. According to those criteria, US troops should withdraw from the Persian Gulf and Central Asia forthwith.

Third, consistent with the just war tradition, the United States should employ force only as a last resort and only in self-defense. The Bush Doctrine of preventive war—the United States bestowing on itself the exclusive prerogative of employing force against ostensible threats even before they materialize—is a moral and strategic abomination, the very inverse of prudent and enlightened statecraft. Concocted by George W. Bush to justify his needless and misguided 2003 invasion of Iraq, this doctrine still awaits explicit abrogation by authorities in Washington. Never again should the United States undertake a "war of choice" informed by fantasies that violence provides a shortcut to resolving history's complexities.

Were this alternative triad to become the basis for policy, dramatic changes in the US national security posture would ensue. Military spending would decrease appreciably. The Pentagon's global footprint would shrink. Weapons manufacturers would see their profits plummet. Beltway bandits would close up shop. The ranks of defense-oriented think tanks would thin. These changes, in turn, would narrow the range of options available for employing force, obliging policy makers to exhibit greater restraint in intervening abroad. With resources currently devoted to rehabilitating Baghdad or Kabul freed up, the cause of rehabilitating Cleveland and Detroit might finally attract a following.

Popular susceptibility to fear-mongering by those always conjuring up new national emergencies might also wane and with it the average American's willingness to allow some freshly discovered "axis of evil" to dictate the nation's priorities. The imperial presidency's ability to evoke awe and command deference would likewise diminish. With that, the possibility of responsible and genuinely democratic government might present itself.

Of fundamental importance, the identity of the American solider would undergo substantial revision. The warrior-professional brought home from distant provinces of empire might once again become the citizen-protector of the nation. Rather than serving as an instrument of the state, the solider might simply defend the country—a cause which Americans, regardless of class or political orientation, might once again see as their own.

This very prospect—the likelihood of any departure from the Washington rules reducing the privileges that Washington has long enjoyed—helps explain the tenacity of those intent on preserving the status quo. If change is to come, it must come from the people. Yet unless Americans finally awaken to the fact that they've been had, Washington will continue to have its way.

So the need for education—summoning Americans to take on the responsibilities of an active and engaged citizenship—has become acute. Americans today must reckon with a contradiction of gaping proportions. Promising prosperity and peace, the Washington rules are propelling the United States toward insolvency and perpetual war. Over the horizon a shipwreck of epic proportions awaits. To acknowledge the danger we face is to make learning—and perhaps even a course change—possible. To willfully ignore the danger is to become complicit in the destruction of what most Americans profess to hold dear.

36

Why Read Clausewitz When Shock and Awe Can Make a Clean Sweep of Things?

(2006)

The events of September 11, 2001, killed thousands, left many thousands more bereft, and horrified countless millions who merely bore witness. But for a few, 9/11 suggested an opportunity. In the inner circles of the United States government, men of ambition seized on that opportunity with alacrity. Far from fearing a "global war on terror," they welcomed it, certain of their ability to bend war to their purposes. Although the ensuing conflict has not by any means run its course, we are now in a position to begin evaluating the results of their handiwork.

To that effort, this very fine book makes an important contribution.[1] A decade ago, Michael Gordon, a reporter with the *New York*

---

1. Michael Gordon and Bernard Trainor, *Cobra II: The Inside Story of the Invasion and Occupation of Iraq* (New York: Vintage Books, 2006).

Times, and Bernard Trainor, a retired US Marine Corps lieutenant general, collaborated on *The Generals' War*, still perhaps the best narrative history of the Persian Gulf War of 1990–91. *Cobra II*, a worthy successor, is packaged as an account of the planning and conduct of Operation Iraqi Freedom. It should be read as a study of the politics of war. Although Gordon and Trainor describe in stirring detail the celebrated "march on Baghdad," their real contribution has been to identify the confluence of factors that inspired the march, shaped it, and produced consequences very different from those expected.

One point above all stands out: the rationale for the war had next to nothing to do with the threat posed by Saddam Hussein. Weapons of mass destruction offered little more than a convenient pretext for a war conjured up to serve multiple ends. Neither the Baath Party regime nor the Iraqi army, crippled by defeat and well over a decade of sanctions, threatened anyone other than the Iraqi people. The hawks in the Bush administration understood this quite well. They hankered to invade Iraq not because Saddam was strong and dangerous but because he was weak and vulnerable, not because he was implicated in 9/11 but because he looked like an easy mark.

For the war's architects, "Iraq was not a danger to avoid but a strategic opportunity," less a destination than a point of departure. In their eyes, 2003 was not 1945, but 1939: not a climax but the opening gambit of a vast enterprise largely hidden from public view. Allusions to Saddam as a new Hitler notwithstanding, they did not see Baghdad as Berlin but as Warsaw—a preliminary objective. For the war's most determined proponents—Cheney, Rumsfeld, and Wolfowitz—toppling Saddam was the first phase of what was expected to be a long campaign. In Iraq they intended to set precedents, thereby facilitating other actions to follow. Although Bush portrayed himself as a reluctant warrior for whom armed conflict was a last resort, key members of his administration were determined that nothing should get in the way of a showdown with Saddam. "In crafting a strategy for Iraq," the undersecretary of defense Douglas Feith insisted to one baffled US general, "we cannot accept surrender." The object of the exercise was to demolish constraints on the subsequent employment of American power. Merely promulgating a doctrine of preventive war would not be enough: it was imperative to implement that doctrine.

The principal players in this game had their eyes fixed on two very different fronts. First, the Persian Gulf. As the Bush administration hawks saw it, the weak and feckless Clinton administration had allowed the once dominant US position in the region to slip in the course of the previous decade. Taking down Saddam promised to restore US preeminence, yielding large economic and political benefits. In the short term, a demonstration of American assertiveness would ease concerns about access to the energy reserves on which the prosperity of the developed world depended. A "friendly" Iraq would reduce the need to cater to Saudi Arabia, whose friendship was looking increasingly problematic given that fifteen of the nineteen 9/11 hijackers had been Saudis. In the longer term, Iraq could serve as a secure operating base or jumping-off point for subsequent US efforts to extend the Pax Americana across the Greater Middle East, a project expected to last decades. American power would eliminate the conditions that bred and sustained violent Islamic radicalism. That was the ultimate strategic rationale for war.

By planting the Stars and Stripes in downtown Baghdad, Gordon and Trainor write, the advocates of war intended not only to "implant democracy in a nation that had never known it" but to "begin to redraw the political map of the region." As "a demonstration of American power for Syria and other wayward regimes," Operation Iraqi Freedom would show the consequences of defying the world's only superpower. Even beyond the Middle East, Saddam's demise was likely to have salutary effects, letting "other adversaries know they should watch their step."

None of this could be done, however, until certain domestic obstacles had been removed. This was the second front, in many respects more challenging than the first. As Bush's more bellicose lieutenants saw it, the principal constraints on the use of American power lay within the US government itself. In a speech to Defense Department employees only a day before 9/11, Rumsfeld had warned of "an adversary that poses a threat, a serious threat, to the security of the United States of America." Who was this adversary? Some evil tyrant or murderous terrorist? No, Rumsfeld announced: "The adversary's closer to home. It's the Pentagon bureaucracy." But the internal threat was not confined to this single bureaucracy. It included Congress and the

Supreme Court, each of which could circumscribe presidential free-dom of action. It extended to the CIA and the State Department, which the hawks viewed as obstructive and hidebound. It even took in the senior leadership of the US military, especially the unimaginative and excessively risk-averse Joint Chiefs of Staff. All these were capable of impeding the greater assertiveness that Cheney, Rumsfeld, and Wolfowitz had yearned for well before the events of 9/11. Everyone had to be neutralized. In other words, unleashing American might abroad implied a radical reconfiguration of power relationships at home. On this score, 9/11 came as a godsend. The hawks, citing the urgent imperatives of national security, set out to concentrate au-thority in their own hands. September 11 inaugurated what became in essence a rolling coup.

Nominally, the object of the exercise was to empower the commander-in-chief to wage his Global War on Terror. Yet with George W. Bush a president in the mold of William McKinley or War-ren Harding—an affable man of modest talent whose rise in national politics could be attributed primarily to his perceived electability— Cheney and his collaborators were engaged in an effort to enhance their own clout. Bush might serve as the front man; but on matters of substance, theirs would be the decisive voices. Gordon and Trainor describe the operative model this way: "The president would pre-side, the vice-president would guide, and the defense secretary would implement"—with Wolfowitz and a handful of others lending the en-terprise some semblance of intellectual coherence.

Step one—bringing Congress to heel—proved remarkably easy. Immediately after 9/11, the Senate and House of Representatives is-sued the executive branch the equivalent of a blank check. A joint reso-lution passed on September 14 not only authorized the president "to use all necessary and appropriate force against those nations, organi-zations or persons" that had perpetrated 9/11, but also called on him "to prevent any future acts of international terrorism against the United States." The notorious Gulf of Tonkin Resolution of 1964 was a straitjacket compared to this spacious grant of authority. Even when the subsequent Global War on Terror produced massive intelligence failures, operational ineptitude, the abuse of detainees and warrantless wiretaps, the White House had little difficulty keeping the legislative branch at bay. As long as Congress stays firmly in Republican hands, executive accountability will remain a theoretical proposition.

As if to drive home its ascendancy, the White House now claimed the prerogative of disregarding any congressional action that it did not like. On at least 750 occasions during his first five years in office, Bush issued so-called signing statements voiding legislative provisions with which he disagreed. When Congress last year roused itself long enough to ban torture as an instrument of US policy, Bush asserted that as commander-in-chief he would abide by this stricture only so far as it suited him to do so. As a result of all this, the aftermath of 9/11 saw the system of checks and balances all but collapse. Individual legislators still quibble and gripe, but as an institution, Congress at present hardly amounts to more than a nuisance. Its chief function is simply to appropriate the ever-more-spectacular sums of money that the Global War on Terror requires and to rubber stamp increases in the national debt. This, of course, it routinely and obligingly does.

Nor, thus far at least, have the courts interfered with this presidential muscle-flexing. The Supreme Court historically has shown little inclination to encroach on presidential turf in time of war. Any prospect of the Court confronting this president was seemingly nipped in the bud by the fortuitous retirement of one justice followed by the death of another. In appointing John Roberts and Samuel Alito, Bush elevated to the court two jurists with track records of giving the executive branch a wide berth on matters relating to national security. (Once on the court, justices don't always perform as expected; whether the Roberts court will actually defer to the chief executive on national security issues remains to be seen.)

Within the executive branch itself, however, efforts by Cheney and Rumsfeld to consolidate authority in their own hands have encountered fierce resistance. Here *Cobra II* confirms much of what we already know. During the months leading up to the Iraq war, Rumsfeld and his aides waged a bureaucratic battle royal to marginalize the State Department and to wrest control of intelligence analysis away from the CIA. Colin Powell was one casualty of that bruising fight. George Tenet, eased out as CIA director, was another. Whether that battle has ended is another matter. With Rumsfeld himself lately under siege and

Condoleezza Rice enjoying Bush's confidence as Powell never did, and with efforts to silence the CIA having yielded a criminal indictment of the vice-president's former chief of staff, a declaration of victory on behalf of the Cheney-Rumsfeld axis might be premature. The overall conclusion, however, is as clear as it is disturbing. To the extent that any meaningful limits on executive power survive, they are almost entirely bureaucratic. This administration has eviscerated the Constitution.

Within the Department of Defense, the hawks were intent on calling the shots. Determined to have a decisive voice in deciding when and where the United States would fight, they also wanted to dictate how it would fight. The team Rumsfeld recruited to assist him in managing the Pentagon contained an unusual number of military zealots, men who believed in the utility of force and viewed the prospect of war with considerable enthusiasm.

In addition to Wolfowitz and Feith, the group included Stephen Cambone, Lawrence Di Rita, William Luti and, on a part-time basis, Richard Perle, who chaired the Defense Policy Board. Several of them had had a hand in rebuilding the armed forces, kicking the Vietnam syndrome, and winning the Cold War in the 1980s in the service of Ronald Reagan and George H. W. Bush. They had, in their own minds, raised American influence and prestige to heights not seen since the end of World War II. Yet they had left office in 1993 with the nagging sense that their mission was unfinished. Although the hegemony of the world's sole superpower was real enough, it wasn't absolute and unquestioned.

Then came the era of Bill Clinton: eight years of drift and stagnation camouflaged by the vaporous talk in which the "Man from Hope" specialized. With his notion of foreign policy as a variant of social work, Clinton had repeatedly misused America's armed forces. Kowtowing to his own generals, he had failed to push through the reforms essential for perpetuating US military dominance. Beguiled by his own rhetoric about globalization, he had ignored threats brewing in East Asia and the Middle East. In the Clinton years, American power had atrophied even as new dangers proliferated. For the zealots, these were wilderness years. Apart from publishing an occasional op-ed or signing the odd manifesto, they were stuck on the sidelines, watching with dismay. The Bush restoration of November-December 2000 offered the chance to reverse this slide towards decline and disarray. Although they had made little headway in promoting their agenda during the administration's first months, the propitious onset of the Global War on Terror promised to change all that. For those intent on establishing beyond doubt and beyond challenge the supremacy of American arms, an expansive, amorphous, open-ended war seemed made to order.

When it came to cementing US military dominion, however, Rumsfeld and his closest associates viewed the Pentagon brass less as part of the solution than as part of the problem. Concerned that the JCS and its staff had emerged "as a rival source of power" during the Clinton years, Rumsfeld intended to put the generals in their place. But this was easier said than done. Before 9/11, the generals pushed back: inside "the Building," Rumsfeld's ideas and his imperious manner touched off a round of nasty civil-military conflict. Questions of personality aside, disagreement centered on what national security aficionados call "transformation," Rumsfeld's vision of a redesigned armed force: lighter, more agile, and more usable than before. As he and his disciples saw it, senior military officers (army officers especially) were still enamored of the Powell Doctrine of overwhelming force— lots of tanks, lots of artillery, and lots of "boots on the ground." Rumsfeld's vision of a new American way of war instead placed the emphasis on quality—precise intelligence, precise weapons, and smaller numbers of troops, primarily elite special operations forces.

Implicit in the Powell Doctrine was the assumption that the wars of the future would be large, uncertain, expensive, and therefore infrequent. Implicit in Rumsfeld's thinking was the expectation that future American wars would be brief and economical, all but eliminating the political risk of opting for force. Rumsfeld believed that technology was rendering obsolete old worries about fog, friction, and chance. Why bother studying Clausewitz when "Shock and Awe" could make a clean sweep of things? For Rumsfeld and his coterie, this was the appeal of having a go at Iraq: a swift victory over Saddam would validate Rumsfeld's "vision" and discredit those who were obstructing his reforms. According to *Cobra II*, he was certain that a "rapid defeat of Iraq on his terms would break the spine of army resistance to his transformation goal once and for all."

Gordon and Trainor describe in detail the process that eventually produced a campaign plan which met with Rumsfeld's approval. The Joint Chiefs of Staff essentially played no role in this. Rumsfeld had little use for their advice. The compliant JCS chairman, General Richard Myers, so much under Rumsfeld's thumb that he was "incapable of expressing an independent view," remained an onlooker. When Eric Shinseki, the army chief of staff, dared to suggest that occupying Iraq might require several hundred thousand troops, Wolfowitz retaliated with a public rebuke and Rumsfeld instantly pushed the general into oblivion.

Rumsfeld's chosen military interlocutor was General Tommy Franks, the commander of United States Central Command. In a best-selling memoir published after his retirement, Franks portrays himself as a "good old boy" from west Texas who also happens to be a military genius. In *Cobra II*, he comes across as Rumsfeld's useful idiot: a coarse, not especially bright, kiss-up, kick-down martinet who mistreats his subordinates but keeps his boss happy. Franks knew that he wasn't in charge, but he pretended otherwise. Appreciating the "political value in being able to stand at the Pentagon podium and say that the Bush administration was implementing the military's plan," Rumsfeld was happy to play along.

The invasion plan that Rumsfeld bludgeoned Franks into drafting foresaw a relatively small force rushing towards Baghdad at breakneck speed, swiftly toppling the Baath regime, and just as quickly extricating itself. "The Iraq War would be like a thunderstorm: a short, violent episode that swept away the enemy but would not entail a burdensome, long-term troop commitment." Underlying these expectations were three key assumptions: that the regular Iraqi army wouldn't fight; that the Iraqi people would greet US and British troops as liberators; and that major Iraqi institutions would survive the war intact, facilitating the rapid withdrawal of all but a small contingent of occupying forces.

In the event, these assumptions proved fallacious, even with Saddam Hussein doing his best to help out: convinced that the United States would never actually try to take Baghdad, Saddam concentrated on threats from Iran and from within Iraq itself; as a consequence, the

Iraqi general staff had no plan worthy of the name to defend against an Anglo-American attack. When that attack began, the anticipated mass defection of Iraqi forces did not occur. The Iraqi army did fight, though poorly—and some US troops found even this level of opposition disconcerting. "Why would the Iraqis shoot at us?" one army captain wondered to himself. "We are the good guys." Iraqi irregulars—the Fedayeen—offered a spirited resistance that caught allied commanders by surprise. Meanwhile, the welcome given to allied forces as they traversed southern Iraq proved to be spotty and less than wholehearted. Worse still, when Baghdad fell, Iraq's political infrastructure collapsed, and mass disorder followed.

These developments (especially the appearance of irregular forces), dismissed by the Pentagon and Central Command as mere blemishes on an otherwise perfect campaign, were a portent of things to come. Neither Franks nor Rumsfeld responded to these warnings. Gordon and Trainor rightly indict Franks for failing the most fundamental responsibility of high command: the general did not "comprehend the nature of the war he was directing." But the charge applies equally to Rumsfeld and his team of zealots. An obdurately conventional soldier, Franks lacked the wit to grasp that the conflict in which he was engaged was anything but conventional. Entranced with his vision of warfare rendered precise by precision weapons, Rumsfeld had little patience with facts that did not fit with his preconceptions.

Although US forces made it to Baghdad, and Bush soon thereafter declared an end to "major combat operations," it was all downhill from there. An incident in Fallujah—troops from the 82nd Airborne Division fired into a crowd of angry demonstrators—kick-started the insurgency. That was on April 24, 2003. Heavy-handed US tactics added fuel to the fire. "The only thing these sand niggers understand is force and I'm about to introduce them to it," a senior officer in the 4th Infantry Division is quoted as saying. Bush's chosen proconsul, Paul Bremer, compounded the problem by dissolving the remnants of the Iraqi army, thereby providing the insurgents with a pool of potential recruits. As Franks made his escape, command in Iraq devolved on Lieutenant General Ricardo Sanchez, an officer of indifferent ability, poorly prepared for the challenges he faced, and unable to forge an amicable relationship with Bremer.

Cobra II provides only the briefest sketch of all the ugly events that followed. The volume concludes with a summary of the administration's myriad errors: underestimating the enemy, failing to understand the fractious nature of Iraqi society, relying excessively on technology, and failing to anticipate the magnitude of the nation-building task that could not be avoided. But one failure stands out. Rumsfeld's grand plan to transform the US military was at odds with the administration's grand plans to transform the Greater Middle East. Imperial projects don't prosper with small armies that leave quickly: they require large armies that stay. Out of this arrogance, incompetence, and sheer stupidity came a policy failure that may yet beggar the debacle of Vietnam.

37

![black bar]

Living Room War

(2005)

The contrast could hardly be more striking.

When Confederates attacked Fort Sumter on April 12, 1861, President Abraham Lincoln responded by immediately quintupling the size of the US Army, calling for 75,000 volunteers to put down the rebellion. As events soon demonstrated, this was a mere down payment. Utterly determined to repair the Union, Lincoln would stop at nothing to achieve his aim. In the bloody Civil War that ensued, virtually every household in the nation, both North and South, found itself called upon to sacrifice.

Similarly, when the Japanese attack of December 7, 1941, thrust the United States into World War II, President Franklin Roosevelt wasted no time in putting the entire nation on a war footing. He directed immediate implementation of the War Department's "Victory Plan," calling for the creation of an army of some eight million. The draft, initiated a year earlier on a limited scale, expanded many times over, the state asserting unconditional authority to order male citizens to serve "for the duration." To outfit fighting forces with the tanks, artillery pieces, fighter planes, and bombers they required, the federal government terminated the production of consumer durables, imposed wage and price controls, rationed scarce materials, and generally made it clear that nothing would impede the war effort. For Americans in and out of uniform, World War II became an all-encompassing enterprise. Other priorities would have to wait.

Not so with the Global War on Terror. The attack of September 11 elicited from the American people a universal sense of shock, anger, and outrage. But when it came to tapping the energies inherent in that instantaneous emotional response, the administration of George W. Bush did essentially nothing.

Instead of a Lincolnesque summons to "think anew and act anew," President Bush instructed his fellow citizens to "enjoy America's great destination spots." Within weeks of the terrorist attack, he was urging folks to "get down to Disney World in Florida." Rather than announcing that the imperative of victory had now transcended all other priorities—in his day, FDR had pointedly retired "Dr. New Deal," making way for "Dr. Win-the-War"—Bush thought it more important for Americans to "enjoy life, the way we want it to be enjoyed."

Americans took heed. Within remarkably short order, the country went back to business as usual. Almost as if 9/11 hadn't happened, ordinary citizens resumed their single-minded pursuit of happiness. Rather than entailing collective sacrifice, "war" this time around meant at most occasional annoyances, the most onerous involving the removal of one's shoes while transiting airport security. Although patriotic Americans acknowledged an obligation to "Support the Troops," fulfilling that obligation generally meant displaying decals on the rear of an SUV. Should preventing another 9/11, or the even more devastating attack that officials ominously hint lurks just around the corner, oblige American consumers to tighten their belts and make do with less? Don't be silly.

Bush the warrior-president has signaled his approval of this response. Instead of a call to service delivered via the local draft board, the commander in chief made a point of easing the burdens of citizenship. Through simultaneous spending hikes and tax cuts, he offloaded onto future generations responsibility to foot the bill for the present generation's security.

Further, even as he declared that the events of 9/11 had thrust the United States into a global conflict likely to last for years, if not decades, and even as he vowed to liberate the Islamic world and to eliminate evil itself, the president carefully refrained from suggesting that such an enterprise might require expanding the US military services. Despite the extraordinary challenges said to lie ahead, the president assumed from the outset that the all-volunteer force as it existed on September 11 provided the United States all that it needed to wage a protracted global war. From the outset, Bush and his lieutenants took it for granted that the regulars—0.5 percent of the entire population—backed up by a modest number of reservists would suffice to get the job done.

On the one hand, according to Bush, the United States after 9/11 embarked upon a mighty endeavor, a life-or-death struggle against an implacable enemy. On the other hand, the president's actual policies suggested that prevailing in that endeavor would not require anything remotely comparable to a mobilization of the nation's resources. Notwithstanding the throwaway line from his second inaugural summoning the nation's youth to "make the choice to serve in a cause larger than your wants, larger than yourself," President Bush clearly expects the nation to triumph even while serenely persisting in its comfortable peacetime routines.

How are we to reconcile this apparent contradiction? How can we explain the disparity between a monumentally ambitious agenda that is making even some dyed-in-the-wool Reaganites squirm and policies seemingly designed to encourage popular complacency and self-indulgence?

One answer might be that in the inner circles of power the Global War on Terror qualifies as a war only in a metaphorical sense, comparable, say, to the War on Poverty or the War on Drugs. But Bush has gone out of his way to correct any such misapprehension, first by invading Afghanistan, then by promulgating a doctrine of preventive war, and finally by implementing that doctrine through his invasion of Iraq. When this president speaks of a global war, he means precisely that—large-scale, open-ended military campaigns conducted in far-flung theaters of operations. Scholars might argue about whether among Muslims jihad refers to war as such or to a form of spiritual struggle. But when it comes to Mr. Bush's jihad, the facts permit no such confusion.

A second, more plausible explanation for the apparent disparity between the president's grandiose agenda and his willingness to let the country coast along undisturbed is to be found in the Bush administration's view of modern war. During the 1990s, Republican Party elites (and more than a few of their Democratic counterparts) convinced themselves that old-fashioned warfare, which relied on large numbers of soldiers and massive arsenals of destructive but not terribly accurate weapons, had gone the way of the steam locomotive and the typewriter. A new model of high-tech warfare, waged by highly skilled professionals equipped with "smart" weapons, had begun to emerge, with the Pentagon far out in front of any potential adversary in grasping the significance of this military revolution.

This image of transformed war derived from, but also reinforced, the technology-hyped mood prevailing during the years just prior to Bush's election in 2000. By common consent, the defining characteristics of this Information Age were speed, control, and choice. Even as it was empowering the individual, information technology was reducing the prevalence of chance, surprise, and random occurrences. Henceforth, everything relevant could be known and, if known, could be taken into account. The expected result was to lessen, if not eliminate, uncertainty, risk, waste, and error and to produce quantum improvements in efficiency and effectiveness.

The potential for applying information technology to armed conflict—long viewed as an area of human endeavor especially fraught with uncertainty, risk, waste, and error—appeared particularly attractive. Given access to sufficient information, man could regain control of war, arresting its former tendency to become total. Swiftness, stealth, agility, and precision would characterize the operations of modern armies. Economy, predictability, and political relevance would constitute the hallmarks of war in the Information Age.

Further, this new style of technowar relied not on the huge, industrial-age armies, but on compact formations consisting of select volunteers. Winning wars during the twentieth century had required guts and muscle. Winning wars in the new century just dawning would emphasize the seamless blending of technology and skill, consigning the average citizen to the role of spectator. Fighting promised to remain something that other people were paid to do.

This vision of surgical, frictionless, postmodern war seemingly offered to the United States the prospect of something like permanent global military supremacy. Better still, at least among the activist neoconservatives who came to exercise great influence in the Bush administration, it held the promise of removing the constraints that had hitherto inhibited the United States in the actual use of its military power. With American society as a whole insulated from the effects of conflict, elites could expect to enjoy greater latitude in deciding when and where to use force.

These militaristic fantasies possessed an intoxicating allure akin to, complementing, and making plausible the ideological fantasies suggesting that the United States after 9/11 was called upon to remake the world in its own image. Hubris in the realm of military affairs meshed neatly with hubris in the realm of international politics.

Alas, as with seemingly brilliant military schemes throughout history, this attractive vision did not survive contact with the enemy. As so often happens, it turns out that our adversaries do not share our views of how modern war is to be conducted. At least, that has been the verdict of the Iraq War thus far. Launched with the breezy expectation that a tidy and decisive preventive war held the prospect of jumpstarting efforts to democratize the Middle East, Operation Iraqi Freedom has transitioned willy-nilly from a demonstration of "shock and awe" into something very old and very familiar: an ugly insurgency conducted by a tough, elusive, and adaptable foe. On the battlefields of the Sunni Triangle, technology and skill have a part to play; but guts and muscle will determine the outcome.

Whether the muscle of the existing all-volunteer force will prove adequate to the task has become an open question. Already, signs of eroding American fighting power, notably a sharp drop in reserve recruiting and retention, have begun to crop up. Steadily accumulating reports of misconduct by US troops suggest that discipline is beginning to unravel.

This situation cannot be sustained indefinitely. Although the armed services today are by no means confronting the sort of crisis that toward the end of Vietnam brought them to the verge of collapse, the process of institutional decay has begun. Unless checked, that process may become irreversible.

The Pentagon is attempting to "manage" the problem, but such efforts can only go so far. A much-touted internal reorganization of the army designed to increase the total number of combat brigades may be the equivalent of trying to get five patties rather than four out of the same pound of ground beef. Increasing re-enlistment bonuses, loosening recruiting standards, recalling retirees to active duty, imposing stop-loss policies to postpone the discharge of soldiers whose enlistments have expired, easing restrictions on the assignment of women to forward areas, increasing the reliance on contractors and mercenaries: all of these are mere stopgaps. None get to the core issue: Mr. Bush has too few soldiers doing too many things, while the rest of the country blissfully contents itself shopping and watching TV.

Some informed observers have argued that in the specific case of Iraq, the presence of large numbers of US troops is exacerbating rather than reducing existing security problems. That said, and recognizing that Iraq forms but one facet of the Bush administration's larger project that aims to purge the globe of tyrants and bring about the final triumph of liberty for all, there can be no denying that a yawning gap exists between US grand strategy and the forces that the Pentagon can call upon to implement that strategy.

In pursuit of the president's goal of eliminating tyranny, American military forces today are badly overstretched. But the nation is not. In this gap between breathtakingly grand ideological goals and the failure to raise up the instruments of power to achieve those goals lies the full measure of this administration's recklessness and incompetence.

38

Bush's Grand Strategy

(2002)

All but lost amidst the heated talk of regime change in Baghdad, the White House in late September issued the Bush administration's US National Security Strategy. In one sense, publication of this document is a routine event, just one more periodic report mandated by Congress. Yet this latest rendering of US grand strategy—the first to appear since 9/11—deserves far greater attention than it has received.

The Bush USNSS offers the most comprehensive statement to date of America's globe-straddling post–Cold War ambitions. In it, the administration makes plain both its intention to perpetuate American military supremacy and its willingness—almost approaching eagerness—to use force to reshape the international order. This new strategy places the approaching showdown with Saddam Hussein in a far wider context, showing that overthrowing the Iraqi dictator is only the next step in a massive project, pursued under the guise of the Global War on Terror, but aimed ultimately at remaking the world in our image.

Calling back into service a phrase first employed by candidate Bush, the USNSS propounds what it refers to as "a distinctly American internationalism." When George W. Bush used that phrase on the campaign trail, it was devoid of content. Here it takes on meaning, at once grandiose and combustible.

The Bush strategy does qualify as truly distinctive in one specific sense—in its fusion of breathtaking utopianism with barely disguised *machtpolitik*. It reads as if it were the product not of sober, ostensibly conservative Republicans but of an unlikely collaboration between Woodrow Wilson and the elder Field Marshal von Moltke.

On the one hand, the document rings with assurances affirming the inevitable triumph of liberty around the world. America's "great mission," President Bush writes in the document's introduction, is to hasten this triumph, by "extend[ing] the benefits of freedom across the globe." Fulfilling that mission obliges the United States to assume responsibility for eliminating the obstacles to freedom everywhere: war and terror, poverty and disease, and "the clashing wills of powerful states and the evil designs of tyrants."

But America's mission has a positive as well as a negative aspect. Fulfilling it requires not only removing obstacles but also creating a new global order conducive to freedom. When it comes to identifying the principles around which to organize that order, George W. Bush harbors no doubts. Like his predecessor Bill Clinton, he is certain that the United States has deciphered the deepest secrets of history and understands its direction and purpose. There is, he declares, only "a single sustainable model for national success," one to which all people aspire and to which all societies must ultimately conform. That model is ours.

Democracy, the rule of law, freedom of speech and worship, respect for private property and for the rights of women and minorities: these comprise the "nonnegotiable demands of human dignity." (Regarding rights of the unborn, the USNSS is silent.) But beyond those principles, the quality that will bind the world together and bring utopia within reach is "openness." In an increasingly interdependent world, one in which "the distinction between domestic and foreign affairs is diminishing," nations—including this nation—have no choice but to "be open to people, ideas, and goods from across the globe."

In an open and integrated world—achieved in the first instance by removing impediments to trade and investment—all things become possible. Without openness, material abundance for those who presently enjoy it becomes unsustainable and for those who yearn for it remains beyond reach. Here too Bush echoes the views of Bill Clinton, who based his foreign policy on the conviction that an "open world" knit together by the forces of globalization offered a sure-fire formula for limitless prosperity, universal freedom, and perpetual peace.

The Johnny Appleseed of globalization, Clinton spent eight years travelling the world, extolling the benefits of openness and exuding good cheer, no doubt expecting peace and prosperity to spring up wherever he trod. But events in the Persian Gulf, Somalia, Rwanda, Haiti, the Balkans, and elsewhere showed such expectations to be illusory. To these indicators that openness might not be quite the panacea that its advocates claimed, Clinton responded by resorting to force, usually belatedly, almost always indecisively, but with remarkable frequency.

Throughout the Clinton era, US military forces marched hither and yon, intervening in a wider variety of places, and for a wider variety of purposes, than at any time in our history. More often than not, once the troops arrived, they stayed. As a result, by the time that Clinton left office in 2001, the defining fact of international politics—albeit one vigorously denied by the outgoing administration—had become not openness and globalization but the emergence of a Pax Americana.

Bringing into office a greater affinity for exercising power and a pronounced belief in the efficacy of coercion—both reinforced by the chastening experience of 9/11—senior members of the Bush administration do not share Bill Clinton's ambivalence about American military might. Hence, the second major theme of the new US National Security Strategy—a candid acknowledgment and endorsement of the progressively greater militarization of US foreign policy.

To state the point bluntly, the Bush administration no longer views force as the last resort; rather, it considers military power to be America's most effective instrument of statecraft—the area in which the United States owns the greatest advantage. Beginning with the premise that "our best defense is a good offense," the USNSS describes how President Bush intends to exploit that advantage to the fullest.

He will do so in two ways. First, he will expand US global power projection capabilities. Already spending roughly as much on defense as the entire rest of the world combined, the United States will spend still more—much, much more. The purpose of this increase is not to respond to any proximate threat. Rather, the Bush administration is boosting the Pentagon's budget with an eye toward achieving a margin of such unprecedented and unsurpassed superiority that no would-be adversary will even consider mounting a future challenge. The United States will thereby secure in perpetuity its status as sole superpower. Old concerns about the "clashing wills of powerful states" will disappear; henceforth, a single power will call the tune.

Second, with the USNSS codifying the concept of "anticipatory self-defense," President Bush claims for the United States the prerogative of using force preemptively and unilaterally, however its interests may dictate. (That prerogative belongs exclusively to the United States; the Bush strategy pointedly warns other nations not to "use preemption as a pretext for aggression.") In contrast to his predecessor's reactive, half-hearted military adventures, Bush will employ America's armed might proactively and on a scale sufficient to achieve rapid, decisive results. The prospect of ever greater US military activism—against terrorists, against rogue states, against evildoers of whatever stripe—beckons.

Nowhere does the Bush administration's national security strategy pause to consider whether the nation's means are adequate to the "great mission" to which destiny has ostensibly summoned the United States. Asserting that American global hegemony is necessarily benign and that Washington can be counted on to use the Bush Doctrine of preemption judiciously, nowhere does it contemplate the possibility that others might take a contrary view. Nowhere does it tally up the costs of shouldering an ever-expanding array of military commitments that flow from efforts to police the world. Nowhere does it convey any awareness that America's power and the world's plasticity may each have limits. Nowhere does it even speculate on when the United States might be able to lay down its imperial burdens and become a normal nation. Indeed, in all likelihood, the zealots who crafted this strategy have no interest in such matters.

The Bush administration's grand strategy reeks of hubris. Yet one may also detect in its saber-rattling occasional notes of desperation. America today is, by any measure, the most powerful nation on earth, enjoying a level of mastery that may exceed that of any great power or any previous empire in all of history. Yet to judge by this extraordinary document, we cannot rest easy, we cannot guarantee our freedom or our prosperity until we have solved every problem everywhere, relying chiefly on armed force to do so. In the end, we have little real choice—as the similarities between this new strategy and the Clinton strategy that Republicans once denounced with such gusto attest. In truth, whatever their party affiliation or ideological disposition, members of the so-called foreign policy elite cannot conceive of an alternative to "global leadership"—the preferred euphemism for global empire.

"In the new world that we have entered," George W. Bush writes, "the only path to peace and security is the path of action." So we must press on, with vigor and determination. Following our president, we must charge down that path until we drop from exhaustion or fling ourselves off the precipice fashioned of our own arrogance.

39

New Rome, New Jerusalem

(2002)

No longer fodder for accusations and denials, American imperialism has of late become a proposition to be considered on its merits. In leading organs of opinion, such as the *New York Times* and the *Washington Post*, the notion that the United States today presides over a global imperium has achieved something like respectability.

This is a highly salutary development. For only by introducing the idea of empire into the mainstream of public discourse does it become possible to address matters far more pressing than mulling over the semantic distinctions between empire and hegemony and "global leadership." What precisely is the nature of the Pax Americana? What is its purpose? What are the challenges and pitfalls that await the United States in the management of its domain? What are the likely costs of empire, moral as well as material, and who will pay them? These are the questions that are now beginning to find a place on the agenda of US foreign policy.

As befits a nation founded on the conviction of its own uniqueness, the American empire is like no other in history. Indeed, the peculiar American approach to empire offers a striking affirmation of American exceptionalism. For starters, that approach eschews direct rule over subject peoples. Apart from a handful of possessions left over from a brief, anomalous land grab in 1898, we have no colonies. We prefer access and influence to ownership. Ours is an informal empire, composed not of satellites or fiefdoms but of nominally coequal states. In presiding over this empire, we prefer to exercise our authority indirectly, as often as not through intermediary institutions in which the United States enjoys the predominant role but does not wield outright control (e.g., the North Atlantic Treaty Organization, the United Nations Security Council, the International Monetary Fund, and the World Bank).

Although we enjoy unassailable military supremacy and are by no means averse to using force, we prefer seduction to coercion. Rather than impose our will by the sword, we count on the allure of the "American way of life" to win over doubters and subvert adversaries. In the imperium's most valued precincts, deference to Washington tends to be rendered voluntarily. Thus, postwar Europe, viewing the United States as both protector and agent of economic revival, actively pursued American dominion, thereby laying the basis for an "empire by invitation" that persists even though European prosperity has long since been restored and threats to Europe's security have all but disappeared. An analogous situation prevails in the Pacific, where Japan and other states, more than able to defend themselves, willingly conform to an American-ordered security regime.

Imperial powers are all alike in their shared devotion to order. Imperial powers differ from one another in the values they purport to inculcate across their realm. To the extent that the empires of Spain, France, and Great Britain defined their purpose (at least in part) as spreading the benefits of Western civilization, the present-day Pax Americana qualifies as their historical successor. But whereas those earlier imperial ventures specialized in converting pagans or enlightening savages, the ultimate value and the ultimate aspiration of the American imperium is freedom. Per Thomas Jefferson, ours is an "empire of liberty."

From the outset, Americans self-consciously viewed the United States as an enterprise imbued with a providential significance extending far beyond the nation's boundaries. America was no sooner created than it became, in the words of the poet Philip Freneau, "a New Jeru-salem sent down from heaven." But the salvation this earthly Zion promised was freedom, not eternal life. Recall George Washington's first inaugural address, in 1789: "The preservation of the sacred fire of liberty," he declared, had been "intrusted to the hands of the American people." The imperative in Washington's day not to promulgate the sacred fire but simply to keep it from being extinguished reflected a realistic appraisal of the young republic's standing among the nations of the world. For the moment, it lacked the capacity to do more than model freedom.

Over the course of the next two hundred years, that would change. By the time the Berlin Wall fell in 1989, effectively bringing to a close a century of epic ideological struggle, the New Jerusalem had ascended to a category of its own among the world's powers. The United States was dominant politically, economically, culturally, and, above all, mili-tarily. In effect, the New Jerusalem had become the New Rome, an identity that did not supplant America's founding purpose but pointed toward its fulfillment—and the fulfillment of history itself. To Presi-dent Bill Clinton, the moment signified that "the fullness of time" was at hand. Thomas Paine's claim that Americans had it in their power "to begin the world over again" no longer seemed preposterous. Salvation beckoned. In Reinhold Niebuhr's evocative phrase, the United States stood poised to complete its mission of "tutoring mankind on its pil-grimage to perfection."

Early Americans saw the task of tutoring mankind as a directive from on high; later Americans shouldered the burden out of a pro-found sense of self-interest. Despite the frequent allusions to liberty in describing that pilgrimage's final destination and in justifying the use of American power, the architects of US policy in the twentieth cen-tury never viewed empire as an exercise in altruism. Rather, at least from the time of Woodrow Wilson, they concluded that only by pro-tecting and promoting the freedom of others could Americans fully guarantee their nation's own well-being. The two were inextricably linked.

In the eyes of Wilson and his heirs, to distinguish between American ideals (assumed to be universal) and American interests (in-creasingly global in scope) was to make a distinction without a difference. It was a plain fact that successive crusades to advance those ideals—against German militarism in 1917, fascism and Japanese imperialism in 1941, and communism after World War II—resulted in the United States accruing unprecedented power. Once the smoke had cleared, the plain fact defined international politics: One nation with its own particular sense of how the world should operate stood like a colossus astride the globe.

Not surprisingly, Americans viewed the distribution of power as a sort of cosmic judgment, an affirmation that the United States was (in a phrase favored by politicians in the 1990s) on "the right side of history." American preeminence offered one measure of humanity's progress toward freedom, democracy, and world peace. Those few who persisted in thinking otherwise—in American parlance, "rogue regimes"—marked themselves not only as enemies of the United States but as enemies of freedom itself.

The barbarous events of September 11 revealed that the pilgrimage to perfection was far from over. But not for a moment did they cause American political leaders to question the project's feasibility. If anything, September 11 reinforced their determination to complete the journey. In offering his own explanation for the attack on the World Trade Center and the Pentagon, George W. Bush refused to countenance even the possibility that an assault on symbols of American economic and military power might have anything to do with how the United States employed its power. He chose instead to frame the issue at hand in terms of freedom. Why do they hate us? "They hate our freedoms," Bush explained. Thus did the president skillfully deflect attention from the consequences of empire.

September 11 became the occasion for a new war, far wider in scope than any of the piddling military interventions that had kept American soldiers marching hither and yon during the preceding decade. In many quarters, that conflict has been described as the equivalent of another world war. The description is apt. As the multifaceted US military campaign continues to unfold, it has become clear that the Bush administration does not intend simply to punish those who perpetrated the attacks on New York and Washington or to preclude the recurrence of any such incidents. America's actual war aims are far more ambitious. The United States seeks to root out terror around the globe. It seeks also to render radical Islam and the nations that make up the "axis of evil" incapable of threatening the international order.

But there is more still: the Bush administration has used the war on terror as an occasion for conducting what is, in effect, a referendum on US global primacy. In this cause, as President Bush has emphasized, all must declare their allegiance: nations either align themselves with the United States or they cast their lot with the terrorists—and, by implication, can expect to share their fate. As a final byproduct of September 11, the administration has seized the opportunity to promulgate a new Bush Doctrine, incorporating such novel concepts as "anticipatory self-defense" and "preemptive deterrence." Through the Bush Doctrine, the United States—now combining, in the words of Stanley Hoffmann, the roles of "high-noon sheriff and proselytizing missionary"—lays claim to wider prerogatives for employing force to reorder the world.

In short, the conflict joined after September 11 may well qualify as a war against terror and against those who "hate our freedoms." But it is no less genuinely a conflict waged on behalf of the American imperium, a war in which, to fulfill its destiny as the New Jerusalem, the United States, as never before, is prepared to exert its authority as the New Rome.

Thus, when the president vowed in December 2001 that "America will lead the world to peace," he was not simply resurrecting some windy Wilsonian platitude. He was affirming the nation's fundamental strategic purpose and modus operandi. The United States will "lead"—meaning that it will persevere in its efforts to refashion the international order, employing for that purpose the preeminent power it acquired during the century of its ascendancy (which it has no intention of relinquishing in the century just begun). And it will do so with an eye toward achieving lasting "peace"—meaning an orderly world, conducive to American enterprise, friendly to American values, and perpetuating America's status as sole superpower. This was the aim of US policy prior to September 11; it remains the aim of the Bush administration today.

How widespread is support for this imperial enterprise? Despite the tendency of American statesmen from Wilson's day to our own to resort to coded language whenever addressing questions of power, the project is not some conspiracy hatched by members of the elite and then foisted on an unsuspecting citizenry. The image of the United States leading the world to peace (properly understood) commands broad assent in virtually all segments of American society. A fringe of intellectuals, activists, and self-described radicals might take umbrage at the prospect of a world remade in America's image and policed by American power, but out on the hustings the notion plays well—so long, at least, as the required exertions are not too taxing. The fact is that Americans like being number one, and since the end of the Cold War have come to accept that status as their due. Besides, someone has to run the world. Who else can do the job?

What are the empire's prospects? In some respects, the qualities that have contributed to the nation's success in other endeavors may serve the United States well in this one. Compared with the citizens of Britain in the age of Victoria or of Rome during the time of the Caesars, Americans wear their imperial mantle lightly. They go about the business of empire with a singular lack of pretense. Although Washington, D.C. has come to exude the self-importance of an imperial capital, those who live beyond its orbit have, thus far at least, developed only a limited appetite for pomp, privilege, and display. We are unlikely to deplete our treasury erecting pyramids or other monuments to our own ostensible greatness. In matters of taste, American sensibilities tend to be popular rather than aristocratic. Our excesses derive from our enthusiasms—frequently vulgar, typically transitory—rather than from any of the crippling French diseases: exaggerated self-regard, intellectual bloat, cynicism, and envy. All things considered, America's imperial ethos is pragmatic and without ostentation, evidence, perhaps, that the nation's rise to great-power status has not yet fully expunged its republican origins. Above all, measured against societies elsewhere in the developed world, American society today seems remarkably vigorous and retains an astonishing capacity to adapt, to recover, and to reinvent itself.

That said, when it comes to sustaining the Pax Americana, the United States faces several challenges.

First, no one is really in charge. Ours is an empire without an emperor. Although in times of crisis Americans instinctively look to the top for leadership—a phenomenon that greatly benefited George W. Bush after September 11—the ability of any president to direct the affairs of the American imperium is limited, in both degree and duration. Though he is routinely described as the most powerful man in the world, the president of the United States in fact enjoys limited authority and freedom of action. The system of government codified by the Constitution places a premium on separation and balance among the three branches that vie with one another in Washington, but also between the federal government and agencies at the state and local levels. Hardly less significant is the impact of other participants in the political free-for-all—parties, interest groups, lobbies, entrenched bureaucracies, and the media—that on any given issue can oblige the chief executive to dance to their tune. The notion of an "imperial presidency" is a fiction, and for that Americans can be grateful. But the fact remains that the nation's political system is not optimally configured for the management of empire.

Second, although popular support for the empire is real, it is, in all likelihood, highly contingent. The heirs of the so-called greatest generation have little stomach for sacrifice. They expect the benefits of empire to outweigh the burdens and responsibilities, and to do so decisively. The garden-variety obligations of imperial policing—for example, keeping peace in the Balkans or securing a US foothold in Central Asia—are not causes that inspire average Americans to hurry down to their local recruiter's office. To put it bluntly, such causes are not the kind that large numbers of Americans are willing to die for.

In this sense, the empire's point of greatest vulnerability is not the prospect of China's becoming a rival superpower or of new terrorist networks' supplanting al-Qaeda—those developments we can handle—but rather the questionable willingness of the American people to foot the imperial bill. Sensitive to the limits of popular support—as vividly demonstrated after a single night's action in Mogadishu in 1993—policymakers over the past decade have exerted themselves mightily to pass that bill off to others. In the process, they have devised imaginative techniques for ensuring that when blood spills, it won't be American blood. Hence, the tendency to rely on high-tech weapons launched from beyond the enemy's reach, on proxies to handle any dirty work on the ground, or, as a last resort, on a cadre of elite professional soldiers who are themselves increasingly detached from civilian society.

Over the past decade, this effort to maintain the American empire on the cheap has (with the notable exception of September 11) enjoyed remarkable success. Whether policymakers can sustain this success indefinitely remains an open question, especially when each victory gained with apparent ease—Bosnia, Kosovo, Afghanistan—only reinforces popular expectations that the next operation will also be neat, tidy, and virtually fault-free.

The third challenge facing the American imperium concerns freedom itself. For if peace (and US security) requires that the world be free as Americans define freedom, then the specifics of that definition complicate the management of empire in ways that thus far have received inadequate attention.

Here's the catch: as Americans continuously reinvent themselves and their society, they also reinvent—and in so doing, radically transform—what they mean by freedom. They mean not just independence, or even democracy and the rule of law. Freedom as Americans understand it today encompasses at least two other broad imperatives: maximizing opportunities for the creation of wealth and removing whatever impediments remain to confine the sovereign self. Freedom has come to mean treating the market and market values as sacrosanct (the economic agenda of the Right) and celebrating individual autonomy (the cultural agenda of the Left).

Without question, adherence to the principles of free enterprise offers the most efficient means for generating wealth. Without question, too, organizing society around such principles undermines other sources of authority. And that prospect mobilizes, in opposition to the United States, those in traditional and, especially, religious societies who are unwilling to abandon the old order. The implications of shedding the last constraints on the individual loom even larger. The contemporary pursuit of freedom has put into play beliefs, arrangements, and institutions that were once viewed as fundamental and unalterable. Gender, sexuality, identity, the definition of marriage and family, and the origins, meaning, sacredness, and malleability of life—in American society, they are all now being re-examined to accommodate the claims of freedom.

Some view this as an intoxicating prospect. Others see it as the basis for a domestic culture war. In either case, pursuant to their present-day understanding of what freedom entails, Americans have embarked on an effort to reengineer the human person, reorder basic human relationships, and reconstruct human institutions that have existed for millennia.

To render a summary judgment on this project is not yet possible. But surely it is possible to appreciate that some in the world liken it to stepping off a moral precipice, and they view the New Jerusalem with trepidation. Their fears, and the resistance to which fear gives birth, all but guarantee that the legions of the New Rome will have their hands full for some time to come.

40

Permanent War for
Permanent Peace

(2001)

In his widely praised appearance before a joint session of Congress on September 20, 2001, George W. Bush put to rest any lingering doubts about the legitimacy of his presidency. After months during which it had constituted a battle cry of sorts, "Florida" reverted to being merely a state.

Speaking with confidence, conviction, and surprising eloquence, Bush reassured Americans that their commander-in-chief was up to the task at hand: they could count on him to see the nation through the crisis that had arrived nine days earlier with such awful and terrifying suddenness. To the extent that leadership contains elements of performance art, this particular performance was nothing short of masterful, delighting the president's supporters and silencing, at least for a time, his critics. The moment had seemingly found the man.

Yet however much the atmospherics surrounding such an occasion matter—and they matter a great deal—the historian's attention is necessarily drawn elsewhere. Long after passions have cooled and anxieties have eased, the words remain, retaining the potential to affect subsequent events in ways large or small.

What did the president actually say? What principles did he enunciate? From which sources did he (or his speechwriters) draw the phrases that he spoke and the aspirations or sentiments that they signified? What unstated assumptions lurked behind? Looking beyond the crisis of the moment, what does this particular rendering of America's relationship to the world beyond its borders portend for the future?

In this case, more than most others, those questions may well matter. Not since the Cold War ended over a decade ago has an American statesman offered an explanation of foreign policy principles and priorities that enjoyed a half-life longer than a couple of news cycles. Bush's father during his single term in office and Bill Clinton over the course of eight years issued countless pronouncements touching on this or that aspect of US diplomacy or security policy. None achieved anything even remotely approaching immortality. (George H. W. Bush's "This will not stand"—uttered in response to Saddam Hussein's invasion of Kuwait in 1990—might have come close. But given the unsatisfactory conclusion of the Persian Gulf War and its frustrating aftermath—with Bush's nemesis evincing a Castro-like knack for diddling successive administrations—the rhetorical flourish that a decade ago sounded brave reads in retrospect like warmed-over Churchill).

George W. Bush's speech outlining his war on terror may prove to be the exception. It qualifies as the first foreign policy statement of the post–Cold War era with a chance of taking its place alongside Washington's Farewell Address, the Monroe Doctrine, the Roosevelt Corollary, and Wilson's Fourteen Points among the sacred texts of American statecraft. Or perhaps a more apt comparison might be to another momentous speech before a joint session of Congress, delivered by Harry Truman on March 12, 1947.

A looming crisis in a part of the world that had only infrequently commanded US attention prompted President Truman to appear before Congress. A faltering British Empire had just announced that it could no longer afford to support Greece, wracked by civil war and deemed acutely vulnerable to communist takeover. Britain's withdrawal would leave a power vacuum in southeastern Europe and the Near East, with potentially disastrous strategic consequences. Filling that vacuum, in Truman's judgment, required immediate and decisive American action.

In short, Truman came to the Capitol not to promulgate some grand manifesto but simply to persuade Congress that the United States should shoulder the burden that Britain had laid down by providing aid to shore up the beleaguered governments of Greece and of neighboring Turkey. But Senator Arthur Vandenberg, a recent convert from isolationism (and thus presumed to possess special insights into the isolationist psyche) had cautioned Truman that enlisting the support of skeptical and tightfisted legislators would require that the president first "scare hell out of the American people." Truman took Vandenberg's counsel to heart.

Thus, the president described the challenges of the moment as nothing short of pivotal. History, he told the Congress and the nation, had reached a turning point, one in which "nearly every nation must choose between alternative ways of life." Alas, in too many cases, the choice was not one that they were at liberty to make on their own. Militant minorities, "exploiting human want and misery" and abetted by "aggressive movements" from abroad, were attempting to foist upon such nations the yoke of totalitarianism. Left unchecked, externally supported subversion would lead to the proliferation of regimes relying upon "terror and oppression, a controlled press and radio, fixed elections, and the suppression of personal freedoms"—the very antithesis of all that America itself stood for. According to Truman, the United States alone could stem this tide. In what came to be known as the Truman Doctrine, he declared that henceforth "it must be the policy of the United States to support free peoples who are resisting attempted subjugation by armed minorities or by outside pressures."

Truman did not spell out detailed guidelines on where this general statement of intent might or might not apply. In the matter at hand, Congress responded positively to the president's appeal, appropriating $400 million of economic and military assistance for Greece and Turkey. But things did not end there. Truman's open-ended commitment to protect governments threatened by subversion continued to reverberate. His successors treated it as a mandate to intervene whenever and wherever they deemed particular US interests to be at risk. America's putative obligation to defend free peoples everywhere (some of them not very free) provided political and moral cover for actions overt and covert, wise and foolish, successful and unsuccessful, in virtually every quarter of the globe. Over the next four decades, in ways that Truman himself could never have anticipated, his eponymous doctrine remained the cornerstone of US foreign policy.

George W. Bush's speech of September 20 bears similar earmarks and may well give birth to a comparable legacy. This is not because Bush, any more than Truman, consciously set out to create such a legacy. But in making his case for a war on terror, Bush articulated something that has eluded policymakers since the collapse of the Soviet Union deprived the United States of a readily identifiable enemy: a coherent rationale for the wide-ranging use of American power on a global scale. Truman had placed the problems besetting Greece and Turkey in a broad strategic context. The threat to those two distant nations implied a threat to US security and to the security of the world at large. On September 20, Bush advanced a similar argument. The events of September 11 may have targeted the United States, but they posed a common danger. The fight was not just America's. "This is the world's fight," Bush said. "This is civilization's fight."

Truman had depicted a planet in the process of dividing into two opposing camps—the free world against totalitarianism. Bush portrayed an analogous division—with "the civilized world" now pitted against a terrorist network intent on "remaking the world—and imposing its radical beliefs on people everywhere." Echoing Truman, Bush insisted that history had reached a turning point. Once again, as at the beginning of the Cold War, circumstances obliged nations to choose sides. "Either you are with us," he warned, "or you are with the terrorists." Neutrality was not an option.

As in 1947 so too in 2001, the stakes were of the highest order. In the course of enunciating the doctrine that would bear his name, President Truman had alluded to freedom—free peoples, free institutions, liberty, and the like—eighteen separate times. President Bush's presentation of September 2001 contained fourteen such allusions. According to Bush, the events of September 11 showed that "freedom itself is under attack."

Casting the US response to that attack not simply in terms of justifiable self-defense or retaliation for an act of mass murder but as necessary to preserve freedom itself imbued Bush's speech with added salience. Although its meaning is both continually shifting and fiercely contested, freedom by common consent is the ultimate American value. In political rhetoric, it is the ultimate code word.

Defining the war on terror as a war on behalf of freedom served the administration's purposes in two important ways, both of them likely to have longer-term implications. First, it enabled President Bush to affirm the nation's continuing innocence—not only in the sense that it is blameless for the events of September 11 but more broadly in the sense that its role in the world cannot be understood except as benign. "Why do they hate us?" the president asked rhetorically. "They hate our freedoms," he replied, "our freedom of religion, our freedom of speech, our freedom to vote and assemble and disagree with each other." In offering this litany of estimable values as the only conceivable explanation for "why they hate us," Bush relieved himself (and his fellow citizens) of any obligation to reassess the global impact of US power—political, economic, or cultural. That others—to include even our friends—view America's actual influence abroad as varied, occasionally problematic, and at times simply wrongheaded is incontrovertible. The president's insistence on describing the United States simply as a beacon of liberty revalidated a well-established national preference for discounting the perceptions of others.

Second, sounding the theme of freedom enabled Bush to situate this first war of the twenty-first century in relation to the great crusades of the century just concluded. Alluding to the perpetrators of the September 11 attack, the president declared, "We have seen their kind before. They are the heirs of all the murderous ideologies of the twentieth century. . . . [T]hey follow the path of fascism, and Nazism, and totalitarianism. And they will follow that path all the way, to where it ends: in history's unmarked grave of discarded lies."

The president did not need to remind his listeners that the dangers posed by those murderous ideologies had legitimized the rise of the United States to great-power status in the first place. It was the mobilization of American might against the likes of Germany, Japan, and the Soviet Union that had hastened the demise of the ideologies they represented. A new war *on behalf of freedom and against evil* provides renewed legitimacy to the exercise of American power both today and until the final elimination of evil is complete.

Furthermore, engagement in such a war removes the fetters that have hobbled the United States in its use of power since the last ideological competitor fell into its grave. The most important of those constraints relates to the use of force. Since the end of the Cold War, military power has emerged as never before as the preferred instrument of American statecraft. Military preeminence forms an integral component of US grand strategy—an effort to create an open and integrated international order, conducive to the values of democratic capitalism, with the United States enjoying a position of undisputed primacy. But absent an adversary on a par with Nazi Germany or the Soviet Union, policymakers during the 1990s found themselves unable to explain to the American people generally exactly why the United States needed to exert itself to remain the world's only superpower—why the need to spend more on defense than the next eight or ten strongest military powers *combined*? With US security seemingly more assured than at any time in recent memory, they found themselves similarly hard-pressed to translate military preeminence into useful policy outcomes in places far from the American homeland—why the need to intervene in Somalia, Haiti, Bosnia, and elsewhere?

The Clinton administration justified its penchant for military intervention by insisting that it acted to succor the afflicted, restore democracy, and prevent genocide. Yet in virtually every case the facts belied such claims. Moreover, even if the purest altruism were motivating Bill Clinton periodically to launch a few cruise missiles or send in the Marines, Americans weren't buying it. Ordinary citizens evinced precious little willingness to support foreign-policy-as-social-work if such efforts entailed even a remote risk to US troops. The hope of salvaging a multi-ethnic Bosnia might stir the hearts of journalists and intellectuals, but the cause was not one that the average American viewed as worth dying for. As a result, during the 1990s, the greatest military power in history found itself hamstrung by its own self-imposed shackles, above all, an obsession with casualty avoidance. The United States could actually employ its military only with advanced assurance that no American lives would be lost. The Kosovo conflict of 1999 epitomized the result: a so-called humanitarian war where US pilots bombed Belgrade from 15,000 feet while Serb forces, largely unmolested, pursued their campaign of ethnic cleansing on the ground.

The fact that these various experiments in peacemaking and peace-keeping almost inevitably resulted in semi-permanent deployments of questionable efficacy, trampling on expectations that armed intervention should produce prompt and clear-cut results, only accentuated popular discontent. Bald-faced lies by senior US officials—remember the fraudulent promises that the troops would be out of Bosnia within a year?—didn't help much.

Now President Bush's declaration of a war on terror offers a way out of that predicament, making it possible for policymakers to reclaim the freedom of action that the Truman Doctrine had provided in earlier decades. Under the terms of the Bush Doctrine, the constraints that hampered the United States in the 1990s need not apply. The calculations governing tolerable risk change considerably. The gloves can come off—not just in the campaign against Osama bin Laden, but against any other group or regime that this administration or any of its successors can plausibly tag with supporting terrorist activity. The Republican Party that had once codified the lessons of the Vietnam War in the Weinberger Doctrine has now chucked that doctrine overboard, telling Americans that they must *expect* war to be a protracted and ambiguous affair, a long twilight struggle with even the definition of victory uncertain.

Furthermore, defining our adversary as "terrorism" itself makes it all the easier to avert our eyes from the accumulating evidence suggesting that it is the quasi-imperial role that the United States has asserted that incites resistance—and that it will continue to do so. In fact, as Daniel Pipes has correctly noted, terror is a tactic, not an enemy. But by insisting that our present quarrel is with terrorism—rather than, for example, with radical Islam—the United States obscures the irreconcilable political differences underlying this conflict. We willfully ignore the fact that bin Laden's actions (however contemptible) represent an expression of strongly held convictions (however warped): a determination by whatever means necessary to overturn the existing American imperium in the Middle East and the Persian Gulf. Thus do we sustain the pretense that America is not an empire.

In the weeks immediately following the terrorist attacks on New York and Washington, a rift about how best to proceed appeared at the highest levels of the Bush administration. Should the United States embark upon what the president, in an unscripted moment, referred to as an all-out "crusade" against global terror? Or should it limit itself to identifying and eliminating the network that had actually perpetrated the September 11 attack? In the near term, the advocates of the narrow approach seemingly prevailed. When Operation Enduring Freedom began on October 7, 2001, the United States singled out bin Laden's apparatus and the Taliban for destruction. Yet US officials also hinted that the just-launched offensive constituted only the first phase of a multi-part campaign—carefully refraining from specifying what phase two or phase three might entail. It turned out that the president had not rejected the idea of a crusade; he had merely deferred it while keeping all options open.

Assuming that the first phase of Operation Enduring Freedom succeeds, the doctrine that President Bush enunciated on September 20 will provide a powerful argument for those eager to move onto the next phase. Finding a suitable candidate to play the roles of al-Qaeda and the Taliban will present few difficulties: the State Department roster of terrorist organizations is a lengthy one; regimes suspected of supporting terror include Iraq, Iran, Syria, Libya, the Palestinian Authority, Sudan, Yemen, North Korea, and perhaps even our new-found ally Pakistan, just for starters.

To put it another way: Operation Enduring Freedom may be the first instance of the United States waging a "war on terror." But it is unlikely to be the last. The quest for "enduring freedom" points where the pursuit of absolutes always has in international relations: toward permanent war waged on behalf of permanent peace. The Bush Doctrine, like the Truman Doctrine that it supersedes, offers policymakers a veritable blank check to fight those wars.

PART 4

Politics and Culture

41

Slouching Toward Mar-a-Lago

(2017)

Like it or not, the president of the United States embodies America itself. The individual inhabiting the White House has become the preeminent symbol of who we are and what we represent as a nation and a people. In a fundamental sense, he is us.

It was not always so. Millard Fillmore, the thirteenth president (1850–53), presided over but did not personify the American republic. He was merely the federal chief executive. Contemporary observers did not refer to his term in office as the Age of Fillmore. With occasional exceptions, Abraham Lincoln in particular, much the same could be said of Fillmore's successors. They brought to office low expectations, which they rarely exceeded. So when Chester A. Arthur (1881–85) or William Howard Taft (1909–13) left the White House, there was no rush to immortalize them by erecting gaudy shrines—now known as "presidential libraries"—to the glory of their presidencies. In those distant days, ex-presidents went back home or somewhere else where they could find work.

Over the course of the past century, all that has changed. Ours is a republic that has long since taken on the trappings of a monarchy, with the president inhabiting rarified space as our king-emperor. The Brits have their woman in Buckingham Palace. We have our man in the White House.

Nominally, the Constitution assigns responsibilities and allocates prerogatives to three co-equal branches of government. In practice, the executive branch enjoys primacy. Prompted by a seemingly endless series of crises since the Great Depression and World War II, presidents have accumulated ever-greater authority, partly through usurpation, but more often than not through forfeiture.

At the same time, they also took on various extra-constitutional responsibilities. By the beginning of the present century, Americans took it for granted that the occupant of the Oval Office should function as prophet, moral philosopher, style-setter, interpreter of the prevailing zeitgeist, and—last but hardly least—celebrity-in-chief. In short, POTUS was the bright star at the center of the American solar system.

As recently as a year ago, few saw in this cult of the presidency cause for complaint. On odd occasions, some particularly egregious bit of executive tomfoolery might trigger grumbling about an "imperial presidency." Yet rarely did such complaints lead to effective remedial action. The War Powers Resolution of 1973 might be considered the exception that proves the rule. Inspired by the disaster of the Vietnam War and intended to constrain presidents from using force without congressional buy-in and support, that particular piece of legislation ranks alongside the Volstead Act of 1919 (enacted to enforce Prohibition) as among the least effective ever to become law.

In truth, influential American institutions—investment banks and multinational corporations, churches and universities, big city newspapers and TV networks, the bloated national security apparatus and both major political parties—have found reason aplenty to endorse a system that elevates the president to the status of demigod. By and large, it's been good for business, whatever that business happens to be.

Furthermore, it's *our* president—not some foreign dude—who is, by common consent, the most powerful person in the universe. For inhabitants of a nation that considers itself both "exceptional" and "indispensable," this seems only right and proper. So Americans generally like it that *their* president is the acknowledged Leader of the Free World rather than some fresh-faced pretender from France or Canada.

Then came the Great Hysteria. Arriving with a Pearl Harbor-like shock, it erupted on the night of November 8, 2016, just as the news that Hillary Clinton was losing Florida and appeared certain to lose much else besides became apparent.

Suddenly, all the habits and precedents that had contributed to empowering the modern American presidency no longer made sense. That a single deeply flawed individual along with a handful of unelected associates and family members should be entrusted with determining the fate of the planet suddenly seemed the very definition of madness.

Emotion-laden upheavals producing behavior that is not entirely rational are hardly unknown in the American experience. Indeed, they recur with some frequency. The Great Awakenings of the eighteenth and early nineteenth centuries are examples of the phenomenon. So also are the two Red Scares of the twentieth century, the first in the early 1920s and the second, commonly known as "McCarthyism," coinciding with the onset of the Cold War.

Yet the response to Donald Trump's election, combining as it has fear, anger, bewilderment, disgust, and something akin to despair, qualifies as an upheaval without precedent. History itself had seemingly gone off the rails. The crude Andrew Jackson's 1828 ousting of an impeccably pedigreed president, John Quincy Adams, was nothing compared to the vulgar Donald Trump's defeat of an impeccably credentialed graduate of Wellesley and Yale who had served as first lady, United States senator, and secretary of state. A self-evidently inconceivable outcome—all the smart people agreed on that point—had somehow happened anyway.

A vulgar, bombastic, thrice-married real-estate tycoon and reality TV host as prophet, moral philosopher, style-setter, interpreter of the prevailing zeitgeist, and chief celebrity? The very idea seemed both absurd and intolerable.

If we have, as innumerable commentators assert, embarked upon the Age of Trump, the defining feature of that age might well be the single-minded determination of those horrified and intent on ensuring its prompt termination. In 2016, *Time* magazine chose Trump as its person of the year. In 2017, when it comes to dominating the news, that "person" might turn out to be a group—all those fixated on cleansing the White House of Trump's defiling presence.

Egged on and abetted in every way by Trump himself, the anti-Trump resistance has made itself the Big Story. Lies, hate, collusion, conspiracy, fascism: rarely has the everyday vocabulary of American politics been as ominous and forbidding as over the past six months. Take resistance rhetoric at face value and you might conclude that Donald Trump is indeed the fifth horseman of the Apocalypse, his presence in the presidential saddle eclipsing all other concerns. Pestilence, War, Famine, and Death will just have to wait.

The unspoken assumption of those most determined to banish him from public life appears to be this: once he's gone, history will be returned to its intended path, humankind will breathe a collective sigh of relief, and all will be well again. Yet such an assumption strikes me as remarkably wrongheaded—and not merely because, should Trump prematurely depart from office, Mike Pence will succeed him. Expectations that Trump's ouster will restore normalcy ignore the very factors that first handed him the Republican nomination (with a slew of competitors wondering what hit them) and then put him in the Oval Office (with a vastly more seasoned and disciplined, if uninspiring, opponent left to bemoan the injustice of it all).

Not all, but many of Trump's supporters voted for him for the same reason that people buy lottery tickets: Why not? In their estimation, they had little to lose. Their loathing of the status quo is such that they may well stick with Trump even as it becomes increasingly obvious that his promise of salvation—an America made "great again"—is not going to materialize.

Yet those who imagine that Trump's removal will put things right are likewise deluding themselves. To persist in thinking that he defines the problem is to commit an error of the first order. Trump is not cause, but consequence.

For too long, the cult of the presidency has provided an excuse for treating politics as a melodrama staged at four-year intervals and centering on hopes of another Roosevelt or Kennedy or Reagan appearing as the agent of American deliverance. Donald Trump's ascent to the office once inhabited by those worthies should demolish such fantasies once and for all.

How is it that someone like Trump could become president in the first place? Blame sexism, Fox News, James Comey, Russian meddling, and Hillary's failure to visit Wisconsin all you want, but a more fundamental explanation is this: the election of 2016 constituted a de facto referendum on the course of recent American history. That referendum rendered a definitive judgment: the underlying consensus informing US policy since the end of the Cold War has collapsed. Precepts that members of the policy elite have long treated as self-evident no longer command the backing or assent of the American people. Put simply, it's the ideas, stupid.

Rabbit Poses a Question

"Without the Cold War, what's the point of being an American?" As the long twilight struggle was finally winding down, Harry "Rabbit" Angstrom, novelist John Updike's late-twentieth-century Everyman, pondered that question. In short order, Rabbit got his answer. So, too, after only perfunctory consultation, did his fellow citizens.

The passing of the Cold War offered cause for celebration. On that point all agreed. Yet, as it turned out, it did not require reflection from the public at large. Policy elites professed to have matters well in hand. The dawning era, they believed, summoned Americans not to think anew, but to keep doing precisely what they were accustomed to doing, albeit without fretting further about Communist takeovers or the risks of nuclear Armageddon. In a world where a "single superpower" was calling the shots, utopia was right around the corner. All that was needed was for the United States to demonstrate the requisite confidence and resolve.

Three specific propositions made up the elite consensus that coalesced during the initial decade of the post-Cold-War era. According to the first, the globalization of corporate capitalism held the key to wealth creation on a hitherto unimaginable scale. According to the second, jettisoning norms derived from Judeo-Christian religious tradition held the key to the further expansion of personal freedom. According to the third, muscular global leadership exercised by the United States held the key to promoting a stable and humane international order.

Unfettered neoliberalism plus the unencumbered self plus unabashed American assertiveness: these defined the elements of the post–Cold War consensus that formed during the first half of the 1990s—plus what enthusiasts called the information revolution. The miracle of that "revolution," gathering momentum just as the Soviet Union was going down for the count, provided the secret sauce that infused the emerging consensus with a sense of historical inevitability.

The Cold War itself had fostered notable improvements in computational speed and capacity, new modes of communication, and techniques for storing, accessing, and manipulating information. Yet however impressive, such developments remained subsidiary to the larger East-West competition. Only as the Cold War receded did they move from background to forefront. For true believers, information technology came to serve a quasi-theological function, promising answers to life's ultimate questions. Although God might be dead, Americans found in Bill Gates and Steve Jobs nerdy but compelling idols.

More immediately, in the eyes of the policy elite, the information revolution meshed with and reinforced the policy consensus. For those focused on the political economy, it greased the wheels of globalized capitalism, creating vast new opportunities for trade and investment. For those looking to shed constraints on personal freedom, information promised empowerment, making identity itself something to choose, discard, or modify. For members of the national security apparatus, the information revolution seemed certain to endow the United States with seemingly unassailable military capabilities. That these various enhancements would combine to improve the human condition was taken for granted; that they would, in due course, align everybody from Afghans to Zimbabweans with American values and the American way of life seemed more or less inevitable.

The three presidents of the post–Cold War era—Bill Clinton, George W. Bush, and Barack Obama—put these several propositions to the test. Politics-as-theater requires us to pretend that our forty-second, forty-third, and forty-fourth presidents differed in fundamental ways. In practice, however, their similarities greatly outweighed any of those differences. Taken together, the administrations over which they presided collaborated in pursuing a common agenda, each intent on proving that the post–Cold War consensus could work in the face of mounting evidence to the contrary.

To be fair, it did work for some. "Globalization" made some people very rich indeed. In doing so, however, it greatly exacerbated inequality, while doing nothing to alleviate the condition of the American working class and underclass.

The emphasis on diversity and multiculturalism improved the status of groups long subjected to discrimination. Yet these advances have done remarkably little to reduce the alienation and despair pervading a society suffering from epidemics of chronic substance abuse, morbid obesity, teen suicide, and similar afflictions. Throw in the world's highest incarceration rate, a seemingly endless appetite for porn, urban school systems mired in permanent crisis, and mass shootings that occur with metronomic regularity, and what you have is something other than the profile of a healthy society.

As for militarized American global leadership, it has indeed resulted in various bad actors meeting richly deserved fates. Goodbye, Saddam. Good riddance, Osama. Yet it has also embroiled the United States in a series of costly, senseless, unsuccessful, and ultimately counterproductive wars. As for the vaunted information revolution, its impact has been ambiguous at best, even if those with eyeballs glued to their personal electronic devices can't tolerate being offline long enough to assess the actual costs of being perpetually connected.

In November 2016, Americans who considered themselves ill-served by the post–Cold War consensus signaled that they had had enough. Voters not persuaded that neoliberal economic policies, a culture taking its motto from the Outback steakhouse chain ("No Rules, Just Right"), and a national security strategy that employs the US military as a global police force were working to their benefit provided a crucial margin in the election of Donald Trump.

The response of the political establishment to this extraordinary repudiation testifies to the extent of its bankruptcy. The Republican

Party still clings to the notion that reducing taxes, cutting government red tape, restricting abortion, curbing immigration, defending the Second Amendment, and increasing military spending will alleviate all that ails the country. Meanwhile, to judge by the promises contained in their recently unveiled (and instantly forgotten) program for a "Better Deal," Democrats believe that raising the minimum wage, capping the cost of prescription drugs, and creating apprenticeship programs for the unemployed will return their party to the good graces of the American electorate.

In both parties embarrassingly small-bore thinking prevails, with Republicans and Democrats equally bereft of fresh ideas. Each party is led by aging hacks. Neither has devised an antidote to the crisis in American politics signified by the nomination and election of Donald Trump.

While our emperor tweets, Rome itself fiddles.

Starting Over

I am by temperament a conservative and a traditionalist, wary of revolutionary movements that more often than not end up being hijacked by nefarious plotters more interested in satisfying their own ambitions than in pursuing high ideals. Yet even I am prepared to admit that the status quo appears increasingly untenable. Incremental change will not suffice. The challenge of the moment is to embrace radicalism without succumbing to irresponsibility.

The one good thing we can say about the election of Donald Trump—to borrow an image from Thomas Jefferson—is this: it ought to serve as a fire bell in the night. If Americans have an ounce of sense, the Trump presidency will cure them once and for all of the illusion that from the White House comes redemption. By now we ought to have had enough of de facto monarchy.

By extension, Americans should come to see as intolerable the meanness, corruption, and partisan dysfunction so much in evidence at the opposite end of Pennsylvania Avenue. We need not wax sentimental over the days when Lyndon Johnson and Everett Dirksen presided over the Senate to conclude that Mitch McConnell and Chuck Schumer represent something other than progress. If Congress continues to behave as contemptibly as it has in recent years, it will, by default, allow the conditions that have produced Trump and his cronies to prevail.

So it's time to take another stab at an approach to governance worthy of a democratic republic. Where to begin? I submit that Rabbit Angstrom's question offers a place to start: What's the point of being an American?

Authentic progressives and principled conservatives will offer different answers to Rabbit's query. My own answer is rooted in an abiding conviction that our problems are less quantitative than qualitative. Rather than simply more—yet more wealth, more freedom, more attempts at global leadership—the times call for something different. In my view, the point of being an American is to participate in creating a society that strikes a balance between wants and needs, that exists in harmony with nature and the rest of humankind, and that is rooted in an agreed-upon conception of the common good.

My own prescription for how to act upon that statement of purpose is unlikely to find favor with many readers. But therein lies the basis for an interesting debate, one that is essential to prospects for stemming the accelerating decay of American civic life.

Initiating such a debate, and so bringing into focus core issues, will remain next to impossible, however, without first clearing away the accumulated debris of the post–Cold War era. Preliminary steps in that direction, listed in no particular order, ought to include the following:

First, abolish the Electoral College. Doing so will preclude any further occurrence of the circumstances that twice in recent decades cast doubt on the outcome of national elections and thereby did far more than any foreign interference to undermine the legitimacy of American politics.

Second, roll back gerrymandering. Doing so will help restore competitive elections and make incumbency more tenuous.

Third, limit the impact of corporate money on elections at all levels, if need be by amending the Constitution.

Fourth, mandate a balanced federal budget, thereby demolishing the pretense that Americans need not choose between guns and butter.

Fifth, implement a program of national service, thereby eliminating the all-volunteer military and restoring the tradition of the citizen-soldier. Doing so will help close the gap between the military and society and enrich the prevailing conception of citizenship. It might even encourage members of Congress to think twice before signing off on wars that the commander-in-chief wants to fight.

Sixth, enact tax policies that will promote greater income equality.

Seventh, increase public funding for public higher education, thereby ensuring that college remains an option for those who are not well-to-do.

Eighth, beyond mere "job" creation, attend to the growing challenges of providing meaningful work—employment that is both rewarding and reasonably remunerative—for those without advanced STEM degrees.

Ninth, end the thumb-twiddling on climate change and start treating it as the first-order national security priority that it is.

Tenth, absent evident progress on the above, create a new party system, breaking the current duopoly in which Republicans and Democrats tacitly collaborate to dictate the policy agenda and restrict the range of policy options deemed permissible.

These are not particularly original proposals and I do not offer them as a panacea. They may, however, represent preliminary steps toward devising some new paradigm to replace a post–Cold War consensus that, in promoting transnational corporate greed, mistaking libertinism for liberty, and embracing militarized neo-imperialism as the essence of statecraft, has paved the way for the presidency of Donald Trump.

We can and must do better. But doing so will require that we come up with better and truer ideas to serve as a foundation for American politics.

42

Not the "Age of Trump"

(2017)

A sampling of recent headlines: "Art in the Age of Trump;" "Truth in the Age of Trump;" "Feminism in the Age of Trump;" "Hate in the Age of Trump;" "Reading Yeats in the Age of Trump;" "Anything At All Can Happen in the Age of Trump." And that's barely scratching the surface.

Concerned about the impact of the "Age of Trump" on science? A wealth of recent literature examining that topic awaits you. Ditto for sex, gay rights, cities, philanthropy, bioethics, foreign policy, fashion, investing, anxiety, faithfulness, the Arctic, and even "vegan activism." The list goes on. In the "Age of Trump," everything is changing, and bigly.

To judge by the avalanche of commentary exploring every aspect of his eponymous "Age," our recently inaugurated president is to the United States what Caesar Augustus was to Rome or Louis XIV was to France. Just months in office, he is already putting a profound mark on virtually every aspect of human endeavor.

So at least hordes of hyperventilating journalists, scholars, activists, bloggers, and opinionated citizens purport to believe. Mark me down as skeptical. My bet is that when future historians render a verdict on Donald Trump they will see him as our least consequential president since Benjamin Harrison, whose signature diplomatic achievement was to persuade Europeans to lift a ban on pork imported from the United States, or even since William Henry Harrison, Benjamin Harrison's grandfather, who died after a mere thirty-one days in office.

Particularly on the home front, the prospect of Trump achieving anything of lasting significance is rapidly diminishing. Barring some domestic equivalent of Pearl Harbor, Trump's own incompetence, compounded by the internal dysfunction besetting his administration, will severely limit his prospect of making much of an impact. Throw in extreme partisanship, relentless sniping from the establishment press, and the obstructions posed by courts and the permanent government, and you end up with a recipe that almost guarantees paralysis.

That Trump will retain the ability to fire up his supporters and enrage his detractors will doubtless be the case. But for the balance of his term, fending off investigations and indictments is likely to absorb the preponderance of his attention. Whatever mischief he succeeds in committing, whether by cutting social programs or conferring favors on major corporations, can be overturned or reversed once he departs the scene. So unless Trump plunges the nation into some disastrous war—a possibility, alas, not to be discounted—Americans will end up mostly remembering their forty-fifth president, fondly or not, for his tweets.

Yet to suggest that Trump will end up on the Harrison end of the presidential spectrum is not to imply that the United States as a whole will remain stuck in neutral as long as he occupies the White House. On the contrary, dramatic, fundamental, and probably irreversible changes are transforming American society day by day before our very eyes. It's just that Trump himself is irrelevant to those changes, which predate his entry into politics and continue today all but unaffected by his ascent to the presidency.

Melodramatic references to an "Age of Trump" that suddenly commenced in November 2016 obscure this reality. Simply put, our collective fixation on the person and foibles of Trump the individual causes us to overlook what is actually going on. And what is actually going on is something that Donald Trump hasn't, won't, and can't affect.

Let me illustrate the point by citing a pair of recent articles in the *New York Times*. Even as other "legacy" outlets become passé, that newspaper continues to serve as an important bellwether of change, cueing political and cultural elites to trends that merit their attention. Nominally, the *Times* provides its readers with "All the News That's Fit to Print." In practice, it prints "All the Views Deemed to Matter." Among the things that matter most at the *Times* are changes in the prevailing definition of freedom.

What we're talking about is not my grandmother's version of freedom, of course. In practice, the *Times* equates freedom with maximizing personal autonomy, a proposition especially applicable to all matters related to race, gender, sex, and sexuality. (When it comes to class, the *Times* is ambivalent, sympathizing with those in need while simultaneously celebrating extravagant consumption.) Choice signifies empowerment. That expanding individual choice ultimately advances the common good is taken as a given.

So the operative principle is this: anything that enlarges choice is commendable. A recent *Times* story about the first women to complete army infantry training—"a towering milestone"—offers a vivid example. Young women "who dreamed of going into the infantry" now can have those dreams come true, the *Times* reports, and with that "are no longer barred from the core combat positions that are the clearest routes to senior leadership." Whether the quality of US senior military leadership leaves something to be desired (it does) and whether gender imbalance at the top contributes to those deficiencies (who knows) are questions that the *Times* does not take up. What counts, and is to be applauded, is that nothing should impede women hankering to serve in combat from making it to the pinnacle of the military hierarchy.

On the other hand, anything that inhibits choice calls for critical examination. The traditional prohibition on suicide offers an example. The front-page treatment given to a story on "medically assisted death," published in the *Times* one day after the feature on female grunts, illustrates the point.

This 7,000-plus word essay, spread across six pages and including photographs, provides a deeply sympathetic account of why and how John Shields chose to arrange for his own death. A former Catholic priest and lifelong spiritual seeker who had lived a full and consequential life, Mr. Shields was suffering from an incurable disease that condemned him to a wretchedly slow and painful demise. So he resolved to determine his own fate. In doing so, this exemplar of decency and virtue became something more: as depicted by the *Times*, in ending his life, Mr. Shields was expanding the very parameters of human freedom.

"Having control over the terms of his death," according to the *Times*, "made him feel empowered over the disease rather than crippled by it." So after bidding farewell to loving family and friends, and with the help of an obliging physician ("I'm coming here and John will be dead, so I guess technically I'm killing John. But that's not how I think of it."), he did it his way, with impressive dignity.

Add to the mix a recent *New York Times Magazine* cover story on non-exclusive coupling—"Is an Open Marriage a Happier Marriage?"—along with the attention the newspaper lavishes on all things LGBT and you get the picture. Whether for good or for ill, and whatever tomfoolery Donald Trump may or may not be plotting, American society is undergoing a profound moral and cultural revolution, of which—irony of ironies—the narcissistic Trump is himself a product.

My argument here is not that the *Times* itself is somehow responsible for this revolution. While it may encourage, approve, or certify, it does not cause. As the paper of record, the principal function of the *Times* is to bear witness. In that regard, it performs an essential service. But if the *Times* went out of business next week, the forces promoting a radically revised conception of freedom would persist, their momentum unchecked.

So to expend energy exploring the implications of the so-called "Age of Trump" is to engage in a fool's errand. Trump's antics serve to obscure the real story. Indeed, in a fundamental sense, the Trump phenomenon represents the embodiment of "fake news."

The real story is this: ours is an "Age of Autonomy," in which received norms—the basis of freedom as my grandmother understood the term—are losing their authority. This is notably the case with regard to norms that derive from religious tradition. How and whether the forces displacing those norms—science, the market, Big Data, social media—will foster a durable basis for a morally grounded community is at present impossible to foresee.

Yet this much is for sure. Long after Trump has retired to Mar-a-Lago, the revolution that predates his rise to prominence will continue, with implications far outweighing anything he—or any other president—may do. Someday even the *New York Times* may notice.

43

The Failure of
American Liberalism

(2016)

Does the election of Donald Trump qualify as a triumph of American conservatism? No, for the simple reason that Trump subscribes to few of the values that conservatives (and by extension the Republican Party) have for decades touted as core principles.

So although the GOP will now control the presidency and both houses of Congress, gaining power has come at a high cost: the party faithful must now declare their fealty to a leader whose convictions, to the extent that any can be identified, are all over the map. In effect, Republicans must now pretend that incoherence and inconsistency are virtues. Rallying to Trump requires conservatives to engage in voluntary acts of self-debasement, all presumably contributing to the overarching goal of "draining the swamp."

Yet if Trump's unexpected triumph is, therefore, rich with contradictions, Hillary Clinton's defeat is precisely what it seems to be: a rejection not only of the Democratic Party but also of contemporary American liberalism.

Democrats today may see themselves as heirs to a progressive tradition that traces its lineage back to Franklin Roosevelt, or even to Williams Jennings Bryan. But that does not describe the Democratic Party that elevated Hillary Clinton to the position of standard bearer. Mrs. Clinton bears no more resemblance to Bryan, the Great Commoner, than does Donald Trump to Abraham Lincoln, the Great Emancipator.

Once upon a time, progressivism meant standing up for the little guy against what another Roosevelt once called "the malefactors of great wealth." Those days have long since passed. The version of progressivism represented by Clinton and her allies accommodates present-day malefactors. Rather than confronting class enemies, it glosses over competing class interests.

True, on the far left, vestiges of an earlier and more radical progressivism persist. We saw it in the primary challenge mounted by Bernie Sanders. We hear it in the language of Elizabeth Warren. We can expect to hear more of that language in the days ahead.

But in the party that chose Hillary Clinton as its nominee, radicalism qualifies as no more than a fringe phenomenon. While paying lip service to the idea of "toppling" the 1 percent, Clinton herself identifies with and assiduously courted members of the moneyed elite. They are her kind of people. In that regard, if ever a picture were worth a thousand words, it's the photograph of both Clintons happily posing alongside Donald Trump at Trump's third wedding. It shows a couple at ease with their surroundings, knowing that they are where they belong.

Yet apart from an affinity for wealth, status, and celebrity, what is the essence of Clinton-style liberalism? As during her husband's presidency, it centers on a theory of political economy. In a paid speech to Brazilian bankers prior to launching her run for the presidency, Hillary Clinton remarked, "My dream is a hemispheric common market, with open trade and open borders, some time in the future with energy that is as green and sustainable as we can get it, powering growth and opportunity for every person in the hemisphere."

Critics jumped on this passage as proof that Clinton intended to permit hordes of undocumented immigrants to flood the United States. It is, instead, a concise summary of the worldview to which leading Democrats subscribe, albeit with this caveat: the scope of that dream is not hemispheric, but global. The Democratic establishment's commitment to openness encompasses not only trade and borders, but also capital and ideas, all flowing without disruption. Raised a Methodist, Hillary Clinton has long since followed the mainstream of her party by putting her faith in globalization.

To be sure, her belief in the transformative effects of globalization is unexceptional. On such matters, she merely parrots conventional wisdom. That removing barriers to technology-charged corporate capitalism will generate wealth on an unprecedented scale has long since become an article of faith everywhere from Washington to Wall Street to Silicon Valley. That given proper oversight these forces will also alleviate problems of inequality, injustice, and environmental degradation, while advancing the cause of world peace—all boats everywhere eventually rising—is liberalism's addendum to globalization's common creed.

Since the end of the Cold War, the American political establishment has committed itself to validating such expectations. This has become the overarching theme of national politics, successive administrations, occasionally differing on specifics, all adhering to the so-called Washington Consensus. From the first Clinton to the second Bush and then on to Barack Obama, each in turn has used American power and influence to pry open the world so that people, goods, and capital can move ever more freely.

Each administration in turn has ignored or downplayed evidence that openness is not a win-win proposition. Along with riches for some have come market crashes, painful recessions, joblessness for citizens hard-pressed to adapt to the rigors of a changing market, and resistance from those opposed to the cultural amalgamation that trails in globalization's wake. Even so, proponents of this ideology remain undeterred.

With its putative "logic" so deeply embedded in the fabric of American politics, globalization appeared—at least until November 8—immune to challenge. Submission to the dictates of a globalizing marketplace appeared all but obligatory, with alternatives such as socialism or distributism or any other -ism rendered inconceivable and therefore not worthy of serious consideration.

Lost along the way were expectations that furthering the common good or promoting human virtue, not simply expanding the economic pie, might figure among the immediate aims of political economy. On the weekend before Election Day, Ross Douthat wrote in the *New York Times* that "technocratic and secular liberalism may simply not be satisfying to a fragmented, atomized society." He got that right. Indeed, he might have gone further: the technocratic and secular liberalism embodied by Hillary Clinton has actually exacerbated the fragmentation and atomization of society, even if elites (until now) were slow to take notice.

In the run-up to the 2016 election, observers without number described it as the most important in recent memory, if not in all of US history. In fact, however, a Hillary Clinton victory, assumed as all but automatic, would have drained the election of significance.

Clinton's supporters looked forward to the prospect of the first woman president as an achievement of cosmic importance. Of course, a half-century ago many attributed comparable significance to the election of our first Catholic president. Yet note that today John F. Kennedy's religious affiliation figures as little more than a footnote to his presidency. So too, I suspect, the novelty of having a woman in charge of the White House would have worn off within weeks. At that point, rather than the president's gender, the been-there, done-that quality of her thinking would have attracted notice.

In that respect, rather than a turning point, installing a second Clinton in the White House would have constituted a postponement of sorts, Americans kicking four years further down the road any recognition of just how bland and soulless their politics had become.

Now that Trump has won, however, the pre-election hyperbole might actually prove justified. The United States finds itself suddenly adrift in uncharted waters. Once Trump takes office, the captain on the bridge will be unlicensed and unqualified. We may hope that he masters his responsibilities before running the ship aground. In the meantime, the rough seas ahead might provide an incentive for liberals and conservatives alike to give a fresh look to some of those ideological alternatives that we just might have discarded prematurely.

44

An Ode to Ike and Adlai

(2016)

My earliest recollection of national politics dates back exactly sixty years to the moment, in the summer of 1956, when I watched the political conventions in the company of that wondrous new addition to our family, television. My parents were supporting President Dwight D. Eisenhower for a second term and that was good enough for me. Even as a youngster, I sensed that Ike, the former supreme commander of Allied forces in Europe in World War II, was someone of real stature. In a troubled time, he exuded authority and self-confidence. By comparison, Democratic candidate Adlai Stevenson came across as vaguely suspect. Next to the five-star incumbent, he seemed soft, even foppish, and therefore not up to the job. So at least it appeared to a nine-year-old living in Chicagoland.

Of the seamy underside of politics I knew nothing, of course. On the surface, all seemed reassuring. As if by divine mandate, two parties vied for power. The views they represented defined the allowable range of opinion. The outcome of any election expressed the collective will of the people and was to be accepted as such. That I was growing up in the best democracy the world had ever known—its very existence a daily rebuke to the enemies of freedom—was beyond question.

Naïve? Embarrassingly so. Yet how I wish that Election Day in November 2016 might present Americans with something even loosely approximating the alternatives available to them in November 1956. Oh, to choose once more between an Ike and an Adlai.

Don't for a second think that this is about nostalgia. Today, Stevenson doesn't qualify for anyone's list of Great Americans. If remembered at all, it's for his sterling performance as President John F. Kennedy's UN ambassador during the Cuban Missile Crisis. Interrogating his Soviet counterpart with cameras rolling, Stevenson barked that he was prepared to wait "until hell freezes over" to get his questions answered about Soviet military activities in Cuba. When the chips were down, Adlai proved anything but soft. Yet in aspiring to the highest office in the land, he had come up well short. In 1952, he came nowhere close to winning and in 1956 he proved no more successful. Stevenson was to the Democratic Party what Thomas Dewey had been to the Republicans: a luckless two-time loser.

As for Eisenhower, although there is much in his presidency to admire, his errors of omission and commission were legion. During his two terms, from Guatemala to Iran, the CIA overthrew governments, plotted assassinations, and embraced unsavory right-wing dictators—in effect, planting a series of IEDs destined eventually to blow up in the face of Ike's various successors. Meanwhile, binging on nuclear weapons, the Pentagon accumulated an arsenal far beyond what even Eisenhower as commander-in-chief considered prudent or necessary.

In addition, during his tenure in office, the military-industrial complex became a rapacious juggernaut, an entity unto itself as Ike himself belatedly acknowledged. By no means least of all, Eisenhower fecklessly committed the United States to an ill-fated project of nation-building in a country that just about no American had heard of at the time: South Vietnam. Ike did give the nation eight years of relative peace and prosperity, but at a high price—most of the bills coming due long after he left office.

The Pathology of US Politics

And yet, and yet . . .

To contrast the virtues and shortcomings of Stevenson and Eisenhower with those of Hillary Rodham Clinton and Donald Trump is both instructive and profoundly depressing. Comparing the adversaries of 1956 with their 2016 counterparts reveals with startling clarity what the decades-long decay of American politics has wrought.

In 1956, each of the major political parties nominated a grown-up for the highest office in the land. In 2016, only one has.

In 1956, both parties nominated likeable individuals who conveyed a basic sense of trustworthiness. In 2016, neither party has done so.

In 1956, Americans could count on the election to render a definitive verdict, the vote count affirming the legitimacy of the system itself and allowing the business of governance to resume. In 2016, that is unlikely to be the case. Whether Trump or Clinton ultimately prevails, large numbers of Americans will view the result as further proof of "rigged" and irredeemably corrupt political arrangements. Rather than inducing some semblance of reconciliation, the outcome is likely to deepen divisions.

How in the name of all that is holy did we get into such a mess?

How did the party of Eisenhower, an architect of victory in World War II, choose as its nominee a narcissistic TV celebrity who, with each successive tweet and verbal outburst, offers further evidence that he is totally unequipped for high office? Yes, the establishment media are ganging up on Trump, blatantly displaying the sort of bias normally kept at least nominally under wraps. Yet never have such expressions of journalistic hostility toward a particular candidate been more justified. Trump is a bozo of such monumental proportions as to tax the abilities of our most talented satirists. Were he alive today, Mark Twain at his most scathing would be hard-pressed to do justice to The Donald's blowhard pomposity.

Similarly, how did the party of Adlai Stevenson, but also of Stevenson's hero Franklin Roosevelt, select as its candidate someone so widely disliked and mistrusted even by many of her fellow Democrats? True, antipathy directed toward Hillary Clinton draws some of its energy from incorrigible sexists along with the "vast right wing conspiracy" whose members thoroughly loathe both Clintons. Yet the antipathy is not without basis in fact.

Even by Washington standards, Secretary Clinton exudes a striking sense of entitlement combined with a nearly complete absence of accountability. She shrugs off her misguided vote in support of invading Iraq back in 2003, while serving as senator from New York. She neither explains nor apologizes for pressing to depose Libya's Muammar Gaddafi in 2011, her most notable "accomplishment" as secretary of state. "We came, we saw, he died," she bragged back then, somewhat prematurely given that Libya has since fallen into anarchy and become a haven for ISIS.

She clings to the demonstrably false claim that her use of a private server for State Department business compromised no classified information. Now opposed to the Trans-Pacific Partnership (TTP) that she once described as the "gold standard in trade agreements," Clinton rejects charges of political opportunism. That her change of heart occurred when attacking the TPP was helping Bernie Sanders win one Democratic primary after another is merely coincidental. Oh, and the big money accepted from banks, Wall Street, and the tech sector for minimal work, and the even bigger money from leading figures in the Israel lobby? Rest assured that her acceptance of such largesse won't reduce by one iota her support for "working class families" or her commitment to a just peace settlement in the Middle East.

Let me be clear: none of these offer the slightest reason to vote for Donald Trump. Yet together they make the point that Hillary Clinton is a deeply flawed candidate, notably so in matters related to national security. Clinton is surely correct that allowing Trump to make decisions related to war and peace would be the height of folly. Yet her record in that regard does not exactly inspire confidence.

When it comes to foreign policy, Trump's preference for off-the-cuff utterances finds him committing astonishing gaffes with metronomic regularity. Spontaneity serves chiefly to expose his staggering ignorance.

By comparison, the carefully scripted Clinton commits few missteps, as she recites with practiced ease the pabulum that passes for right thinking in establishment circles. But fluency does not necessarily connote soundness. Clinton, after all, adheres resolutely to the highly militarized "Washington playbook" that President Obama himself has disparaged—a faith-based belief in American global primacy to be pursued regardless of how the world may be changing and heedless of costs.

On the latter point, note that Clinton's acceptance speech in Philadelphia included not a single mention of Afghanistan. By Election Day, the war there will have passed its fifteenth anniversary. One might think that a prospective commander-in-chief would have something to say about the longest conflict in American history, one that continues with no end in sight. Yet, with the Washington playbook offering few answers, Mrs. Clinton chooses to remain silent on the subject.

So while a Trump presidency holds the prospect of the United States driving off a cliff, a Clinton presidency promises to be the equivalent of banging one's head against a brick wall without evident effect, wondering all the while why it hurts so much.

Pseudo-Politics for an Ersatz Era

But let's not just blame the candidates. Trump and Clinton are also the product of circumstances that neither created. As candidates, they are merely exploiting a situation—one relying on intuition and vast stores of brashness, the other putting to work skills gained during a life spent studying how to acquire and employ power. The success both have achieved in securing the nominations of their parties is evidence of far more fundamental forces at work.

In the pairing of Trump and Clinton, we confront symptoms of something pathological. Unless Americans identify the sources of this disease, it will inevitably worsen, with dire consequences in the realm of national security. After all, back in Eisenhower's day, the IEDs planted thanks to reckless presidential decisions tended to blow up only years—or even decades—later. For example, between the 1953 US-engineered coup that restored the Shah to his throne and the 1979 revolution that converted Iran overnight from ally to adversary, more than a quarter of a century elapsed. In our own day, however, detonation occurs so much more quickly—witness the almost instantaneous and explosively unhappy consequences of Washington's post-9/11 military interventions in the Greater Middle East.

So here's a matter worth pondering: How is it that all the months of intensive fundraising, the debates and speeches, the caucuses and primaries, and the avalanche of TV ads and annoying robocalls have produced two presidential candidates who tend to elicit from a surprisingly large number of rank-and-file citizens disdain, indifference, or at best hold-your-nose-and-pull-the-lever acquiescence?

Here, then, is a preliminary diagnosis of three of the factors contributing to the erosion of American politics, offered from the conviction that, for Americans to have better choices next time around, fundamental change must occur—and soon.

First, and most important, the evil effects of money: Need chapter and verse? For a tutorial, see this essential 2015 book by Professor Lawrence Lessig of Harvard: *Republic Lost, Version 2.0*. Those with no time for books might spare eighteen minutes for Lessig's brilliant and deeply disturbing TED talk. Professor Lessig argues persuasively that unless the United States radically changes the way it finances political campaigns, we're pretty much doomed to see our democracy wither and die.

Needless to say, moneyed interests and incumbents who benefit from existing arrangements take a different view and collaborate to maintain the status quo. As a result, political life has increasingly become a pursuit reserved for those like Trump who possess vast personal wealth or for those like Clinton who display an aptitude for persuading the well to-do to open their purses, with all that implies by way of compromise, accommodation, and the subsequent repayment of favors.

Second, the perverse impact of identity politics on policy: Observers make much of the fact that, in capturing the presidential nomination of a major party, Hillary Clinton has shattered yet another glass ceiling. They are right to do so. Yet the novelty of her candidacy starts and ends with gender. When it comes to fresh thinking, Donald Trump has far more to offer than Clinton—even if his version of "fresh" tends to be synonymous with "wacky," "off-the-wall," "ridiculous," or "altogether hair-raising."

The essential point here is that in the realm of national security Hillary Clinton is utterly conventional. She subscribes to a worldview (and view of America's role in the world) that originated during the Cold War, reached its zenith in the 1990s when the United States proclaimed itself the planet's "sole superpower," and persists today remarkably unaffected by actual events. On the campaign trail, Clinton attests to her bona fides by routinely reaffirming her belief in American exceptionalism, paying fervent tribute to "the world's greatest military," swearing that she'll be "listening to our generals and admirals," and vowing to get tough on America's adversaries. These are, of course, the mandatory rituals of the contemporary Washington stump speech, amplified if anything by the perceived need for the first female candidate for president to emphasize her pugnacity.

A Clinton presidency, therefore, offers the prospect of more of the same—muscle-flexing and armed intervention to demonstrate American global leadership—albeit marketed with a garnish of diversity. Instead of different policies, Clinton will offer an administration that has a different look, touting this as evidence of positive change.

Yet while diversity may be a good thing, we should not confuse it with effectiveness. A national security team that "looks like America" (to use the phrase originally coined by Bill Clinton) does not necessarily govern more effectively than one that looks like President Eisenhower's. What matters is getting the job done.

Since the 1990s women have found plentiful opportunities to fill positions in the upper echelons of the national security apparatus. Although we have not yet had a female commander-in-chief, three women have served as secretary of state and two as national security adviser. Several have filled Adlai Stevenson's old post at the United Nations. Undersecretaries, deputy undersecretaries, and assistant secretaries of like gender abound, along with a passel of female admirals and generals.

So the question needs be asked: Has the quality of national security policy improved compared to the bad old days when men exclusively called the shots? Using as criteria the promotion of stability and the avoidance of armed conflict (along with the successful prosecution of wars deemed unavoidable), the answer would, of course, have to be no. Although Madeleine Albright, Condoleezza Rice, Susan Rice,

Samantha Power, and Clinton herself might entertain a different view, actually existing conditions in Afghanistan, Iraq, Libya, Syria, Somalia, Sudan, Yemen, and other countries across the Greater Middle East and significant parts of Africa tell a different story.

The abysmal record of American statecraft in recent years is not remotely the fault of women, yet neither have women made a perceptibly positive difference. It turns out that identity does not necessarily signify wisdom or assure insight. Allocating positions of influence in the State Department or the Pentagon based on gender, race, ethnicity, or sexual orientation—as Clinton will assuredly do—may gratify previously disenfranchised groups. But little evidence exists to suggest that doing so will produce more enlightened approaches to statecraft, at least not so long as adherence to the Washington playbook figures as a precondition to employment. (Should Clinton win in November, don't expect the redoubtable ladies of Code Pink to be tapped for jobs at the Pentagon and State Department.)

In the end, it's not identity that matters but ideas and their implementation. To contemplate the ideas that might guide a President Trump along with those he will recruit to act on them—Ivanka as national security adviser?—is enough to elicit shudders from any sane person. Yet the prospect of Madam President surrounding herself with an impeccably diverse team of advisers who share her own outmoded views is hardly cause for celebration.

Putting a woman in charge of national security policy will not in itself amend the defects exhibited in recent years. For that, the obsolete principles with which Clinton along with the rest of Washington remains enamored will have to be jettisoned. In his own bizarre way (albeit without a clue as to a plausible alternative), Donald Trump seems to get that; Hillary Clinton does not.

Third, the substitution of "reality" for reality: Back in 1962, a young historian by the name of Daniel Boorstin published *The Image: A Guide to Pseudo-Events in America*. In an age in which Donald Trump and Hillary Clinton vie to determine the nation's destiny, it should be mandatory reading. *The Image* remains, as when it first appeared, a warning that we ignore at our peril.

According to Boorstin, more than five decades ago the American people were already living in a "thicket of unreality." By relentlessly indulging in ever more "extravagant expectations," they were forfeiting their capacity to distinguish between what was real and what was illusory. Indeed, Boorstin wrote, "We have become so accustomed to our illusions that we mistake them for reality."

While ad agencies and PR firms had indeed vigorously promoted a world of illusions, Americans themselves had become willing accomplices in the process.

> The American citizen lives in a world where fantasy is more real than reality, where the image has more dignity than its original. We hardly dare to face our bewilderment, because our ambiguous experience is so pleasantly iridescent, and the solace of belief in contrived reality is so thoroughly real. We have become eager accessories to the great hoaxes of the age. These are the hoaxes we play on ourselves.

This, of course, was decades before the nation succumbed to the iridescent allure of Facebook, Google, fantasy football, *Real Housewives of* _____, selfies, smartphone apps, *Game of Thrones*, Pokémon GO—and, yes, the vehicle that vaulted Donald Trump to stardom, *The Apprentice*.

"The making of the illusions which flood our experience has become the business of America," wrote Boorstin. It's also become the essence of American politics, long since transformed into theater, or rather into some sort of (un)reality show.

Presidential campaigns today are themselves, to use Boorstin's famous term, "pseudo-events" that stretch from months into years. By now, most Americans know better than to take at face value anything candidates say or promise along the way. We're in on the joke—or at least we think we are. Reinforcing that perception on a daily basis are media outlets that have abandoned mere reporting in favor of enhancing the spectacle of the moment. This is especially true of the cable news networks, where talking heads serve up a snide and cynical complement to the smarmy fakery that is the office-seeker's stock in trade. And we lap it up. It matters little that we know it's all staged and contrived—Megyn Kelly getting under Trump's skin, Trump himself denouncing "lyin' Ted" Cruz, etc., etc.—as long as it's entertaining.

This emphasis on spectacle has drained national politics of whatever substance it still had back when Ike and Adlai commanded the scene. It hardly need be said that Donald Trump has demonstrated an extraordinary knack—a sort of post-modern genius—for turning this phenomenon to his advantage. Yet in her own way Clinton plays the same game. How else to explain a national convention organized around the idea of "reintroducing to the American people" someone who served eight years as First Lady, was elected to the Senate, failed in a previous high-profile run for the presidency, and completed a term as secretary of state? The Democratic conclave in Philadelphia was, like the Republican one that preceded it, a pseudo-event par excellence, the object of the exercise being to fashion a new "image" for the Democratic candidate.

The thicket of unreality that is American politics has now become all-enveloping. The problem is not Trump and Clinton, per se. It's an identifiable set of arrangements—laws, habits, cultural predispositions—that have evolved over time and promoted the rot that now pervades American politics. As a direct consequence, the very concept of self-government is increasingly a fantasy, even if surprisingly few Americans seem to mind.

At an earlier juncture back in 1956, out of a population of 168 million, we got Ike and Adlai. Today, with almost double the population, we get—well, we get what we've got. This does not represent progress. And don't kid yourself that things really can't get much worse. Unless Americans rouse themselves to act, count on it, they will.

45

War and Culture,
American Style

(2016)

In the dispiriting summer of 1979, a beleaguered President Jimmy Carter tried to sell his fellow citizens on a radical proposition: having strayed from the path of righteousness, the nation was in dire need of moral and cultural repair.

Carter's pitch had a specific context: an "oil shock"—this one a product of the Iranian Revolution—had once more reminded Americans that their prevailing definition of the good life depended on the indulgence of others. The United States was running out of oil and was anxiously counting on others to provide it.

Yet the problem at hand, Carter insisted, went far beyond "gasoline lines or energy shortages." A "mistaken idea of freedom" had led too many Americans "to worship self-indulgence and consumption." The nation therefore faced a fundamental choice. Down one path lay "fragmentation and self-interest," pointing toward "constant conflict" and "ending in chaos and immobility." Down the other lay a "path of common purpose and the restoration of American values." By choosing rectitude over profligacy, the nation could save itself. Making the sacrifices needed to end their dependence on foreign oil would enable Americans to "seize control again of our common destiny."

Alas, members of the congregation weren't buying what Pastor Carter was selling. They had no interest in getting by with less. Ronald Reagan, sunny where Carter was dour and widely expected to challenge the president for reelection, was offering an alternative view: for Americans, there is always more. Besides, austerity didn't sound like much fun. Soon enough Carter himself got the message. In January 1980, he capitulated, declaring Persian Gulf oil a cause worth fighting for.

The implications of the Carter Doctrine were not immediately apparent. Yet what unfolded over the course of subsequent decades was a vast military enterprise that today finds US forces engaged in something approximating permanent war, not only in the Persian Gulf but across large parts of the Islamic world.

At odd intervals during this very long conflict, Carter's theme of moral and cultural restoration resurfaced, albeit with a twist. Observers expressed hopes that war itself might somehow provide the instrument of national redemption.

George W. Bush was eloquent on this point. In his 2002 State of the Union address, Bush depicted 9/11 itself as an occasion for cultural transformation. "This time of adversity," he announced, offers "a moment we must seize to change our culture." Indeed, the change was already happening. "After America was attacked, it was as if our entire country looked into a mirror and saw our better selves. We were reminded that we are citizens with obligations. . . . We began to think less of the goods we can accumulate and more about the good we can do." For too long, Americans had adhered to the dictum "if it feels good, do it." Now, even as Bush was urging his fellow citizens to shop and take vacations, he commended them for embracing "a new culture of responsibility."

This was mostly nonsense, of course. Just as we had ignored Carter's critique of their "mistaken idea of freedom," so too we passed on Bush's "culture of responsibility." To avoid getting sucked into the Middle East, Carter had admonished Americans to change their ways.

The response: piss off. With the United States now wading into a Middle Eastern quagmire, Bush revived Carter's call for a cultural Great Awakening. Although 9/11 briefly induced a mood of "United We Stand," the invasion of Iraq, with all the mournful consequences that ensued, terminated that feel-good moment and demolished Bush's standing as moral arbiter.

In truth, the inclinations, habits, and mores that Carter bemoaned and that Bush fancied war might banish are immune to presidential authority. Presidents don't control the culture; they cope with it. In times of war, they abide by what the culture permits and adhere to what it requires. Simply put, culture shapes the American way of war.

Certainly this was the case during prior conflicts of US history such as the Civil War and World War II. During each conflict, a widely shared (if imperfect) collective culture imbued the war effort with effectiveness that contributed directly to victory. From the very outset of the war that the United States has for decades waged in various parts of the Islamic world, just the reverse has been true. An absence of cultural solidarity has undermined military effectiveness.

These days, American culture posits a minimalist definition of citizenship. It emphasizes choice rather than duty and self-gratification over sacrifice—except where sacrifice happens to accord with personal preference. Individuals enjoy wide latitude in defining the terms of their relationship to the state. Pay your taxes and obey the law; civic obligation extends that far and no further.

So in conducting military campaigns in the Islamic world, presidents from Carter's day to our own have asked little—indeed, next to nothing—from the vast majority of citizens. They are spectators rather than participants.

The people find this arrangement amenable. On occasion, some exceptionally egregious calamity such as the Beirut bombing of 1983, the "Black Hawk down" debacle of 1993, or the botched occupation of Iraq following the invasion of 2003 may briefly command their attention. But in general, they tune out what they view as not their affair.

As recently as the 1960s, antipathy toward a misguided and failing war generated mass protest. Today, instead of protest there is accommodation, with Americans remarkably untroubled by the inability of those presiding over the ebb and flow of military actions across the

Greater Middle East to explain when, how, or even whether they will end.

To be sure, even today we retain a residual capacity for outrage, as the Occupy Wall Street and Black Lives Matter movements have demonstrated. When the issue is inequality or discrimination based on race, gender, or sexuality, we still take to the streets. When it comes to war, however, not so much. The "peace movement," to the extent that it can be said to exist, is anemic and almost entirely devoid of clout. Our politics allows no room for anything approximating an antiwar party. Instead, the tacit acceptance of war has become a distinguishing feature of the contemporary American scene.

With The People opting out, the burden of actually conducting the various campaigns launched pursuant to the Carter Doctrine falls to those who willingly make themselves available to fight. We may compare these volunteers to fighter pilots during the Battle of Britain: they are the Few. The many have other options and act accordingly.

Given the choice between a job in finance and the chance to carry an assault rifle, Harvard grads opt for Wall Street, destination of roughly one-third of graduating seniors in recent years. In 2015, by comparison, participants in Harvard's annual military commissioning ceremony numbered exactly four. Offered the opportunity to sign with the pros or the Army, top athletes opt for the playing field rather than the battlefield. The countercultural Tillman Exception awaits replication.

So a central task for field commanders has been to figure out how to fight wars that the political class deems necessary but to which the rest of us are largely indifferent. In 2007, Admiral Mike Mullen, the Joint Chiefs of Staff chairman, neatly summarized the problem. "In Afghanistan, we do what we can," he remarked. "In Iraq, we do what we must." Implicit in Mullen's can/must formulation was the fact that in neither Afghanistan nor Iraq were commanders able to do what they wished. The constraint they labored under was not money or equipment, which were available and expended in prodigious quantities, but troops.

We tend to rank those two conflicts among this nation's "big wars." In reality, except as measured by duration, both qualify as puny. The total number of troops committed to both Operation Iraqi

Freedom and Operation Enduring Freedom together peaked at one-third the total number of Americans in Vietnam in 1968. However much commanders in Iraq and Afghanistan might have wanted more troops—and they did—more were not forthcoming.

For an explanation, look not to need but to availability. In truth, the pool of the willing is not deep. Sustaining what depth there is requires incentives. Since 9/11, new recruit pay has jumped by 50 percent. Reenlistment bonuses can run as high as $150,000. In a material culture, appeals to patriotism don't suffice to elicit and retain volunteers. Inducing people to put their lives on the line requires upfront compensation. Even then, the Few remain few.

In practice, roughly 1 percent of the population bears the burden of actually fighting our wars. A country that styles itself a democracy ought to find this troubling. Yet unlike the inequitable distribution of income, which generates considerable controversy, this inequitable distribution of sacrifice generates almost none. Even in a presidential election year, it finds no place on the nation's political agenda. In the prevailing culture of choice, those choosing to remain on the sidelines are not to be held accountable for the fate that befalls those choosing to go fight.

Yet while the availability of warriors may be limited, money is another matter. Ours is not a pay-as-you-go culture. It's go now and worry about the bills later. So it has been with the funding of recent military operations. Rather than defraying war costs through increased taxation—thereby drawing public attention to the war's progress or lack thereof—the government borrows, with the sums involved hardly trivial. Since 9/11 alone, the national debt has nearly quadrupled. By and large, Americans are OK with sloughing off onto future generations the responsibility of paying for wars presumably undertaken on their own behalf—a bit like buying a pricey car and sticking your grandkids with the payments.

Granted, money partially offsets the shortage of troops. In Iraq and Afghanistan, the Pentagon found it expedient to contract out functions traditionally performed by soldiers. When each of those wars was at its height, contractors in the employ of profit-minded security firms outnumbered G.I.s. Privatizing war provides a workaround to the predicament caused by having a large appetite for war while the people nurse appetites of a different sort.

In some quarters, as a sort of hangover from Vietnam, the belief persists that American culture, at least in those quarters where professors and artsy types congregate, is intrinsically anti-military. Nothing could be further from the truth. American culture is decidedly pro-military. All it asks is that military institutions get in step with the culture's core requirements.

And so they have, becoming open to all as venues for individual self-actualization. The Pentagon has embraced diversity—the very signature of contemporary culture. In today's military, overt racism has ceased to exist. Women wear four stars, fly fighter jets, graduate from Ranger school, and enlist as combat Marines. Barriers preventing members of the LGBT community from serving openly? On the way out.

This is to the good. Yet where it really counts, our culturally compliant military falls short. Thrust into a series of wars to make good on the people's expectations of more, while respecting their aversion to sacrifice, the Few—admirable in so many ways—find themselves unable either to win and or to get out.

Whether Carter's "restoration of American values" or Bush's "culture of responsibility" would find us today in a different place is a moot point. Our culture remains on a fixed trajectory.

When it comes to making war, that culture hinders rather than helps. Rather than fighting the problem, policy makers should consider turning it to US advantage. Instead of promoting American-style freedom at the point of a bayonet, they should pursue alternatives to war. Instead of coercion, perhaps it's time to try seduction.

46

Under God

(2015)

Whether Americans today sin more frequently or less frequently than they did when I was a boy growing up in the 1950s is difficult to say. Yet this much is certain: back then, on matters related to sex and family, a rough congruity existed between prevailing American cultural norms and the traditional teachings of the Catholic Church. Today that is no longer the case. If any doubts persisted on that point, the Supreme Court decision in the case of *Obergefell v. Hodges*, legalizing gay marriage, demolished them once and for all.

During the early days of the Cold War, when it came to marriage, divorce, abortion, and sex out of wedlock—not to mention a shared antipathy for communism—Washington and Rome may not have been in lockstep, but they marched to pretty much the same tune. As for homosexuality, well, it ranked among those subjects consigned to the category of unmentionables.

No doubt the hypocrisy quotient among those upholding various prohibitions on what Americans could do in the privacy of their own bedroom or the backseat of their father's car was considerable. But for a nation locked in an existential struggle against a godless adversary, paying lip service to such norms was part of what it meant to be "under God."

Cold War–era sexual mores had implications for US foreign policy. Even if honored only in the breach, the prevailing code—sex consigned to monogamous heterosexual relationships sanctified by marriage— imparted legitimacy to the exercise of American power. In measured doses, self-restraint and self-denial offered indicators of collective moral fiber. By professing respect for God's law, we positioned ourselves on his side. It followed that he was on ours. Here was American chosenness affirmed. Certainty that the United States enjoyed divine favor made it possible to excuse a multitude of transgressions committed in the name of defending a conception of freedom ostensibly mindful of God's own strictures.

The justices who voted in favor of gay marriage don't care a lick about whether the United States is "under God" or not. On that score, however dubious their reading of the Constitution, they have accurately gauged the signs of the times. The people of "thou shall not" have long since become the people of "whatever," with obligations deriving from moral tradition subordinated to claims of individual autonomy. That's the way we like it. August members of the Supreme Court have now given their seal of approval.

Their decision highlights just how attenuated the putative link between God's law and American freedom has become. As a force in American politics, religion is in retreat. True, even today politicians adhere to rituals that retain religious overtones. For example, the National Prayer Breakfast that President Eisenhower instituted in 1953 remains a fixture on Washington's calendar. Yet this is an exercise in nostalgia, devoid of substance. Some symbols matter—like displaying the Confederate battle flag, for example. Others—like emblazoning your currency with "In God We Trust"—don't mean squat.

On balance, we may judge this a clarifying moment. The irreversibility of the cultural revolution that has unfolded across the past half-century now becomes apparent to all. The trajectory of change that this revolution mandates will continue, even if its ultimate destination remains hidden. For some the transformation underway may be a source of regret, for others cause for celebration, but there is no denying its profound significance, reaching into every corner of American existence.

A nation once purportedly "under God" has decisively rejected the hierarchical relationship that phrase implies. Those who interpret the nation's laws have dropped all pretense of deferring to guidance from above. From here on out, we've got the green light to chart our own course.

Again, however, there are likely to be foreign policy implications. For Americans, as the *Obergefell* case vividly testifies, freedom is not a fixed proposition. It evolves, expands, and becomes more inclusive, bringing freedom's prevailing definition (at least in American eyes) ever closer to perfection.

But a nation founded on universal claims—boldly enumerating rights with which "all men" are endowed—finds intolerable any conception of freedom that differs from its own. The ongoing evolution of American freedom creates expectations with which others are expected to comply.

Recall that for the first two centuries of this nation's existence, American diplomats were indifferent to discrimination against women. Then gender equality found a place on the American political agenda. Now the State Department maintains an Office of Global Women's Issues devoted to "empowering women politically, socially, and economically around the world."

We should anticipate something similar occurring in relation to LGBT communities worldwide. Their plight, which is real, will necessarily emerge as a matter of official US concern. Today the United States condemns the racism, sexism, and anti-Semitism that Americans once found eminently tolerable. Tomorrow standing in principled opposition to anti-LGTB discrimination wherever it exists will become a moral imperative, Americans declaring themselves rid of sins they themselves had committed just yesterday.

Whether or not US support for LGBT rights goes beyond the rhetorical, societies still viewing themselves as "under God" will bridle at this sudden turnabout. Especially in the Islamic world, demands to conform to the latest revision of American (and therefore universal) freedom will strike many as not only unwelcome but also unholy encroachments. Whether the upshot will contribute to the collective well-being of humankind or sow the seeds of further conflict remains to be seen. At least in the near term, the latter seems more likely than the former.

In any case, we are witnessing a remarkable inversion in the relationship between religion and American statecraft. Rather than facilitating the pursuit of America's liberating mission, faith now becomes an impediment, an obstacle to freedom's further advance. It's no longer the godless who pose a problem, but the God-fearing with their stubborn refusal to accommodate truths that Americans have ever-so-recently discovered. Almost without anyone noticing, God himself has moved from our side to theirs.

47

Thoughts on a
Graduation Weekend

(2014)

"We have a world bursting with new ideas, new plans, and new hopes. The world was never so young as it is today, so impatient of old and crusty things." So wrote Walter Lippmann in 1912. Of course, the world seemed young because Lippmann himself was young, a wunderkind journalist in his early twenties when he penned those words.

Lippmann embodied the optimism of the progressive era, animated by a faith in democracy, liberal reform, and charismatic leadership. Here was the triumvirate that would redeem a corrupt, unjust, and hidebound political system. Progressives looked to the likes of Theodore Roosevelt and Woodrow Wilson to do just that.

Within two years, of course, war erupted, beginning in Europe, but eventually enveloping the United States. The ideas, plans, and hopes to which Progressives such as Lippmann subscribed turned into ash. Old and crusty things—hatred, bloodlust, fanaticism—returned with a vengeance, bringing in their trail revolution, totalitarian ideologies, economic calamity, and genocide. Lippmann later recanted his youthful enthusiasms, viewing his fling with progressivism as a never-to-be-repeated folly.

Fast-forward a half-century and members of another notably self-assured generation of young people—my fellow baby boomers— discovered their own world bursting with new ideas, plans, and hopes. In 1962, a boomer manifesto laid out its blueprint for doing away with old and crusty things. The authors of the Port Huron Statement envisioned "a world where hunger, poverty, disease, ignorance, violence, and exploitation are replaced as central features by abundance, reason, love, and international cooperation." Ours was the generation that would repair a broken world.

Yet several decades later, progress toward fulfilling such grandiose aspirations remains fitful. Boomer achievements have fallen well short of their own youthful expectations. In practice, power harnessed to advance the common good took a backseat to power wielded to remove annoying curbs on personal behavior. To navigate the path marked "liberation," boomers took their cues not from philosophers and priests, but from rockers, dopers, and other flouters of convention.

No doubt the boomer triumvirate of radical autonomy, self-actualization, and contempt for authority, a.k.a., sex, drugs, and rock-and-roll, has left an indelible mark on contemporary culture. Even so, the old and crusty things against which they passionately inveighed persist, both at home and abroad. Love and reason have not supplanted violence and exploitation. Viewed in retrospect, the expectations that boomers voiced back in the Sixties appear embarrassingly naïve and more than a little silly.

Now, with the passing of yet another half-century, another youthful cohort purports to see big change in the making. With Progressives gone and forgotten and boomers preparing to exit the stage, here come the so-called millennials, bursting with their own ideas, plans, and hopes. They too believe that the world was never so young (or so plastic) and they seem intent on making their own run at banishing all that is old and crusty.

Millennials boast their own triumvirate, this one consisting of personal electronic devices in combination with the internet and social media. In addition to refashioning politics (the Progressives' goal) and expanding personal choice (a boomer priority), this new triumvirate offers much more. It promises something akin to limitless, universal empowerment.

Today's young welcome that prospect as an unvarnished good. "You're more powerful than you think," Apple assures them. "You have the power to create, shape, and share your life. It's right there in your hand. Or bag. Or pocket. It's your iPhone 5s."

Here for millennials is what distinguishes their generation from all those that have gone before. Here is their Great Truth. With all the gullibility of Progressives certain that Wilson's Fourteen Points spelled an end to war and of boomers who fancied that dropping acid promised a short cut to enlightenment, millennials embrace this truth as self-evident. The power that they hold in their hand, carry in their bag, or stuff in the pocket of their jeans is transforming human existence.

To a historian, the credulity of the millennials manages to be both touching and pathetic. It is touching as a testimonial to an enduring faith in human ingenuity as panacea. It is pathetic in its disregard for the actual legacy of human ingenuity, which is at best ambiguous.

In that regard, the so-called Information Age is unlikely to prove any different than, say, the Nuclear Age or the Industrial Age. Touted as a vehicle for creating wealth, it increases the gap between haves and have-nots. Promising greater consumer choice, it allows profit-minded corporations to shape the choices actually made. While facilitating mass political action, it enhances the ability of the state to monitor and control citizens. By making weapons more precise, it eases restraints on their use, contributing not to the abolition of war but to its proliferation.

While empowering *me*, in other words, information also empowers *them*. Thus do the old and crusty things gain a new lease on life.

"There is no arguing with the pretenders to a divine knowledge and to a divine mission," an older and wiser Walter Lippmann reflected. "They are possessed with the sin of pride. They have yielded to the perennial temptation." Having thus yielded, the pretenders will in their own turn be obliged to pay for their transgressions.

48

One Percent Republic

(2013)

In evaluating the Global War on Terror, the overriding question is necessarily this one: Has more than a decade of armed conflict enhanced the well-being of the American people? The wars fought by citizen-soldiers at the behest of Abraham Lincoln and Franklin Roosevelt did so. Can we say the same for the war launched by George W. Bush and perpetuated in modified form by Barack Obama?

Before taking stock of what a decade of war has actually produced, recall the expectations that prevailed shortly before war began. On the eve of World War II, the mood was anxious. For a nation still caught in the throes of a protracted economic slump, the prospect of a European war carried limited appeal; the previous one, just two decades earlier, had yielded little but disappointment. By comparison, expectations on the near side of the Global War on Terror were positively bullish. For citizens of the planet's "sole remaining superpower," the twentieth century had ended on a high note. The twenty-first century appeared rich with promise.

Speaking just before midnight on December 31, 1999, President Bill Clinton surveyed the century just ending and identified its central theme as "the triumph of freedom and free people." To this "great story," Clinton told his listeners, the United States had made a pivotal contribution. Contemplating the future, he glimpsed even better days ahead—"the triumph of freedom wisely used." All that was needed to secure that triumph was for Americans to exploit and export "the economic benefits of globalization, the political benefits of democracy and human rights, [and] the educational and health benefits of all things modern." At the dawning of the new millennium, he concluded confidently, "the sun will always rise on America as long as each new generation lights the fire of freedom."

What the president's remarks lacked in terms of insight or originality they made up for in familiarity. During the decade following the Cold War, such expectations had become commonplace. Skillful politician that he was, Clinton was telling Americans what they already believed.

The passing of one further decade during which US forces seeking to ignite freedom's fire flooded the Greater Middle East reduced Bill Clinton's fin de siècle formula for peace and prosperity to tatters. In Iraq, Afghanistan, and Pakistan, the United States touched off a conflagration of sorts, albeit with results other than intended. Yet for the average American, the most painful setbacks occurred not out there in wartime theaters but back here on the home front. Instead of freedom wisely used, the decade's theme became bubbles burst and dreams deflated.

Above all, those dreams had fostered expectations of unprecedented material abundance—more of everything for everyone. Alas, this was not to be. Although "crisis" ranks alongside "historic" atop any list of overused terms in American political discourse, the Great Recession that began in 2007 turned out to be the real deal: a crisis of historic proportions.

With the ongoing "war" approaching the ten-year mark, the US economy shed a total of 7.9 million jobs in just three years. For only the second time since World War II, the official unemployment rate topped 10 percent. The retreat from that peak came at an achingly slow pace. By some estimates, actual unemployment—including those who had simply given up looking for work—was double the official figure. Accentuating the pain was the duration of joblessness; those laid off during the Great Recession stayed out of work substantially longer than the unemployed during previous postwar economic downturns. When new opportunities did eventually materialize, they usually came with smaller salaries and either reduced benefits or none at all.

As an immediate consequence, millions of Americans lost their homes or found themselves "underwater," the value of their property less than what they owed on their mortgages. Countless more were thrown into poverty, the number of those officially classified as poor reaching the highest level since the Census Bureau began tracking such data. A drop in median income erased gains made during the previous fifteen years. Erstwhile members of the great American middle class shelved or abandoned outright carefully nurtured plans to educate their children or retire in modest comfort. Inequality reached gaping proportions with 1 percent of the population amassing a full 40 percent of the nation's wealth.

Month after month, grim statistics provided fodder for commentators distributing blame, for learned analysts offering contradictory explanations of why prosperity had proven so chimerical, and for politicians absolving themselves of responsibility while fingering as culprits members of the other party. Yet beyond its immediate impact, what did the Great Recession signify? Was the sudden appearance of hard times in the midst of war merely an epiphenomenon, a period of painful adjustment and belt-tightening after which the world's sole superpower would be back in the saddle? Or had the Great Recession begun a Great Recessional, with the United States in irreversible retreat from the apex of global dominion?

The political response to this economic calamity paid less attention to forecasting long-term implications than to fixing culpability. On the right, an angry Tea Party movement blamed Big Government. On the left, equally angry members of the Occupy movement blamed Big Business, especially Wall Street. What these two movements had in common was that each cast the American people as victims. Nefarious forces had gorged themselves at the expense of ordinary folks. By implication, the people were themselves absolved of responsibility for the catastrophe that had befallen them and their country.

Yet consider a third possibility. Perhaps the people were not victims but accessories. On the subject of war, Americans can no more claim innocence than they can regarding the effects of smoking or excessive drinking. As much as or more than Big Government or Big Business, popular attitudes toward war, combining detachment, neglect, and inattention, helped create the crisis in which the United States is mired.

A "country made by war"—to cite the title of a popular account of US military history—the United States in our own day is fast becoming a country undone by war. Citizen armies had waged the wars that made the nation powerful (if not virtuous) and Americans rich (if not righteous). The character of those armies—preeminently the ones that preserved the Union and helped defeat Nazi Germany and Imperial Japan—testified to an implicit covenant between citizens and the state. According to its terms, war was the people's business and could not be otherwise. For the state to embark upon armed conflict of any magnitude required informed popular consent. Actual prosecution of any military campaign larger than a police action depended on the willingness of large numbers of citizens to become soldiers. Seeing war through to a conclusion hinged on the state's ability to sustain active popular support in the face of adversity.

In their disgust over Vietnam, Americans withdrew from this arrangement. They disengaged from war, with few observers giving serious consideration to the implications of doing so. Events since, especially since 9/11, have made those implications manifest. In the United States, war no longer qualifies in any meaningful sense as the people's business. In military matters, Americans have largely forfeited their say.

As a result, in formulating basic military policy and in deciding when and how to employ force, the state no longer requires the consent, direct participation, or ongoing support of citizens. As an immediate consequence, Washington's penchant for war has appreciably increased, without, however, any corresponding improvement in the ability of political and military leaders to conclude its wars promptly or successfully. A further result, less appreciated but with even larger implications, has been to accelerate the erosion of the traditional concept of democratic citizenship.

In other words, the afflictions besetting the American way of life derive in some measure from shortcomings in the contemporary American way of war. The latter have either begotten or exacerbated the former.

Since 9/11, Americans have, in fact, refuted George C. Marshall by demonstrating a willingness to tolerate "a Seven Years [and longer] War." It turns out, as the neoconservative pundit Max Boot observed, that an absence of popular support "isn't necessarily fatal" for a flagging war effort. For an inveterate militarist like Boot, this comes as good news. "Public apathy," he argues, "presents a potential opportunity," making it possible to prolong "indefinitely" conflicts in which citizens are not invested.

Yet such news is hardly good. Apathy toward war is symptomatic of advancing civic decay, finding expression in apathy toward the blight of child poverty, homelessness, illegitimacy, and eating disorders also plaguing the country. Shrugging off wars makes it that much easier for Americans—overweight, overmedicated, and deeply in hock—to shrug off the persistence of widespread hunger, the patent failures of their criminal justice system, and any number of other problems. The thread that binds together this pattern of collective anomie is plain to see: unless the problem you're talking about affects me personally, why should I care?

For years after 9/11, America's armed force floundered abroad. Although the invasions of Afghanistan and Iraq began promisingly enough, in neither case were US forces able to close the deal. With the fall of Richmond in April 1865, the Civil War drew to a definitive close. No such claim could be made in connection with the fall of Kabul in November 2001. When it came to dramatic effect, the staged April 2003 toppling of Saddam Hussein's statue in Baghdad's Firdos Square stands on a par with the September 1945 surrender ceremony on the deck of the USS *Missouri*. There, however, the comparison ends. The one event rang down the curtain; the other merely signified a script change. Meanwhile, Americans at home paid little more than lip service to the travails endured by the troops.

Beginning in 2007—just as the "surge" was ostensibly salvaging the Iraq War—a sea of troubles engulfed the home front. From those troubles, the continuation of war offered no escape. If anything, the perpetuation (and expansion) of armed conflict plunged the nation itself that much more deeply underwater. Once again, as in the 1860s and 1940s, war was playing a major role in determining the nation's destiny. Yet this time around, there was no upside. Virtually all of the consequences—political, economic, social, cultural, and moral—proved negative. To a nation gearing up for global war, FDR had promised jobs, help for the vulnerable, an end to special privilege, the protection of civil liberties, and decisive military victory over the nation's enemies. To a considerable degree, Roosevelt made good on that promise. Judged by those same criteria, the Bush-Obama global war came up short on all counts.

The crux of the problem lay with two symmetrical 1 percents: the 1 percent whose members get sent to fight seemingly endless wars and that other 1 percent whose members demonstrate such a knack for enriching themselves in "wartime." Needless to say, the two 1 percents neither intersect nor overlap. Few of the very rich send their sons or daughters to fight. Few of those leaving the military's ranks find their way into the ranks of the plutocracy. Rather than rallying to the colors, Harvard graduates these days flock to Wall Street or the lucrative world of consulting. Movie star heroics occur exclusively on screen, while millionaire professional athletes manage to satisfy their appetite for combat on the court and playing field.

Yet a people who permit war to be waged in their name while offloading onto a tiny minority responsibility for its actual conduct have no cause to complain about an equally small minority milking the system for all it's worth. Crudely put, if the very rich are engaged in ruthlessly exploiting the 99 percent who are not, their actions are analogous to that of American society as a whole in its treatment of soldiers: the 99 percent who do not serve in uniform just as ruthlessly exploit the 1 percent who do.

To excuse or justify their conduct, the very rich engage in acts of philanthropy. With a similar aim, the not-so-rich proclaim their undying admiration of the troops.

As the bumper sticker proclaims, freedom isn't free. Conditioned to believe that the exercise of global leadership is essential to preserving their freedom, and further conditioned to believe that leadership best expresses itself in the wielding of military might, Americans have begun to discover that trusting in the present-day American way of war to preserve the present-day American way of life entails exorbitant and unexpected costs.

Yet as painful as they may be, these costs represent something far more disturbing. As a remedy for all the ailments afflicting the body politic, war—at least as Americans have chosen to wage it—turns out to be a fundamentally inappropriate prescription. Rather than restoring the patient to health, war (as currently practiced pursuant to freedom as currently defined) constitutes a form of prolonged ritual suicide. Rather than building muscle, it corrupts and putrefies.

The choice Americans face today ends up being as straightforward as it is stark. If they believe war is essential to preserving their freedom, it's incumbent upon them to prosecute war with the same seriousness their forebears demonstrated in the 1940s. Washington's war would then truly become America's war with all that implies in terms of commitment and priorities. Should Americans decide, on the other hand, that freedom as presently defined is not worth the sacrifices entailed by real war, it becomes incumbent upon them to revise their understanding of freedom. Either choice—real war or an alternative conception of freedom—would entail a more robust definition of what it means to be a citizen.

Yet the dilemma just described may be more theoretical than real. Without the players fully understanding the stakes, the die has already been cast. Having forfeited responsibility for war's design and conduct, the American people may find that Washington considers that grant of authority irrevocable. The state now owns war, with the country consigned to observer status. Meanwhile, the juggernaut of mainstream, commercial culture continues to promulgate the four pop gospels of American freedom: novelty, autonomy, celebrity, and consumption. Efforts to resist or reverse these tendencies, whether by right-leaning traditionalists (many of them religiously inclined) or left-leaning secular humanists (sometimes allied with religious radicals) have been feeble and ineffective.

Americans must therefore accept the likelihood of a future in which real, if futile, sacrifices exacted of the few who fight will serve chiefly to facilitate metaphorical death for the rest who do not.

49

Counterculture Conservatism

(2013)

How to revive the flagging fortunes of the Republican Party might matter to some people, but it's not a question that should concern principled conservatives. Crypto-conservatives aplenty stand ready to shoulder that demeaning task. Tune in to Fox News or pick up the latest issue of *National Review* or the *Weekly Standard* and you'll find them, yelping, whining, and fingering our recently reelected president as the Antichrist.

Conservatives who prefer thinking to venting—those confident that a republic able to survive eight years of George W. Bush can probably survive eight years of Barack Obama—confront a question of a different order. To wit: Does authentic American conservatism retain any political viability in this country in the present age? That is, does homegrown conservatism have any lingering potential for gaining and exercising power at the local, state, or national levels? Or has history consigned the conservative tradition—as it has Marxism—to a status where even if holding some residual utility as an analytical tool, it no longer possesses value as a basis for practical action?

To which a properly skeptical reader may respond, perhaps reaching for a sidearm: Exactly whose conservative tradition are you referring to, bucko?

Well, I'll admit to prejudices, so let me lay them out.

(Fans of Ayn Rand or Milton Friedman will want to stop reading here and flip to the next essay. If Ronald Reagan's your hero, sorry—you won't like what's coming. Ditto regarding Ron Paul. And if in search of wisdom you rely on anyone whose byline appears regularly in any publication owned by Rupert Murdoch, then what follows might give you indigestion.)

The conservative tradition I have in mind may not satisfy purists. It doesn't rise to the level of qualifying as anything so grandiose as a coherent philosophy. It's more of a stew produced by combining sundry ingredients. The result, to use a word that ought to warm the cockles of any conservative's heart, is a sort of intellectual slumgullion.

Here's the basic recipe. As that stew's principal ingredients, start with generous portions of John Quincy Adams and his grandson Henry. Fold in ample amounts of Randolph Bourne, Reinhold Niebuhr, and Christopher Lasch. For seasoning, throw in some Flannery O'Connor and Wendell Berry—don't skimp. If you're in a daring mood, add a dash of William Appleman Williams. To finish, sprinkle with Frank Capra—use a light hand: too sweet and the concoction's ruined. Cook slowly. (Microwave not allowed.) What you get is a dish that is as nutritious as it is tasty.

This updated conservative tradition consists of several complementary propositions:

As human beings, our first responsibility lies in stewardship, preserving our common inheritance and protecting that which possesses lasting value. This implies an ability to discriminate between what is permanent and what is transient, between what ought to endure and what is rightly destined for the trash heap. Please note this does not signify opposition to all change—no standing athwart history, yelling Stop—but fostering change that enhances rather than undermines that which qualifies as true.

Conservatives, therefore, are skeptical of anything that smacks of utopianism. They resist seduction by charlatans peddling the latest Big Idea That Explains Everything. This is particularly the case when that

Big Idea entails launching some armed crusade abroad. Conservatives respect received wisdom. The passage of time does not automatically render irrelevant the dogmas to which our forebears paid heed. George Washington was no dope.

In private life and public policy alike, there exists a particular category of truths that grown-ups and grown-up governments will respectfully acknowledge. For conservatives this amounts to mere common sense. Actions have consequences. Privileges entail responsibility. There is no free lunch. At day's end, accounts must balance. Sooner or later, the piper will be paid. Only the foolhardy or the willfully reckless will attempt to evade these fundamental axioms.

Conservatives take human relationships seriously and know that they require nurturing. In community lies our best hope of enjoying a meaningful earthly existence. But community does not emerge spontaneously. Conservatives understand that the most basic community, the little platoon of family, is under unrelenting assault from both left and right. Emphasizing autonomy, the forces of modernity are intent on supplanting the family with the hyper-empowered—if also alienated—individual, who exists to gratify their own appetite and ambition. With its insatiable hunger for profit, the market is intent on transforming the family into a cluster of consumers who just happen to live under the same roof. One more thing: conservatives don't confuse intimacy with sex.

All of that said, conservatives also believe in original sin, by whatever name. They know, therefore, that the human species is inherently ornery and perverse. Hence, the imperative to train and educate young people in the norms governing civilized behavior. Hence, too, the need to maintain appropriate mechanisms to restrain and correct the wayward who resist that training or who through their own misconduct prove themselves uneducable.

Conversely, conservatives are wary of concentrated power in whatever form. The evil effects of original sin are nowhere more evident than in Washington, on Wall Street, or in the executive suites of major institutions, sadly including churches and universities. So conservatives reject the argument that correlates centralization with efficiency and effectiveness. In whatever realm, they favor the local over the distant. Furthermore, although conservatives are not levelers, they believe that a reasonably equitable distribution of wealth—property held in private hands—offers the surest safeguard against Leviathan. A conservative's America is a nation consisting of freeholders, not of plutocrats and proletarians.

Finally, conservatives love and cherish their country. But they do not confuse country with state. They know that America is neither its military nor any of the innumerable three-lettered agencies comprising the bloated national security apparatus. America is amber waves of grain, not SEAL Team Six.

Given such a perspective, American conservatives cannot view the current condition of their country and their culture with anything but dismay. Yet apart from mourning, what can they do about it?

My vote is for taking a page from the playbook of our brethren on the radical left. Remember the "long march through the institutions"? It's time to mobilize a countercultural march in an entirely different direction.

Conservatism—the genuine article, not the phony brand represented by the likes of Mitt Romney, Karl Rove, or Grover Norquist—has now *become* the counterculture. This is a mantle that committed conservatives should happily claim. That mantle confers opportunity. It positions conservatives to formulate a compelling critique of a status quo that few responsible Americans view as satisfactory or sustainable.

Put simply, the task facing conservatives is to engineer a change in the zeitgeist through patient, incremental, and thoughtful action. Effecting such a change presents a formidable challenge, one likely to entail decades of effort. Yet the task is not an impossible one. Consider the astonishing successes achieved just since the 1960s by left-leaning proponents of women's rights and gay rights. There's the model.

The key to success will be to pick the right fights against the right enemies, while forging smart tactical alliances. (By tactical, I do not mean cynical.) Conservatives need to discriminate between the issues that matter and those that don't, the contests that can be won and those that can't. And they need to recognize that the political left includes people of goodwill whose views on some (by no means all) matters coincide with our own.

So forget about dismantling the welfare state. Social Security, Medicare, Medicaid, and, yes, Obamacare are here to stay. Forget about outlawing abortion or prohibiting gay marriage. Conservatives may judge the fruits produced by the sexual revolution poisonous, but the revolution itself is irreversible.

Instead, the new conservative agenda should emphasize the following:

- Protecting the environment from the ravages of human excess. Here most emphatically, the central theme of conservatism should be to *conserve*. If that implies subordinating economic growth and material consumption in order to preserve the well-being of planet Earth, so be it. In advancing this position, conservatives should make common cause with tree-hugging, granola-crunching liberals. Yet in the cultural realm, such a change in American priorities will induce a tilt likely to find particular favor in conservative circles.
- Exposing the excesses of American militarism and the futility of the neo-imperialist impulses to which Washington has succumbed since the end of the Cold War. When it comes to foreign policy, the conservative position should promote modesty, realism, and self-sufficiency. To the maximum extent possible, Americans should "live within," abandoning the conceit that the United States is called upon to exercise "global leadership," which has become a euphemism for making mischief and for demanding prerogatives allowed to no other nation. Here the potential exists for conservatives to make common cause with members of the impassioned antiwar left.
- Insisting upon the imperative of putting America's fiscal house in order. For starters, this means requiring government to live within its means. Doing so will entail collective belt-tightening, just the thing to curb the nation's lazily profligate tendencies. Conservatives should never cease proclaiming that trillion-dollar federal deficits are an abomination and a crime committed at the expense of future generations.
- Laying claim to the flagging cause of raising children to become responsible and morally centered adults. Apart from the pervasive deficiencies of the nation's school system, the big problem here is not gay marriage but the collapse of heterosexual marriage as an enduring partnership sustained for the well-being of offspring. We

know the result: an epidemic of children raised without fathers. Turning this around promises to be daunting, but promoting economic policies that make it possible to support a family on a single income offers at least the beginnings of a solution. Yes, just like in the 1950s.

- Preserving the independence of institutions that can check the untoward and ill-advised impulses of the state. Among other things, this requires that conservatives mount an adamant and unyielding defense of religious freedom. Churches—my own very much included—may be flawed. But conservatives should view their health as essential.

Who knows, perhaps in 2016 or 2020 the existing Republican Party's formula of protecting the well-to-do and promoting endless war while paying lip-service to traditional values and pandering to the Israel lobby will produce electoral success. But I doubt it. And even if the party does make a comeback on that basis, the conservative cause itself won't prosper. Reviving that cause will require a different formula altogether.

50

Ballpark Liturgy

(2011)

Fenway Park, Boston, July 4, 2011. On this warm summer day, the Red Sox will play the Toronto Blue Jays. First come pre-game festivities, especially tailored for the occasion. The ensuing spectacle—a carefully scripted encounter between the armed forces and society—expresses the distilled essence of present-day American patriotism. A masterpiece of contrived spontaneity, the event leaves spectators feeling good about their baseball team, about their military, and not least of all about themselves—precisely as it was meant to do.

In this theatrical production, the Red Sox provide the stage, and the Pentagon the props. In military parlance, it is a joint operation. In front of a gigantic American flag draped over the left-field wall, an Air Force contingent, clad in blue, stands at attention. To carry a smaller version of the Stars and Stripes onto the playing field, the Navy provides a color guard in crisp summer whites. The United States Marine Corps kicks in with a choral ensemble that leads the singing of the national anthem. As the anthem's final notes sound, four US Air Force F-15C Eagles scream overhead. The sellout crowd roars its approval.

But there is more to come. "On this Independence Day," the voice of the Red Sox booms over the public address system, "we pay a debt of gratitude to the families whose sons and daughters are serving our country." On this particular occasion the designated recipients of that gratitude are members of the Lydon family, hailing from Squantum, Massachusetts. Young Bridget Lydon is a sailor—Aviation Ordnance-man Airman is her official title—serving aboard the carrier USS *Ronald Reagan*, currently deployed in support of the Afghanistan War, now in its tenth year.

From Out of Nowhere

The Lydons are Every Family, decked out for the Fourth. Garbed in random bits of Red Sox paraphernalia and Mardi Gras necklaces, they wear their shirts untucked and ball caps backwards. Neither sleek nor fancy, they are without pretension. Yet they exude good cheer. As they are ushered onto the field, their eagerness is palpable. Like TV game show contestants, they know that this is their lucky day and they are keen to make the most of it.

As the Lydons gather near the pitcher's mound, the voice directs their attention to the 38-by-100-foot Jumbotron mounted above the centerfield bleachers. On the screen, Bridget appears. She is aboard ship, in duty uniform, posed below deck in front of an F/A-18 fighter jet. Waiflike, but pert and confident, she looks directly into the camera, sending a "shout-out" to family and friends. She wishes she could join them at Fenway.

As if by magic, wish becomes fulfillment. While the video clip is still running, Bridget herself, now in dress whites, emerges from behind the flag covering the leftfield wall. On the Jumbotron, in place of Bridget below deck, an image of Bridget marching smartly toward the infield appears. In the stands pandemonium erupts. After a moment of confusion, members of her family—surrounded by camera crews—rush to embrace their sailor, a reunion shared vicariously by the 38,000 fans in attendance along with many thousands more watching at home on the Red Sox television network.

Once the Lydons finish with hugs and kisses and the crowd settles down, Navy veteran Bridget (annual salary approximately $22,000) throws the ceremonial first pitch to aging Red Sox veteran Tim Wakefield (annual salary $2,000,000). More cheers. As a souvenir, Wakefield gives her the baseball along with his own hug. All smiles, Bridget and her family shout "Play Ball!" into a microphone. As they are escorted off the field and out of sight, the game begins.

Cheap Grace

What does this event signify?

For the Lydons, the day will no doubt long remain a happy memory. If they were to some degree manipulated—their utter and genuine astonishment at Bridget's seemingly miraculous appearance lending the occasion its emotional punch—they played their allotted roles without complaint and with considerable élan. However briefly, they stood in the spotlight, quasi-celebrities, all eyes trained on them, a contemporary version of the American dream fulfilled. And if off-stage puppet-masters used Bridget herself, at least she got a visit home and a few days off—no doubt a welcome break.

Yet this feel-good story was political as well as personal. As a collaboration between two well-heeled but image-conscious institutions, the Lydon reunion represented a small but not inconsequential public relations triumph. The Red Sox and the Navy had worked together to perform an act of kindness for a sailor and her loved ones. Both organizations came away looking good, not only because the event itself was so deftly executed, but because it showed that the large for-profit professional sports team and the even larger military bureaucracy both care about ordinary people. The message conveyed to fans/taxpayers could not be clearer: the corporate executives who run the Red Sox have a heart. So, too, do the admirals who run the Navy.

Better still, these benefits accrued at essentially no cost to the sponsors. The military personnel arrayed around Fenway showed up because they were told to do so. They are already "paid for," as are the F-15s, the pilots who fly them, and the ground crews that service them. As for whatever outlays the Red Sox may have made, they are trivial and easily absorbed. For the 2011 season, the average price of a ticket at Fenway Park had climbed to $52. A soft drink in a commemorative plastic cup runs you $5.50 and a beer $8. Then there is the television ad revenue, all contributing the previous year to corporate profits exceeding $58 million. A decade of war culminating in the worst economic crisis since the Great Depression hasn't done much good for the country but it has been strangely good for the Red Sox—and a no-less well-funded Pentagon. Any money expended in bringing Bridget to Fenway and entertaining the Lydons had to be the baseball/military equivalent of pocket change.

And the holiday festivities at Fenway had another significance as well, one that extended beyond burnishing institutional reputations and boosting bottom lines. Here was America's civic religion made manifest.

In recent decades, an injunction to "support the troops" has emerged as a central tenet of that religion. Since 9/11 this imperative has become, if anything, even more binding. Indeed, as citizens, Americans today acknowledge no higher obligation.

Fulfilling that obligation has posed a challenge, however. Rather than doing so concretely, Americans—with a few honorable exceptions—have settled for symbolism. With their pronounced aversion to collective service and sacrifice (an inclination indulged by leaders of both political parties), Americans resist any definition of civic duty that threatens to crimp lifestyles.

To stand in solidarity with those on whom the burden of service and sacrifice falls is about as far as they will go. Expressions of solidarity affirm that the existing relationship between soldiers and society is consistent with democratic practice. By extension, so, too, is the distribution of prerogatives and responsibilities entailed by that relationship: a few fight, the rest applaud. Put simply, the message that citizens wish to convey to their soldiers is this: although choosing not to be *with* you, we are still *for* you (so long as being for you entails nothing on our part). Cheering for the troops, in effect, provides a convenient mechanism for voiding obligation and easing guilty consciences.

In ways far more satisfying than displaying banners or bumper stickers, the Fenway Park Independence Day event provided a made-to-order opportunity for conscience easing. It did so in three ways.

First, it brought members of Red Sox Nation into close proximity (even if not direct contact) with living, breathing members of the armed forces, figuratively closing any gap between the two. (In New England, where few active duty military installations remain, such encounters are increasingly infrequent.) Second, it manufactured one excuse after another to whistle and shout, whoop and holler, thereby allowing the assembled multitudes to express—and to be seen expressing—their affection and respect for the troops. Finally, it rewarded participants and witnesses alike with a sense of validation, the reunion of Bridget and her family, even if temporary, serving as a proxy for a much larger, if imaginary, reconciliation of the American military and the American people. That debt? Mark it paid in full.

The late German theologian Dietrich Bonhoeffer had a name for this unearned self-forgiveness and undeserved self-regard. He called it cheap grace. Were he alive today, Bonhoeffer might suggest that a taste for cheap grace, compounded by an appetite for false freedom, is leading Americans down the road to perdition.

51

The Great Divide

(2008)

Regardless of who wins the presidency in November 2008, rethinking the premises of US military policy will be an urgent priority. Grasping the scope of the problem requires an appreciation of three overarching themes that have shaped the narrative of American military experience since Vietnam.

The post-Vietnam narrative began with the "Great Divorce," engineered in the early 1970s by President Richard Nixon. When Nixon abolished the draft, he severed the relationship between citizenship and military service. Although that was not Nixon's purpose, it was one very clear result of ending conscription. Contributing to the country's defense now became not a civic duty but a matter of individual choice. That choice carried no political or moral connotations.

The Great Divorce gave birth to a new professional military with an ethos that emphasized the differences between soldiers and civilians. Out of differences came distance: after Vietnam, members of the officer corps saw themselves as standing apart from (or perhaps even above) the rest of society. More than a few members of the public

endorsed that view. In the lexicon of the Founders, the nation now relied on a "standing army," although Americans during the last quarter
of the twentieth century chose to call it the all-volunteer force.

The second narrative thread emerged during the 1980s. This was
the "Great Reconstitution," largely the handiwork of Ronald Reagan.
Throughout his presidency, Reagan lavished attention and funding
on the armed forces. Over the course of that decade, soldiers shed their
post-Vietnam malaise and gradually recovered their sense of self-
confidence. New weapons, revised doctrine, and improved training
techniques endowed US forces with an unusually high level of compe-
tence, at least in the arena of conventional conflict.

Above all, the Great Reconstitution converted the officer corps to
the view that technology held the secret to future military victories.
The ultimate expression of this view was the "Revolution in Military
Affairs." According to this concept, information technology was transforming the very nature of war itself, with the United States uniquely
positioned to exploit this transformation. By the end of the 1980s, the
United States had achieved military preeminence; something like outright and unchallengeable supremacy now seemed to lay within its
grasp.

By the time of Operation Desert Storm in 1991, the restoration of
US military might had captured popular attention and gained widespread public approval. Citizens again professed to admire soldiers.
They certainly admired the missile-through-the-window capabilities
of advanced military technology. Although admiration did not annul
the Great Divorce brought on by the end of the draft, it made the
separation more amicable. Expressions of public support for the troops
became commonplace. Yet "support" in this context was akin to what
sports fans provide to their local professional baseball or football franchise. Offered from a safe distance, it implies no obligation and entails
no risks. It is more rhetorical than real.

During the 1990s, the first two narrative threads combined to produce a third. This was the theme of "Great Expectations," which found
members of the political elite looking for new ways to tap the potential of this technologically sophisticated, highly professional military. Armed force accrued positive connotations: hitherto employed
to wreak mayhem, it now became an instrument for fixing things. One

result was the discovery of new missions like peacemaking, peacekeeping, and "humanitarian intervention." Another result was to remove any lingering reluctance about employing military force abroad.

During his single term as president, George H. W. Bush made substantial headway in dismantling the inhibitions implied by the Vietnam Syndrome. Bill Clinton completed the task: during his eight years in the Oval Office, armed intervention became so frequent that it almost ceased to be newsworthy. Yet George W. Bush did the most to promote the theme of Great Expectations. After 9/11, the forty-third president committed the United States to a policy of preventive war, the so-called Bush Doctrine. As part of his "Freedom Agenda," he also vowed to use American power to liberate the Greater Middle East, end tyranny, and vanquish evil from the face of the earth.

Tacitly affirming the Great Divorce, Bush committed the nation to these breathtaking goals without calling on Americans themselves to play a role or make any sacrifices. Bush intended to remake the world without mobilizing the country. The people would remain spectators.

Responsibility for implementing the Freedom Agenda, therefore, fell almost entirely on the shoulders of the all-volunteer force. As commander-in-chief, Bush did not even press Congress to expand the size of the force. Apparently, he assumed that the Great Reconstitution had made the standing army unstoppable. Even as he embarked on an open-ended global war, the president did not question that assumption.

This proved to be a serious miscalculation, as events in Iraq and Afghanistan have shown. The indisputable lesson of those two wars is this: the United States lacks sufficient military power to achieve the objectives outlined in Bush's Freedom Agenda. Means and ends are wildly out of whack. We have too much war and too few warriors. No amount of technology can close that gap.

To put it another way: the Great Expectations of the 1990s are exhausting the military created by the Great Reconstitution of the 1980s. Meanwhile, abiding by the Great Divorce of the 1970s, the American people content themselves with cheering from the sidelines.

For the next president, restoring US military policy to a sound basis is likely to prove a daunting proposition. Change will not come easily. On the one hand, the president will have to contend with advocates of the Bush Doctrine and Freedom Agenda who even now—with the Iraq War five years old and the Afghanistan War halfway through its seventh year—stubbornly insist that everything will come out all right. On the other hand, the president will have to deal with an officer corps that remains deeply wedded to habits developed over the past several decades.

The president will need new themes to replace the now-discredited themes of the post-Vietnam era. Here are three possibilities, one related to the use of force, one to basic national security strategy, and a third to civil-military relations.

With regard to the use of force, the United States should revert to the just-war tradition. The next president should explicitly abrogate the Bush Doctrine, which is both normatively and pragmatically defective. Put simply, preventive war is wrong and it doesn't work. Never again should the United States wage a war of aggression. Instead, we should treat force as a last resort, to be used only after exhausting all other options. We should wage war exclusively for defensive purposes. Adhering to the just-war tradition will go far toward alleviating the current disparity between ends and means.

When it comes to strategy, the United States should adopt a policy of containment. The next president should give up any fantasies about ending tyranny or expunging evil. Those tasks fall within God's purview. While violent Islamic radicalism does pose a serious (although not existential) threat to our security and that of our allies, the proper response to that threat is not global war but a concerted effort to prevent the Islamists from doing us harm. This implies an emphasis on effective defenses, comprehensive intelligence collection and surveillance, and aggressive international police work—not the invasion and occupation of countries in the Islamic world.

With regard to civil-military relations, the next president will face an especially daunting challenge. What we need appears quite clear: American citizens must acknowledge their own accountability for what American soldiers are sent to do and for all that occurs as a consequence. To classify Iraq as "Bush's war" is to perpetrate a fraud. Whether that conflict is moral or immoral, essential or unnecessary, winnable or beyond salvaging, it is very much the nation's war. Vacuously "supporting the troops" while carrying on for all practical purposes as if the war did not exist amounts to an abdication of basic civic responsibility.

As long as Americans persist in seeing national security as a function that others are contracted to perform, they will persist in this unaccountability. In this regard, the restoration of civic responsibility will require first restoring some connection between citizenship and military service. We need to reinvent the concept of the citizen-soldier. Yet we need to do so in a way that precludes conscription, for which next to no support exists in the Pentagon or in the public at large.

This is a tall order. Yet until we repair our democracy, repairing the defects in our military policy will remain a distant prospect.

Acknowledgments

I am grateful to the following publications for permitting me to include in this collection materials that originally appeared in their pages.

"The Age of Great Expectations and the Great Void: History after 'the End of History.'" *TomDispatch*, January 8, 2017, http://www.tomdispatch.com/blog/176228.

"Always and Everywhere: The *New York Times* and the Enduring 'Threat' of Isolationism." *TomDispatch*, October 24, 2013, http://www.tomdispatch.com/blog/175764.

"American Imperium." *Harper's Magazine*, May 2016, 29–38.

"Angst in the Church of America the Redeemer." *TomDispatch*, February 23, 2017, http://www.tomdispatch.com/post/176246.

"Ballpark Liturgy: America's New Civic Religion; Cheap Grace at Fenway." *TomDispatch*, July 28, 2011, http://www.tomdispatch.com/blog/175423.

"Boykinism: Joe McCarthy Would Understand." *TomDispatch*, September 25, 2012, http://www.tomdispatch.com/post/175597.

"Breaking Washington's Rules." *The American Conservative*, January 2011, 23–26.

"Bush's Grand Strategy." *The American Conservative*, November 4, 2002, 12–14.

"Counterculture Conservatism." *The American Conservative*, January/February 2013, 12–14.

"The Decay of American Politics: An Ode to Ike and Adlai." *TomDispatch*, August 4, 2016, http://www.tomdispatch.com/blog/176172.

"The Duplicity of the Ideologues." *Commonweal*, July 11, 2014, 10–12.

"Election 2016: A Postmortem." *Commonweal*, January 6, 2017, 15–17.

"The Elusive American Century." *Harper's Magazine*, February 2012, 13–16.

"The End of (Military) History? The United States, Israel, and the Failure of the Western Way of War." *TomDispatch*, July 29, 2010, http://www.tomdispatch.com/archive/175278.

"Family Man: Christopher Lasch and the Populist Imperative." Review of *Hope in a Scattering Time: A Life of Christopher Lasch*, by Eric Miller. *World Affairs*, May/June 2010, 81–84.

"Fault Lines: Inside Rumsfeld's Pentagon." Review of *War and Decision: Inside the Pentagon at the Dawn of the War on Terrorism*, by Douglas J. Feith, and *Wiser in Battle: A Soldier's Story*, by Ricardo S. Sanchez. *Boston Review*, July/August 2008, 21–24.

"The Folly of Albion." *The American Conservative*, January 17, 2005, 11–13.

"The Great Divide." *Commonweal*, March 28, 2008, 10.

"History that Makes Us Stupid." *Chronicle of Higher Education*, November 6, 2015, 15.

"How We Became Israel." *The American Conservative*, September 2012, 16–18.

"Kennan Kvetches: The Diplomat's Life in Doomsaying." Review of *The Kennan Diaries*, edited by Frank Costigliola. *Harper's Magazine*, April 2014, 86–110.

"Kissing the Specious Present Goodbye: Did History Begin Anew Last November 8th?" *TomDispatch*, June 22, 2017, http://www.tomdispatch.com/blog/176299.

"A Letter to Paul Wolfowitz: Occasioned by the Tenth Anniversary of the Iraq War." *Harper's Magazine*, March 2013, 48–50.

"Living Room War." *The American Conservative*, March 14, 2005, 11–13.

"The Man in the Black Cape." *The American Interest*, January/February 2009, 116–18.

"A Modern Major General." Review of *American Soldier*, by Tommy Franks with Malcolm McConnell. *New Left Review* 29 (September–October 2004): 123–34.

"Naming Our Nameless War: How Many Years Will It Be?" *TomDispatch*, May 28, 2013, http://www.tomdispatch.com/blog/175704.

"The New Normal." *Commonweal*, July 7, 2017, 8–9.

"New Rome, New Jerusalem." *Wilson Quarterly* 26, no. 3 (2002): 50–58.

"One Percent Republic." *The American Conservative*, November/December 2013, 20–23.

"'Permanent War for Permanent Peace': American Grand Strategy since World War II." *Historically Speaking* 3, no. 2 (2001): 2–5.

"The Real World War IV." *Wilson Quarterly* 29, no. 1 (2005): 36–61.

Review of *Known and Unknown: A Memoir*, by Donald Rumsfeld. *Financial Times*, February 11, 2011–15.

"The Revisionist Imperative: Rethinking Twentieth Century Wars." *Journal of Military History* 76, no. 2 (2012): 333–42.

"Save Us from Washington's Visionaries: In (Modest) Praise of a Comforting Mediocrity." *TomDispatch*, January 29, 2015, http://www.tomdispatch.com/blog/175949/.

"Saving 'America First': What Responsible Nationalism Looks Like." *Foreign Affairs*, September/October 2017, 56–57.

"Schlesinger and the Decline of Liberalism." Review of *Schlesigner: The Imperial Historian*, by Richard Aldous. *Boston Review*, October 10, 2017.

"Selling Our Souls." *Commonweal*, August 12, 2011, 11–13.

"Slouching toward Mar-a-Lago: The Post-Cold-War Consensus Collapses." *TomDispatch*, August 8, 2017, http://www.tomdispatch.com/post/176316.

"Tailors to the Emperor." *New Left Review* 69 (May–June 2011): 101–24.

"Thoughts on a Graduation Weekend." *Front Porch Republic*, May 19, 2014, http://www.frontporchrepublic.com/2014/05/thoughts-graduation-weekend/.

"Tom Clancy, Military Man." *The Baffler*, no. 24 (2014): 157–60.

"Tragedy Renewed: William Appleman Williams." *World Affairs*, Winter 2009, 62–72.

"Twilight of the Republic?" *Commonweal*, December 1, 2006, 10–16.

"The Ugly American Telegram." *The New York Times*, August 23, 2013.

"'Under God': Same-Sex Marriage and Foreign Policy." *Commonweal*, August 14, 2015, 11–12.

"War and Culture, American Style." *The Boston Globe*, April 24, 2016, K8.

"A War of Ambition." *America*, February 10, 2014, 13–15.

"What Happened at Bud Dajo: A Forgotten Massacre—and Its Lessons." *The Boston Globe*, March 12, 2006, C2.

"Why Read Clausewitz When Shock and Awe Can Make a Clean Sweep of Things?" Review of *Cobra II: The Inside Story of the Invasion and Occupation of Iraq*, by Michael Gordon and Bernard Trainor. *London Review of Books*, June 8, 2006, 3–5.

I want to express my gratitude to the University of Notre Dame Press for making this volume possible, above all to Steve Wrinn for suggesting the possibility of collecting my recent essays. But Steve's colleagues have been nothing short of splendid: responsive and supremely professional. They include Susan Berger, Matt Dowd, Wendy McMillan, and Kathryn Pitts. My thanks to all.

Index

Clark, Wesley, 120
Clarke, Richard, 122, 123, 323
Clausewitz, Carl von, 130, 371
client states, 315
climate change, 215, 330, 357, 414
Clinton, Bill, 102, 187, 247, 344,
    410–11
  on America's historic mission, 26,
    28, 237, 388, 448
  foreign policy of, 370–71, 383, 422
  on globalization, 370, 383, 448
  military interventions under,
    317–20, 351–52, 383, 400–401,
    467
Clinton, Hillary Rodham, 29, 227,
    421–22
  belief in globalization, 208, 421–22
  in election of 2016, 208, 407, 409,
    420, 423, 426–28, 429–31, 433
  moneyed interests and, 421, 427
  national security views of, 28, 430
  on Trump "deplorables," 187
Cobra II (Gordon and Trainor),
    365–74
Cohen, Richard, 70
Cohen, Roger, 241
Cohen, William, 101–2
Cold War, 143, 184–85, 300, 410
  American military and, 6–7, 267
  binary definitions during, 61,
    135–36, 322–23, 355, 398
  containment strategy during, 40,
    177, 343
  Eisenhower on, 357–58
  Kagan on, 54–56
  Kennan and, 41, 43, 44, 46
  as name and label, 301, 342
  nuclear strategy during, 85–86
  preventive war argument during,
    175
  Reagan and, 71, 155, 224, 302
  real history of, 71–72

standard narratives of, 71, 236–37,
    259, 301–3
  Truman and, 322, 343, 398
  two phases of, 302
  Vietnam and, 221, 302, 333
  war for Europe during, 224
  Wohlstetter School on, 85–89, 100
  as World War III, 238, 298, 301,
    302, 343
Cold War ending, 69, 201–3, 299–300
  as "end of history," 136, 202, 237,
    266
  fall of Berlin Wall, 7, 43, 155, 201,
    202, 231, 259, 388
  need for revisionist narrative on,
    259–60
  "peace dividend" from, 185
Comey, James, 409
Commager, Henry Steele, 32
Commentary, 298
Commission on Integrated Long-
    Term Strategy, 86
Committee to Maintain a Prudent
    Defense Policy, 86
Congress, 368–69
conservatism, 11, 24, 144, 279, 455
  basic tenets of, 454–58
  new agenda proposed for, 458–59
consumerism, 282
containment, 80–81, 468
  Cold War strategy of, 40, 177, 343
  of Iraq under Saddam Hussein, 99,
    317–18
Costigliola, Frank
  The Kennan Diaries, 40, 42, 45,
    46, 47
covert action, 227, 304, 312, 398
Cross, Gary, 281–82
Cruz, Ted, 28, 48, 49, 227, 432
Cuba, 55, 64, 218, 357
Cuban Missile Crisis, 55, 90–92, 154,
    302, 425

USS *Cole*, 103, 319
USS *Stark*, 311
utopian globalism, 185, 186, 188, 189,
    190, 192
utopianism, 184–87, 455–56

Vandenberg, Arthur, 397
Venezuela, 241, 357, 358
Vietnam Syndrome, 370, 467
Vietnam War, 5, 22, 56, 57, 157, 229,
    276
    anti-war movement, 154–55
    Cold War conceptions of, 221, 302,
        333
    Diem overthrow and, 71, 250–52
    "new isolationism" and, 245–46
    Rumsfeld on, 74–75
    Wohlstetter School on, 21, 96–97
Vinnell Corporation, 304
Volstead Act of 1919, 406
von Moltke, Helmuth (elder), 382
von Moltke, Helmuth (younger),
    127

Waging Modern War (Clark), 120
Wakefield, Tim, 462
Wallace, Henry A., 243
Wall Street Journal, 204, 241
war
    American people and, 450–51
    Bourne on, 148, 149–51
    culture and, 434–39
    in God's name, 62–63
    high-tech, 97, 378–79
    living room, 376–80
    opposition to, within United
        States, 154–55, 214
    politics and, 129–30
    See also Civil War; Global War on
        Terror; Iraq War; Mexican War;
        Spanish-American War; Vietnam
        War; World War I; World War II

War and Decision (Feith), 105–13,
    116
war on terror. *See* Global War on
    Terror
War Powers Resolution of 1973, 406
Warren, Elizabeth, 421
Washington, George, 191, 332, 361,
    388, 396
Washington Consensus, 422
Washington Naval Conference
    (1921–22), 92n, 219
Washington Post, 51–52, 86–87, 204,
    249, 386
Waugh, Evelyn, 11
wealth
    globalization's creation of, 69, 99,
        188, 203, 207, 409, 411
    inequality, 207, 448–49, 452
weapons of mass destruction
    (WMD), 19, 77, 107, 108, 126
Weekly Standard, 25, 204, 454
Weinberger, Caspar, 312
Weinberger Doctrine, 401
Westmoreland, William, 129
West Point, 1–2, 6
Why We Were in Vietnam
    (Podhoretz), 325
Williams, William Appleman, 11,
    153–65, 455
    on American *Weltanschauung*,
        159–60
    as historian, 156, 158–59
    left-wing views of, 154–55, 161
    on Open Door strategy, 160–61
    *The Tragedy of American Diplo-
        macy*, 153–54, 156, 158, 159, 162,
        165
    on war, 156–57
Wills, Garry, 307
Wilson, Woodrow, 92n, 229, 444
    on America's mission, 169, 388
    Fourteen Points of, 396, 446

Index   491